Linda Crawford
1974

THE BOOK OF DANIEL

Daniel

Verse by Verse Study

by

Oliver B. Greene

The Gospel Hour, Inc., Oliver B. Greene, Director
P.O. Box 2024, Greenville, South Carolina

Daniel

Verse by Verse Study

Printed in the United States of America

First printing, October 1964—10,000 copies
Second printing, January 1966—10,000 copies
Third printing, August 1966—10,000 copies
Fourth printing, November 1967—10,000 copies
Fifth printing, December 1968—15,000 copies
Sixth printing, September 1969—15,000 copies
Seventh printing, February 1971—15,000 copies
Eighth printing, February 1972—15,000 copies
Ninth printing, April 1973—15,000 copies
Tenth printing, November 1973—15,000 copies
Eleventh printing, March 1974—15,000 copies

$5.95

CONTENTS

PART ONE

Chapters 1–6

Personal History of the Prophet Daniel
Under the Reign of
Nebuchadnezzar, Belshazzar, Darius, and Cyrus

PART TWO

Chapters 7–12

Strictly Prophetic

CONTENTS

INTRODUCTION

None other of the sixty-six books of our Bible has been attacked by so many enemies of the Word of God as has the book of Daniel. For sixteen centuries the enemies of God have violently attacked and tried to discredit this precious book.

Porphyry, a Syrian critic of the third century, claimed that the book was not written by the prophet Daniel. He asserted that it was not written 533 B. C., but 168 B. C. The reason for the writing, says Porphyry, was the fierce persecution under Antiochus Epiphanes, and the book was written by one of the Maccabees to encourage the Jews in those trying days of suffering.

Some of the modern critics claïm that Daniel (if such a person ever existed) had nothing to do with writing the prophecy that bears his name. They claim that a gifted Jew who lived after the time of Antiochus Epiphanes wrote the book in 165 B. C., and that the book of Daniel is pure fiction.

However, those of us who love and study the Word of God know that this is just another attack of the devil on this great book—a book recognized by the Lord Jesus Himself. Daniel is one of the most important books in the Bible, and for that reason the devil has done his utmost to discredit this prophecy—but to no avail. In the minds of those of us who love God and honor His Word, there is no question but that the book of Daniel existed long before the days of Antiochus Epiphanes, who lived 175 B. C.

Josephus, the Jewish historian, gives a history in his writings of the Jewish people from Abraham down to the destruction of Jerusalem by Titus, in 70 A. D. In his account of the bitter persecutions and the struggle with Antiochus Epiphanes, Josephus tells us that these things came to pass "according to the prophecy of Daniel which was given 408 years before." According to this great historian, the book of Daniel was written about 573 B. C. Josephus also tells us that when Alexander the Great (foretold in the prophecies of Daniel 8:5–8) came against Jerusalem in conquest 332 B. C., Juddua, the high priest at that time, showed him the reference to himself in the book of Daniel, which so pleased Alexander that he spared the city.

These facts are recorded by Josephus, an accepted authority on Jewish history; and *according to these facts* the book of Daniel *must* have been written before 332 B. C.

The prophet Ezekiel was a contemporary of Daniel, and (in Babylon) he wrote the book which bears his name in our Bible. Ezekiel was held in high esteem by his brothers in exile, and they consulted him often. Since Daniel was in Babylon at that time, and since he occupied a position near the top rank of governors and rulers, Ezekiel must have known these facts. However, this would not have made it necessary for him to mention Daniel in his writings–yet he *does* mention Daniel–not once, but *three times*:

"Though these three men, Noah, Daniel, and Job, were in it, they should deliver but their own souls by their righteousness, saith the Lord God" (Ezek. 14:14). "Though Noah, Daniel, and Job, were in it, as I live, saith the Lord God, they shall deliver neither son nor daughter; they shall but deliver their own souls by their righteousness" (Ezek. 14:20). "Behold, thou art wiser than Daniel; there is no secret that they can hide from thee" (Ezek. 28:3).

Thus the prophet Ezekiel testifies to the fact that Daniel DID live, and that he was noted for his righteousness along with Noah; and for his wisdom he was classified with Job. But the highest authority who could possibly declare that such a man as Daniel actually lived, was none other the Lord Jesus Christ:

"When ye therefore shall see the abomination of desolation, spoken of by Daniel the prophet, stand in the holy place, (whoso readeth, let him understand)" (Matt. 24:15). Jesus referred to Daniel as "the prophet," an actual person; and to deny that Daniel lived, to say that the book of Daniel is but fiction, is to insult the integrity and wisdom of the Son of God, the Lord Jesus Christ!

In the Scripture just quoted from Matthew, Jesus testifies that *there was a prophet named Daniel*, and that he foretold that such a thing as the "abomination of desolation" would appear and would stand in the temple in the holy place. When anyone–teacher, preacher, evangelist, or college professor–states that Daniel never lived and that the book of Daniel is fiction, that person has insulted Almighty God and is on the verge of committing the unpardonable sin!

"*All Scripture is given by inspiration*," and men spoke as the Holy Ghost breathed upon them the words of inspiration. Therefore, to attribute the Holy Scriptures to the pen of a writer of fiction is to insult God the Father, God the Spirit, and God the Son, who said, "When ye therefore shall see the abomination of desolation, spoken of by Daniel the prophet, stand in the holy place, (whoso readeth, let him understand)." God forbid that I keep company with or give comfort to any preacher, teacher, or professor who would dare suggest that the book of Daniel should not be included in the sacred library of the sixty-six books of our Bible!

Of all the beloved characters found in the Word of God, there is none more interesting, appealing, lovable and pure than Daniel. He and Joseph stand among the heroes of the Old Testament as the Siamese twins of purity, and against these two men there is practically no evil recorded. With the exception of Joseph, I find no other character in the Bible who compares so closely with Daniel in purity. Both of these young men lived pure, dedicated lives, yielding their all to God in service, in love, and in obedience. Yet Daniel was a sinner, and he needed the grace of God just as much as did Peter or Mary Magdalene. Daniel clearly acknowledged his need of repentance in the tremendous prayer recorded in the ninth chapter of the book that bears his name.

The book of Daniel is most remarkable, it matters not from what standpoint you study it or analyze it. Like Daniel, it is unique and extraordinary. It records for us the course of the history of the nations from Daniel's day until the end—and that record is accurate. Higher critics and skeptics have groaned in despair in their attempts to discredit the book of Daniel, but there is no other book in all of our Bible that has been so completely and accurately vindicated by history as has Daniel.

Every prophecy in Daniel up until this very hour has been meticulously, accurately, and minutely fulfilled in every detail. Why then should we not expect the prophecies which have not yet *been fulfilled*, TO BE fulfilled just as accurately and meticulously as the many that have already come to pass? No wonder the book of Daniel is a target for critics. Men who reject the supernatural verbal inspiration of the Bible, the infallible dictation of the Scriptures by the Spirit of God to holy men, must somehow destroy the book if they hope ever to disprove the Word of God.

Daniel wrote concerning things of the future which would occur after his days on earth were ended; and since his prophecies concerning the kingdom of Nebuchadnezzar and the kingdoms of Persia, Greece, and Rome all came true *just AS prophesied*, the enemies of the Word of God have put forward the explanation that Daniel was NOT an actual historic character at all, and that he was NOT a prophet who wrote the book that bears his name. They maintain that Daniel was written long *after* the events prophesied in the book had taken place—and critics therefore claim that the book of Daniel is history, *NOT prophecy*, and that it was written by some impostor who simply took Daniel as his pen name.

In spite of all hell has hurled at the book of Daniel, it still stands; but the attack upon it is much more serious than appears on the surface. If Daniel can be discredited by the critics, then the Satanic attack upon the Word of God will continue until the whole body of Scripture has been declared to be—not the Word of God at all—but simply another book, written by historians, poets, and writers of fiction! You may believe the critics if you care to; but as for me, *since Ezekiel and Jesus Christ both testified to the inspiration and authenticity of the book of Daniel*, I will *accept* the word of Ezekiel and the Lord Jesus Christ.

As we begin our verse by verse study of these twelve tremendous chapters, let me point out several things for you to keep in mind which will lessen your difficulty in understanding and accepting the message of Daniel. We will never understand *all* of it, but we *can* understand all that God would have us to understand until we sit in the heavenly Bible class and Jesus makes known to us the things we could not bear while here upon this earth in flesh.

1. First and foremost, *discount any suggestion that Daniel was a character of fiction or a pen name, instead*

of a prophet. Ezekiel 14:20 plainly declares that Daniel was a historic character, and that he actually lived in the days of Nebuchadnezzar, king of Babylon.

2. Keep uppermost in your mind the fact that *Jesus declared Daniel to be a prophet* (Matt. 24:15), and that he prophesied concerning things of the future–even things that have not as yet come to pass, such as the "abomination of desolation" who will in the future stand in the temple in Jerusalem. Since Jesus said Daniel was a prophet, *you believe it,* regardless of what the critics and those of higher learning have to say.

3. Daniel deals with things which *have happened,* which are going on *now,* and which *will happen* during the Gentile Age and in the tribulation period known in the Word of God as the time of "Jacob's trouble" or the time of "great tribulation."

4. Daniel and his godly companions, Shadrach, Meshach, and Abed-nego, were historical characters; but they were also *a type of the nation of Israel*–the nation to which they belonged. The experience of the three Hebrew children in the fiery furnace and the experience of Daniel in the lions' den typify the history of Israel during the time of the Gentiles, the reign of the Antichrist, the time of Jacob's trouble, when the devil will make his last all-out, *but futile,* drive to annihilate Israel.

The reign of Nebuchadnezzar was a type and a shadow of the reign of Antichrist. The deliverance of the three Hebrew children from the fiery furnace and the deliverance of Daniel from the lions' den are pictures of Jehovah's present protection of Israel, of their ultimate deliverance from the devil and all the emissaries of hell, and their restoration to the land of Palestine. God will bring them back to their land and plant them, never to be plucked up again: "For I will set mine eyes upon them for good, and I will bring them again to this land: and I will build them, and not pull them down; and I will plant them, and not pluck them up" (Jer. 24:6).

5. One of the primary rules for Bible study is that ALL Scripture has but *one primary interpretation*; but ANY Scripture may have *several practical applications*, and many Scriptures have *a prophetic revelation.* Whether you are studying Daniel or I John, Matthew or Revelation, always keep this simple rule in mind—and always remember that if the devil cannot make a liberal or modernist of you, he will do his utmost to cause you to become a bigot, narrow and conceited; or he will run you down a blind alley and cause you to spend time majoring on the minor, running with nothing to say when you arrive, advertising great swelling subjects but delivering sermons that are like clouds without water (Jude 12).

Some dear teachers can tell you all about the image Nebuchadnezzar saw in his dream. They can describe every toe, every toenail, and every wrinkle in the toes, going into great detail in explaining what all of this means; but if their pastor should ask them to lead a soul into the knowledge of salvation at the altar in their church, they would be at a complete loss as to how to instruct a dear sinner to be saved by God's grace through faith!

Some people are "sponge-Christians," always soaking up, but never giving out anything that is a blessing to the unsaved or to the cause of Christ.

When one dogmatically insists that his primary interpretation is correct, and then rejects the practical applications of the Scripture, that person may be saved—but such practices will lead him into cold, lifeless, spiritless orthodoxy! On the other hand, to take only the practical applications of the Scripture, refusing to see the primary doctrinal interpretation of it, will lead to religious fanaticism.

When one ignores the prophetic revelation of the Scriptures, he closes his eyes to the future and refuses to see the plain facts recorded in God's Word concerning events that lie ahead. There are many top-heavy, one-sided, warped religionists. Some of them are saved, but they will lose their reward because they emphasize their ability, depend upon their own wisdom and knowledge, and they do not yield to the Holy Spirit–the One who dictated the Scriptures to holy men of old and who is able to make known to us the deep things of God.

"We have also a more sure word of prophecy; whereunto ye do well that ye take heed, as unto a light that shineth in a dark place, until the day dawn, and the day star arise in your hearts: Knowing this first, that no prophecy of the Scripture is of any private interpretation. For the prophecy came not in old time by the will of man: but holy men of God spake as they were moved by the Holy Ghost" (II Pet. 1:19–21).

"But the anointing which ye have received of Him (the Holy Spirit) abideth in you, and ye need not that any man teach you: but as the same anointing teacheth you of all things, and is truth, and is no lie, and even as it hath taught you, ye shall abide in Him" (I John 2:27).

A minister, teacher, or layman yielded to the Spirit and led by Him, will not teach the Scriptures for vainglory or to advertise his personal ability and knowledge. On the contrary, if the teacher is led by the Spirit he will magnify the Christ in whom God the Father is well pleased. Study John 16:12–15.

Let me point out one special part of the Scripture: "Howbeit when He, the Spirit of truth, is come, He will guide you into all truth: for He shall not speak of Himself; but whatsoever He shall hear, that shall He speak: and He will shew you things to come. He shall glorify me: for He shall receive of mine, and shall shew it unto you" (John 16:13,14).

Always keep in mind that God the Father is highly pleased with His Son, the Lord Jesus. The Holy Ghost came into the world to glorify Jesus; and when the Holy Ghost abides in the bosom of a believer, that believer (yielded to the Holy Spirit) will glorify JESUS—not himself, not his religion, not his experience or denomination. If you want to know whether or not a person is spiritual, listen to his message and see to whom he gives glory. Then you will know whether that person is led by the Holy Spirit, or whether he is carnal.

Daniel lived before and during the captivity of Judah, as testified in verses 1 and 2 of chapter 1: "In the third year of the reign of Jehoiakim king of Judah came Nebuchadnezzar king of Babylon unto Jerusalem, and besieged it. And the Lord gave Jehoiakim king of Judah into his hand . . . ."

To the casual reader of the Word of God this statement may seem unimportant; but to the spiritually minded *student* of the Word, it is *very important.* Please notice: ". . . *And the Lord GAVE Jehoiakim king of Judah into his hand.*"

In II Kings 20:17,18 we read: "Behold, the days come, that all that is in thine house, and that which thy fathers have laid up in store unto this day, shall be carried into Babylon: nothing shall be left, saith the Lord. And of thy sons that shall issue from thee, which thou shalt beget, shall they take away; and they shall be eunuchs in the palace of the king of Babylon."

The same prophecy is recorded by Isaiah in chapter 39. God gives this record because He had declared this very thing to happen many, many years before it came to pass. Through the pen of Daniel, the Holy Ghost reminds us that God never breaks His Word—*cannot* break His Word—whether it is a promise of blessing and plenty, or a solemn warning of judgment. God will always do exactly what He says He will do.

Many years before Daniel's time, Hezekiah, king of Judah, had put the holy vessels of the temple on exhibition in order that a heathen, in his pride and eagerness, might ally with him. As a result of this act of the flesh, God sent His prophet Isaiah to Hezekiah and warned him. Read II Kings 20:17,18 and Isaiah 39.

The events in Daniel occurred more than one hundred years after God dictated these words to Isaiah and he delivered them to the king; but even though the judgment was delayed for more than a century, God never fails to do what He promises. Notice in the Scriptures how accurately and meticulously this prophecy was fulfilled in every detail. The temple was spoiled as promised, and the royal princes—descendants of Hezekiah—were taken into Babylon and made slaves, serfs, and eunuchs in the house of the king of Babylon! The literal fulfillment of this prophecy is recorded in Daniel 1:3.

There are many, many lessons to be learned from the book of Daniel. God does visit evil with judgment. The wages of sin is death, and whatsoever a man soweth, that shall he also reap. God forgave Hezekiah—but he had to pay a tremendous price and reap the harvest of seed sown. God delayed the judgment for a hundred years, but finally it came. The royal princes were taken into Babylon to become slaves, serfs, and eunuchs in the king's court—and Daniel was among the royal seed who suffered for the sins of their ancestor, King Hezekiah.

The name *Daniel* comes from the word *Dan*, meaning "to judge," and from the fragment *El*, meaning "God."

Thus the name Daniel means "God will judge." So the first lesson God would have us learn from the book of Daniel is that God *will*, God *does*–yea, God *MUST* judge sin and evil. Daniel had no part in the sins of King Hezekiah, but nevertheless he suffered; he reaped the bitter harvest. The sins of the fathers are visited upon the children, even "unto the third and to the fourth generation" (Ex. 34:7). We fathers should be careful how we live!

Daniel suffered because of the sins of his fathers, but God showed mercy toward him and his friends because they *remembered* the sins of their fathers. They confessed those sins and begged for mercy from the God of mercy. God forgave, and He exalted Daniel and his three friends because they acknowledged their sin and repented. They *believed* God; they were willing to *serve* God, even to the extent of being placed in a den of lions–and in a fiery furnace heated seven times hotter than ever before!

I am not surprised that the critics of the Bible and the enemies of Almighty God have done everything in their ungodly, crooked power to destroy the book of Daniel. But I would call your attention to the fact that some of that crowd are already roasting in hell today, while the book of Daniel stands–and WILL BE STANDING when all of its enemies are dead and in the lake of fire! The Word of God cannot, and shall not, be discredited or destroyed. "*For ever, O Lord, thy Word is settled in heaven*" (Psalm 119:89).

PART I

Chapters 1 through 6

PERSONAL HISTORY OF THE PROPHET DANIEL

UNDER THE REIGN OF
NEBUCHADNEZZAR, BELSHAZZAR,
DARIUS AND CYRUS

CHAPTER ONE

THE CONQUEST OF JERUSALEM

1. In the third year of the reign of Jehoiakim king of Judah came Nebuchadnezzar king of Babylon unto Jerusalem, and besieged it.

2. And the Lord gave Jehoiakim king of Judah into his hand, with part of the vessels of the house of God: which he carried into the land of Shinar to the house of his god; and he brought the vessels into the treasure house of his god.

3. And the king spake unto Ashpenaz the master of his eunuchs, that he should bring certain of the children of Israel, and of the king's seed, and of the princes;

4. Children in whom was no blemish, but well favoured, and skilful in all wisdom, and cunning in knowledge, and understanding science, and such as had ability in them to stand in the king's palace, and whom they might teach the learning and the tongue of the Chaldeans.

5. And the king appointed them a daily provision of the king's meat, and of the wine which he drank: so nourishing them three years, that at the end thereof they might stand before the king.

6. Now among these were of the children of Judah, Daniel, Hananiah, Mishael, and Azariah:

7. Unto whom the prince of the eunuchs gave names: for he gave unto Daniel the name of Belteshazzar; and to Hananiah, of Shadrach; and to Mishael, of Meshach; and to Azariah, of Abednego.

8. But Daniel purposed in his heart that he would not defile himself with the portion of the king's meat, nor with the wine which he drank: therefore he requested of the prince of the eunuchs that he might not defile himself.

9. Now God had brought Daniel into favour and tender love with the prince of the eunuchs.

10. And the prince of the eunuchs said unto Daniel, I fear my lord the king, who hath appointed your meat and your drink:

for why should he see your faces worse liking than the children which are of your sort? then shall ye make me endanger my head to the king.

11. Then said Daniel to Melzar, whom the prince of the eunuchs had set over Daniel, Hananiah, Mishael, and Azariah,

12. Prove thy servants, I beseech thee, ten days; and let them give us pulse to eat, and water to drink.

13. Then let our countenances be looked upon before thee, and the countenance of the children that eat of the portion of the king's meat: and as thou seest, deal with thy servants.

14. So he consented to them in this matter, and proved them ten days.

15. And at the end of ten days their countenances appeared fairer and fatter in flesh than all the children which did eat the portion of the king's meat.

16. Thus Melzar took away the portion of their meat, and the wine that they should drink; and gave them pulse.

17. As for these four children, God gave them knowledge and skill in all learning and wisdom: and Daniel had understanding in all visions and dreams.

18. Now at the end of the days that the king had said he should bring them in, then the prince of the eunuchs brought them in before Nebuchadnezzar.

19. And the king communed with them; and among them all was found none like Daniel, Hananiah, Mishael, and Azariah: therefore stood they before the king.

20. And in all matters of wisdom and understanding, that the king enquired of them, he found them ten times better than all the magicians and astrologers that were in all his realm.

21. And Daniel continued even unto the first year of king Cyrus.

In the first chapter of Daniel we find the account of the conquest of Jerusalem by Nebuchadnezzar, king of Babylon, and the personal history of Daniel.

Verses 1 and 2: "In the third year of the reign of Jehoiakim king of Judah came Nebuchadnezzar king of Babylon unto Jerusalem, and besieged it. And the Lord gave Jehoiakim king of Judah into his hand, with part of the vessels of the house of God: which he carried into the land of Shinar to the house of his god; and he brought the vessels into the treasure house of his god."

In Jeremiah 25:1–11, Jeremiah points out that the Babylonian captivity occurred in the *fourth* year of Jehoiakim's reign. Daniel declares that it happened in the *third* year. This is not a discrepancy in the Word of God.*

**I have given much time and study in research on these dates; and in any of the groups of dates used there is much which leaves question marks in the mind, and much lack of harmony. We know that the Word of God is not wrong; there are no discrepancies there—and were God to give us, by divine revelation, the key to each portion of Scripture dealing in numbers and dates, all would be co-ordinated into perfect harmony.*

I give you here the most accepted dates concerning Nebuchadnezzar—his ascension to the throne when he became king, and his taking captive Daniel and other young men of Israel.

Nebuchadnezzar was made head of his aged father's armies in 609 B. C. He took Palestine in 606 B. C., and that is when he took Daniel and his contemporaries captive and transported them to Babylon. Nebuchadnezzar put the king back on the throne in Jerusalem, and in that same year (606 B. C.) he became co-regent with his father. The reference in Jeremiah 25:1 is Nebuchadnezzar's first year as co-regent. It was during his co-regency in 605 B. C. that he broke the power of Egypt. His first year as sole ruler was 604 B. C., and in Daniel 2:1 his second year as sole ruler is 603 B. C. Nebuchadnezzar made other attacks upon Jerusalem and finally carried away all but the very poorest (II Kings 24:11–14).

Give or take a year, these dates are as nearly correct as it is possible to ascertain. Please bear in mind that the seeming differences have nothing to do with the message of Daniel.

The fact is that Nebuchadnezzar set out on his expedition near the *close of the third year* of Jehoiakim's reign, and this is the point from which Daniel reckons the time. However, the conquest of Jerusalem was not fully accomplished until the ninth month of the following year, and Jeremiah reckons the time of the conquest from that point. Thus, the critics have no ground to stand on when they say that Daniel speaks of the third year of the reign of Jehoiakim, while Jeremiah speaks of the fourth year. *Both are correct.* The conquest began in the third year and was finished in the fourth year of the reign of Jehoiakim, king of Judah.

God had a plan and a purpose: It was His divine plan to make the descendants of Abraham the leading nation of the world, but through their disobedience and idolatry the Hebrew nation prevented God's doing this. In the year 721 B. C. the ten tribes were carried into captivity by the king of Assyria, but even this did not cure them of their sin and idolatry. One hundred and fifteen years later–in 606 B. C. (Ussher)–began the seventy years of captivity in Babylon of the other two tribes, known as Judah, as prophesied in Jeremiah 25:11.

Lest this seem confusing, let me point out that the *ten* tribes were taken into Assyrian captivity in 721 B. C.; and the remaining two tribes known as Judah were taken into Babylonian captivity in 606 B. C., one hundred and fifteen years later. This is the prophecy of Jeremiah 25:11.

After the confusion of languages at the tower of Babel there were still those who were striving for world supremacy, and among these nations was Babylon. The Babylonian empire had already swallowed up Assyria. Pharaoh-Necho, king of Egypt, led his armies against Babylon and was defeated by Nebuchadnezzar in the battle of Carchemish–a city located on the west bank of the great river Euphrates. This victory won by Nebuchadnezzar over Pharaoh-Necho made Babylon the most powerful ruler of the then known world. (This battle was prophesied by Jeremiah in Jeremiah 46:1–26.) Not only did Nebuchadnezzar *defeat* Pharaoh-Necho, but he pushed him all the way back into Egypt and completely conquered that nation. He then marched against Jerusalem, and in the third year of the reign of Jehoiakim Nebuchadnezzar conquered that city. The power of his armies overran Jerusalem, and Jehoiakim surrendered to Nebuchadnezzar, but was again placed on the throne.

But Nebuchadnezzar did not return to Babylon empty handed; he plundered the temple in Jerusalem, confiscated the golden vessels, and took captive the princes of royal blood and those who were most intellectual of the Hebrew young men to convey them to Babylon, that they might be instructed in the language and tongue of the Chaldeans. After three years, Jehoiakim rebelled against Nebuchadnezzar, and the Lord sent neighboring bands of Chaldeans, Syrians, Moabites, and Ammonites to destroy Judah:

"In his days Nebuchadnezzar king of Babylon came up, and Jehoiakim became his servant three years: then he turned and rebelled against him. And the Lord sent against him bands of the Chaldees, and bands of the Syrians, and bands of the Moabites, and bands of the children of Ammon, and sent them against Judah to destroy it, according to the word of the Lord, which He spake by His servants the prophets. Surely at the commandment of the Lord came this upon Judah, to remove them out of His sight, for the sins of Manasseh, according to all that he did; and also for the innocent blood that he shed: for he filled Jerusalem with innocent blood; which the Lord would not pardon" (II Kings 24:1–4).

In the eleventh year of Jehoiakim's reign Nebuchadnezzar captured Jerusalem, put Jehoiakim in chains, and probably killed him (II Chron. 36:5–7). Jehoiakim died a most disgraceful death: "But thine eyes and thine heart are not but for thy covetousness, and for to shed innocent blood, and for oppression, and for violence, to do it. Therefore thus saith the Lord concerning Jehoiakim the son of Josiah king of Judah; They shall not lament for him, saying, Ah my brother! or, Ah sister! they shall not lament for him, saying, Ah lord! or, Ah his glory! He shall be buried with the burial of an ass, drawn and cast forth beyond the gates of Jerusalem" (Jer. 22:17–19).

At the death of Jehoiakim, his son Jehoiachin reigned in his stead. However, his reign lasted only three months, and he did that which was evil and ungodly in the sight of the Lord: "Jehoiachin was eighteen years old when he began to reign, and he reigned in Jerusalem three months. And his mother's name was Nehushta, the daughter of Elnathan of Jerusalem. And he did that which was evil in the sight of the Lord, according to all that his father had done. At that time the servants of Nebuchadnezzar king of Babylon came up against Jerusalem, and the city was besieged. And Nebuchadnezzar king of Babylon came against the city, and his servants did besiege it. And Jehoiachin the king of Judah went out to the king of Babylon, he, and his mother, and his servants, and his princes, and his officers: and the king of Babylon took him in the eighth year of his reign. And he carried out thence all the treasures of the house of the Lord, and the treasures of the king's house, and cut in pieces all the vessels of gold which Solomon king of Israel had made in the temple of the Lord, as the Lord had said. And he carried away all Jerusalem, and all the princes, and all the mighty men of valour, even ten thousand captives, and all the craftsmen and smiths:

none remained, save the poorest sort of the people of the land. And he carried away Jehoiachin to Babylon, and the king's mother, and the king's wives, and his officers, and the mighty of the land, those carried he into captivity from Jerusalem to Babylon. And all the men of might, even seven thousand, and craftsmen and smiths a thousand, all that were strong and apt for war, even them the king of Babylon brought captive to Babylon" (II Kings 24:8–16).

This is often referred to as "the captivity" because of the great number—and the character—of those carried away. However, the *seventy years'* captivity began in 606 B. C. and ran out at the fall of Babylon when King Cyrus began to reign. It was he who issued the edict (in 536 B. C.) for the Jews to return to Jerusalem.

Before Nebuchadnezzar left for Babylon with his captives, he made the uncle of Jehoiachin king and changed his name from Mattaniah to Zedekiah. But Zedekiah did that which was evil and ungodly in the sight of Jehovah and also rebelled against the king of Babylon. Therefore, in the ninth year of Zedekiah's reign Nebuchadnezzar again besieged Jerusalem, and took it after two years of battle.

At that time he destroyed the temple and the city, and from that time forward the Jewish people ceased to exist *as a nation*: "And the king of Babylon made Mattaniah his father's brother king in his stead, and changed his name to Zedekiah. Zedekiah was twenty and one years old when he began to reign, and he reigned eleven years in Jerusalem. And his mother's name was Hamutal, the daughter of Jeremiah of Libnah. And he did that which was evil in the sight of the Lord, according to all that Jehoiakim had done. For through the anger of the Lord it came to pass in Jerusalem and Judah, until he had cast them out from his presence, that Zedekiah rebelled against the king of Babylon" (II Kings 24:17–20). Please study also II Kings 25:1–21.

The city of Jerusalem and the land were left in a desolate condition for seventy years, as prophesied by "the weeping prophet," Jeremiah: "And this whole land shall be a desolation, and an astonishment; and these nations shall serve the king of Babylon seventy years" (Jer. 25:11). Nebuchadnezzar's becoming king marked the beginning of "the times of the Gentiles."

Verses 3–7: "And the king spake unto Ashpenaz the master of his eunuchs, that he should bring certain of the children of Israel, and of the king's seed, and of the princes; children in whom was no blemish, but well favoured, and skilful in all wisdom, and cunning in knowledge, and understanding science, and such as had ability in them to stand in the king's palace, and whom they might teach the learning and the tongue of the Chaldeans. And the king appointed them a daily provision of the king's meat, and of the wine which he drank: so nourishing them three years, that at the end thereof they might stand before the king. Now among these were of the children of Judah, Daniel, Hananiah, Mishael, and Azariah: Unto whom the prince of the eunuchs gave names: for he gave unto Daniel the name of Belteshazzar; and to Hananiah, of Shadrach; and to Mishael, of Meshach; and to Azariah, of Abed-nego."

These verses give the names of some of the Hebrew captives of royal blood who were carried into Babylon. Isaiah, speaking to King Hezekiah, said, "Hear the word of the Lord of hosts: Behold, the days come, that all that is in thine house, and that which thy fathers have laid up in store until this day, shall be carried to Babylon: nothing shall be left, saith the Lord. And of thy sons that shall issue from thee, which thou shalt beget, shall they take away; and they shall be eunuchs in the palace of the king of Babylon" (Isa. 39:5–7).

From this passage we learn that Daniel, Shadrach, Meshach, and Abed-nego were of royal blood, descendants of good King Hezekiah, and that they were made eunuchs in the palace of Nebuchadnezzar. They were placed under the supervision of the prince of the eunuchs, who had charge over them for a period of three years, and who also changed their names.

Daniel's name, which meant "God is my judge," was changed to *Belteshazzar*, a heathen name meaning "Whom Bel favors." Hananiah's name, which meant "Beloved of the Lord," was changed to *Shadrach*, meaning "Illumined by the sun god." The name of Mishael, meaning "Who is as God," was changed to *Meshach*, a pagan name meaning "Who is like Venus." Azariah's name, meaning "The Lord is my help," was changed to *Abed-nego*, a heathen name meaning "The servant of Nego."

On the surface, the changing of these names may not mean much to the casual reader of the Word of God; but those who are spiritually minded will recognize it as a scheme of the devil to gradually wean these young men away from their land, their religion, and their God, and to lead them little by little to adopt the religion and habits of the heathen people among whom they would be living in future months and years. But changing a person's name does not change the character of that person. These young men had Christian character; they were rooted and grounded in the faith of their fathers, and they were not to be led into the practices of the heathen.

In the outset of this study I stated that Daniel and Joseph were Siamese twins as pertaining to purity. There is also a very striking similarity between these two men in their experiences with God and with the enemy, the devil . . . Joseph and his experiences in Egypt, Daniel and his experiences in Babylon. Both of them were Hebrews; both were prisoners in a strange land among heathen people. Both were dreamers; both understood and made known the *interpretation* of dreams. Both underwent severe moral testing—*and both won the victory*!

Joseph was taken to the house of Potiphar (Genesis chapter 39). Daniel was taken into King Nebuchadnezzar's palace and exposed to everything that existed in the palace of the heathen king. Both of these men were young, which made their temptations especially severe. Most Bible scholars believe that both Daniel and Joseph were about twenty years of age when they were taken captive, and those of us who have studied their lives know that they refused to compromise to even the smallest degree. They refused to forsake their faith and their God.

Both of these young men proved to be a great blessing to the homes in which they lived; and because of their devotion to God, because of their character and their unusual abilities, both were promoted to positions of power, honor, and glory. The secret of the success and blessings in the lives of Joseph and Daniel was their loyalty to their God—the God of their fathers, the God whom they knew personally.

The first thing Satan did in his attempt to lead Daniel and his friends astray was to cause them to be commanded to eat the dainties of the king's table and drink the wine from the king's wine cellar: *"And the king appointed them a daily provision of the king's meat, and of the wine which he drank: so nourishing them three years, that at the end thereof they might stand before the king."*

To the average youth, such a temptation in the house of a king would be extremely attractive and appealing. The carnal nature craves popularity and those physical, material things that money can provide. Daniel and his friends, though prisoners, were exalted to a most honorable position–they were invited to sit at the king's table. Out of all the other captives *they* had been selected to spend their lives in the king's court, enjoying the comforts and luxuries that only a king could provide.

They could have found many excuses for yielding to the king's command. They could have considered the fact that they were captives, and as such they had no choice but to obey their captors. As prisoners of that country, they would be forced to adopt the pagan habits–or lose the favor of the king. They could forfeit their promotions–or even their lives. But if Satan put these suggestions into the minds of the four young Hebrews, they were not allowed to remain there long enough to materialize.

Their strongest argument could have been: "WE are not responsible for the judgment that came upon us. We did not commit the sin. We are suffering for the sins of our fathers, and God will not hold US responsible. We will therefore yield to the king and make the best of it." But they did not use that argument. They faced the lions' den, they faced the blazing furnace, they faced criticism and ridicule–but they did not yield to the king and compromise their faith.

They could have said, "After all, what would be so sinful about eating the king's meat? And if we are temperate, what would be so terrible about drinking a little of the king's wine?" Today young theologians are taught that they should *coexist.* The modern advice given to young men in the position of Daniel, Shadrach, Meshach and Abed-nego would be, "Participate! Sit at the king's table, nibble on his meat, sip his wine. *You might be able to win him.*" But these young men, thank God, did not have the modern professors in schools of theology to advise them. They had the God of their fathers and the Spirit of Jehovah!

They knew that the meat on the king's table would sometimes be meat strictly forbidden by the law of their God. They knew that the king would serve the flesh of swine, or meat from which the blood had not been drawn. They knew he would serve meat which had first been offered to idols, and to eat such meat would be against the laws of Jehovah God:

"Whatsoever parteth the hoof, and is clovenfooted, and cheweth the cud, among the beasts, *that shall ye eat*. . . . And the swine, though he divide the hoof, and be clovenfooted, yet he cheweth not the cud; he is unclean to you. *Of their flesh ye shall NOT eat*, and their carcase shall ye not touch; they are unclean unto you. These SHALL ye eat of all that are in the waters: *whatsoever hath fins and scales in the waters*, in the seas, and in the rivers, *them shall ye eat. . . Whatsoever hath no fins nor scales in the waters, that shall be an abomination unto you*. . . This is the law of the beasts, and of the fowl, and of every living creature that moveth in the waters, and of every creature that creepeth upon the earth: *To make a difference between the unclean and the clean, and between the beast that may be eaten and the beast that may NOT be eaten*" (Lev. 11:3, 7–9, 12, 46 and 47). It would be well for you to read the entire eleventh chapter of Leviticus and become acquainted with the laws of a holy God concerning the food for his people.

"And whatsoever man there be of the house of Israel, or of the strangers that sojourn among you, that eateth any manner of blood; I will even set my face against that soul that eateth blood, and will cut him off from among his people. For the life of the flesh is in the blood: and I have given it to you upon the altar to make an atonement for your souls: for it is the blood that maketh an atonement for the soul. Therefore I said unto the children of Israel, No soul of you shall eat blood, neither shall any stranger that sojourneth among you eat blood. And whatsoever man there be of the children of Israel, or of the strangers that sojourn among you, which hunteth and catcheth any beast or fowl that may be eaten; he shall even pour out the blood thereof, and cover it with dust. For it is the life of all flesh; the blood of it is for the life thereof: therefore I said unto the children of Israel, Ye shall eat the blood of no manner of flesh: for the life of all flesh is the blood thereof: whosoever eateth it shall be cut off" (Lev. 17:10–14).

"As concerning therefore the eating of those things that are offered in sacrifice unto idols, we know that an idol is nothing in the world, and that there is none other God but one. . . But meat commendeth us not to God: for neither, if we eat, are we the better; neither, if we eat not, are we the worse" (I Cor. 8:4 and 8). Read the entire eighth chapter of I Corinthians.

Daniel knew that if he ate meat forbidden by the law of his God, he would be ceremonially defiled. Therefore, there was only one course to follow: He and his friends must be total abstainers regardless of cost or consequence. They could not, they WOULD not, eat at the king's table!

I personally believe that Daniel was the leader of the group and the strongest of the four. I do not doubt that Shadrach, Meshach, and Abed-nego leaned on him to a great extent, that they watched his every move and listened to his every word. Just as Paul said many times to his children in the Lord, "Follow me as I follow Jesus," I believe Shadrach, Meshach, and Abed-nego followed

Daniel as Daniel followed the leading of his God.

Verse 8: "But Daniel purposed in his heart that he would not defile himself with the portion of the king's meat, nor with the wine which he drank: therefore he requested of the prince of the eunuchs that he might not defile himself."

Knowing that he must not yield to the king's command, Daniel *"purposed in his heart"* that he would not defile himself. He did not know what his stand might cost him, but I am sure he knew that it could easily cost him his life. But the day Daniel purposed in his heart that he would not eat the king's meat nor drink his wine, was the crowning day, the day of crisis, in the life of the young Hebrew. When he took his stand that day, the rest of the way was not hard to plan and follow.

Had Daniel NOT "purposed in his heart that he would not defile himself with the portion of the king's meat, nor with the wine which he drank," there is a good chance that we would never have heard his name again. It is probable that his name would never have been recorded in another verse in the sacred library of God's Word.

Like Paul, Daniel was determined to eat, drink, and do whatsoever he did "to the glory of God," in full obedience to Him. He knew the restrictions concerning clean and unclean foods imposed upon the covenant nation of Israel, and he refused to defile himself, even at the cost of his life. The book of Daniel is *rich* in lessons and instructions for present day believers. We need to study it carefully and prayerfully.

How I wish believers today would, like Daniel, purpose in their hearts to obey the Lord, even though they would suffer persecution, rather than coexisting with liberals, modernists, and religionists! Thank God *all* have not sold out; many are *willing* to suffer, and many HAVE purposed in their hearts that they will not defile themselves with the religious trends of the times.

Daniel certainly stands among the heroes of the Word of God. His whole life was pure, obedient, and blessed. I repeat: *The crowning day of his experience with God was the day he purposed in his heart to remain clean and separate*—and he did it under the most trying conditions one could imagine! Everything seemed against him; from the human standpoint he could not win, he could only suffer loss. But with dark clouds all around him, seemingly fighting a losing battle, he faced it all and purposed in his heart that he would TOUCH NOT the king's meat and wine.

The book of Daniel is a prophetic book, but it is more than that: It contains some of the most precious and important lessons in practical Christianity that can be found anywhere in all of the Word of God. Today as never before we need to emphasize the necessity for living an obedient, Spirit-filled, separated life, dedicated unto the Lord, and the *reward* for such a life. I believe the greatest need in the Church today is the need for men, consecrated to God as Daniel was when he purposed in his heart that he would be obedient to God regardless of the cost to himself.

God's message to the Church today cries out, "Come out from among them and be ye separate, saith the Lord, and touch not the unclean!" To the Ephesians Paul said: "Have no fellowship with the unfruitful works of darkness, but rather reprove them." Ministers need to use this text often, and to sound out this solemn warning as never before.

Many times preachers miss the practical teachings of the Scriptures while dealing with the prophetic interpretation. Hair-splitting theologians, experts in prophecy, have spent precious hours and much of the Lord's money trying to enlighten the multitudes concerning certain symbols and objects in the Scriptures; but those same men are spiritually as cold as an iceberg and as spiritually dead as last year's bird's-nest—and just as empty! While splitting hairs over who will be the Antichrist, or what may be the meaning of the ten toes of Nebuchadnezzar's image, they miss the practical lessons contained in the prophecies of Daniel and Revelation. I believe in prophecy; I preach and teach prophecy—but there is no need to teach people concerning the prophetic truths of the Bible if they do not practice righteousness and practical Christianity in their daily life.

Certainly we need to preach doctrine and we need to preach prophecy; but we dare not neglect the practical lessons of personal spirituality, holiness, and separation. May God help us to escape the preaching of empty sermons while sinners pour into hell by the thousands and Christians are more excited about the circus or the county fair than they are about the church revival! We ministers must be fed before we can feed others. We must see the light before we can point others to it. We must be clean before we can give forth the message that will cause others to become clean, pure, and sanctified.

It is a solemn Bible fact that the Holy Spirit will not reveal the deep things of God, nor will He open the door of truth and reveal God's precious Word, to those who are defiled by sin. No church will climb any higher spiritually, nor go any deeper into truths revealed in the Scriptures, than their pastor leads them.

Daniel was an extraordinary young man, a man of character. He "purposed in his heart," and there was no weakness in his decision. With his whole heart he vowed that he *would* not–*and he DID not*! Yet he did not speak to the prince of the eunuchs in a haughty, dogmatic way. He did not say, "I simply *will not* participate in your drunken feasts!" Had he done that he would never have won the favor of the prince of the eunuchs. God put the right spirit into Daniel's heart and gave him the right words to make known his request. Instead of commanding or demanding, with a sanctimonious air and a great display of his religious views, Daniel "*requested* of the prince of the eunuchs that he might not defile himself." God honored his loyalty by preparing in advance the heart of the eunuch, for the eunuch gave him a courteous, sympathetic reply.

Daniel could have taken a text and preached an hour-long sermon to this man. He could have denounced the idols and the religious views of the Babylonians; he could have preached long and loud concerning their rebellion against Jehovah God; but he did not. He simply requested the eunuch to allow him to choose his own diet and not be compelled to eat the king's meat and drink his wine.

Verses 9 and 10: "Now God had brought Daniel into favour and tender love with the prince of the eunuchs. And the prince of the eunuchs said unto Daniel, I fear my lord the king, who hath appointed your meat and your drink: for why should he see your faces worse liking than the children which are of your sort? Then shall ye make me endanger my head to the king."

God looks out for His own. The God of Israel neither slumbers nor sleeps; and if God be FOR us, *who can be against us*? Dear believer, YOU and GOD are a majority over any crowd–including kings! God brought Daniel into "*favour and tender love*" with the man who had charge over him. It did not take the eunuch long to see in Daniel something out of the ordinary; and with God working on his heart, the sweet spirit (yet deep determination) of Daniel won his favor, and he was willing to reason with him.

The prince of the eunuchs said, "I fear my lord the king, who hath appointed your meat and your drink." In other words, "Daniel, this is not *my* idea. I am only doing what I have been ordered to do–and I confess I fear the king. Suppose that when you stand before him, your face is worse than the faces of the others who are of your sort? *Then shall ye make me endanger my head to the king*! I will lose my life."

"A soft answer turneth away wrath." Daniel had made his request in a humble way and in all the kindness God had planted in his heart. The prince of the eunuchs, in turn, had a sensible argument to present to Daniel, and he spoke without becoming boisterous or commanding. Again, Daniel could have replied, "What do I care about your head? Suppose you DO lose your life? I am not going to dishonor my God just to save your neck!" But Daniel did not say that.

Verses 11–14: "Then said Daniel to Melzar, whom the prince of the eunuchs had set over Daniel, Hananiah, Mishael, and Azariah, Prove thy servants, I beseech thee, ten days; and let them give us pulse to eat, and water to drink. Then let our countenances be looked upon before thee, and the countenance of the children that eat of the portion of the king's meat: and as thou seest, deal with thy servants. So he consented to them in this matter, and proved them ten days."

Daniel's suggestion was a fair test. He did not want to get the prince into trouble with the king and cause him to lose his life; so he offered to work with him in a satisfactory way and suggested that he and his friends be allowed to eat their chosen diet for a trial period of ten days: "*Then let our countenances be looked upon before thee, and the countenance of the children that eat of the portion of the king's meat: and as thou seest, deal with thy servants."* In response to this suggestion, Melzar the steward consented to allow Daniel and his friends to eat pulse and water for ten days.

"Pulse" refers to "something sown, which signifies primarily vegetables in general and more particularly edible seeds which are cooked, as lentils, horse beans, beans, chick peas and the like" (Unger's Bible Dictionary). Daniel was asking for a simple vegetable diet in the palace of a king! He was not a vegetarian because he thought it a sin to eat meat, for certain meats were NOT sinful to the Hebrews. However, some religions have majored on the fact that Daniel refused to eat the king's meat, and they have incorporated into their doctrines the teaching that it is a sin to eat meat.

These people miss the point of Daniel 1 altogether. The Hebrews were not denied these unclean foods because they were not good to eat–for after Calvary and the Dispensation of the Law, this prohibition was removed from the Church, and we today are not under the dietary laws of the Law. Read Acts 10:12–15.

Daniel did not make his request for the sake of diet or health alone, but for spiritual and moral reasons. He knew the king would place on the table meats that the Hebrews could not eat without being defiled. He did not refuse the king's meat because he was a vegetarian or a religious fanatic, but because he was an obedient child of God–and God had forbidden the eating of certain meats which were termed unclean to His chosen people.

The God of Israel had forbidden them to eat unclean foods or to mix and mingle with other nations, which was a sign of their separation and peculiar relationship to Jehovah God. He had segregated them from the Moabites (and from all other "ites"). They were a separated people, and God wanted them to *remain* separate from the Gentile nations round about them. He gave them an isolated land and a peculiar form of worship and ritual. He gave them only one place in which to worship, and they were to observe peculiar regulations of dress and diet which would segregate them from fellowship with unclean nations who worshipped idols and practiced sin in its most abhorrent forms.

A Hebrew who was faithful to his God could not have social fellowship with heathen nations. Daniel was a faithful Hebrew, a consecrated servant of God; and he could not have social intercourse with those around the king's table. If he did, he would be called upon to eat with them—and they ate unclean food! Thus he would defile himself and lose his separated position as one of those chosen of God.

God imposed severe restrictions upon His people, and these restrictions were God's own provision to keep Israel in the place of blessing. When His chosen people failed to observe God's laws, He brought judgment upon the nation: "A people that provoketh me to anger continually to my face; that sacrificeth in gardens, and burneth incense upon altars of brick; which remain among the graves, and lodge in the monuments, which eat swine's flesh, and broth of abominable things is in their vessels" (Isa. 65:3,4).

Even though the Israelites were God's chosen people, when they rebelled against His commandments and disobeyed Him, He sent judgment upon them: "Behold, it is written before me: I will not keep silence, but will recompense, even recompense into their bosom, your iniquities, and the iniquities of your fathers together, saith the Lord, which have burned incense upon the mountains, and blasphemed me upon the hills: therefore will I measure their former work into their bosom" (Isa. 65:6,7).

Daniel knew that it was a serious thing to bring upon one's self the displeasure of the king—especially such a king as Nebuchadnezzar was; but regardless of the king's greatness and power, Daniel refused to compromise in order to gain his favor. As we study chapter by chapter of this great book, we will learn that Daniel's determination paid off.

I stated earlier in this study that Daniel contains many practical lessons for believers today. Born again Christians, like the Hebrews, are a "peculiar people" in many respects: "But ye are a chosen generation, a royal priesthood, an holy nation, *a peculiar people*; that ye should shew forth the praises of Him who hath called you out of darkness into his marvellous light" (I Pet. 2:9).

The English word "peculiar" comes from the latin *peculium*, which means "private possession." This latin word was applied to things which were particularly *one's own personal property or possession*; it was not used when referring to public property. In that day, if one referred to his *peculium*, he was referring to something which was his very own private property, his private possession.

Believers are GOD'S *peculium*. We are God's purchased, private possession. We are not our own; we are purchased with the tremendous, inestimable price of the precious blood of the Lamb of God. God has a very definite claim upon us, and we need to realize that we are His and *His alone*. We are His *peculium*—His peculiar possession, His pearl of great price. We have no right to share our love or our allegiance with the archenemy of God, the devil and his followers.

In the spiritual sense, the word "peculiar" does not mean that we are to be odd, queer, fanatical or "funny." It does not mean that we are to conduct ourselves in a strange manner or dress in an odd fashion. Christians are not to be known by a garb so outlandish as to attract the attention of all who see it, nor are we to be a group of silly, pious eccentrics. The word "peculiar" applied to Christians means that *we are God's private possession,* and we need to own that fact and live accordingly.

We need to face God's claim upon us, refusing all else that would lead us away from Him in devotion and stewardship. We need to determine in our hearts that we will not go along with anything sinful or questionable, anything that will bring reproach upon the name of Jesus or displease the heart of God. We need to determine that we will not give comfort to the enemies of Jesus Christ by fellowshipping with them or supporting them in any way.

We are not to love the world, nor the things that are IN the world. We are to come out from among them and be a separate people, having no fellowship with the unfruitful works of darkness. We are to prove all things and hold fast to that which is good. We are to USE this world, but not abuse it, for "the fashion of this world passeth away" (I Cor. 7:31).

God is a reasonable God; He will withhold no good thing from them who walk uprightly. At His right hand are pleasures forevermore, and it is the joy of God to give to all who will trust and obey. Abundant life is the birthright of every believer. We are entitled to the fullness and unsearchable riches of His grace if we are willing to admit that we are His *peculium* and yield wholly to Him, determining in our hearts, as Daniel did, that our habits of life will be entirely to the glory of God.

"I beseech you therefore, brethren, by the mercies of God, that ye present your bodies a living sacrifice, holy, acceptable unto God, which is your reasonable service. And be not conformed to this world: but be ye transformed by the renewing of your mind, that ye may prove what is that good, and acceptable, and perfect, will of God" (Rom. 12:1,2).

"Prove all things; hold fast that which is good. Abstain from all appearance of evil. And the very God of peace sanctify you wholly; and I pray God your whole spirit and soul and body be preserved blameless unto the coming of our Lord Jesus Christ" (I Thess. 5:21–23).

Verses 15–17: "And at the end of ten days their countenances appeared fairer and fatter in flesh than all the children which did eat the portion of the king's meat. Thus Melzar took away the portion of their meat, and the wine that they should drink; and gave them pulse. As for these four children, God gave them knowledge and skill in all learning and wisdom: and Daniel had understanding in all visions and dreams."

These verses clearly tell what happened. Daniel and his friends were allowed to eat their diet of herbs and vegetables for ten days; and at the end of that time they were brought before the prince of the eunuchs, "*and their countenances appeared fairer and fatter in flesh than all the children which did eat the portion of the king's meat.*" Melzar therefore took away their portion of meat and wine, and gave them pulse.

God took care of Daniel, Meshach, Shadrach, and Abed-nego. He gave them knowledge, skill, all learning and wisdom. God is still on the throne—and He watches over His children, regardless of where they are or what conditions they may be called upon to live under.

"*. . . And Daniel had understanding in all visions and*

dreams." It seems that God bestowed this *special gift* upon Daniel. God knew that in the very near future, Daniel would have need of this understanding–and God always supplies the need of His servant. If we preachers, teachers, and evangelists would study and apply ourselves as we should and leave the rest to God, He would take care of every detail of our ministry!

God knew that Daniel would be faced with the unreasonable task of recalling and interpreting a dream the king had forgotten, and He provided the ability before the need arose. God always provides for His own.

Like Joseph, Daniel and his companions were trained in the palace of a king. They were chosen from among others to learn the language, literature, and customs of the Chaldeans so that they could act as wise men and counsellors in the king's court. There was nothing wrong with that. There is nothing wrong with young men studying today–provided they keep God uppermost in their studies. It is not wrong for the Christian young man or young woman to acquire knowledge by studying science, literature, the arts and professions; but if they are attending a school that attempts to undermine their faith and destroy their God, then they should pray and seek God's will concerning the continuation of study in such a university.

In Daniel's case, there were no adverse results. The fact that he and his companions underwent a three-year course of instruction implies that there was a "*palace school*" for the instruction of youth of noble descent. The school could not have been far from the palace, for they were fed from the king's table.

Archeologists have uncovered clay libraries of Nineveh and Babylon which prove that the Chaldeans were a learned people–extremely so, considering the times in which they lived. They made great advances in mathematics, astronomy, and grammar. They were well educated people. Babylon was built on the site of Babel, where Nimrod attempted to build a tower to heaven—and the Babylonians were similar, in skills and wisdom, to the antediluvians who were the inventors of musical instruments, and were skilled workers in iron and brass. We learn this from Genesis 4:20–22:

"And Adah bare Jabal: he was the father of such as dwell in tents, and of such as have cattle. And his brother's name was Jubal: he was the father of all such as handle the harp and organ. And Zillah, she also bare Tubal-cain, an instructer of every artificer in brass and iron . . . ."

Verses 18–21: "Now at the end of the days that the king had said he should bring them in, then the prince of the eunuchs brought them in before Nebuchadnezzar. And the king communed with them; and among them all was found none like Daniel, Hananiah, Mishael, and Azariah: therefore stood they before the king. And in all matters of wisdom and understanding, that the king enquired of them, he found them ten times better than all the magicians and astrologers that were in all his realm. And Daniel continued even unto the first year of king Cyrus."

"Now at the end of the days . . . ." This was the three-year period referred to in verse 5. These men had been on a special diet, trained by special instructors, and having finished their course, they appeared personally before Nebuchadnezzar to stand the final test. The king talked with them, asked them many questions, examined them: *"And among them all was found none like Daniel, Hananiah, Mishael, and Azariah: therefore stood they before the king."*

"It pays to serve Jesus/ It pays every day/ It pays every step of the way." Christianity does not pay in eternity only: It pays to be a Christian in *this life*, in more ways than tongue can tell.

"*And in all matters of wisdom and understanding* . . . ." Notice: "*ALL matters* of wisdom and understanding." (Those fellows had quite an extensive course. I wonder how many of us could pass such a test today?) In *all matters* of wisdom and understanding that the king inquired of them, he found the young Hebrews TEN TIMES BETTER than all the magicians and astrologers that were in his realm!

Beautiful, marvelous lesson for believers today! Daniel and his friends had no hope of returning to their homeland for at least seventy years—because they knew the Scripture; they knew that God's sentence was upon them and that He could not, *would not*, change His mind. These young men had every reason to agree among themselves that the only sensible thing for them to do was to fall in line, coexist, and yield—at least in part—to the customs of this heathen land; but they did not do that. They knew God, and they knew that somehow the God of their fathers would work this thing out to His glory and their good: "And we know that all things work together for good to them that love God, to them who are the called according to His purpose. . . What shall we then say to these things? If God be for us, who can be against us?" (Rom. 8:28, 31).

It was not the thought of promotion that caused Daniel and his friends to refuse to yield to the king's wishes; they had every reason to believe that they would forfeit their lives. But in spite of what might happen to them for resisting the command of the king, they refused to deny their God and yield to Nebuchadnezzar's command. (Later in our study we will learn that Daniel was made chief of the governors and his friends were promoted in the palace. God took care of His own!)

We need more Daniels today. We need the *spirit* of Daniel, the *conviction and determination* of Daniel, and we need *the love for God* that Daniel had. Believers today are not captives in Babylon, literally speaking, but we ARE in the Babylon of worldliness and pleasure. Many Christians are conformed to the world, instead of being *transformed* to the image of God's dear Son. Many have succumbed to the spirit of this present evil age, living lives of coexistence and compromise, the outcome of which is powerless spiritual living and spiritual barrenness!

The work of the Lord suffers because of these conditions; the church of the living God is losing the respect of men and women, and instead of making disciples of them and teaching them, we are standing in the way of sinners and sitting in the seat of the scornful. May God help us to repent and return unto Him. He will then reward and bless us after the fashion in which He took care of Daniel and his friends in the land of the enemies of God! Our God is the same God who watched over Daniel–and if we will dare to BE a Daniel, God will do for US what He did for Daniel.

Wonderful, is it not? These Hebrew children were not just *better* students, but they were TEN TIMES better! God honored Daniel and his friends because THEY honored GOD. "*And Daniel continued even unto the first year of king Cyrus.*"

CHAPTER TWO

THE VISIONS OF NEBUCHADNEZZAR; RESULTS OF THE VISIONS

1. And in the second year of the reign of Nebuchadnezzar Nebuchadnezzar dreamed dreams, wherewith his spirit was troubled, and his sleep brake from him.

2. Then the king commanded to call the magicians, and the astrologers, and the sorcerers, and the Chaldeans, for to shew the king his dreams. So they came and stood before the king.

3. And the king said unto them, I have dreamed a dream, and my spirit was troubled to know the dream.

4. Then spake the Chaldeans to the king in Syriack, O king, live for ever: tell thy servants the dream, and we will shew the interpretation.

5. The king answered and said to the Chaldeans, The thing is gone from me: if ye will not make known unto me the dream, with the interpretation thereof, ye shall be cut in pieces, and your houses shall be made a dunghill.

6. But if ye shew the dream, and the interpretation thereof, ye shall receive of me gifts and rewards and great honour: therefore shew me the dream, and the interpretation thereof.

7. They answered again and said, Let the king tell his servants the dream, and we will shew the interpretation of it.

8. The king answered and said, I know of certainty that ye would gain the time, because ye see the thing is gone from me.

9. But if ye will not make known unto me the dream, there is but one decree for you: for ye have prepared lying and corrupt words to speak before me, till the time be changed: therefore tell me the dream, and I shall know that ye can shew me the interpretation thereof.

10. The Chaldeans answered before the king, and said, There is not a man upon the earth that can shew the king's matter: therefore there is no king, lord, nor ruler, that asked such things at any magician, or astrologer, or Chaldean.

11. And it is a rare thing that the king requireth, and there is none other that can shew it before the king, except the gods, whose dwelling is not with flesh.

12. For this cause the king was angry and very furious, and commanded to destroy all the wise men of Babylon.

13. And the decree went forth that the wise men should be slain; and they sought Daniel and his fellows to be slain.

14. Then Daniel answered with counsel and wisdom to Arioch the captain of the king's guard, which was gone forth to slay the wise men of Babylon:

15. He answered and said to Arioch the king's captain, Why is the decree so hasty from the king? Then Arioch made the thing known to Daniel.

16. Then Daniel went in, and desired of the king that he would give him time, and that he would shew the king the interpretation.

17. Then Daniel went to his house, and made the thing known to Hananiah, Mishael, and Azariah, his companions:

18. That they would desire mercies of the God of heaven concerning this secret; that Daniel and his fellows should not perish with the rest of the wise men of Babylon.

19. Then was the secret revealed unto Daniel in a night vision. Then Daniel blessed the God of heaven.

20. Daniel answered and said, Blessed be the name of God for ever and ever: for wisdom and might are his:

21. And he changeth the times and the seasons: he removeth kings, and setteth up kings: he giveth wisdom unto the wise, and knowledge to them that know understanding:

22. He revealeth the deep and secret things: he knoweth what is in the darkness, and the light dwelleth with him.

23. I thank thee, and praise thee, O thou God of my fathers, who hast given me wisdom and might, and hast made known unto me now what we desired of thee: for thou hast now made known unto us the king's matter.

24. Therefore Daniel went in unto Arioch, whom the king had ordained to destroy the wise men of Babylon: he went and said thus unto him; Destroy not the wise men of Babylon: bring me in before the king, and I will shew unto the king the interpretation.

25. Then Arioch brought in Daniel before the king in haste, and said thus unto him, I have found a man of the captives of Judah, that will make known unto the king the interpretation.

26. The king answered and said to Daniel, whose name was Belteshazzar, Art thou able to make known unto me the dream which I have seen, and the interpretation thereof?

27. Daniel answered in the presence of the king, and said, The secret which the king hath demanded cannot the wise men, the astrologers, the magicians, the soothsayers, shew unto the king;

28. But there is a God in heaven that revealeth secrets, and maketh known to the king Nebuchadnezzar what shall be in the latter days. Thy dream, and the visions of thy head upon thy bed, are these;

29. As for thee, O king, thy thoughts came into thy mind upon thy bed, what should come to pass hereafter: and he that revealeth secrets maketh known to thee what shall come to pass.

30. But as for me, this secret is not revealed to me for any wisdom that I have more than any living, but for their sakes that shall make known the interpretation to the king, and that thou mightest know the thoughts of thy heart.

31. Thou, O king, sawest, and behold a great image. This great image, whose brightness was excellent, stood before thee; and the form thereof was terrible.

32. This image's head was of fine gold, his breast and his arms of silver, his belly and his thighs of brass,

33. His legs of iron, his feet part of iron and part of clay.

34. Thou sawest till that a stone was cut out without hands, which smote the image upon his feet that were of iron and clay, and brake them to pieces.

35. Then was the iron, the clay, the brass, the silver, and the gold, broken to pieces together, and became like the chaff of the summer threshingfloors; and the wind carried them away, that no place was found for them: and the stone that smote the image became a great mountain, and filled the whole earth.

36. This is the dream; and we will tell the interpretation thereof before the king.

37. Thou, O king, art a king of kings: for the God of heaven hath given thee a kingdom, power, and strength, and glory.

38. And wheresoever the children of men dwell, the beasts of the field and the fowls of the heaven hath he given into thine hand, and hath made thee ruler over them all. Thou art this head of gold.

39. And after thee shall arise another kingdom inferior to thee, and another third kingdom of brass, which shall bear rule over all the earth.

40. And the fourth kingdom shall be strong as iron: forasmuch as iron breaketh in pieces and subdueth all things: and as iron that breaketh all these, shall it break in pieces and bruise.

41. And whereas thou sawest the feet and toes, part of potters' clay, and part of iron, the kingdom shall be divided; but there shall be in it of the strength of the iron, forasmuch as thou sawest the iron mixed with miry clay.

42. And as the toes of the feet were part of iron, and part of clay, so the kingdom shall be partly strong, and partly broken.

43. And whereas thou sawest iron mixed with miry clay, they shall mingle themselves with the seed of men: but they shall not cleave one to another, even as iron is not mixed with clay.

44. And in the days of these kings shall the God of heaven set up a kingdom, which shall never be destroyed: and the kingdom shall not be left to other people, but it shall break in pieces and consume all these kingdoms, and it shall stand for ever.

45. Forasmuch as thou sawest that the stone was cut out of the mountain without hands, and that it brake in pieces the iron, the brass, the clay, the silver, and the gold; the great God hath made known to the king what shall come to pass hereafter: and the dream is certain, and the interpretation thereof sure.

46. Then the king Nebuchadnezzar fell upon his face, and worshipped Daniel, and commanded that they should offer an oblation and sweet odours unto him.

47. The king answered unto Daniel, and said, Of a truth it is, that your God is a God of gods, and a Lord of kings, and a revealer of secrets, seeing thou couldest reveal this secret.

48. Then the king made Daniel a great man, and gave him many great gifts, and made him ruler over the whole province of Babylon, and chief of the governors over all the wise men of Babylon.

49. Then Daniel requested of the king, and he set Shadrach, Meshach, and Abed-nego, over the affairs of the province of Babylon: but Daniel sat in the gate of the king.

This chapter of Daniel deals with the period of time known in Scripture as "*the times of the Gentiles.*" This period began with the captivity of Judah under Nebuchadnezzar six centuries before the birth of Christ, and will end with the second coming of Jesus Christ at the beginning of the Millennium–the thousand years of peace on earth with Jesus on the throne in Jerusalem and the Church reigning with Him over the earth.

Daniel was faithful to God, and through Daniel God now prepares to reveal the course of this age from Judah's captivity to the time when the kingdom will be set up here on earth and King Jesus will reign over the house of David from His throne in Jerusalem. God gave this revelation to Daniel at the very outset of the Gentile age. He did not give it by chance, but definitely and for a very specific reason.

Among the Israelite captives carried into Babylon was a group of faithful Hebrews who had not been guilty of the gross sins committed by the nation of Israel–sins that brought about the seventy years of Babylonian captivity. Undoubtedly these faithful ones were extremely disturbed at the breaking up of the kingdom of Israel and Judah. God had made a specific promise to Abraham, Isaac, Jacob, and David; and through all of His prophets it had been revealed that Israel was God's covenant nation, and that in the plan and program of God, Israel would be the head among the nations of the world, and their Messiah would come at the appointed time to set up the kingdom of Israel, which would never come to an end.

These faithful Hebrews well knew that the land of Palestine, given to Israel by divine covenant, promised to Abraham by Jehovah God, was to be their safe and peaceful home forever and ever. Under the reign of David and Solomon it seemed that the glorious age had finally come; but a few hundred years later the entire nation was taken captive and carried away into pagan lands to serve as slaves, held in bondage by the enemies of the God of Abraham, Isaac, Jacob and David!

Having looked for the hope of Israel, having lived for the day when the King would put down their enemies and give them that glorious Utopia, and now facing their predicament in Babylon, surely Daniel and his friends must have asked themselves, "Has God forgotten His promise? Has He forgotten His covenant? *Has He forgotten US*? Will the promises of God concerning the kingdom never be fulfilled? Has He put an end to the nation of Israel and the chosen people to whom He made such glorious promises? Was God mistaken—or did Israel misunderstand Him? Had He ever really intended to give them a literal kingdom?"

If such questions tormented the minds of these young Hebrews, it was not for long, because in the very outset of the seventy years of captivity God revealed to Daniel the answer to any and all questions that might arise in their troubled hearts and minds. God had not forgotten His people; He had not forgotten His promise; He had not forgotten His covenant with Abraham. God cannot break His word—and although His chosen people were in bondage and would be scattered to every nation and every island because of their sins, in the fulness of time God would plant them in their own land, never to pluck them up again (Jer. 24:6). In the process of time, God will set up the kingdom, Jesus will sit on the throne, the knowledge of the Lord will cover the earth as the waters cover the sea, and there will be peace on earth, good will toward men (Isaiah 11).

The centuries to elapse between the dispersion of the people of Israel among all the nations and their regathering into their own land at the coming of Messiah were the burden and the message of Daniel's prophecy. God gave the revelation to him at that particular time, in the very outset of the seventy years of captivity, to encourage and reassure the faithful Hebrews that although they were captives in a heathen land, in the end they would be regathered to their own land and the God of their fathers would keep every promise made to Father Abraham and his descendants. The period of time is "the times of the Gentiles," beginning with Nebuchadnezzar and running through the reign of the Antichrist.

God committed the government of earth to His chosen people, Israel. His plan for earth's government was to be administered through priests, prophets, and kings—men who feared God and lived godly lives; but the Israelites disobeyed Him and turned aside after strange gods. Therefore Jehovah interrupted the kingdom, allowing Gentile nations to take over the reins of the governments of earth.

The Gentiles have been ruling since the days of Nebuchadnezzar, but the Gentile Age is rapidly drawing to a close. The nations are at this moment engaged in a death struggle to prevent the destruction of the world and the annihilation of the human race. God will allow man to run his limit—and when he has come to the place of such utter hopelessness that it seems there will be no flesh saved, *Jesus will come*; the times of the Gentiles will end, and God will set up His glorious kingdom of peace and righteousness here on earth. There will be peace—the Utopia that man has *talked* about, but has never been able to *bring* about. The best is just ahead, for God has permitted man to go just about as far as He *will permit* him to go. As we study the last chapter of Daniel, we will see that surely we are living in the last moments of "the times of the Gentiles."

Verse 1: "And in the second year of the reign of Nebuchadnezzar, Nebuchadnezzar dreamed dreams, wherewith his spirit was troubled, and his sleep brake from him."

Some may ask, "Why did God choose *a heathen king* to whom He would reveal the tremendous prophecies concerning the 'times of the Gentiles'? He could have given the revelation to Daniel or to any one of his friends, or to some other prophet." In the Bible we read of the "divine rights of kings"—and if ever a king *had a divine right* to rule upon this earth, it was Nebuchadnezzar, king of Babylon. He did not gain the position he held: *God gave it to him.*

"Thus saith the Lord of hosts, the God of Israel; Thus shall ye say unto your masters; I have made the earth, the man and the beast that are upon the ground, by my great power and by my outstretched arm, and have given it unto whom it seemed meet unto me. And now have I given all these lands into the hand of Nebuchadnezzar the king of Babylon, my servant; and the beasts of the field have I given him also to serve him. And all nations shall serve him, and his son, and his son's son, until the very time of his land come: and then many nations and great kings shall serve themselves of him. And it shall come to pass, that the nation and kingdom which will not serve the same Nebuchadnezzar the king of Babylon, and that will not put their neck under the yoke of the king of Babylon, that nation will I punish, saith the Lord, with the sword, and with the famine, and with the pestilence, until I have consumed them by his hand" (Jer. 27:4–8).

Here, from the inspired pen of Jeremiah, we learn that Nebuchadnezzar was chosen by Jehovah God for the work he did in Babylon; but the Bible does not tell us whether or not Nebuchadnezzar himself knew this. However, we do know that he was greatly puffed up and filled with pride by his greatness and his overwhelming power. One day as he walked in his palace, he looked out over the great city and the country over which he was king, and said, "Is not this great Babylon, that I have built for the house of the kingdom by the might of my power, and for the honour of my majesty?" (Dan. 4:29,30).

Since the king was filled with pride and puffed up because of his greatness in Babylon, it seems proper that he should have had a dream which could have (and *should have*) enlightened him and made known to him that his greatness was not because of his own ability nor because of his own power–but GOD had made him great. The glories of Babylon would soon pass away, but the God who gave him glory and power was able to take away that which He had given.

The Forgotten Dream

Early in the reign of Nebuchadnezzar, as he lay on his sumptuous couch in his magnificent palace one day thinking about the great kingdom over which he ruled, perhaps wondering what the future of that kingdom would be, thus daydreaming–he fell asleep; but the thoughts of his waking hours did not leave him, and he began to visualize in a dream. He saw a great image "whose brightness was excellent." The form of this monstrous image "was terrible." (This probably refers to its colossal size.) Its brightness was the result of supernatural light that fell from heaven and was reflected upon the metals of which the image was composed.

While Nebuchadnezzar looked upon the image in awe and amazement, he saw another spectacular sight: A stone, cut out of the neighboring mountain–cut out without hands–smote the image upon its feet. The massive image collapsed and was ground into powder, and the wind blew it away. And as the king gazed in wonder, the stone began to grow—larger and larger—until it covered the whole plain upon which the great image had stood but a short time before.

There is a difference between dreams and visions. *Dreams* occur while we sleep, and are often remembered when we awake. Sometimes, however, if the dream is not a vivid one, it fades from the mind and we cannot recall it afterward. *Visions* are ocular phenomena and occur while one is awake. The mind becomes absorbed with some thought, and the one seeing a vision is not conscious of the things going on around him at that moment. I personally believe God warns believers in dreams, and it is clear in the Bible that some spiritually minded people have visions; but we are warned to *try* the spirits and see if they be of God. We must be very careful about dreams and visions.

Dreamers dream of things with which they are familiar. A hundred years ago people did not dream about automobiles and airplanes, nor about satellites orbiting the earth, for there were no such things then. A hundred years ago, if one dreamed of making a trip, it would not be by deisel locomotive or by flying through the air; it would be by oxcart or horse and buggy. It was natural for Nebuchadnezzar to dream of images, because in his day there were many such. Archeologists have unearthed many giant statues of kings and rulers who lived before and during that time. Nebuchadnezzar had just returned from Egypt, having overrun the Egyptians and conquered that country. What would be more natural than for this proud king to be thinking of the massive statues he had seen in Egypt, perhaps thinking of erecting one to himself in Babylon?

The images in Egypt were made of stone, whereas the great image Nebuchadnezzar saw in his dream was made of metal—not just one kind of metal, but several different kinds. Nebuchadnezzar was deeply interested in knowing just what the dream meant, but the image was so frightful, so overwhelming, that when the king awoke in terror, perplexed and troubled, he could not remember the dream; it had faded completely from his memory.

Verses 2 and 3: "Then the king commanded to call the magicians, and the astrologers, and the sorcerers, and the Chaldeans, for to shew the king his dreams. So they came and stood before the king. And the king said unto them, I have dreamed a dream, and my spirit was troubled to know the dream."

The heathen king did not believe in God, and the only ones to whom he *could* turn for help were the magicians, astrologers, sorcerers, and Chaldeans. These were the advisors who unraveled mysteries for the king. They practiced all the superstitious rites and ceremonies commonly associated with fortunetellers and witchdoctors. The magicians were supposed to make mysteries known. They were supposed to have power to interpret dreams.

The astrologers were men who pretended to foretell events of the future. They claimed they were able to do this by studying the stars. There were many astrologers in the eastern nations before, during, and after the time of Nebuchadnezzar and Daniel.

The sorcerers claimed to have the ability to communicate with the dead. They claimed to possess supernatural power gained in many ways, especially through evil spirits. Modern spiritualism is an example of what the sorcerers were in Daniel's day.

The Chaldeans were a sect of philosophers who made the sciences their special study. They claimed to have degrees in science and to be authorities on scientific information.

The king was in serious trouble, the most serious trouble he had ever encountered. He had dreamed a dream, but the dream had left him. It had been a terrible dream, but he could not make known what was so terrible about it because the design of it was completely erased from his memory.

The Failure of the Wise Men

The magicians, the astrologers, the sorcerers and the Chaldeans appeared before the king:

Verses 4–9: "Then spake the Chaldeans to the king in Syriack, O king, live for ever: tell thy servants the dream, and we will shew the interpretation. The king answered and said to the Chaldeans, The thing is gone from me: if ye will not make known unto me the dream, with the interpretation thereof, ye shall be cut in pieces, and your houses shall be made a dunghill. But if ye shew the dream, and the interpretation thereof, ye shall receive of me gifts and rewards and great honour: therefore shew me the dream, and the interpretation thereof. They answered again and said, Let the king tell his servants the dream, and we will shew the interpretation of it. The king answered and said, I know of certainty that ye would gain the time, because ye see the thing is gone from me. But if ye will not make known unto me the dream, there is but one decree for you: for ye have prepared lying and corrupt words to speak before me, till the time be changed: therefore tell me the dream, and I shall know that ye can shew me the interpretation thereof."

I do not discount the fact that there have always been spiritualists who were demon-possessed, sold to the devil, and who could communicate with evil spirits. There have been witch doctors and fortunetellers who were indeed *in union* with evil spirits and the power of the devil; but most of these fellows in Daniel's day were fakes.

The ancient magicians, fortunetellers, and interpreters of dreams and visions were shrewd in the art of drawing from their victim enough information to form a foundation for some acceptable answer, giving the answer in such a way as to make it believable, regardless of what might happen concerning their predictions or interpretations. The wise men of Babylon figured among themselves that if they could get the king to tell them enough about his dream to give them a starting place, they could then agree on an interpretation and give the king an answer that seemed reasonable, thus saving their reputations and remaining on the royal payroll.

Nebuchadnezzar had called upon them to perform such a task as they had never before encountered! He wanted them to *reveal* his dream—and then give the interpretation of it. In spite of their claim to superhuman powers, the king had called upon them to do something which, according to them, only the gods could do.

Nebuchadnezzar then recognized his wise men as fakers. He said, *"Ye have prepared lying and corrupt words to speak before me."* He accused them of stalling for time. They were hoping that the king would forget the whole matter if they could put him off long enough, and that he would dismiss them from the obligation he had placed upon them.

The Chaldeans claimed to be able to communicate with the gods and to receive from them wisdom and knowledge not given to ordinary men; but the fact that they could not tell the king his dream proved that they were false. They confessed as much in their statement to the king:

Verses 10 and 11: "The Chaldeans answered before the king, and said, There is not a man upon the earth that can shew the king's matter: therefore there is no king, lord, nor ruler, that asked such things at any magician, or astrologer, or Chaldean. And it is a rare thing that the king requireth, and there is none other that can shew it before the king, except the gods, whose dwelling is not with flesh."

Thus the Chaldeans announced to Nebuchadnezzar that they were a group of impostors, liars, and counterfeits. No wonder the king flew into a rage and commanded that the Chaldeans and the wise men of Babylon be destroyed!

Verses 12 and 13: "For this cause the king was angry and very furious, and commanded to destroy all the wise men of Babylon. And the decree went forth that the wise men should be slain; and they sought Daniel and his fellows to be slain."

Let us sum up the episodes recorded in the first thirteen verses of our present chapter and see why the Holy Spirit dictated these verses to Daniel to be penned down for our instruction and admonition:

King Nebuchadnezzar was the most powerful monarch on earth at that time. His kingdom was majestic in size; his palace no doubt was the last word in luxury and comfort. The king was resting on his couch, his thoughts dwelling upon his huge kingdom and his exalted position, remembering the images he had seen in Egypt during his successful conquest there. Having seen the ruins of the great Egyptian images, he no doubt had this in mind when he fell asleep; and while sleeping he dreamed dreams—dreams so disturbing to his spirit that sleep left him.

Immediately he called his wise men, who were supposed to possess such supernatural wisdom as to be capable of interpreting dreams and making known the answers to any and all questions the king might present to them.

The Chaldeans, magicians, soothsayers, and astrologers all appeared before the king in his court; and he told them that he had dreamed a dream that troubled his spirit and he must know the dream. They replied, "O king, live forever! Tell thy servants the dream—and we will shew thee the interpretation."

Undoubtedly, in times past the king had told the wise men what he had dreamed, and they had always been able to agree on an answer that would please him; but this time, the dream had left him and he could not remember what it was about. He could only remember that the dream was horrible, and that it disturbed him as nothing had ever disturbed him in all of his life.

The king had been paying these wise men well; he had been feeding and sheltering them for many years—and now when he needed them most, he was disappointed to learn that they were unable to reveal what he had forgotten. He said to them, "If ye will not make known unto me the dream, with the interpretation thereof, *ye shall be cut in pieces*, and your houses shall be made a dunghill! However, if you will show me the dream and interpret it for me, you will receive gifts, rewards, and great honor. Therefore, show me the dream, and the interpretation thereof!"

A *second* time the wise men called upon the king to make known his dream and they would then make known the interpretation of it; but the king was not to be put off. He realized that they *could* not make known his dream and its interpretation, and that they were only making a play for extra time. If these men actually were in contact with spirits that could make known the *interpretation* of the dream, then the same spirits should make known the forgotten *dream*. He knew they wanted time to prepare "lies and corrupt words" in an attempt to satisfy him concerning the dream that had so disturbed him and brought terror to his spirit.

The wise men told the king that there was not a man

upon the face of the earth who could grant his request, "except the gods, whose dwelling is not with flesh." Thus by their own confession they revealed that they were not connected with the gods in any way, and that they did not have access to the wisdom and knowledge that only the gods could supply. The king therefore issued a decree that the wise men of Babylon should be slain. Since Daniel and his friends were in this group, the decree meant that these God-fearing Hebrews would also be put to death.

All Scripture is given by inspiration of God, and is profitable for instruction, for correction, edification and doctrine. What could these thirteen verses contain that will enlighten us in this day? I believe the primary truth God would have us to see here is that while the devil and his evil spirits are not *omnipotent*, they ARE very, very powerful. There are millions of them throughout the universe, and the devil is the prince of the power of the air. Satan is not omniscient–he does not know and understand all things–but he knows much, much more than we give him credit for, even about the saints of God!

The king's dream had left him; and even though some of the wise men and magicians might have been genuine, might actually have been in touch with evil spirits, those evil spirits could not make known Nebuchadnezzar's dream–*because that dream was of God*. It revealed "the times of the Gentiles" and the fact that the Gentiles would reign over the earth until their time should come to an end. King Jesus would then call His people from the four corners of the earth and from the islands of the sea; He would plant them in their own land never to be plucked up again, and He, their Messiah, would reign over them. God gave the dream to Nebuchadnezzar, and ONLY God could bring it to the minds of the wise men and give the interpretation of it. It was God's doing, and demons and evil spirits could not make known that which God had shown Nebuchadnezzar in his dream.

But all hell cannot stop the program of Almighty God. He always has His representative in the right place at the right time. "*In the beginning*" God blueprinted the plan of the ages–even the eternity of eternities. He knew the end in the beginning. God is sovereign–He puts up whom He will, and He puts down whom He will. God had a plan–but the king, being a sinner, could not understand that his dream was a revelation from God. His wise men *could not* make known his dream; because if they were empowered by any spirit at all, it was the spirit of the devil–and certainly the spirit of Satan cannot make known the things of God! The wise men of Babylon were helpless; and had it not been for the God of heaven, they could not have been delivered when the sentence of execution was passed upon them by the king.

There is another important fact that should be pointed out here: In these thirteen verses we learn that because of a few righteous people, God has, on many occasions, spared multitudes of ungodly people. The lives of the wise men were spared because there was a man of God in the kingdom who was capable of *contacting* God, getting the right answer from Him, and giving that answer to the king. Had it not been for Daniel and his godly brethren, the wise men of Babylon would have been cut to pieces under the king's decree. (If Abraham could have found only ten righteous men in Sodom, God would have delivered that whole city for the sake of ten righteous people.)

Jesus said, "Ye are the salt of the earth. Ye are the light of the world." The only thing that keeps the judgment of God from falling upon this great land of ours are the few godly, God-fearing men and women left in the United States of America. God spares this country for the sake of the righteous.

From the human standpoint, things looked dark for Daniel and his friends. Daniel had stood firm in the very outset of his stay in the king's court and had purposed in his heart that he would not deny his God to please a heathen king. He remembered His God; he refused the king's meat and wine, and God would now remember Daniel as He had remembered Noah, Abraham, and Moses. God remembered Joseph; He remembered David. God has always remembered His faithful servants–and He always will. God's man is indestructible. All hell cannot destroy God's prophet or servant until God has finished with that man here on earth!

For some reason which we do not know, Daniel and his friends knew nothing of the entire episode until the captain of the king's guard came to arrest them. God wanted the impostors to have their chance to reveal the dream; they were proven false, declared counterfeit, and forced to confess that they could not do what only the supernatural was capable of doing. If Daniel had been called first, he would have called upon the God of heaven, he would have interpreted the dream, and the Babylonian wise men would have escaped the test which exposed them for what they really were.

Whether the wise men should have been slain or not is a good question. We know they were not what they claimed to be, but magicians, astrologers, sorcerers and wise men were numerous in Babylon. They were more or less human parasites, because they were considered to be superior, they were wealthy and influential, they had great power in the kingdom–and for that reason the king feared them. These men were the *learned* men of Babylon, and to destroy them was to weaken the great Babylonian empire, from the standpoint of human power. But had not Daniel made known Nebuchadnezzar's dream, the king would have had these men butchered.

There is another parallel between Daniel and Joseph in evidence here: When the magicians and the sorcerers of Egypt could not interpret the dreams of Pharaoh, Joseph (God's man) was there in jail prepared for the task. Joseph made known the interpretation of Pharaoh's dreams —and saved the land from starvation.

Nothing can happen to a child of God without God's permission. Even though Joseph and Daniel did not have Romans 8:28 written in a book, they had it in their hearts because they knew that God is the Word and the Word is God. They knew that the God of their fathers would take care of them, in His own way, in His own time.

When the wise men of Babylon could not make known the forgotten dream of Nebuchadnezzar, God had another Hebrew captive on the scene to do the job as only God's man can:

Verses 14–16: "Then Daniel answered with counsel and wisdom to Arioch the captain of the king's guard, which was gone forth to slay the wise men of Babylon: He answered and said to Arioch the king's captain, Why is the decree so hasty from the king? Then Arioch made the thing known to Daniel. Then Daniel went in, and desired of the king that he would give him time, and that he would shew the king the interpretation."

Notice: "*Daniel answered with counsel and wisdom* to Arioch the captain of the king's guard." Had Daniel been hot-headed he might have been the cause of great tragedy; but he was a man of godly character, and he used wisdom and faith in dealing with the captain. Daniel did not ask the king to describe his dream; he simply asked for time, having unshakable confidence that if the king would give him time to pray, he could reproduce the dream and give the king its meaning. Nebuchadnezzar granted the request.

God will not, He cannot, forsake His own. If we trust Him, He will never let us down. If we are true to God, He will stand by us in time of danger and pull us back from the very verge of destruction–and that is where Daniel stood. But he had faith in God to such great extent that he simply asked for time to pray, and promised to then make known the king's forgotten dream.

Verses 17 and 18: "Then Daniel went to his house, and made the thing known to Hananiah, Mishael, and Azariah, his companions: That they would desire mercies of the God of heaven concerning this secret; that Daniel and his fellows should not perish with the rest of the wise men of Babylon."

I do not doubt that Daniel and his friends had an all night prayer meeting, for this was a matter of life and death! If God heard and answered their prayers, their lives would be spared; but if He refused to hear and answer, their lives would be forfeited along with the other wise men.

I personally believe Daniel would have been heard had he prayed by himself, but evidently he believed in united prayer. He had high regard for his three Hebrew companions–and they were as concerned in this matter as he was, for their lives, too, were at stake. If Daniel could not keep his promise to the king, all four of them would die.

There was more at stake here than the lives of these four men. Had Daniel failed God, the world would have missed the great revelation locked up in the king's dream and the interpretation thereof. Nebuchadnezzar's dream held the prophetic and the historical blueprint of "the times of the Gentiles."

The Holy Spirit did not see fit to reveal to us just when this prayer meeting began nor when it ended, but we know that Daniel and his friends did not cease praying until they had the assurance that God would give them the answer they needed. We are not told HOW God revealed the dream to Daniel. Perhaps as Daniel *slept* the dream was revealed to him. Perhaps the angel Gabriel appeared as he did in another of Daniel's visions, and revealed both the dream and its interpretation. The record simply states, "*Then was the secret revealed unto Daniel in a night vision*"—and we know that GOD gave Daniel the revelation.

Verses 19–23: "Then was the secret revealed unto Daniel in a night vision. Then Daniel blessed the God of heaven. Daniel answered and said, Blessed be the name of God for ever and ever: for wisdom and might are His: and He changeth the times and the seasons: He removeth kings, and setteth up kings: He giveth wisdom unto the wise, and knowledge to them that know understanding: He revealeth the deep and secret things: He knoweth what is in the darkness, and the light dwelleth with Him. I thank thee, and praise thee, O thou God of my fathers, who hast given me wisdom and might, and hast made known unto me now what we desired of thee: for thou hast now made known unto us the king's matter."

These verses record one of the most beautiful, wonderful outbursts of praise and adoration to God in all of the Bible. It is noteworthy that God's prophet did not rush in haste to the court of Nebuchadnezzar, demanding that the king leave his bedchamber and appear for a conference. Daniel was a man of wisdom—wise as a serpent, harmless as a dove. God had given him the answer, the burden had left his soul, and he was jubilant in his heart. He believed in giving thanks to God for blessings, and especially for answered prayer.

Let us analyze the prayer of thanksgiving and praise that Daniel sent up to heaven in thanksgiving to God for answering their prayer:

1. Daniel praised God because wisdom and might *belong* to God. Daniel knew that His God was omniscient, that He was sovereign, that He knew all things and was able to make all things known. He knew that God was omnipotent, that all power in heaven and on earth belonged to HIM. Therefore, Daniel blessed the name of his God and praised Him for wisdom and power. "If any of you lack wisdom, let him ask of God, that giveth to all men liberally, and upbraideth not; and it shall be given him" (James 1:5). Jesus said, "All power is given unto me in heaven and in earth" (Matt. 28:18). "If God be for us, who can be against us?" (Rom. 8:31).

2. Daniel praised God that He alone "changeth the times and the seasons." The object of this is to assert that God has general control in reference to all of the changes which occur. Particularly is this assertion made in reference to the changes in the empire which Daniel had now seen in the dream. "There is no essential difference between the words *times* and *seasons.* The words in Chaldee denote stated or appointed seasons; and the idea of times *appointed, set, determined* enters into both." Times and seasons are not under the control of chance, but are regulated by established laws; yet God, who appointed these laws, has power to change them, and all the changes which occur under these laws are produced under His power and control. God is the God of time and of eternity, the God of heaven and earth, the God of all seasons. *He is the sovereign God over the earth and all creation.*

3. Daniel blessed the God of heaven and praised Him because "He removeth kings, and setteth up kings."

God puts up whom He will and puts down whom He will. Daniel was in Babylon by God's permission, and even though a captive, he was there on business for the King of all kings.

4. He praised God and thanked Him because "He giveth wisdom unto the wise." God had blessed Daniel with wisdom and had made known to him the dream which the heathen wise men and astrologers could NOT make known to Nebuchadnezzar. The wisdom of this world is foolishness to God, and the foolishness of God is wiser than the wisdom of men. When all the astrologers, magicians, and wise men of this earth fail, the God of wisdom is able to reveal what man could never fathom nor understand.

5. Not only does God give wisdom unto the wise, but He also gives knowledge *"to them that know understanding."* That is, God gives knowledge to men who understand that "the fear of the Lord is the *beginning* of knowledge" (Prov. 1:7). Until a man fears God he is ignorant, regardless of how many universities he may have attended or how many college degrees he holds. To fear God and to trust Him is to be on grounds to receive knowledge and understanding FROM God. Therefore, Daniel gave thanks to the God of heaven for knowledge and understanding.

6. Daniel praised God in prayer with thanksgiving in his heart and jubilance in his soul, that God *"revealeth the deep and secret things."* Moses declared, "The secret things belong unto the Lord our God" (Deut. 29:29); but God is able to *reveal* the deep and secret things. Nebuchadnezzar's dream had departed from his mind; he could not recall it, and not one of his wise men could reproduce it—but the God of ALL secrets made known to Daniel the dream and the interpretation of it.

Daniel knew that within himself he could never have brought the dream to light nor have given the interpretation, and he gave God the praise, honor, adoration and thanksgiving to which He was entitled.

7. Daniel blessed the God of heaven because "*He knoweth what is in the darkness, and the light dwelleth with Him.*" I John 1:5 tells us, "God is light, and in Him is no darkness at all." God is light. God's kingdom is the kingdom of light. God had brought to Daniel's mind the dream that was shrouded in darkness, which the king had forgotten—and had made known to him the interpretation thereof.

Daniel closes his prayer: "*I thank thee, and praise thee, O thou God of my fathers, who hast given me wisdom and might, and hast made known unto me now what we desired of thee: for thou hast now made known unto us the king's matter.*"

Notice that Daniel did not forget his friends. He said, "Thou hast made known what WE desired of thee . . . Thou hast now made known unto US the king's matter." Daniel's heart was filled with the Spirit of God, and he was not interested in making a name for himself. Pride had no place in his life. He was humble, surrendered fully to the will of God. He had called on his friends to help him pray, and when God gave him the revelation of the king's dream, he did not claim the honor and glory for answered prayer. He included his friends.

I would that we might be delivered today from religious pride and have a unified church—not that we might compromise, but that we might stop "splitting hairs" over the minor and spend more time on the major. If God's people would stand together in this hour as did Daniel, Shadrach, Meshach, and Abed-nego in Babylon, we would have revival in our great land today. But too many Christians are interested only in their own denomination, their own church, and their own little circle of fellowship. Christians today are too busy debating their differences to have time for hearts united in prayer for revival.

Daniel was in no hurry to get to the king. He praised God to his heart's content, and then he sought Arioch and made known to him the good news.

Verse 24: "Therefore Daniel went in unto Arioch, whom the king had ordained to destroy the wise men of Babylon: he went and said thus unto him; Destroy not the wise men of Babylon: bring me in before the king, and I will shew unto the king the interpretation."

In view of the fact that the dream was now disclosed to him, he proposed to lay the solution before the king. But Daniel did not go directly to the king. He approached him through Arioch, the one to whom was intrusted the decree to slay all of the wise men of Babylon. That officer would naturally have access to the king, and it was only proper that Daniel go first to the officer in charge.

Notice Daniel's *first* request of Arioch: "*Destroy not the wise men of Babylon.*" If Daniel had had the spirit of selfishness and greed, I wonder if he would not have requested that Arioch go ahead and destroy all of the wise men except himself and his friends? On one occasion the disciples asked Jesus if they should call down fire from heaven and destroy His enemies. He replied that He had not come to destroy men's lives, but to save them. God has no pleasure in the death of the wicked, and it is not His will that any perish. Daniel knew God, and I do not doubt that he had a prayer in his heart for each of the wise men, that God might use this experience to cause them to be converted. At least we know that he did not want them executed. Whether the wise men gave him thanks or not, they *should have*, for certainly their lives were spared because of him.

On another occasion (Acts 27) a group of unsaved men were spared because of a man of God: "For there stood by me this night the angel of God, whose I am, and whom I serve, saying, Fear not, Paul; thou must be brought before Caesar: and, lo, *God hath given thee all them that sail with thee*" (Acts 27:23,24). On this occasion, Paul was a prisoner enroute by ship to Rome to appear before Caesar. A terrible storm arose, and because Paul knew God, *he prayed* while members of the ship's crew panicked. God heard and answered him, and the next day he stood on the deck of the ship and announced to the sailors that not one of them would perish. God kept His promise to Paul; the sailors were all spared. But had not Paul been on board the ship there is no doubt that the men would all have perished.

The Word of God teaches us that the wicked are blessed for righteousness' sake. The house of Potiphar was blessed for Joseph's sake (Gen. 39:5), and the Lord would have spared Sodom and Gomorrah if Abraham could have found even ten righteous people in those cities. The world is spared today because of the righteous people in it; and when the Rapture occurs and the Church is taken out, all hell will break loose right here on this earth under the reign of the devil in flesh—the Antichrist. The wise men of Babylon were spared for Daniel's sake. WE are *saved* for Jesus' sake (Eph. 4:32).

Verses 25 and 26: "Then Arioch brought in Daniel before the king in haste, and said thus unto him, I have found a man of the captives of Judah, that will make known unto the king the interpretation. The king answered and said to Daniel, whose name was Belteshazzar, Art thou able to make known unto me the dream which I have seen, and the interpretation thereof?"

Please note: Arioch said, "*I* have found a man."

He attempted to win favor with Nebuchadnezzar by claiming to have found an interpreter—but HE had not found the man at all! Arioch forgot, if he had ever known, that Daniel had appeared earlier in the presence of the king, and had requested time to pray, promising that he would afterward reveal the dream and its interpretation.

Daniel was not seeking self-glory; he did not covet position or power. He was simply doing the will of God; he was acting in obedience to the God of his fathers. And if Nebuchadnezzar slapped Arioch on the back and said, "Well done," it is not recorded.

It is worthy of our notice that Arioch must have had faith in Daniel, for he was taking a chance when he took Daniel before the king, saying, "This man can tell you the dream." Remember in verse 12 the king was furious with the wise men and their excuses. Suppose Daniel should give a similar answer. Would not Arioch's life have been in danger also? The king was already disgusted and his patience was exhausted with the "lying, corrupt words" of the wise men. Knowing this, Arioch could have thought, "Daniel is only stalling for time; he knows no more than the rest. And if I take him before the king I may forfeit my head!"

But he did not hesitate. *"In haste"* he brought Daniel before the king. He believed Daniel had the answer. It was remarkable in the first place that this captain was disposed to delay the execution even for a little while, so that Daniel could have time to pray for an answer. It was, of course, God's divine intervention; but it seems that all of the circumstances in the case imply that, in addition to his desire to please his king, Arioch was not a cruel, blood-thirsty man.

The king at once turned to Daniel and asked, *"Art thou able* to make known unto me the dream which I have seen, and the interpretation thereof?" Whether the king realized it or not, he was asking Daniel, "Was *your God* able to help you? Did He hear your prayers? Is *your* God more powerful and wiser than the gods of the astrologers and wise men of Babylon?"

Verse 27: "Daniel answered in the presence of the king, and said, The secret which the king hath demanded cannot the wise men, the astrologers, the magicians, the soothsayers, shew unto the king."

Picture Daniel as he stood in the presence of Nebuchadnezzar—a king who had conquered all the known kingdoms of his day, a king who was the most powerful ruler on earth. Yet the humble Hebrew boy who had been brought captive to Babylon and forced to serve in the king's court did not falter before him. Daniel said, "The secret which you have demanded made known cannot be shown by the wise men, the astrologers, the magicians, or the soothsayers."

It might seem that there was a note of sarcasm in Daniel's answer to the king, but I do not think so. I believe he was trying to drive home to the heart of Nebuchadnezzar the fact that he had been looking to the wrong gods, the wrong power. I believe he was making a desperate effort to point the king to the God whom Daniel loved and served. The Scripture does not tell us *how many* wise men Nebuchadnezzar had—there might have been scores of them—but Daniel reminded him that the *best* Babylon could produce in wise men, magicians, astrologers and soothsayers could not do what Daniel's God had done. Then to the king he said:

Verse 28: "But there is a God in heaven that revealeth secrets, and maketh known to the king Nebuchadnezzar what shall be in the latter days. Thy dream, and the visions of thy head upon thy bed, are these."

Daniel took no credit for himself and his friends.

He wanted the king to understand that it was God in heaven who had made known the secrets and revealed Nebuchadnezzar's forgotten dream which all the wise men in Babylon could not reproduce. The God of heaven was the Revelator. It was not through wisdom or ability on the part of Daniel and his three Hebrew friends that the revelation had been given. The God of gods, the King of kings, had made known the secrets Nebuchadnezzar had forgotten.

Verse 29: "As for thee, O king, thy thoughts came into thy mind upon thy bed, what should come to pass hereafter: and He that revealeth secrets maketh known to thee what shall come to pass."

"*Thy thoughts came into thy mind upon thy bed.*" It would seem most likely, from this phrase, that Nebuchadnezzar's thoughts before he fell asleep had been occupied with his kingdom, his possible successor, changes that would possibly be made in other kingdoms, etc. The dream was then grafted onto these thoughts, showing him what was to be hereafter. If this be true, then Daniel, in referring to these thoughts, would do much to confirm the king's belief in his revelation—for even though the king had forgotten his dream, he would surely not have forgotten his thoughts while awake.

"*. . . What should come to pass hereafter: and He that revealeth secrets maketh known to thee what shall come to pass.*" In other words, "King Nebuchadnezzar, your dream was no ordinary dream; it was a revelation from the God of heaven concerning things that shall come to pass."

Verse 30: "But as for me, this secret is not revealed to me for any wisdom that I have more than any living, but for their sakes that shall make known the interpretation to the king, and that thou mightest know the thoughts of thy heart."

Daniel said in verse 29, "As for THEE, O king." Now he says, "But as for ME . . . this secret is not revealed to me for any wisdom that I have, more than any living." In other words, "King, it is not *my* wisdom that will make known these secrets to you. It is not *my* understanding, nor *my ability*. I have no more wisdom than other men . . . but for their sakes that shall make known the interpretation to the king, that thou mightest know the thoughts of thy heart."

Daniel wanted Nebuchadnezzar to understand that the God of heaven had revealed the interpretation to him, and that *the only reason God had made that revelation* was that the king might know the future of his kingdom, and that he might know the things that were to come to pass in the far distant future—even until the consummation of the times of the Gentiles!

If ever a person had a right to be proud, from the human standpoint, Daniel was that person. But, like John the Baptist, Daniel was not interested in fame and fortune. He was God's prophet, God's servant; and the joy of his heart and life was to do the will of God. John the Baptist said, "I am NOT that Light; I am only a voice crying in the wilderness. I have come to announce the coming of the King. Make His path straight. He must increase, I must decrease." True servants of God have that same humble spirit. They are possessed by the Holy Spirit, who always points men to the God of heaven, the Christ of God, the Saviour of sinners.

Nebuchadnezzar's Dream

Verses 31–35: "Thou, O king, sawest, and behold a great image. This great image, whose brightness was excellent, stood before thee; and the form thereof was terrible. This image's head was of fine gold, his breast and his arms of silver, his belly and his thighs of brass, his legs of iron, his feet part of iron and part of clay.

Thou sawest till that a stone was cut out without hands, which smote the image upon his feet that were of iron and clay, and brake them to pieces. Then was the iron, the clay, the brass, the silver, and the gold, broken to pieces together, and became like the chaff of the summer threshingfloors; and the wind carried them away, that no place was found for them: and the stone that smote the image became a great mountain, and filled the whole earth."

It would be useless for us to try to imagine how Nebuchadnezzar felt as this young Hebrew made known, word by word and step by step, the details of the dream the king could not remember. As Daniel reconstructed the dream, the great image stood out in perfect clarity just as the king had seen it in his dream. And what must he have thought of Daniel, and of his spiritual insight and wisdom?

It would have been interesting to have watched the wise men, the astrologers, the soothsayers and the Chaldeans as Daniel unfolded the mystery of the dream which they and their heathen gods had been unable to reproduce and interpret. The king must have been amazed at Daniel's wisdom, but he demonstrated faith in that wisdom by accepting the interpretation of the dream. And why not? Daniel had unfolded it before his very eyes!

Three of the expressions used in verses 28 and 29 give us the key that unlocks the meaning of the vision with its colossal image:

"*Latter days . . . .*"

"*Should come to pass hereafter . . . .*"

"*What shall come to pass . . . .*"

All three expressions emphasize a fact which we must keep in mind: *The image Nebuchadnezzar saw in his dream was a picture (God's blueprint) of future things.* Wrapped up in that dream was a prophecy dealing with things which had not happened up to that time, but *would* happen—even in the "latter days."

Skeptics and infidels have attacked the book of Daniel. Some have declared that it is not a prophetic book, but was written *after* these things occurred. Some declare that Daniel was not the author of it. If we will bear in mind that Jesus declared Daniel to be a prophet, and therefore the book that bears his name *is* a prophetic book, we will be more likely to keep in mind the prophetic aspect of Nebuchadnezzar's dream.

Daniel makes it very clear that the image of gold, silver, brass, iron and clay is definitely a picture of events yet future. His interpretation of the dream was divinely revealed, and if we will read the book of Daniel as it is, *literally*; if we will read it with an open mind, without prejudice and without preconceived conclusions, forgetting what we have read and heard from the critics, we will find it easy to believe, and we can clearly understand all of it that God would *have* us to understand.

We are two thousand five hundred years this side of Daniel's day; but we can turn to the pages of history and check the accuracy of his prophecies, which have been—and are being—fulfilled in detail, even in the morning headlines of our newspapers day by day! Most of the book of Daniel has already been literally fulfilled, and there is no reason to suppose that the rest of it will NOT be fulfilled with the same amazing accuracy.

In verses 31 through 35 Daniel recounts for the king exactly what he dreamed—the great image whose brightness was "excellent" and whose form was "terrible." Its head was of fine gold, the breast and arms were of silver, the belly and thighs were of brass, the legs were of iron and the feet were a mixture of iron and clay.

As Nebuchadnezzar gazed upon the image in his

dream, a stone was cut out of the mountain–cut out without the use of hands or tools–and the stone smote the image upon its feet of iron and clay, breaking them to pieces. Then the entire image–iron, clay, brass, silver, and gold–was broken until it became like chaff on a summer threshingfloor. (In Psalm 1:4 David tells us, "*The ungodly are not so: but are like the chaff which the wind driveth away.*")

Nebuchadnezzar watched as the stone ground the massive image into bits, "and the wind carried them away, that no place was found for them." Then he gazed upon the stone in wonder and amazement as it began to grow. It grew until it "became a great mountain, and filled the whole earth!" Daniel revealed the king's dream in all of its impressive magnitude, and then began to give the king the interpretation of it.

The Interpretation of the Dream

Verse 36: "This is the dream; and we will tell the interpretation thereof before the king."

Please note that Daniel did not say, "*I* will tell the interpretation," but "*WE will tell the . . . .*" Daniel included his friends. What a big heart he had! Would to God we had more men today with a heart like the heart of Daniel.

The Head of Gold – the Babylonian Empire:

Verses 37 and 38: "Thou, O king, art a king of kings: for the God of heaven hath given thee a kingdom, power, and strength, and glory. And wheresoever the children of men dwell, the beasts of the field and the fowls of the heaven hath He given into thine hand, and hath made thee ruler over them all. *Thou art this head of gold.*"

The Arms and Breast of Silver – the Media-Persian Empire:

Verse 39a: "And after thee shall arise another kingdom inferior to thee . . . ."

The Abdomen of Brass – the Grecian Empire:

Verse 39b: "... And another third kingdom of brass, which shall bear rule over all the earth."

The Legs of Iron – the Roman Empire:

Verses 40–43: "And the fourth kingdom shall be strong as iron: forasmuch as iron breaketh in pieces and subdueth all things: and as iron that breaketh all these, shall it break in pieces and bruise. And whereas thou sawest the feet and toes, part of potters' clay, and part of iron, the kingdom shall be divided; but there shall be in it of the strength of the iron, forasmuch as thou sawest the iron mixed with miry clay. And as the toes of the feet were part of iron, and part of clay, so the kingdom shall be partly strong, and partly broken. And whereas thou sawest iron mixed with miry clay, they shall mingle themselves with the seed of men: but they shall not cleave one to another, even as iron is not mixed with clay."

The Stone Cut Out of the Mountain Without Hands–
The Kingdom of Christ on Earth:

Verses 44 and 45: "And in the days of these kings shall the God of heaven set up a kingdom, which shall never be destroyed: and the kingdom shall not be left to other people, but it shall break in pieces and consume all these kingdoms, and it shall stand for ever. Forasmuch as thou sawest that the stone was cut out of the mountain without hands, and that it brake in pieces the iron, the brass, the clay, the silver, and the gold; the great God hath made known to the king what shall come to pass hereafter: and the dream is certain, and the interpretation thereof sure."

Note the closing words of Daniel to the king: "... *The dream is certain, and the interpretation thereof sure*!" If Nebuchadnezzar was astonished and amazed beyond words as Daniel made known the dream he had forgotten, he must have been "thunderstruck" when Daniel finished the *interpretation* of the dream! His heart no doubt swelled with pride at the interpretation of the first part of the dream, having to do with the head of gold; but imagine the sinking of his heart within him as Daniel made known the prophecy that his kingdom would fall and be succeeded by inferior ones, until all world kingdoms should be ground into chaff!

"The Times of the Gentiles" Revealed

This phrase does not occur in the book of Daniel nor in any other book in the Old Testament. It is definitely a New Testament phrase, and was used by the Lord Jesus Himself in reference to the destruction of the Holy City in 70 A. D. by Titus the Roman: ". . . And Jerusalem shall be trodden down of the Gentiles, until *the times of the Gentiles* be fulfilled" (Luke 21:24).

According to the words of Jesus in this verse, "the times of the Gentiles" had a beginning and will have an ending. The chronological limit of "the times of the Gentiles" corresponds to the time Israel shall be without a king. Hosea prophesied concerning this period of time: "For the children of Israel shall abide many days without a king, and without a prince, and without a sacrifice, and without an image, and without an ephod, and without teraphim: Afterward shall the children of Israel return, and seek the Lord their God, and David their king; and shall fear the Lord and His goodness IN THE LATTER DAYS" (Hos. 3:4,5).

After this passage of time, when these "*many days*" of Israel without a king are expired, the children of Israel will return to Jehovah their God and they will seek the Lord. They will seek David their king, and they will FEAR the Lord. This will take place "in the latter days" when "the times of the Gentiles" be fulfilled and God turns again to His chosen people, Israel.

"The times of the Gentiles" began in 606 B. C. when Daniel was carried to Babylon, and not in 70 A. D. when Titus destroyed Jerusalem—and will continue until Jesus comes back to set up His kingdom and reign for one thousand glorious years right here on this earth . . . the "stone" kingdom represented by the stone cut out of the mountain without hands.

We should not confuse "the *times* of the Gentiles" with "the *fulness* of the Gentiles" mentioned by Paul in Romans 11:25: "For I would not, brethren, that ye should be ignorant of this mystery, lest ye should be wise in your own conceits; that blindness in part is happened to Israel, until *the fulness* of the Gentiles be come in."

The "*fulness* of the Gentiles" refers to the Gentile bride now being called out by the Holy Spirit in this dispensation of grace, and has nothing whatsoever to do with the "*times* of the Gentiles." Since Pentecost, the Holy Spirit has been calling out a bride—the body of Christ, the New Testament Church; and when that number is complete (or FULL), Jesus will descend from heaven with a shout, with the trumpet of God and the voice of the archangel. The dead in Christ will be raised incorruptible, and the living born again will put on incorruption and be caught up to meet Jesus in the clouds in the air.

Jesus will take His Church out of this earth and "the fulness of the Gentiles" will be complete. God gave us this program, minutely outlined, in Acts 15:13–18: "And after they had held their peace, James answered, saying, Men and brethren, hearken unto me: Simeon hath declared how God at the first did visit the Gentiles, to take out of them a people for His name. And to this agree the words of the prophets; as it is written, After this I will return, and will build again the tabernacle of

David, which is fallen down; and I will build again the ruins thereof, and will set it up: That the residue of men might seek after the Lord, and all the Gentiles, upon whom my name is called, saith the Lord, who doeth all these things. Known unto God are all His works from the beginning of the world."

The "*fulness* of the Gentiles" will end at the Rapture. The "*times* of the Gentiles" will come to a close at the Battle of Armageddon when the Antichrist and his armies are annihilated and King Jesus sets up His kingdom on earth and sits on the throne in Jerusalem to reign for one thousand glorious years!

THIS IS MAN'S DAY

Bible scholars refer to this present dispensation as "man's day." However, the term can be applied to the entire period of the "times of the Gentiles." God has permitted and is permitting man to run his course. If I believed in evolution, I would be forced to preach it in reverse—because, as prophesied, evil men and seducers are waxing worse and worse. Man is NOT becoming better and better. He will continue to become worse until Jesus comes and puts down all rule, Himself taking over the reins of the governments of earth.

When Isaiah prophesied concerning the coming of Messiah, he said, "For unto us a child is born, unto us a son is given: and the government shall be upon His shoulder: and His name shall be called Wonderful, Counsellor, The mighty God, The everlasting Father, The Prince of Peace. Of the increase of His government and peace there shall be no end, upon the throne of David, and upon His kingdom, to order it, and to establish it with judgment and with justice from henceforth even for ever. The zeal of the Lord of hosts will perform this" (Isa. 9:6,7).

When Gabriel announced to Mary that she would be the mother of God's Son, Gabriel said, "And, behold, thou shalt conceive in thy womb, and bring forth a son, and shalt call His name JESUS.

HE SHALL BE GREAT,
AND SHALL BE CALLED THE SON OF THE HIGHEST:
AND THE LORD GOD SHALL GIVE UNTO HIM THE THRONE OF HIS FATHER DAVID:
AND HE SHALL REIGN OVER THE HOUSE OF JACOB FOR EVER;
AND OF HIS KINGDOM THERE SHALL BE NO END" (Luke 1:31–33).

Man has done all in his power to produce such conditions as these without God's help. He has talked about Utopia, a lasting peace; but it will never be until Jesus comes. As long as the governments of earth are in the hands of men, there will be wickedness, war, and deterioration. Finally, if God did not shorten the horrible days of the reign of the false Messiah, there would be no flesh saved. But for the sake of God's elect, He will shorten those days: "And except those days should be shortened, there should no flesh be saved: but for the elect's sake *those days shall be shortened*" (Matt. 24:22).

In Daniel 3:1 Nebuchadnezzar set up a golden image (typifying himself) and commanded worship of the image by all the people. From that day until the False Prophet makes an image in honor of the Beast (the Antichrist) and commands all men, under penalty of death, to worship *that image*, the only suitable description for the character of "the times of the Gentiles" is "*Man's Day*"—times when the image of man, not God, is uppermost in the minds of the majority. For some unknown and unexplainable reason, man has always desired to by-pass God his Creator and run his own affairs in his own way.

When Adam and Eve sinned, when their eyes were

opened and they saw the despicable sight of their nakedness, instead of crying out to God for forgiveness they immediately set about to correct their wrong through their own wisdom and ability by making aprons of fig leaves to hide their shame. You know the sad story.

Cain paid no attention to God. He brought a bloodless offering, which God rejected; but God assured Cain that if he would only bring the *right kind* of an offering he would be forgiven and accepted. Cain refused to obey God; he was exceedingly wroth, and he later murdered his brother—and lied about it! In the flood, God was forced to destroy *all the descendants* of Cain.

Nimrod planned to build a tower to heaven and bypass God; but God came down, looked at the tower, and stopped it by confusing the languages. Time after time down through the ages, man has rebelled against God; and this will continue until Antichrist leads the last all-out revolt against the God of heaven, only to be defeated and destroyed. Then King Jesus will sit on the throne, the knowledge of the Lord will cover the earth as the waters cover the sea, and there will be peace on earth, good will toward men—*but not UNTIL then.*

How suitable was the golden-headed image of Nebuchadnezzar's dream, to picture and describe the character of the period known as "the times of the Gentiles." The image clearly points out the deterioration of the Gentile age. We see it in the diminishing value of the metals in the image: The head of gold, the breast of silver, the abdomen of brass, the legs of iron, the feet of iron and clay. Considering this picture of the times of the Gentiles, certainly we have no right to teach that the world is becoming better and better. If this were true, the *head* should have been iron and clay and the FEET should have been of fine gold.

Not only do the metals of the image decline in value, they also decline in weight. Gold is much heavier than silver, silver is heavier than brass, brass is heavier than iron, and iron is heavier than clay. Nebuchadnezzar's golden-headed image was top-heavy. It was weak in the foundation where it should have been strong. It portrayed degeneration, deterioration, and devaluation from head to foot.

The image of Nebuchadnezzar's dream symbolized the four great world empires in their unity and historical succession. There are to be four world-wide empires on this earth (no more, no less) from Nebuchadnezzar to the second coming of Jesus Christ, and these four world empires are represented by the four metals in the image. Men like Napoleon, Hitler, Mussolini, and others have hoped, planned, plotted, warred and slaughtered in an attempt to establish a fifth world empire—but all have failed. These four world empires are not only made known as to number, but their names are given in the order of their succession.

1. The Babylonian Empire

The first empire Daniel pointed out in his interpretation was the Babylonian empire over which Nebuchadnezzar was king: "*Thou art this head of gold.*" You will notice as we study the interpretation of the dream that Daniel uses the words "king" and "kingdom" interchangeably. Nebuchadnezzar reigned over Babylon for forty-four years. He died in 561 B. C. and was succeeded by his son, Evil-Merodach, who reigned through two years of terror. He was assassinated by his brother-in-law, Neriglissar, who then seized the throne, reigned for almost four years and was killed in battle in 556 B. C. Neriglissar was succeeded by his son, Laborosoarched, who reigned for nine months and was beaten to death. Then Nabonidus, another son-in-law of Nebuchadnezzar who had married the widow of Neriglissar, seized the throne by force and reigned for seventeen years. During his entire reign, Babylon was threatened by invasion from the Persians; and while Nabonidus was away from Babylon on a military expedition, the Persians conquered Babylon. (Nabonidus had made Belshazzar, his son, second ruler while he was away on the expedition. That is why Belshazzar had to make Daniel "third ruler," because he himself was second–Daniel 5:29.)

Certainly through all of this we can clearly see that Nebuchadnezzar was properly called "the head of gold," because all who succeeded him in Babylon were inferior to him. They degraded step by step after his death until the reign of Belshazzar, the ungodly drunk who was in power when Babylon finally fell and ceased to exist as a world empire.

2. The Media-Persian Empire

"Thou art this head of gold," Daniel said to Nebuchadnezzar; but Babylon was not long to continue in her role as ruler of the known world. Another power would rise and conquer her.

This second power is represented by the chest and arms of silver. History reveals that this kingdom was Persia. The two arms represent the coalition of the Medes and Persians in one great, powerful empire. Although the Medes and the Persians subdued Babylon, Media-Persia was *inferior* to the great Babylon, both in wealth and in power. Silver is inferior to gold; and the head of gold, most powerful of all, was followed by silver–a little weaker, a little less powerful. Daniel points out Media-Persia in his account of the fall of the Babylonian empire, in these dynamic words: "In that night was Belshazzar the king of the Chaldeans slain. And Darius the Median took the kingdom . . ." (Dan. 5:30,31).

The Media-Persian empire is also symbolized in the vision of the ram and the he-goat: "The ram which thou sawest having two horns are the kings of Media and Persia. And the rough goat is the king of Grecia: and the great horn that is between his eyes is the first king" (Dan. 8:20,21). The two horns of the ram correspond to the two arms of the great image. The two horns and the two arms are the kings of Media and Persia. The Babylonian empire was single-headed–the powerful head of gold–Nebuchadnezzar. But the next kingdom (Media-Persia) was a dual empire, represented by two arms, two horns. The Media-Persian empire was inferior to Babylon in wealth, in luxury, and in magnificence.

King Cyrus has the honor of being named in the Scriptures almost two centuried before he conquered Babylon and became king in the second world empire: "That saith of CYRUS, He is my shepherd, and shall perform all my pleasure: even saying to JERUSALEM, Thou shalt be built; and to the TEMPLE, Thy foundation shall be laid" (Isa. 44:28). "Thus saith the Lord to His anointed, to CYRUS, whose right hand I have holden, to subdue nations before him; and I will loose the loins of kings" (kings such as Belshazzar, whose knees smote one against the other when the hand appeared, writing on the wall) "to open before him (Cyrus) the *two leaved gates*"; (These gates were in Babylon.) "and the gates shall not be shut." (Josephus tells us that the inner gates of Babylon were not shut in the river walls on the night of the siege.) ". . . For Jacob my servant's sake, and ISRAEL mine elect, I have even called thee by thy name: I HAVE SURNAMED THEE, THOUGH THOU HAST NOT KNOWN ME" (Isa. 45:1–4).

What a tremendous prophecy, spoken by Isaiah concerning a king who did not know God–spoken over one hundred years before that king conquered Babylon and became the right arm of silver in the Media-Persian empire, declaring that he was surnamed by God (even though he did not know God). We see here that God puts up whom He will and puts down whom He will–and we dare not question the wisdom of God and His doings. Cyrus was foreordained over a hundred years before his birth to do two things as ordered by God Almighty–the God whom Cyrus did not even know.

The first thing he was to do was to conquer Babylon. This he did the night Belshazzar was slain at a drunken party. The second thing foreordained of God that Cyrus would do was to issue an edict at the close of the Babylonian captivity, giving the Jews the right to return to Jerusalem and rebuild their temple. This edict was given by Cyrus in 536 B. C.*

When Cyrus took Babylon in 538 B. C., his uncle, Darius, was king of Media. Because Media was the older of the two kingdoms of Media and Persia, and also because Cyrus had other unfinished military campaigns that he desired to finish, he made Darius governor of Babylon. He ruled for two years.

That same year (536 B. C.) Cambyses, king of Persia, who was the father of Cyrus, also died, and Cyrus became the sole ruler of the dual kingdom of Media-Persia. He reigned as the sole ruler for seven years, then left the empire to his son (also named Cambyses), who reigned for seven years and five months. Therefore, eight rulers, whose reign varied from seven months to forty-six years, followed in succession until 335 B. C., at which time Darius Codomanus became the last of the long line of Persian kings to reign over the second world empire of Media-Persia, represented by the silver breast and arms.

---

* These dates taken from International Standard Bible Encyclopedia.

Darius was a noble king. Compared with those who had preceded him, he was a *good* king, and no doubt would have had a long and prosperous reign had it not been time for the silver to give way to brass. Nothing could prevent the change, because it was foreordained of God; it had been declared, and *it had to be.* In 331 B. C. Alexander the Grecian conquered Media-Persia, and the third world empire came into being.

3. The Grecian Empire

By way of refreshing our memory, suppose we look again at the image: "Thou, O king, sawest, and behold a great image. This great image, whose brightness was excellent, stood before thee; and the form thereof was terrible. This image's head was of fine gold, his breast and his arms of silver, his belly and his thighs of brass."

The third kingdom is represented by the belly and thighs of brass—and brass is inferior to silver. The kingdoms are degenerating. In Daniel 8:20 and 21 the angel Gabriel also identifies the Grecian empire as the he-goat that destroyed the ram which represented Media-Persia: "The ram which thou sawest having two horns are the kings of Media and Persia. And the rough goat is the king of Grecia: and the great horn that is between his eyes is the first king."

This third empire, under King Alexander, was to enjoy a short life. After eight years Alexander died of intemperance and fever, in 323 B. C. He was a young man, only 33 years of age when he died; and his world-wide empire was at that time divided among four of his top generals.

Lest someone misunderstand, let me point out here that the Scriptures do not teach that the four world empires are to succeed each other without a break. From the death of Alexander the Great in 323 B. C., until 30

B. C., the Grecian empire was not a single world-wide empire. It was a fourfold empire made up of the kingdoms of Thrace, Macedonia, Syria and Egypt. These four segments of the Grecian empire fell, one by one, over this period of time, from 323 B. C. until 30 B. C.; and finally the Romans conquered Egypt in 30 B. C., which made *them* the conquerors of the world. The fact that the Grecian empire would be divided into four parts is not pointed out in the image Nebuchadnezzar saw, but it IS pointed out in the prophecy of Daniel 8:21–25:

"And the rough goat is the king of Grecia: and the great horn that is between his eyes is the first king. Now that being broken, whereas four stood up for it, four kingdoms shall stand up out of the nation, but not in his power. And in the latter time of their kingdom, when the transgressors are come to the full, a king of fierce countenance, and understanding dark sentences, shall stand up. And his power shall be mighty, but not by his own power: and he shall destroy wonderfully, and shall prosper, and practise, and shall destroy the mighty and the holy people. And through his policy also he shall cause craft to prosper in his hand; and he shall magnify himself in his heart, and by peace shall destroy many: he shall also stand up against the Prince of princes; but he shall be broken without hand."

The four kingdoms of Thrace, Macedonia, Syria, and Egypt were conquered one by one over a period of almost three hundred years, when Egypt finally fell to the Romans.

4. *The Roman Empire*

". . . His legs of iron, his feet part of iron and part of clay" (Dan. 2:33). The fourth empire, the mixture of iron and clay, is not named in Daniel as the Roman empire, but it is so clearly pointed out that we could not miss the identity. In Daniel's vision of the seventy weeks

of years to finish God's dealings with His people and the Holy City (Dan. 9:26), we read that after the crucifixion of Christ (the "cutting off" of Messiah), Jerusalem—which was the city of worship, the city of the temple—was to be destroyed; and from the people who were to destroy the Holy City there was to proceed *a prince.* This prince will be the man of sin, the *Antichrist.*

From history we know that the city of Jerusalem and the temple actually WERE utterly destroyed by the Romans in 70 A. D. as prophesied by Jesus in Mark 13:2. Titus the Roman overran the city, and not one stone was left upon another. The last emperor of the Roman empire, the Antichrist (the "little horn" . . . the "king of fierce countenance"), corresponds to the iron of Nebuchadnezzar's image, the fourth world empire . . . *Rome*, as we know it in Bible and secular history.

History proves that Rome swept across the known world in mighty conquest and ruled for centuries. I have traveled throughout the Bible lands—Israel, Trans-Jordan, Greece, Egypt, Rome and throughout Italy—and I have seen the marks of Rome wherever she touched with her conquering power. Even in the days before our Lord, Rome was a gigantic empire.

Finally the Roman empire divided into the eastern and western empires and thus became the *two legs* of the image. United Rome was in power in the days of the Lord Jesus, still holding sway the world over under the shrewd and cruel leadership of the Caesars. All of this is history, but we do not necessarily depend upon history to prove that Daniel's interpretation of the king's dream was authentic. The Word of God proves it. We are not dependent upon history for our interpretation. Daniel himself, in a vision recorded in chapter seven, names the four world empires that succeeded each other. He names them under the symbols of four fearful beasts:

First, the lion—*Babylon*; second, the bear—*Persia*; third, the leopard—*Greece*; and the nameless, horrible, powerful monstrosity—*Rome*! We will deal with these beasts later in our study.

The legs are the longest limbs of the body. Could it be that since Rome is symbolized by the legs of the image, God thus signified that Rome would rule longer than any of the other three world empires? Be that as it may, history records that Rome did rule the world longer than did Babylon, Media-Persia, or Greece. I believe the two legs symbolize the two parts of the Roman empire—the eastern division, and the western division. Constantinople was the capital of the eastern division; Rome was the capital of the west.

It is noteworthy that the two feet of the image are divided into five toes each. The ten toes have not until our day manifested themselves; therefore, the fulfillment of the image is not yet complete. Remember, this colossal image is a symbol of "the times of the Gentiles"—from the reign of Nebuchadnezzar until the time when Antichrist and his armies are put down forever by the King of kings, never to rise again.

The first world empire was singular—*one unit*. The second empire was divided—*dual Media-Persia*. The third empire was quadruple—*four generals* ruled in four sections. The fourth empire in its final form will be a *"ten-toed" kingdom*.

It is true that the Roman empire, as a visible, world-ruling power, does not exist today; but its laws, its rituals, its pagan religion have an unseen grip on this world that it is humanly impossible to evaluate! There is no power on earth today, apart from the power of Almighty God, the Holy Ghost, and the Bible, that will equal the evil influence of pagan Rome. As a political, ruling world empire, Rome does not exist today; but the underlying current of evil has never *ceased* to exist—and never will, until King Jesus destroys the revived ten federated kingdoms which will operate under the leadership of Antichrist after the Rapture.

The Feet and Toes of the Image

The head—pure gold. The chest and arms—silver. The belly and thighs—brass. The legs—iron. The feet and toes—part iron, part potters' clay. The ten federated kingdoms represented by the feet and toes of part iron and part clay will continue until the stone cut from the mountain without hands destroys them. That will be when Jesus comes with His saints to execute judgment upon this earth, and to make His enemies His footstool.

The character of the governments of the four world empires reveals to us that the image becomes more and more unstable. For instance, Babylon, the head of gold, was an absolute autocracy. We read of Nebuchadnezzar, ". . . All people, nations, and languages, trembled and feared before him: Whom he would he slew; and whom he would he kept alive; and whom he would he set up; and whom he would he put down" (Dan. 5:19). *Nebuchadnezzar was the government.* When he spoke, the people obeyed.

However, the second empire, Media-Persia, was not an autocracy. The emperor of Media-Persia was bound by certain laws which Daniel refers to as "the laws of the Medes and the Persians." If the emperor of the Medes and Persians signed an edict, he could not recall it. He was bound by certain laws and was compelled to obey them. This was the case when Daniel was put into the lions' den. Darius was in power at that time, and he did all he could to save Daniel from such a fate, but he could not; he had signed the decree, and he was forced to carry it out.

Another such example is the case of Ahasuerus when he attempted to save the slaughter of the Jews, but could not issue a counter-decree saving their lives. He *did* issue a decree permitting them to defend themselves and, if they could, slay those who would attempt to kill them:

"On that day did the king Ahasuerus give the house of Haman the Jews' enemy unto Esther the queen. . . Then the king Ahasuerus said unto Esther the queen and to Mordecai the Jew, Behold, I have given Esther the house of Haman, and him they have hanged upon the gallows, because he laid his hand upon the Jews. Write ye also for the Jews, as it liketh you, in the king's name, and seal it with the king's ring: for the writing which is written in the king's name, and sealed with the king's ring, may no man reverse. . . Wherein the king granted the Jews which were in every city to gather themselves together, and to stand for their life, to destroy, to slay, and to cause to perish, all the power of the people and province that would assault them, both little ones and women, and to take the spoil of them for a prey. . . And in every province, and in every city, whithersoever the king's commandment and his decree came, the Jews had joy and gladness, a feast and a good day. And many of the people of the land became Jews; for the fear of the Jews fell upon them" (Esther 8:1, 7, 8, 11, 17).

The third world empire (the Grecian empire) was a monarchy supported by a military aristocracy. This government was weak because the leaders were weak. The governments decreased in power one by one, and when the Romans came into power their emperors were elected by the people—but the people were not allowed to legislate for them nor to interfere with them. In most cases the emperors were despotic, and the empire is well symbolized by iron. Rome is noted in history for her "iron rule."

But the iron rule of Rome grows weaker when we reach the feet and the toes composed of iron and clay. Here we have imperialism mixed with democracy—the iron representing imperialism, the clay representing the softer form of government, democracy. The governments of the world kingdoms pass from absolute autocracy (Nebuchadnezzar), to a democratic monarchy; from the rule of the head of pure gold down to the weakness of the feet of iron and clay; from the powerful Nebuchadnezzar (who slew whom he would and kept alive whom he would, put up whom he would and put down whom he would), to a government controlled by the masses of the people, swayed by crooked, evil politicians and demagogues who think only of their own selfish desires and interests. They control the government to bring gain into their own pockets, regardless of the suffering it may bring upon mankind. Such a form of government is the weakest, most degenerate possible. It opens the way for socialism, communism, bolshevism, and anarchy.

We know that such phases of government are growing by leaps and bounds all over the world today—and sad but so, their influence is visible even in our great beloved United States of America. All we need do to know that we are living in the day of the beginning of the fulfillment of the last phase of Nebuchadnezzar's great image is to read the papers, listen to the radio, and look around us. We see that the stage is set, and surely the coming of the King of kings for His Church is imminent.

The false messiah (the "little horn"), the Antichrist, will then take over the reins of the governments of this earth, and soon the ten federated kingdoms will be set up, with ten puppet kings who will give their power, worship, and homage to the Antichrist, the devil in flesh. He will sit in the temple of God announcing that he IS God (II Thess. 2).

The Stone Kingdom

"Thou sawest till that a stone was cut out without hands, which smote the image upon his feet that were of iron and clay, and brake them to pieces. Then was the iron, the clay, the brass, the silver, and the gold, broken to pieces together, and became like the chaff of the summer threshingfloors; and the wind carried them away, that no place was found for them: and the stone that smote the image became a great mountain, and filled the whole earth" (Dan. 2:34, 35).

We find the interpretation of the stone cut out of the mountain without hands in verse 44: "And in the days of these kings shall the God of heaven set up a kingdom, which shall never be destroyed: and the kingdom shall not be left to other people, but it shall break in pieces and consume all these kingdoms, and it shall stand for ever."

The king's dream climaxed with the unbelievable sight of a stone, seemingly small at first, being cut out of the side of the mountain—but there were no hands or tools involved, thereby showing clearly the supernatural origin of the stone. This stone did not fill the earth by degrees—slowly, a little each day, each month, each year or each century—and *crowd* out the image, eventually bringing world peace.

The stone cut out of the mountain without hands, in one tremendous blow demolishes the image so completely that its remains, like chaff, are blown away! The action of the stone is not grace, but *bitter judgment*! The stone does not spread over the earth in spiritual revival, setting up a spiritual kingdom such as that taught by post-millennialists. The stone does not convert the world and bring in a visible earthly kingdom. On the contrary, in one giant blow the stone *destroys* the image of world power and government. This stone does not symbolize Christianity, as suggested by some. It is none other than the Lord Jesus Christ!

There is another thing we need to see clearly if we would understand the Word of God and rightly divide it: *The image is not destroyed until after the formation of the ten-toed kingdom.* The legs of the image did not appear until 364 A. D., when the Roman empire was divided into two parts; and up to your day and mine, the ten toes have not developed into the ten kingdoms to be ruled over by ten puppet kings. When the stone falls on the feet of the colossal image, it is "IN THE DAYS OF THESE KINGS."

What kings do those words refer to? Certainly not the kings who reigned over the four world empires of Babylon, Media-Persia, Greece, and Rome–for that would bring us only to the *birth* of Christ. Rome, the fourth of the world empires, was reigning when Jesus was born. She will NOT be reigning when He comes the second time, but she *will come into power* very rapidly after the Rapture of the Church.

"*These kings,*" then, refer to the ten federated kingdoms represented by the toes of the image, kingdoms which will be set up immediately after the Rapture of the Church. The time of the smiting of the stone cut out of the mountain without hands was not when Jesus was born, but will be when He comes the second time as described in Revelation 19:11.*

Oh, yes, *Christ is the stone* throughout Scripture.

---

* You might like to order the author's 550-page book on *Revelation.*

He is the stone that produced water in the desert for the children of Israel. God told Moses to smite the stone with his rod. Moses obeyed—and water gushed forth from the rock. (I had the privilege of drinking water from what is believed to be that very spot when I toured the Holy Land. What a thrill to see a mighty stream of water gushing from the very rock which is supposed to have been struck by Moses at the command of the Lord!)

To the Jews, Christ was "a stone of stumbling, a rock of offence." He was the stone the builders "disallowed," but God made Him the chief cornerstone. Jesus undoubtedly had in mind the stone cut from the mountain, the falling stone of Nebuchadnezzar's dream, when He said, "Whosoever shall fall on this stone (Christ) shall be broken (melted into repentance): but on whomsoever it shall fall, it will grind him to powder" (Matt. 21:44). The stone cut out of the mountain smote the image—the image did not smite the stone.

When we walk with Jesus we walk with victory. ("If God be for us, who can be against us?") When Jesus came as a babe in a manger, He did not destroy the Roman empire; on the contrary, the power of the Roman empire nailed Him to the cross. It was the Jews who demanded his death, *but Pilate consented to it.* When Jesus came the first time, He was not the falling stone cut out of the mountain without hands. He came then as a babe in a manger; but one day He is coming as the falling stone, and He will grind the enemies of the Gospel into powder! When He comes the second time, He will not be wrapped in swaddling clothes. He will appear in the sky riding a giant white stallion, and the armies of heaven will follow Him! The kings of the earth will see Him, and they will hide themselves in the dens and in the rocks of the mountains. They will beg the rocks and the mountains to fall on them and hide them "from the face of Him that sitteth on the throne, and from the wrath of the Lamb" (Rev. 6:16). But the rocks and mountains will not obey them. They must face the King of kings and Lord of lords!

Post-millennialists object to this interpretation of the Gentile powers just before the setting up of the kingdom of heaven on earth, saying that the Scriptures declare that the metals (gold, silver, brass, iron) are destroyed together at the same time, when the stone cut out of the mountain strikes the feet of the image. Those who object say that the empires represented by gold, silver, brass and iron have passed away already, and therefore could not be destroyed at the same time as the feet and the ten-toed kingdoms are destroyed. I agree that the *visible empires* represented by gold, silver, brass and iron have ceased to exist; but *the spirit of these empires has never ceased to exist.* Those empires were incorporated into their successors, and all of them will be found in the last phase of the revived Roman empire. The spirit of Babylon moved into Media-Persia, and on down the line to Rome. There is no power on earth, not even Communism, that has so strong a grip upon mankind as does Rome.

After the Rapture, the Roman empire will be revived, and will be made up of the ten puppet kings who sit on thrones for a season, until they give their power and dominion over to the beast that comes up from the sea:

"And I stood upon the sand of the sea, and saw a beast rise up out of the sea, having seven heads and ten horns, and upon his horns ten crowns, and upon his heads the name of blasphemy. And the beast which I saw was like unto a leopard, and his feet were as the feet of a bear, and his mouth as the mouth of a lion: and the dragon gave him his power, and his seat, and great authority" (Rev. 13:1,2). (In the book of Revelation, the sea is a symbol of peoples or nations.)

When we reach chapter 7 of Daniel and study the vision of the four wild beasts, we will see that these beasts correspond to the metals in Nebuchadnezzar's image. The head of gold corresponds to the lion; the breast and arms of silver correspond to the bear; the abdomen of brass corresponds to the leopard; and the iron corresponds to the fourth beast in chapter 7.

In Revelation, John describes the beast that comes up out of the sea as having a body like the body of a leopard, feet like those of a bear, a mouth like that of a lion, the fourth wild beast being represented by the whole of this monstrosity. This is the revived Roman empire which, after the Rapture of the Church, will be composed of the spirit of Babylon (the lion), the spirit of Media-Persia (the bear), the spirit of Greece (the leopard)—and the beast itself will be Rome. Study Revelation chapter 17 carefully.

Daniel is definitely the *Revelation* of the Old Testament, and Revelation is the *Daniel* of the NEW Testament. To understand either of these books, we must study them both, in relationship to each other. Believers are not looking for the revived Roman empire: *We are looking for the Lord Jesus Christ*! The revival of the Roman empire is in the making, though not visibly seen.

Those of us who read the papers and stay abreast of current events know that Rome is courting the peoples of earth today, willing to "give and take" to bring the *departed brethren* (as they call us) back into the fold. When the time is ripe, when the last soul is converted to complete the Bride of Christ, the Church will be instantaneously taken out of this earth. Every born again person will be caught up to meet Jesus in the air.

The superman will then come immediately on the scene, and will present the Antichrist to the world. The Antichrist (the devil in flesh) will offer to the peoples of earth a peace program guaranteeing world peace—and this will actually come about for the space of approximately three and one-half years. Then all hell will break out, as is clearly seen in studying Revelation.

The mountain out of which the stone was cut without hands is a symbol of Israel. We know the Lord Jesus Christ came through Israel, through the lineage of Abraham. (He was the Son of God, conceived of the Holy Ghost; but from the human side, He came through Israel.) This fact is definitely confirmed by the words of Jacob when he blessed his sons: "But his bow abode in strength, and the arms of his hands were made strong by the hands of the mighty God of Jacob; (from thence is the Shepherd, the stone of Israel)" (Gen. 49:24).

Certainly "*the Shepherd*" could refer to none other than the Lord Jesus Christ. He is the Shepherd; He is also the stone—the chief cornerstone. Nebuchadnezzar witnessed the stone, growing and continuing to grow, until it filled the whole earth. This definitely represents the millennial kingdom of Christ—the time when Jesus will sit on the throne of David in Jerusalem, the knowledge of the Lord will cover the earth as the waters cover the sea, and there will be peace throughout the earth. There will be no more war, no more bloodshed. Men will beat their swords into plowshares and their spears into pruning hooks. We will then have the peace which man has promised but has never been able to bring. The Prince of peace, the Shepherd, the King of kings and Lord of lords will bring lasting peace when His millennial kingdom is set up here on earth. Read Isaiah 11 and Revelation 20:5, 6.

There are those who spiritualize the kingdom of Christ. They believe the four kingdoms of Babylon, Media-Persia, Greece and Rome were literal kingdoms–they cannot deny that, because history proves it. Post-millennialists and others accept these kingdoms as being literal, and then they spiritualize the STONE kingdom. But just as surely as the four world empires were literal, the kingdom of God on earth will be literal and Jesus in a body will sit on a throne and reign over the earth literally. We, the Bride of Christ, will reign with Him.

When the disciples said to Jesus, "Teach us to pray," the prayer Jesus taught them was, and is, the Kingdom Prayer. It does not ask for the needs of a spiritual kingdom, but for those of a *literal* kingdom:

". . . Our Father which art in heaven, Hallowed be thy name. Thy kingdom come. Thy will be done in earth, as it is in heaven. Give us this day our daily bread. And forgive us our debts, as we forgive our debtors. And lead us not into temptation, but deliver us from evil: For thine is the kingdom, and the power, and the glory, for ever. Amen" (Matt. 6:9–13).

"THY KINGDOM COME. THY WILL BE DONE *IN EARTH* . . . ." There is no mistake that the kingdom about which Jesus was praying will be a literal kingdom; for instance: *"Give us this day our daily bread."* Would you suggest that angels and spiritual beings in heaven eat bread? I firmly believe that we who will have glorified bodies can eat. Jesus ate broiled fish and honeycomb in His resurrected body, and we will have a body like unto HIS body. It will be possible for us to eat if we desire to do so–but it will not be necessary. However, in the kingdom, the people of Israel will be in their natural bodies and they will eat, even as they eat today. The Jews had not rejected their King and the setting up of the kingdom had not been postponed when Jesus taught the disciples to pray, "Thy kingdom come. Thy will be done in earth . . . Give us this day our daily bread." Yes, the kingdom WILL come. God's will SHALL be done on earth. Peace will cover the earth, and men will study war no more. The curse will be lifted, and even vegetation and the air above us will be delivered from the curse:

"For I reckon that the sufferings of this present time are not worthy to be compared with the glory which shall be revealed in us. For the earnest expectation of the creature waiteth for the manifestation of the sons of God. For the creature was made subject to vanity, not willingly, but by reason of him who hath subjected the same in hope. Because the creature itself also shall be delivered from the bondage of corruption into the glorious liberty of the children of God. For we know that the whole creation groaneth and travaileth in pain together until now. And not only they, but ourselves also, which have the firstfruits of the Spirit, even we ourselves groan within ourselves, waiting for the adoption, to wit, the redemption of our body" (Rom. 8:18–23).

"Blessed and holy is he that hath part in the first resurrection: on such the second death hath no power, but they shall be priests of God and of Christ, and shall reign with Him a thousand years" (Rev. 20:6).

The Effect of the Interpretation of the Dream Upon Nebuchadnezzar

Verses 46–49: "Then the king Nebuchadnezzar fell upon his face, and worshipped Daniel, and commanded that they should offer an oblation and sweet odours unto him. The king answered unto Daniel, and said, Of a truth it is, that your God is a God of gods, and a Lord of kings, and a revealer of secrets, seeing thou couldest reveal this secret. Then the king made Daniel a great man, and gave him many great gifts, and made him ruler over the whole province of

Babylon, and chief of the governors over all the wise men of Babylon. Then Daniel requested of the king, and he set Shadrach, Meshach, and Abed-nego, over the affairs of the province of Babylon: but Daniel sat in the gate of the king."

You may rest assured that it was not easy for Daniel to stand before the proud world-ruler Nebuchadnezzar and make the divine announcement that his empire would not stand much longer, but was destined to crumble by divine revelation and order. It took courage for Daniel to give the interpretation of the dream to Nebuchadnezzar. From the natural standpoint, an announcement such as Daniel made to the king could have caused him to fly into a rage and order this upstart Hebrew killed! But the interpretation of the dream had the exact reverse effect upon Nebuchadnezzar. Instead of declaring that he did not believe a word of it and demanding that Daniel be punished, he fell upon his face and worshipped Daniel, commanding that oblations and sweet odours should be offered unto him.

I personally believe God softened the heart of Nebuchadnezzar. Daniel had purposed in his heart that he would not deny his God, he would not bow to the king, he would not defile himself with the king's meat and wine. Whatsoever he did in Babylon, he would do to the glory of God and not to the glory of the heathen king. Daniel remembered God—and God remembered Daniel! He will never allow anything to befall His faithful servants without His permission. Even in Daniel's day, *all things worked together for good to them who loved God*!

Someone may ask, "Why did Daniel allow the king to fall on his face before him and worship him? Why would he allow the king to offer oblations and sweet odours unto him?" It seems to me that the beginning of verse 47 indicates that Daniel did protest. The verse begins, "*The king answered unto Daniel*, and said . . . ." Daniel had said nothing since he finished the interpretation of the dream, so surely he must have said something to the king about the impropriety of offering *him* homage which belonged to *God.* Whatever he might have said is not recorded; but it is clear that the king's thoughts were soon turned from the homage he was about to render to Daniel, for Nebuchadnezzar immediately began to give testimony–not concerning the character of Daniel, but concerning the GOD of Daniel, who had made known to the prophet the dream and the interpretation thereof. Nebuchadnezzar said, "*Of a truth it is, that your God is a God of gods, and a Lord of kings, and a revealer of secrets, seeing thou couldest reveal this secret.*"

Notice the words Nebuchadnezzar used: "God of gods . . ." (Jehovah, sovereign, God the Father). "Lord of kings . . . ." (Jesus is the Lord Jesus Christ, King of kings, and He will be king of this earth during the Millennium.) Nebuchadnezzar then said, "A revealer of secrets"–and certainly it is the Holy Ghost who reveals the deep, secret things of God. The Holy Ghost makes known unto us the mysteries, the secrets, the deep things of spiritual nature:

"But God hath revealed them unto us by His Spirit: for the Spirit searcheth all things, yea, the deep things of God. For what man knoweth the things of a man, save the spirit of man which is in him? Even so the things of God knoweth no man, but the Spirit of God" (I Cor. 2:10,11).

"But the anointing which ye have received of Him abideth in you, and ye need not that any man teach you: but as the same anointing teacheth you of all things, and is truth, and is no lie, and even as it hath taught you, ye shall abide in Him" (I John 2:27).

Whether Nebuchadnezzar knew it or not, in his testimony concerning the God of Daniel he testified to the Trinity.

I have often wondered what effect this miracle of Daniel had upon the magicians, astrologers, and other wise men of Babylon. We are not told in the Scriptures how they reacted, what they said, nor how Daniel's revelation of the forgotten dream and its interpretation affected them; but one thing is certain: They realized that Daniel knew a God they did NOT know, and he had understanding and wisdom of which they knew nothing. The fact was evident that Daniel succeeded where they failed, and their failure almost cost them their lives. They were spared only because of the success of Daniel.

Nebuchadnezzar Rewards Daniel

Verse 48: "Then the king made Daniel a great man, and gave him many great gifts, and made him ruler over the whole province of Babylon, and chief of the governors over all the wise men of Babylon."

I am sure there are few men who could have stood the promotion Daniel received, without being affected toward their fellowmen. Daniel was human, though wholly dedicated to God and an unusual servant of the Most High; but he was still in the flesh, and it was not impossible for him to become proud—but he did not. Daniel was promoted to a very exalted position. The king made him "a great man." What that meant in Babylon, only God knows. He did not see fit to reveal it to us here. Nebuchadnezzar gave Daniel many great gifts; how many and how valuable they were, we are not told; but that is not important. Daniel was made ruler over the whole province of Babylon—certainly a position of exaltation that could have made most men very proud. He was made chief of the governors *over all the wise men* of Babylon.

Daniel was promoted in every way possible, and

every gift the king could bestow upon him was given him. But such honors did not change him. He was still the same devoted, humble, God-fearing prophet that he was the day he purposed in his heart that he would not drink the king's wine nor eat the king's meat.

When the king had finished promoting Daniel and all the honors that could possibly be heaped upon him had been given and all the expensive gifts had been laid at his feet, Daniel made one request: "Then Daniel requested of the king, and he set Shadrach, Meshach, and Abed-nego, over the affairs of the province of Babylon: but Daniel sat in the gate of the king."

Daniel did not forget his friends and prayer partners—those who had stood with him when he had refused to drink the king's wine and eat the king's meat. Not all men who are promoted are as considerate as Daniel was. To me, Daniel was one of the most extraordinary characters, one of the most outstanding persons, this earth ever afforded.

This is one of the most remarkable and important chapters in all of the Word of God. In it we have a prophetic outline of the history of the Gentile nations from Nebuchadnezzar to the end of the Gentile rule on this earth. We also have an outline of the history of the Gentiles in relationship to the nation of Israel. Writing to the Corinthians, Paul said, "Give none offence, neither to the Jews, nor to the Gentiles, nor to the church of God" (I Cor. 10:32).

If the rulers of earth would read this chapter today with an open mind and an open heart, and permit Jehovah God to speak to them as He spoke to Nebuchadnezzar, they would change their plans immediately. Instead of making a mad rush to reach the moon, instead of attempting to build bombs more powerful and deadly, they would see that man's day is about to run out and that we are nearing the end of the "times of the Gentiles." They would recognize that the coming of Jesus Christ is imminent.

The signs of the times are all around us; and according to God's time clock, it is just about time for Jesus to come. In the process of His second coming, He will set up the kingdom that will fill the whole earth—the Kingdom of Heaven on earth.

Those of us who know the Lord Jesus and who study our Bibles, should pray daily, "Even so, come quickly, Lord Jesus."

CHAPTER THREE

NEBUCHADNEZZAR'S PRIDE

1. Nebuchadnezzar the king made an image of gold, whose height was threescore cubits, and the breadth thereof six cubits: he set it up in the plain of Dura, in the province of Babylon.

2. Then Nebuchadnezzar the king sent to gather together the princes, the governors, and the captains, the judges, the treasurers, the counsellors, the sheriffs, and all the rulers of the provinces, to come to the dedication of the image which Nebuchadnezzar the king had set up.

3. Then the princes, the governors, and captains, the judges, the treasurers, the counsellors, the sheriffs, and all the rulers of the provinces, were gathered together unto the dedication of the image that Nebuchadnezzar the king had set up; and they stood before the image that Nebuchadnezzar had set up.

4. Then an herald cried aloud, To you it is commanded, O people, nations, and languages,

5. That at what time ye hear the sound of the cornet, flute, harp, sackbut, psaltery, dulcimer, and all kinds of musick, ye fall down and worship the golden image that Nebuchadnezzar the king hath set up:

6. And whoso falleth not down and worshippeth shall the same hour be cast into the midst of a burning fiery furnace.

7. Therefore at that time, when all the people heard the sound of the cornet, flute, harp, sackbut, psaltery, and all kinds of musick, all the people, the nations, and the languages, fell down and worshipped the golden image that Nebuchadnezzar the king had set up.

8. Wherefore at that time certain Chaldeans came near, and accused the Jews.

9. They spake and said to the king Nebuchadnezzar, O king, live for ever.

10. Thou, O king, hast made a decree, that every man that shall hear the sound of the cornet, flute, harp, sackbut, psaltery,

and dulcimer, and all kinds of musick, shall fall down and worship the golden image:

11. And whoso falleth not down and worshippeth, that he should be cast into the midst of a burning fiery furnace.

12. There are certain Jews whom thou hast set over the affairs of the province of Babylon, Shadrach, Meshach, and Abed-nego; these men, O king, have not regarded thee: they serve not thy gods, nor worship the golden image which thou hast set up.

13. Then Nebuchadnezzar in his rage and fury commanded to bring Shadrach, Meshach, and Abed-nego. Then they brought these men before the king.

14. Nebuchadnezzar spake and said unto them, Is it true, O Shadrach, Meshach, and Abed-nego, do not ye serve my gods, nor worship the golden image which I have set up?

15. Now if ye be ready that at what time ye hear the sound of the cornet, flute, harp, sackbut, psaltery, and dulcimer, and all kinds of musick, ye fall down and worship the image which I have made; well: but if ye worship not, ye shall be cast the same hour into the midst of a burning fiery furnace; and who is that God that shall deliver you out of my hands?

16. Shadrach, Meshach, and Abed-nego, answered and said to the king, O Nebuchadnezzar, we are not careful to answer thee in this matter.

17. If it be so, our God whom we serve is able to deliver us from the burning fiery furnace, and he will deliver us out of thine hand, O king.

18. But if not, be it known unto thee, O king, that we will not serve thy gods, nor worship the golden image which thou hast set up.

19. Then was Nebuchadnezzar full of fury, and the form of his visage was changed against Shadrach, Meshach, and Abed-nego: therefore he spake, and commanded that they should heat the furnace one seven times more than it was wont to be heated.

20. And he commanded the most mighty men that were in his army to bind Shadrach, Meshach, and Abed-nego, and to cast them into the burning fiery furnace.

21. Then these men were bound in their coats, their hosen, and their hats, and their other garments, and were cast into the midst of the burning fiery furnace.

22. Therefore because the king's commandment was urgent, and the furnace exceeding hot, the flame of the fire slew those

men that took up Shadrach, Meshach, and Abed-nego.

23. And these three men, Shadrach, Meshach, and Abed-nego, fell down bound into the midst of the burning fiery furnace.

24. Then Nebuchadnezzar the king was astonied, and rose up in haste, and spake, and said unto his counsellors, Did not we cast three men bound into the midst of the fire? They answered and said unto the king, True, O king.

25. He answered and said, Lo, I see four men loose, walking in the midst of the fire, and they have no hurt; and the form of the fourth is like the Son of God.

26. Then Nebuchadnezzar came near to the mouth of the burning fiery furnace, and spake, and said, Shadrach, Meshach, and Abed-nego, ye servants of the most high God, come forth, and come hither. Then Shadrach, Meshach, and Abed-nego, came forth of the midst of the fire.

27. And the princes, governors, and captains, and the king's counsellors, being gathered together, saw these men, upon whose bodies the fire had no power, nor was an hair of their head singed, neither were their coats changed, nor the smell of fire had passed on them.

28. Then Nebuchadnezzar spake, and said, Blessed be the God of Shadrach, Meshach, and Abed-nego, who hath sent his angel, and delivered his servants that trusted in him, and have changed the king's word, and yielded their bodies, that they might not serve nor worship any god, except their own God.

29. Therefore I make a decree, That every people, nation, and language, which speak any thing amiss against the God of Shadrach, Meshach, and Abed-nego, shall be cut in pieces, and their houses shall be made a dunghill: because there is no other God that can deliver after this sort.

30. Then the king promoted Shadrach, Meshach, and Abed-nego, in the province of Babylon.

The Image of Gold

Verse 1: "Nebuchadnezzar the king made an image of gold, whose height was threescore cubits, and the breadth thereof six cubits: he set it up in the plain of Dura, in the province of Babylon."

The exact time that Nebuchadnezzar did this is not mentioned, nor is it stated in whose honor it was erected.

Most Bible scholars agree that Nebuchadnezzar built this tremendous golden image between 19 and 23 years after his dream of the great image with head of gold. The king's heart had undergone a tremendous change since he had fallen upon his face before Daniel and worshipped him, commanding an oblation to be made to him with an offering of sweet odors. At that time, Nebuchadnezzar had declared that Daniel's God was the God of gods, the Lord of kings, and the revealer of secrets (Dan. 2:47); but it was quite another story now. In the intervening years the impression made upon Nebuchadnezzar by the events in chapter 2 seems to have been entirely effaced—which proves again that human nature is totally depraved; and unless we allow God to control us, soul, spirit, and body, we are capable of committing as hideous sins as any other human has ever committed.

The golden image set up by Nebuchadnezzar and described in our present chapter is not said to be the result of what he had seen in his dream; but if it did result from his dream, in his pride he resolved to go a bit further in erecting HIS image, and he not only made the *head* of gold—*the entire image was of gold*! It is not impossible that Nebuchadnezzar was led to the construction of this image by what he had seen in Egypt. Bear in mind that shortly before this, Nebuchadnezzar had conquered and ravaged Egypt, and no doubt was impressed by the great images set up by the kings of Egypt to commemorate their reign and perpetuate their names after death. What would be more natural than that now Nebuchadnezzar would wish to emulate the Egyptian kings who, while still alive, sought through massive images to keep their memory alive and keep the glory of their reign before the people by setting up images of themselves, carved from solid rock?

Babylon was situated in a level country, and there

was no granite or rock from which the image of Nebuchadnezzar could be carved. He therefore decided to erect a statue the magnificence of which would surpass anything that had ever been built. He decided to build an image which would correspond in grandeur to other buildings of Babylon, such as the Tower of Baal and the hanging gardens: The image would be made of gold.

Notice where Nebuchadnezzar erected the image. He did not build it on Main Street nor in the city square; he built it *in the plain of Dura.* No doubt he did not want the other buildings of Babylon to detract from the magnificence of the image which was to commemorate his glory. Also, in the wide open spaces he would have room for all the great men of the many provinces of Babylon whom he proposed to invite. It seems probable that he knew that if he continued as ruler, since his great kingdom was comprised of many peoples of many lands and many religions, he must weld them together with some form of unified religion or national worship. Therefore he invited the rulers and the people from all the provinces of his great world-empire to try to bring about this "state religion." And the setting up of his idol in the plain of Dura would give ample space to accomodate the multitudes so that they could fall down before it in homage and worship.

Nebuchadnezzar's image is one of the sweet morsels of the critics of the book of Daniel. They claim that this image is beyond reason–ninety feet tall, nine feet wide, made of gold. (When we say ninety feet tall and nine feet wide we are assuming the cubit to be eighteen inches.) Critics say there was not enough gold in Babylon to build such a structure of solid gold.

However, the Bible does not say that it was solid gold, and we have no reason to assume that it was. It could have been made of other materials and overlaid with gold. But it is not impossible that there was sufficient gold in Babylon to build a solid gold image ninety feet high and nine feet wide, for Nebuchadnezzar had conquered the known world. He had conducted a successful campaign in Egypt; the Egyptians had vast quantities of gold, and this would have been transported to Babylon. It would certainly not have been impossible, therefore, for the image to have been solid gold, although the Bible does not give us this detail.

It could be that the image was placed on a pedestal, and thus the image within itself would not have been ninety feet tall and not out of proportion to the width, since the pedestal upon which it rested would have taken up a good part of that measurement. Undoubtedly Nebuchadnezzar had erected the image on a pedestal high enough for the multitudes to see it even from a distance.

Those of us who believe the Word of God have no trouble believing that Nebuchadnezzar built such an image of gold; and the critics of the Word who spend their time trying to prove that such a thing was impossible would find it much more profitable to study the Bible with an open mind and permit the Spirit of God to speak to their hearts in saving faith, instead of wasting their time trying to discredit the Word of God. Then they would *rejoice* in the things of the Word of God, rather than trying to disprove them as being beyond reason and human ability.

In Genesis 1:1 we read, "*In the beginning, GOD . . .*" and personally, I have no trouble believing the rest. If God is in it, then God can handle the impossible and accomplish what seems impossible to the mind of man. We are finite; God is infinite. He had a purpose in all that He allowed Nebuchadnezzar to do.

We may rest assured that *whatever* Nebuchadnezzar

constructed was magnificent. History verifies the stupendous walls of Babylon as never having been equalled, and the hanging gardens of Babylon are still a mystery to modern man. Yet history authenticates the fact that these structures existed.

The Bible is composed of sixty-six books, each of which is a book within itself, each with a specific message. ALL the books of the Bible are inspired and are profitable for us. There is not one book, chapter, verse, or word in our Holy Scriptures that was put there for the purpose of filling space. Every word, every statement, every name, has a meaning; every mountain and every river has a significance. The image Nebuchadnezzar built was not *fifty-nine* cubits high, nor *sixty-one* cubits high: *It was sixty cubits high.* It was not *four* cubits wide, nor *twelve* cubits wide: *It was six cubits wide.* In the Scriptures, six is the number of man, seven is God's number–the perfect number in the Bible. *Six* stops short of *seven* and is therefore imperfect. *Seven* is the number of God's completeness; *six* is the number of human incompleteness. Man was created on the sixth day of creation, and God rested on the seventh.

In Revelation 13:18 we read the number of the beast–six hundred, threescore, and six–which adds up to 666; and the Bible clearly states that this is the number of a man:

"And he doeth great wonders, so that he maketh fire come down from heaven on the earth in the sight of men, and deceiveth them that dwell on the earth by the means of those miracles which he had power to do in the sight of the beast; saying to them that dwell on the earth, that they should make an image to the beast, which had the wound by a sword, and did live. And he had power to give life unto the image of the beast, that the image of the beast should both speak, and cause that as many as would not worship the image of the beast should be killed. And he causeth all, both small and great, rich and poor, free and bond, to receive a mark in their right hand, or in their foreheads: And that no man might buy or sell, save he that had the mark, or the name of the beast, or the number of his name. Here is wisdom. Let him that hath understanding count the number of the beast: for it is the number of a man; and his number is Six hundred three score and six" (Rev. 13:13–18).

Nebuchadnezzar did not know that he was blueprinting and erecting an image that measured up to prophetic size—sixty cubits tall and six cubits wide. He did not know that his image was a type of the false prophet who will appear in the end of the age during the reign of the beast—the Antichrist, the Satanic trinity. Nebuchadnezzar did not know that his gigantic statue of gold was a symbol of prophecy, and that one day a greater one than he would cause an image to speak, and that all would be killed who would not worship the beast and his image.

Those who refused to worship the image set up by Nebuchadnezzar were to be thrown into the fiery furnace; but those who refuse to worship the image of the beast during the reign of Antichrist will be killed by guillotine:

"And I saw thrones, and they sat upon them, and judgment was given unto them: and I saw the souls of them that *were beheaded* for the witness of Jesus, and for the word of God, and which had not worshipped the beast, neither his image, neither had received his mark upon their foreheads, or in their hands; and they lived and reigned with Christ a thousand years" (Rev. 20:4).

During the reign of the beast, no one will be permitted to buy or sell except those who wear the mark of the beast or the number of his name (666) in their hand or in their forehead.

When this image is set up in the end-time during the reign of the Antichrist and all peoples are commanded to worship it, those who refuse to worship will be killed. That day is the beginning of the end of "*MAN'S DAY*"—or the beginning of the end of "the times of the Gentiles." At that time the stone cut out of the mountain without hands will be on the verge of crushing the enemies of Jesus into chaff, destroying the Antichrist and his armies, and making ready for the setting up of the "Stone Kingdom"—the last kingdom seen by Nebuchadnezzar in his dream.

The actions of Nebuchadnezzar in this third chapter of Daniel are definitely prophetic. As we go along, we will see, step by step, how this image plays a part in making known the things that will happen during the last week of the seventy weeks of prophecy in the book of Daniel, the last week being the seven years when the Antichrist will reign here upon this earth, sitting in the temple in Jerusalem announcing to the world (no doubt via Tel-Star) that he is God, and the multitudes will fall at his feet and worship him AS God. But there will be a faithful remnant who will be beheaded because, like Daniel, they will purpose in their hearts that they will not receive the mark of the beast, they will not worship his image—and they will lose their lives. In the end, they will reign with Christ (Rev. 20:4, 6).

The Dedication of Nebuchadnezzar's Image

Verses 2 and 3: "Then Nebuchadnezzar the king sent to gather together the princes, the governors, and the captains, the judges, the treasurers, the counsellors, the sheriffs, and all the rulers of the provinces, to come to the dedication of the image which Nebuchadnezzar the king had set up. Then the princes, the governors, and captains, the judges, the treasurers, the counsellors, the sheriffs, and all the rulers of the provinces, were gathered together unto the dedication of the image that Nebuchadnezzar the king had set up; and they stood before the image that Nebuchadnezzar had set up."

Nebuchadnezzar believed in doing things in a big way, and arrangements for dedication of the image were as elaborate as the image itself. All the known nations of earth in that day had become subject to Babylon, and therefore they were called upon to send a delegation to the ceremony, at which time the golden image would be dedicated. The city of Babylon was alive and crowded with great men–governors and rulers from all the nations and provinces over which Babylon ruled.

We can well imagine that the city was decorated in a style magnificent beyond words, and that the day of dedication was probably pronounced to be the greatest day in the history of Babylon. Spirits were running high and tension could be felt throughout the city. But there was a quartet of Hebrews who did not share in the excitement. They knew the king was a powerful monarch, they knew the image had been set up, they knew the day had arrived for its dedication, and they knew what was expected of them; but *they also knew God*, and they were not afraid. They saw a Ruler who was invisible to human eyes, and they feared HIM much more than they feared Nebuchadnezzar!

The Announcement Is Made

Verses 4–7: "Then an herald cried aloud, To you it is commanded, O people, nations, and languages, that at what time ye hear the sound of the cornet, flute, harp, sackbut, psaltery, dulcimer, and all kinds of musick, ye fall down and worship the golden image that Nebuchadnezzar the king hath set up: And whoso falleth not down and worshippeth shall the same hour be cast into the midst of a burning fiery furnace. Therefore at that time, when all the people heard the sound of the cornet, flute, harp, sackbut, psaltery, and all kinds of musick, all the people, the nations, and the languages, fell down and worshipped the golden image that Nebuchadnezzar the king had set up."

The cry rang aloud through the plain: "To you it is *commanded*, O people, nations, and languages . . . ." *Everybody* was commanded. Everybody was there. What a crowd! What a mass of humanity! The herald cried out, "At what time ye hear the sound of the cornet, the flute, the harp, etc., YE FALL DOWN AND WORSHIP the golden image that Nebuchadnezzar the king hath set up!"

There is a question in my mind as to whether or not the invitation sent out included the announcement that this would be a religious service rather than a political rally or the dedication of a monument to commemorate the reign of a powerful king. Personally, I believe the masses were in ignorance concerning the real nature of this great gathering in the plain of Dura; but the king knew well what he was doing. He had made his plans carefully . . . no loopholes were left, no dangling ends untied. Nations and people, great or small, ALL were to fall down and worship the golden image.

If you read these verses carefully you cannot miss the fact that this affair was planned in every detail. The king had declared–and his cohorts had agreed–that anyone who failed to obey the command to fall down and worship the image would immediately ("that same hour") be cast into the midst of a burning, fiery furnace.

The king meant business. Pride had mastered him; power and wealth had gone to his head. God had GIVEN him the kingdom of Babylon; God had blessed him and had even allowed him to see and understand what lay ahead as revealed by Daniel in the interpretation of the king's dream. But Nebuchadnezzar had changed his mind about "the God of heaven, the Lord of kings, and the revealer of secrets"; he himself had made a god and had commanded the people to worship at his shrine. He declared that if anyone *refused* to worship as he commanded, that person would be cremated by being thrown alive into the furnace. The order in verse 6 is tyrannical and is contrary to all of our notions of freedom of worship. But it was much in the spirit of that age, and indeed of almost every age.

Nebuchadnezzar would naturally know the power of religion—and, energized by the pride in his heart, he knew that if he could unify the many peoples, languages, and nations in religion, he could hold his huge empire together and continue to rule the world. He decided to set up a national religion of Babylonian type.

We are not in ignorance concerning Nimrod and his attempt to build a tower to heaven, as recorded in the tenth and eleventh chapters of Genesis—and Nebuchadnezzar was at this point walking in the footsteps of Nimrod, by-passing the God of heaven to set up his own god, drawing his own blueprints for a world-wide kingdom that should never crumble and fall. He did not face the fact that whether it be king or peasant, God Almighty rules in the affairs of men. God puts up whom He will, and puts down whom He will.

The people outside Babylon were idolaters, and the religions of the provinces were also those of idolatry. They were all accustomed to idol worship—and the worship of one idol would not prevent their bowing to another. No one but the Hebrews who worshipped one God would have any scruples on the subject. Though these idolaters might worship other gods in their own countries, they would have no great objection to worshipping the image set up by Nebuchadnezzar.

The king was acquainted with these facts, but even then he was guilty of intolerance concerning religion, because he decreed the penalty of death to all who refused to worship his image. He was shrewd; he knew that all men are religious by nature, easily carried away by whatever excites and appeals to their emotions and feelings. He placed orchestras and musicians in strategic locations throughout the plain of Dura, along with ritualistic paraphernalia to carry out idolatrous worship in the most elaborate, magnificent way.

Religion is powerful, regardless of how pagan it may be. A person will fight for his religion as quickly as he will fight for his life. The bloodiest wars in history have been wars over religion. Nebuchadnezzar knew that if he could get all peoples to accept his state religion and to bow at the shrine of his magnificent golden idol, he would indeed have the entire world at his feet. That is what he wanted. That is the end toward which he was working.

When we look about us today and see the false religions that major on images, "gimmicks" in worship, magnificence in dress and in buildings, when we see religions of *works* growing by leaps and bounds, then we know surely that the church of Antichrist is in the making and it cannot be long until the true Church is caught out and the lukewarm church is spewed out–and from that lukewarm group, neither cold nor hot, never having been born again but strictly "religious," *the church of Antichrist will be formed.* In this day of the spectacular, people want to *see* something, *feel* something, *participate in something*; they are not willing to walk by faith. (Paul said, "The just shall LIVE by faith"–Rom. 1:17).

Nebuchadnezzar was making an all-out attempt to

weld the peoples of earth together in one mind and heart, religiously–on their faces before his magnificent idol of gold; and even as I prepare these messages, headlines in newspapers, magazines, periodicals and newscasts are crying out for union in religion today! The World Council of Churches and the Ecumenical Council are doing all humanly possible to bring denominations together in unity and universal religion, making the whole world of one religious group known as the World Church.

The groups who are striving to unite all religions under one head and one name, deny the virgin birth, the atoning blood of Jesus Christ, and the verbal inspiration of the Scriptures. They advocate a man-made religion, and this will terminate in the church of Antichrist, which will be destroyed when Jesus returns to set up His kingdom.

Writing to Timothy, Paul describes the movements under way today to bring the world under one powerful head religiously:

"This know also, that in the last days perilous times shall come. For men shall be lovers of their own selves, covetous, boasters, proud, blasphemers, disobedient to parents, unthankful, unholy, without natural affection, trucebreakers, false accusers, incontinent, fierce, despisers of those that are good, traitors, heady, highminded, lovers of pleasures more than lovers of God; having a form of godliness, but denying the power thereof: from such turn away. For of this sort are they which creep into houses, and lead captive silly women laden with sins, led away with divers lusts, ever learning, and never able to come to the knowledge of the truth" (II Tim. 3:1–7).

This is the day of form without power. Preachers are "ever learning"; they boast of college degrees, but they are "never able to come to the knowledge of the truth." Evil men and seducers wax worse and worse, and men who live godly lives suffer in the process. These are the days Paul described to Timothy. Surely it cannot be long until the Church will be caught out, the lukewarm church of the Laodiceans will immediately take over the reins of religion, and the whole world will quickly unite to form the universal church out of which Antichrist will appear:

"And there came one of the seven angels which had the seven vials, and talked with me, saying unto me, Come hither; I will shew unto thee the judgment of the great whore that sitteth upon many waters: With whom the kings of the earth have committed fornication, and the inhabitants of the earth have been made drunk with the wine of her fornication. So he carried me away in the spirit into the wilderness: and I saw a woman sit upon a scarlet coloured beast, full of names of blasphemy, having seven heads and ten horns. And the woman was arrayed in purple and scarlet colour, and decked with gold and precious stones and pearls, having a golden cup in her hand full of abominations and filthiness of her fornication: And upon her forehead was a name written, MYSTERY, BABYLON THE GREAT, THE MOTHER OF HARLOTS AND ABOMINATIONS OF THE EARTH" (Rev. 17:1–5).

Nebuchadnezzar believed that an ounce of prevention was worth a pound of cure. He left no stone unturned to insure the success of his plan to set up a state religion. He took every precaution. He did not wait until someone refused to obey his command and then make a law to deal with that person or persons; he made the law *before* the dedication. He intended for this plan of worship to be universal. There could be no discord; cooperation must be one hundred percent. So he declared a penalty for any and all who refused to worship the image. While the image was being set up, a giant furnace was being prepared. The fire was burning, smoke was rolling. Those near the furnace could feel the heat from it.

The announcement was made; the furnace was pointed out. If anyone, regardless of rank or position, refused to obey the king's command to fall down and worship at the sound of the music, in the very same hour that person would be thrown into the blazing furnace. There would be no trial, no pleading for mercy. Nebuchadnezzar thought that everyone loved life so much and would so fear the burning furnace, that they would never entertain the thought of refusing to worship his golden image. He thought the roaring furnace with the fire already hotter than was customary, would be a sure cure for opposition to his plan. But he reckoned without considering the intervention of Almighty God.

In my mind's eye I can see the plain of Dura, swarming with humanity, like ants on a giant anthill. There must have been hundreds of thousands of people gathered to do homage to Nebuchadnezzar. There stood the shining image of gold. The orchestras were seated on bandstands around the plain. The master of ceremonies proclaimed the time of worship. There was a blast from the musical instruments—and the people hit the dirt! What a sight! What a sound! Yes, the multitudes fell down before the image—but there were three Hebrews who did not bow: Shadrach, Meshach, and Abed-nego. Although they were prominent officials in the king's court, they refused to obey the king's command.

The Scripture does not tell us where Daniel was at this time. He could have been sitting next to the king, or it is possible that he was absent from the dedication on official business in some other part of the empire. After all, he was next to the king in power, and perhaps he was not required to bow to the image, since he held such a high position and it would naturally be expected that he would be loyal to the king. It is true that Daniel had given the allegiance of service to Nebuchadnezzar; but his first love and loyalty was to God, and the king knew it. For some unexplainable reason, Daniel was not named with those who would not bow when the command was given to fall in worship before the golden image.

Shadrach, Meshach, and Abed-nego, standing instead of falling down before the image, must have created excitement among the Chaldeans. Probably Nebuchadnezzar had appointed spies or had placed officials in fixed positions through the crowds. Perhaps some of the politicians were jealously watching the three Hebrews, hoping that they would not bow, wanting to see them thrown into the fiery furnace. At any rate, they were reported immediately for their disobedience to the order of the king.

Three Who Dared Defy the King

Verses 8–12: "Wherefore at that time certain Chaldeans came near, and accused the Jews. They spake and said to the king Nebuchadnezzar, O king, live for ever. Thou, O king, hast made a decree, that every man that shall hear the sound of the cornet, flute, harp, sackbut, psaltery, and dulcimer, and all kinds of musick, shall fall down and worship the golden image: And whoso falleth not down and worshippeth, that he should be cast into the midst of a burning fiery furnace. There are certain Jews whom thou hast set over the affairs of the province of Babylon, Shadrach, Meshach, and Abed-nego; these men, O king, have not regarded thee: they serve not thy gods, nor worship the golden image which thou hast set up."

The charges against the Hebrews were threefold:

1. "These men, O king, have not regarded thee. . . ."
2. "They serve not thy gods . . . ."
3. "Nor worship the golden image which thou hast set up."

When Nebuchadnezzar heard the charges against the Hebrews he was furious. It was beyond imagination that anyone would be so stupid and reckless as to show disrespect for his commands! And not only had they been disrespectful of his commands, but they did not respect HIM. They did not respect his gods; they did not respect the enormous golden image he had set up in the plain.

It would seem that after a moment of consideration, the king said to himself, "Undoubtedly there is some mistake. Surely these men did not hear the command—and if they did hear, they evidently misunderstood." So Nebuchadnezzar summoned the three Hebrews to appear in his presence:

Verses 13–15: "Then Nebuchadnezzar in his rage and fury commanded to bring Shadrach, Meshach, and Abed-nego. Then they brought these men before the king. Nebuchadnezzar spake and said unto them, Is it true, O Shadrach, Meshach, and Abed-nego, do not ye serve my gods, nor worship the golden image which I have set up? Now if ye be ready that at what time ye hear the sound of the cornet, flute, harp, sackbut, psaltery, and dulcimer, and all kinds of musick, ye fall down and worship the image which I have made; well: but if ye worship not, ye shall be cast the same hour into the midst of a burning fiery furnace; and who is that God that shall deliver you out of my hands?"

"Nebuchadnezzar in his rage and fury . . . ." The word rendered *fury* means "wrath." It seems that all we learn of this monarch shows that he was a man of violent passions and that he was easily excited. It is remarkable that Nebuchadnezzar gave the three Hebrews the benefit of the doubt. He said, "Is it true that you have disobeyed my command?" I suspect, down deep in his heart, he was hoping that the report had been untrue. For the sake of Daniel, the king probably disliked being forced to cremate these three friends of the man whom he had promoted to the highest office in the land beside his own–the one who had shown more wisdom and understanding than all the wise men in his kingdom. At any rate, the fact that these men were not immediately thrown into the furnace shows that he still had some respect for them. It is proper also to recognize the providence of God in this questioning of Nebuchadnezzar, for we now have the noble reply of the three Hebrew children–and we see the strength of character of these three, even to the last.

The king continued: "Is it true, Shadrach, Meshach, and Abed-nego? Do you not serve my gods, nor worship the golden image that I have set up?" The king found it unbelievable that anyone would dare refuse to worship his gods or bow before the image he had set up in the plain–an image that had cost so much and required so much time, talent, and craftsmanship to set up. The king had then gone to the expense of bringing in unknown numbers of musicians to play for the gala event, and it seemed unthinkable that anyone would defy him and his command when the music began to play.

The king said to the three Hebrew boys, "I am going to give you another chance. Whether or not you realized what you were doing is not important. Perhaps you heard the command, and perhaps you understood it–but we will forget that. We will give you the benefit of the doubt, and when all the instruments begin to play, YOU FALL DOWN AND WORSHIP THE IMAGE WHICH I HAVE MADE! If you men will do as you are told, we will put out the fire. But if you WORSHIP NOT, then we will *build up* the fire and you will be thrown into the midst of it. And *who is that God that shall deliver you out of MY hands?"*

This does not sound like the same king who testified before Daniel after the interpretation of his dream: "Then the king Nebuchadnezzar fell upon his face, and worshipped Daniel, and commanded that they should offer an oblation and sweet odours unto him. The king answered unto Daniel, and said, Of a truth it is, that *your God is a God of gods, and a Lord of kings, and a revealer of secrets*, seeing thou couldest reveal this secret" (Dan. 2:46, 47).

Could it be possible that from the same lips and the same heart now proceeded these cutting, threatening words: "WHO IS THAT GOD THAT SHALL DELIVER YOU OUT OF MY HANDS?"

King Nebuchadnezzar felt his importance that day; he defied the God of heaven! What caused this radical change in the king? He had once recognized the God of Daniel, worshipping at his feet and praising the God of heaven and declaring Him to be sovereign. What was it that drove him into such reckless fanaticism and scorn as he now displayed? Was he not sincere when he confessed that Daniel's God was the God of gods and Lord of kings? And if he *had been* sincere, what subsequent events had caused him to so completely change his mind?

The dream of Nebuchadnezzar had occurred about twenty years earlier. In the meantime, he had overrun Jerusalem a second time, in 598 B. C., and during this second conquest, he had carried the majority of the inhabitants of Jerusalem captive, confiscating many of the sacred vessels of the temple and taking them back to Babylon.

Then in 587 B. C. Nebuchadnezzar overran Jerusalem for the third time and completely destroyed it, burning the temple and leaving the Holy Land in utter desolation. It is a historical fact that oriental monarchs gave credit to their gods for their victories over their enemies. When they conquered a people, they believed that *their* gods were greater than the gods of those whom they conquered. It could be that since Nebuchadnezzar had completely destroyed the Holy Land, he sincerely believed that his gods had overcome the God of Daniel, because he had been able to destroy the temple and confiscate its golden vessels. Did this victory make him believe that Jehovah was not supreme, that He was not sovereign—and that Merodach, chief of the heathen gods of Babylonia, was more powerful than He?

If we consider this sincerely, it seems that it is the only reasonable argument and that Nebuchadnezzar had come to feel that his god was more powerful than Jehovah. He therefore asked the Hebrews, "Who IS that God that shall deliver you out of my hands? Your God is the God of Jerusalem, the God of the temple there; but He did not deliver the temple with its golden vessels, nor did He deliver Jerusalem and its people out of my hands; so why should He deliver YOU? Your God has weakened. MY god is now more powerful than yours. You will now disown your God and bow down to mine!"

I do not doubt that Nebuchadnezzar expected these three young men to obey him. But if he thought they would really surrender to his commands, fall down before the golden image and worship there, he had a great surprise in store; for Shadrach, Meshach, and Abed-nego were of the same faith as Daniel, and they, too, had purposed in their hearts that they would not defile themselves and worship the king's image—and they did not.

The Hebrews Accept the King's Challenge

Verses 16–18: "Shadrach, Meshach, and Abed-nego, answered and said to the king, O Nebuchadnezzar, we are not careful to answer thee in this matter. If it be so, our God whom we serve is able to deliver us from the burning fiery furnace, and He will deliver us out of thine hand, O king. But if not, be it known unto thee, O king, that we will not serve thy gods, nor worship the golden image which thou hast set up."

What a thrill it would have been to witness the next few moments after Nebuchadnezzar poured forth his burning words of final command to the three Hebrews! If they trembled before him, it is not recorded in the Word of God. If they were afraid, it is not suggested in the answer they gave the king. They stood as the Rock of Gibraltar–straight and tall, and their faces shone like the gold on the king's image. Whether they spoke in unison or not, they were agreed in their purpose:

"O Nebuchadnezzar, we are not careful to answer thee in this matter. We are not going to ask for time to make up our minds. We do not need hours–nor even moments–of grace. You have given your command; we have given you our answer: If your decree be so, *OUR GOD is able to deliver us*!"

The king had asked, "Who IS that God that shall deliver you out of my hands?" and the young men had replied, "OUR God is able to deliver us, and He WILL deliver us if it is in accord with His divine will. BUT IF NOT, it will make no difference in our decision concerning your command. WE WILL NOT SERVE THY GODS, NOR WORSHIP THE GOLDEN IMAGE WHICH THOU HAST SET UP." These three Hebrews loved not their lives. They were resolved to be faithful to their God–even unto death.

Daniel 3:16–25

They Would Not Bow;
They Would Not Budge;
They DID NOT Burn.

Verses 19–25: "Then was Nebuchadnezzar full of fury, and the form of his visage was changed against Shadrach, Meshach, and Abed-nego: therefore he spake, and commanded that they should heat the furnace one seven times more than it was wont to be heated. And he commanded the most mighty men that were in his army to bind Shadrach, Meshach, and Abed-nego, and to cast them into the burning fiery furnace. Then these men were bound in their coats, their hosen, and their hats, and their other garments, and were cast into the midst of the burning fiery furnace. Therefore because the king's commandment was urgent, and the furnace exceeding hot, the flame of the fire slew those men that took up Shadrach, Meshach, and Abed-nego. And these three men, Shadrach, Meshach, and Abed-nego, fell down bound into the midst of the burning fiery furnace. Then Nebuchadnezzar the king was astonied, and rose up in haste, and spake, and said unto his counsellors, Did not we cast three men bound into the midst of the fire? They answered and said unto the king, True, O king. He answered and said, Lo, I see four men loose, walking in the midst of the fire, and they have no hurt; and the form of the fourth is like the Son of God."

The dedication of Nebuchadnezzar's great golden image was brief; it ended abruptly. It is not likely that many of the people saw the Hebrews who refused to bow to the image; but the news spread rapidly, and the mob began moving toward the furnace. The king was in a rage. His countenance changed, and he roared out the unmistakable sentence of execution of the three Hebrews. The furnace was to be heated seven times hotter than it had ever been. The most mighty men of Babylon, men from Nebuchadnezzar's army, were commanded to bind Shadrach, Meshach, and Abed-nego. What a foolish command on the part of the king! Placing three men in a furnace hot enough to melt iron, but commanding that they be securely bound before they were cast into the fire!

Deep down in the innermost soul of Nebuchadnezzar there must have been a spark of fear–fear that perhaps the God whom he had defied really *would* attempt to get these three men out of the furnace alive; and that fear caused him to take all possible precautions. The strongest men in the army of Babylon were called; the Hebrews "were bound in their coats, their hosen, and their hats, and their other garments." Nebuchadnezzar meant to be rid of these fellows and everything they owned. He wanted no trace of them left in Babylon!

At the king's command the furnace was heated exceedingly hot–so hot that the flames burned those who were designated to put Shadrach, Meshach, and Abednego into the fire! The spellbound crowd gazed toward the mouth of the furnace; a proud monarch stood with determination in his heart to destroy the three little Hebrew upstarts who had dared defy him. The mighty men of Babylon seized the young men and cast them into the furnace–only to be cremated themselves by the excessive heat from the furnace as they carried out Nebuchadnezzar's order of execution!

Then even a more astonishing thing happened. The king "rose up in haste," and asked in amazement and unbelief, *"Did not we cast THREE men bound into the midst of the fire?"* The counsellors answered, "True, O king." Nebuchadnezzar then said, "Lo, I see FOUR men loose, walking, in the midst of the fire–and they have no hurt. AND THE FORM OF THE FOURTH IS LIKE THE SON OF GOD!" Even though the king spoke the truth concerning the fourth man, there is no evidence that he knew he was referring to the One whom we know in our New Testament as the Son of God. It is doubtful even that the title "The Son of God" was then commonly given to the Messiah by the Jews–and if so, then we must assume that through Daniel Nebuchadnezzar had learned of the coming Messiah–the Son of Jehovah God. Another possibility is that the form and figure of the fourth man was so majestic, His countenance so bright, that the king immediately declared Him to be of heavenly origin. If this be so, then Nebuchadnezzar gave Him the right title without realizing it.

The deliverance of Shadrach, Meshach, and Abednego from the fiery furnace was a great miracle; no one would question that. The heat of the furnace was of sufficient temperature to melt iron–so hot that it consumed those who cast the Hebrews into it; yet those three men walked up and down in the furnace and came forth uninjured! Such an experience is incredible–and apart from God Almighty, it is impossible!

But our God is the God of miracles–such miracles as this; and it *took* such a miracle to counteract the worship of the colossal golden image set up by Nebuchadnezzar, and put an end to the persecution of the Jewish captives in Babylon. No one would doubt now that these men were loyal to their God and to their religion. The fact that they were willing to face the flames rather than deny their God proved that they did not intend to compromise their convictions.

"All things were made by Him; and without Him was not any thing made that was made" (John 1:3). This verse refers to Jesus, the Son of God–the fourth person in the furnace. "All things were made by Him"–including the fire; and the God whom Nebuchadnezzar defied and insulted was the same God who walked in the furnace with the faithful Hebrews–the Person of whom Nebuchadnezzar said, "His form is like the Son of God." All things are possible to HIM. He can do the unbelievable;

He can do far more than we could ever imagine.

It was not hard for the God who created heaven and earth and all that therein is, to deliver three men, created in His image, out of a furnace of fire. When we believe in God—the sovereign, almighty "God of gods, Lord of kings, and revealer of secrets"—we have no trouble believing that He could allow three men to live in a fiery furnace, a furnace hot enough to destroy those who came near it!

King Nebuchadnezzar was a wise man; he was a great and powerful man; but in his rage and fury he outdid himself. When he commanded his executioners to heat the furnace seven times hotter than it had ever been heated, he defeated his own purpose. The heat would only have shortened the sufferings of Shadrach, Meshach, and Abednego, and hastened their destruction; but even more than that, the king's fanaticism cost him the strongest men in his army, because the men who bound the Hebrews and cast them into the furnace were destroyed in the process.

Seven is God's number, the number of perfection. The furnace was heated "seven times hotter"; therefore it was as hot as hot could be, and that fact testified that a supernatural miracle was performed before the king's very eyes—for only the God of supernatural intelligence and power could control the flames and keep men alive in such a fire. There was no way to explain away the survival of the young men. Their *God* had delivered them.

There was no need to say that the *burning* was removed from the fire, because the cords with which the men were bound were consumed. I do not know what kind of cords were used to bind them—but you may rest assured that they were strong, and the men were bound securely. The fire burned the cords from their bodies, but when they emerged from the furnace, their coats were not burned, their hair was not singed, they did not even *smell* like smoke.

It is noteworthy that when Shadrach, Meshach, and Abed-nego realized that their bonds were burned away and they were free, they made no attempt to get out of the furnace. They were willing to remain there with their Lord. They had said, "He is able to deliver us if He so desires. But if He does NOT deliver us, we will not bow to the golden image, nor worship the heathen gods." Whatever God's decision in the matter, they knew He was ABLE to deliver them, and they faced the king's wrath unafraid.

These young Hebrews had, up to this point, known God only as a historical God. They had no doubt learned of Him at their mother's knee. They had known Him as a sovereign God, the God who had been with their fathers; but now they knew Him personally in the Person of His Son, who walked with them in the fiery furnace. Many times, believers come to know God better and come into closer fellowship with Him when passing through the fiery furnace of trials, heartaches, disappointment, and bereavement. Shadrach, Meshach, and Abed-nego chose to walk in a furnace of fire with the Lord Jesus Christ, rather than sit at Nebuchadnezzar's right hand in his magnificent palace!

Shadrach, Meshach, and Abed-nego did not have Romans 8:31: "What shall we then say to these things? If God be for us, who can be against us?" Nor did they have Hebrews 13:5, 6: "Let your conversation be without covetousness; and be content with such things as ye have: for He hath said, I will never leave thee, nor forsake thee. So that we may boldly say, The Lord is my helper, and I will not fear what man shall do unto me." They did not have these tremendous promises in writing, but they knew the God who MADE the promises. He dwelt in their hearts, and they exercised unshakable faith in Him. Even though they did not have His promises in writing, they stood on them by faith.

"When thou passest through the waters, I will be with thee; and through the rivers, they shall not overflow thee: when thou walkest through the fire, thou shalt not be burned; neither shall the flame kindle upon thee" (Isa. 43:2).

In Hebrews 11 we find the roll call of the faithful. Many are named–Abel, Enoch, Noah, Abraham and Sarah, Isaac and Jacob, Joseph, Moses, Joshua, Rahab. And then the Holy Spirit continues:

"And what shall I more say? for the time would fail me to tell of Gedeon, and of Barak, and of Samson, and of Jephthae; of David also, and Samuel, and of the prophets: Who through faith subdued kingdoms, wrought righteousness, obtained promises, stopped the mouths of lions, QUENCHED THE VIOLENCE OF FIRE, escaped the edge of the sword, out of weakness were made strong, waxed valiant in fight, turned to flight the armies of the aliens. Women received their dead raised to life again: and others were tortured, not accepting deliverance; that they might obtain a better resurrection: And others had trial of cruel mockings and scourgings, yea, moreover of bonds and imprisonment: They were stoned, they were sawn asunder, were tempted, were slain with the sword: They wandered about in sheepskins and goatskins; being destitute, afflicted, tormented; (Of whom the world was not worthy:) they wandered in deserts, and in mountains, and in dens and caves of the earth. And these all, having obtained a good report through faith, received not the promise: God having provided some better thing for us, that they without us should not be made perfect" (Heb. 11:32–40).

"Quenched the violence of fire . . . ." There is no doubt that the Holy Spirit here refers to the three Hebrew children—and probably others; but especially to these three brave Hebrew lads.

The Word of God teaches, "The just shall live by faith" (Rom. 1:17). The Word of God declares that without faith it is impossible to please God (Heb. 11:6). *God honors faith*—and the three Hebrew children had unshakable faith in God. If we would allow God to control our lives and supply our needs as these three young men did, we would be far better off—physically, spiritually, and eternally. The joy of God is to come to the defense of His faithful servants. God never changes; He would do for us today what He did for the three Hebrew children if we should have such a need and if that need should occur as a result of our faithfulness to Him.

Nebuchadnezzar had burned with anger and his face had been contorted with fury as he stormed at these young men, "WHO IS that God that shall deliver you out of my hands?" But now he knew that there IS a God who is able to deliver out of even *his* powerful hands. What a rebuke to the king's pride and arrogance! The deliverance of the three Hebrew children was a vindication of the course they had taken by refusing to bow to the king's image or to compromise with him in any way whatsoever. There was not a god in Babylon known to the king or any of his wise men who had ever wrought such a deliverance, nor was there a god who was able to perform such a miracle as the king had just witnessed; and that miracle was the means of his conversion. Nebuchadnezzar recognized, in the miracle of the fiery furnace, that the God of Shadrach, Meshach, and Abednego was certainly more powerful than the gods of Babylon.

Nebuchadnezzar Convinced of a God More Powerful Than the Gods of Babylon

Verses 26–30: "Then Nebuchadnezzar came near to the mouth of the burning fiery furnace, and spake, and said, Shadrach, Meshach, and Abed-nego, ye servants of the most high God, come forth, and come hither. Then Shadrach, Meshach, and Abed-nego, came forth of the midst of the fire. And the princes, governors, and captains, and the king's counsellors, being gathered together, saw these men, upon whose bodies the fire had no power, nor was an hair of their head singed, neither were their coats changed, nor the smell of fire had passed on them. Then Nebuchadnezzar spake, and said, Blessed be the God of Shadrach, Meshach, and Abed-nego, who hath sent His angel, and delivered His servants that trusted in Him, and have changed the king's word, and yielded their bodies, that they might not serve nor worship any god, except their own God. Therefore I make a decree, That every people, nation, and language, which speak any thing amiss against the God of Shadrach, Meshach, and Abed-nego, shall be cut in pieces, and their houses shall be made a dunghill: because there is no other God that can deliver after this sort. Then the king promoted Shadrach, Meshach, and Abed-nego, in the province of Babylon."

You will note that when Shadrach, Meshach, and Abed-nego realized that the cords were burned from their bodies and they were free to walk around, they did not make haste to leave the fiery furnace. However, when Nebuchadnezzar came near to the mouth of the fiery furnace and called them, they walked out of the furnace; and Nebuchadnezzar's princes, governors, captains and counsellors were all there to inspect these amazing young men. They touched them, they examined them and looked them over carefully. These wise and mighty men of Babylon wanted optical and tangible proof that these were really the men whom they had cast into the furnace and who had lived to walk out of the sevenfold heat of that furnace. They were convinced. They saw with their eyes, they touched with their hands, and they could not deny the fact that three men of flesh stood before them—unharmed.

The king then made another pronouncement, quite different from the one he had made only a short time ago. He said, "Blessed be the God of Shadrach, Meshach, and Abed-nego, who sent His angel, and delivered His servants that trusted in Him."

What the Hebrews dared to do in refusing to obey the king's command "changed the king's word." Nebuchadnezzar had made a decree—but the God of the Hebrews set that decree aside. There is only ONE King whose word cannot be changed, and that is the King of kings and Lord of lords. The Word of God is forever settled in heaven; it never changes.

The fact that Shadrach, Meshach, and Abed-nego were willing to yield their bodies to the fiery furnace rather than worship another god moved King Nebuchadnezzar as he had never been moved, and led him to make public announcement of a new decree: "That every people, nation, and language, which speak any thing amiss against the God of Shadrach, Meshach, and Abed-nego, shall be cut in pieces, and their houses shall be made a dunghill: *because there is no other God that can deliver after this sort!*"

Nebuchadnezzar had had some very intimate dealings with the Babylonian wise men, astrologers, and soothsayers, but they had never performed a miracle such as he had just witnessed. He therefore confessed that there IS a God who is more powerful than anything Babylon could produce.

"THEN THE KING PROMOTED SHADRACH, MESHACH, AND ABED-NEGO, IN THE PROVINCE OF

BABYLON." The believer is never *DEmoted* for being faithful to God. God always promotes—though not always as in the case of Shadrach, Meshach, and Abed-nego. It may not be a physical promotion; it may be unseen by those who know us on this earth—but if we dare to be different, and purpose in our hearts that we will not bow at the king's command, then the King of kings will reward us and promote us for being faithful. Our God is the God of Daniel, Shadrach, Meshach, and Abed-nego.

If these three young Hebrews were living today and were facing the same test, if they sought the advice of the religious leaders of our day, they would be advised to "go along" with the king, bow to the image, "coexist" with the idolaters, and, by so doing, perhaps lead the king into a better life. That would be the route suggested by the religious heads of our day. But these young men were dedicated wholeheartedly to their God, and they did not believe in coexisting with His enemies.

The purpose of the miracle of the fiery furnace was not just to deliver three young men from being cremated at the hands of Nebuchadnezzar. The heart of this Scripture goes much deeper than deliverance from physical death: It points to the final deliverance of Israel from the furnace of the nations.

The Prophetic Significance of the Three Hebrews in the Fiery Furnace

The third chapter of Daniel is given over to the record of the great image of Nebuchadnezzar and the refusal of Shadrach, Meshach, and Abed-nego to fall down and worship the king's golden god. Because they refused to obey the king's decree, they were cast into the fiery furnace; but they were miraculously preserved and delivered by the angel of the Lord; and after they were delivered by so great a miracle, the king exalted them.

To see in this most extraordinary narrative simply a picture of how God cares for His own, is to miss the heart of the great message contained in this chapter. It is comforting, wonderful, and encouraging to KNOW that God cares for His own, and that He will protect those who dare to stand true to Him regardless of the cost. We thank God for the promise that He will never leave us nor forsake us. God honors faithfulness in His children in all ages; we glory in the fact that He never changes—and what He did for the three Hebrew children He will do for us if we are faithful to Him. But there is much, much more in this chapter of Daniel. Jesus said that Daniel was a prophet, and that the prophecies of Daniel deal with future events. And beyond the *immediate* lesson here, God has a *prophetic* lesson concerning the future.

Paul tells us, "And without controversy great is the mystery of godliness: God was manifest in the flesh, justified in the Spirit, seen of angels, preached unto the Gentiles, believed on in the world, received up into glory" (I Tim. 3:16).

From the first verse in Genesis to the last verse in Revelation, all Scripture is God-breathed and is profitable to us; but we must study and rightly divide the Word (II Tim. 2:15). Let me point out three rules which will help us here, as well as in all phases of Bible study:

1. All Scripture has *only one primary interpretation*—never two, three, or more.
2. All Scripture has *several practical applications*. Believers of all ages can profit from Scripture, from Genesis through Revelation.
3. Almost all Scripture has *a prophetic revelation*—very little Scripture is not connected, directly or indirectly, with prophecy and future events.

The primary interpretation of the experience of Shadrach, Meshach, and Abed-nego in Nebuchadnezzar's fiery furnace teaches us of God's care for His chosen people, Israel, in the days of Nebuchadnezzar. The devil was trying to use Babylon as a furnace to annihilate the elect of God, the chosen people, through whom the seed of the woman would be born—the seed that would bruise the head of Satan. From the day in Eden when God said to the serpent, ". . . I will put enmity between thee and the woman, and between thy seed and her seed; it shall bruise thy head, and thou shalt bruise his heel," (Gen. 3:15) until the day Jesus said from the cross, "It is finished," (John 19:30), the devil did all in his diabolical power to stop the seed of the woman; and he was using Babylon in an all-out attempt to wipe out Israel, through whom the Messiah would come.

The fiery furnace episode, *by application*, teaches us that God cares for His own whenever and wherever the need arises; but there is definitely the *prophetic revelation* of that episode, and I personally believe this is the most important part of the fiery furnace miracle. Since Jesus acclaimed Daniel as a prophet and said that his book was prophetic, I gather that the number one message of Daniel is the message of prophecy—things that will occur in the future.

The prophetic lesson set forth concerns Israel among the Gentiles until "the times of the Gentiles" comes to an end. The three young Hebrews are a picture of the nation Israel, moving in the furnace of Gentile power but never consumed. From the human standpoint and by human standards, Israel should have been wiped out as a nation; but God has miraculously preserved that nation in the fiery furnace of race hatred and persecution.

Study the history of the Jew and you will find that no other nation has suffered such bloodshed. When Pilate said, "I have two prisoners: Jesus and Barabbas; whom shall I release?" the Jews cried, "Barabbas!" Pilate then asked, "What shall I do then with Jesus, who is called the Christ?" and they shouted, "Crucify Him! *Let His blood be upon us and upon our children*!"

"Now at that feast the governor was wont to release unto the people a prisoner, whom they would. And they had then a notable prisoner, called Barabbas. Therefore when they were gathered together, Pilate said unto them, Whom will ye that I release unto you? Barabbas, or Jesus which is called Christ? For he knew that for envy they had delivered Him. When he was set down on the judgment seat, his wife sent unto him, saying, Have thou nothing to do with that just man: for I have suffered many things this day in a dream because of Him. But the chief priests and elders persuaded the multitude that they should ask Barabbas, and destroy Jesus. The governor answered and said unto them, Whether of the twain will ye that I release unto you? They said, Barabbas. Pilate saith unto them, What shall I do then with Jesus which is called Christ? They all say unto him, Let Him be crucified. And the governor said, Why, what evil hath He done? But they cried out the more, saying, Let Him be crucified. When Pilate saw that he could prevail nothing, but that rather a tumult was made, he took water, and washed his hands before the multitude, saying, I am innocent of the blood of this just person: see ye to it. *Then answered all the people, and said, HIS BLOOD BE ON US, AND ON OUR CHILDREN*!" (Matt. 27:15–25).

The Jews asked for a blood-bath—and *they have had it*! Yet, God has miraculously preserved the Jew—in the lions' den, in the fiery furnace, even in the furnaces of

Adolph Hitler where literally millions of them were cremated. In spite of persecutions down through the centuries, the Jew marches on. Israel is God's covenant nation, and will finally be miraculously delivered and exalted among the nations. This is the deeper prophetic teaching of the fiery furnace episode.

"The times of the Gentiles" began when Israel was taken captive by the king of Babylon, and will continue until the Lord Jesus Christ comes at the end of the tribulation. The Jews will see Him, will recognize Him, and will ask, "What are these wounds in thine hands? Then He shall answer, Those with which I was wounded in the house of my friends" (Zech. 13:6).

The great image of Nebuchadnezzar was symbolic of the image which will be set up in honor of the Antichrist in Revelation 13, just as Nebuchadnezzar himself was a type of Antichrist. And as in the case of the three Hebrews who refused to worship the image of Nebuchadnezzar, so will there be a remnant of faithful Jews who will refuse to worship the beast or receive his mark in their hands or foreheads, and many of them will be killed. But God will preserve a remnant of His covenant people, and they will finally be delivered when Jesus comes at the end of the tribulation in the battle of Armageddon; and then the faithful remnant will be exalted to reign with Jesus in the Millennium.

Daniel 3 and Revelation 13 are identical as having to do with God's dealings with the chosen people Israel and the Gentiles. Daniel 3 marks the *beginning* of "the times of the Gentiles"; Revelation 13 marks the *ending* of "the times of the Gentiles." From Daniel 3 through the reign of Antichrist, Gentile power will rule the world and the nation Israel will suffer.

However, if we are to thoroughly understand the

prophetic teaching of the image in Daniel 3 and the image in Revelation 13, we must go back further than the book of Daniel. Babylonianism began in the days immediately following the flood; we have the record in Genesis 10 and 11. A man named Nimrod (meaning "the Rebel") who was also a type of Antichrist, built a city, named it Babylon, and in the city he built a great tower. On top of the tower he placed an image of his god (*Belus*–or Baal). Genesis 10 and 11 gives the first picture of Babylon, but the heart and spirit of that city have never changed, and never will. Babylon (or Babel) is definitely a system–both political and religious; and that system is the exact opposite of true religion–Christianity.

The system of Babylon is the devil's counterfeit of the kingdom of God. That same spirit has reigned in Egypt, Assyria, Babylon, Persia, Greece, and Rome. All of these empires had different names, but their hearts were the same. All of them were in different localities and were in power at different times; but they were engineered by the same mastermind–the devil. Babylonianism is a religion–an ideology. It is Satan's attempt to set up a kingdom on earth in opposition to the *kingdom of heaven* on earth, when King Jesus will sit on the throne of David in Jerusalem. Babylonianism had its beginning under Nimrod. He built the city–one of the wonders of the world. It is beyond human imagination how, in his day, he could build such a structure as the Tower of Babel.

The city of Babylon represented religion and politics. It was Nimrod's aim for all people to have one religion and dwell in one place–in the land of Shinar. Space will not permit me to give the entire text of Genesis chapters 10 and 11, but please study those two portions of Scripture very carefully.

The Tower of Babel represented the *religion* of

Babylon. How does the desire of Nimrod for one government and one religion compare with the headlines of your newspaper, magazines, radio broadcasts, and other forms of news media today? What are we hearing? "One world . . . the United States of the World . . . the World Market . . . the World Church . . . everything is to be ONE." The spirit of Nimrod still exists and will continue to exist until Jesus comes in flaming fire, "taking vengeance on them that know not God."

The word "Babel" comes from two fragments: *Bab* and *El*. These two fragments mean "Gate of God." In the account of Nimrod's plan and attempt to build a tower into heaven, we read: "And the Lord came down to see the city and the tower, which the children of men builded. And the Lord said, Behold, the people is one, and they have all one language; *and this they begin to do: AND NOW NOTHING WILL BE RESTRAINED FROM THEM, WHICH THEY HAVE IMAGINED TO DO.* Go to, let us go down, and there confound their language, that they may not understand one another's speech. So the Lord scattered them abroad from thence upon the face of all the earth: and they left off to build the city. Therefore is the name of it called Babel; because the Lord did there confound the language of all the earth: and from thence did the Lord scatter them abroad upon the face of all the earth" (Gen. 11:5–9).

God here testified that man would do whatever he had planned to do—unless divinely hindered. Man wanted to build a tower to heaven, by-pass God, and through his own works set up a religion of his own thinking. But God put a stop to it, confused the tongues, scattered the people, and the place was called Babel—or Babylon.

The ancient city of Babylon was destroyed, but its ruins remain to this day; and the *spirit* of Babylon lives on, though existing under new names and in different forms. *One world* religiously, one world in government, has been the plan and program of the devil since he was thrown out of heaven by Almighty God when as Lucifer the "Shining One" he brainwashed some of the angels and led them in rebellion against the throne of God (Ezek. 28:11–15; Isa. 14:12–15).

Study history, and you will see that down through the centuries, each time an ambitious ruler planned and sought to conquer the world, his conquest always began with persecution of God's chosen people, Israel; and each time they were cast into the furnace of persecution and affliction, they were delivered through God's miraculous power.

Egypt, as the Pharaohs knew Egypt with its horrible persecution of God's chosen people, is gone. *Assyria*, with its blast of persecution directed against Israel, is gone as a great empire. Nebuchadnezzar's Babylon, with its dream of one-world power, is no more. We will study the record of Babylon's fall in Daniel 5. God's people have continued on while their persecutors have been destroyed. Like Daniel, Shadrach, Meshach, and Abed-nego, there have always been those who refused to bow to the gods of this world.

The next form of Babylonianism was under Darius the Mede–a different name, but the same story. When Media-Persia fell, Greece appeared–another name, but the same spirit, the same Satanic soul. How nearly Greece succeeded in gaining her objective may be gathered from the fact that so universal was the Greek language, even in the days of Jesus, that our New Testament was written almost entirely in Greek. But Greece crumbled–and Rome came on the scene. In the same Satanic spirit Rome persecuted God's chosen people. Today, Rome is gone as a world power–but the nation of Israel moves on!

In spite of Pharaoh's attempt to drown Israel, Nebuchadnezzar's attempt to cremate them, in spite of Haman's gallows, Caesar's guillotine, Mussolini's hatred, Stalin's wholesale butchering and Hitler's ovens, *Israel lives on, moves on*, and will in the final analysis fulfill God's ultimate aim for them. The hand of God is upon them, and He will protect a remnant until the consummation of all things. Every promise God made to Abraham will be literally and abundantly fulfilled.

We must get the deeper meaning of the fiery furnace fixed in our minds if we hope to understand the book of Daniel. As previously stated, Nebuchadnezzar's image was a type of the image of the beast which will be set up in the tribulation described in Revelation 13:13–15. The image of the beast will be set up in Jerusalem in the closing days of this dispensation, after the Rapture, during the reign of the Antichrist. The three Hebrew children who would not worship the golden image of Nebuchadnezzar are a type of the Jewish remnant that will be on earth during the reign of the Antichrist, and they are seen in Revelation as the 144,000 sealed ones:

"And I saw another angel ascending from the east, having the seal of the living God: and he cried with a loud voice to the four angels, to whom it was given to hurt the earth and the sea, Saying, Hurt not the earth, neither the sea, nor the trees, till we have sealed the servants of our God in their foreheads. And I heard the number of them which were sealed: and there were sealed an hundred and forty and four thousand of all the tribes of the children of Israel. Of the tribe of Juda were sealed twelve thousand. Of the tribe of Reuben were sealed twelve thousand. Of the tribe of Gad were sealed twelve thousand. Of the tribe of Aser were sealed twelve thousand. Of the tribe of Nepthalim were sealed twelve thousand. Of the tribe of Manasses were sealed twelve thousand. Of the tribe of Simeon were sealed twelve thousand. Of the tribe of Levi were sealed twelve thousand. Of the tribe of Issachar were sealed twelve thousand. Of the tribe of Zabulon were sealed twelve thousand. Of the tribe of Joseph were sealed twelve thousand. Of the tribe of Benjamin were sealed twelve thousand" (Rev. 7:2–8).

The 144,000 will *pass through* the great tribulation; they will not be annihilated. Later (Rev. 15:2), we see them on the other side of the tribulation, standing on a sea of glass mingled with fire. They have gone through the fiery trials of the tribulation, having won the victory over the beast, over his image, and over his mark. They were delivered by the power of Jehovah God. They are Israelites, and they sing the new song of Moses and the Lamb–a song which can be sung only by the redeemed of Israel! And just as Shadrach, Meshach, and Abed-nego were promoted by the king in the province of Babylon after having been delivered from the fiery furnace by the hand of their God, just so shall the Jewish remnant, delivered out of the hand of the Antichrist, be promoted and given positions of power and influence in the kingdom of heaven on earth.

The last one who will attempt to revive the dreams of Nimrod will be the devil in flesh, known in the New Testament as the Antichrist, the Man of Sin, and spoken of by Jesus as "the abomination of desolation":

"When ye therefore shall see the abomination of desolation, spoken of by Daniel the prophet, stand in the holy place, (whoso readeth, let him understand:) then let them which be in Judaea flee into the mountains . . . For then shall be great tribulation, such as was not since the beginning of the world to this time, no, nor ever shall be. And except those days should be shortened, there should no flesh be saved: but for the elect's sake those days shall be shortened" (Matt. 24:15, 16, 21, 22).

In these verses Jesus clearly tells us that in the tribulation period Daniel's prophecy concerning the "*abomination of desolation*" will be literally fulfilled. The record is in Daniel 9:27; 11:31; and 12:11. When the Rapture occurs, all born again people will be taken out of the earth. The Antichrist will then come on the scene and offer a solution to the terrible chaos that will reign. He will ride out on a beautiful white horse, and in his hand he will carry a bow without an arrow—a symbol of peace. He will offer peace to the peoples of the earth, and will *give* them peace for three and one-half years. After that brief period of peace, he will break his covenant with Israel (back in their own land), and the "abomination of desolation" will be set up in the temple—and all who refuse to worship the beast will be killed.

John gives a clear picture of this in Revelation 13:13–17: "And he doeth great wonders, so that he maketh fire come down from heaven on the earth in the sight of men, and deceiveth them that dwell on the earth by the means of those miracles which he had power to do in the sight of the beast; saying to them that dwell on the earth, that they should make an image to the beast, which had the wound by a sword, and did live. And he had power to give life unto the image of the beast, that the image of the beast should both speak, and cause that as many as would not worship the image of the beast should be killed. And he causeth all, both small and great, rich and poor, free and bond, to receive a mark in their right hand, or in their foreheads: And that no man might buy or sell, save he that had the mark, or the name of the beast, or the number of his name."

But again, God will remember His covenant people, and will seal 144,000 who cannot be destroyed by Antichrist and all his forces of hell. When we study the Word, comparing spiritual things with spiritual and rightly dividing the word of truth, how clear the picture becomes! When we study Revelation and the words of Jesus in Matthew 24, we see the prophetic picture God gave us by recording the account of the image of Nebuchadnezzar and the three Hebrews in the fiery furnace.

Not a hair on the heads of the three young men was singed in the fiery furnace, but the men who put them into the fire were burned to a crisp. This points to the final and absolute annihilation of the enemies of God's covenant people.

The Burning Bush, Moses, and Israel

There are several incidents in the history of Israel which parallel events in the third chapter of Daniel. The account of Moses and the burning bush is a beautiful picture of God's protection, preservation, and deliverance of Israel:

"Now Moses kept the flock of Jethro his father in law, the priest of Midian: and he led the flock to the backside of the desert, and came to the mountain of God, even to Horeb. And the angel of the Lord appeared unto him in a flame of fire out of the midst of a bush: and he looked, and, behold, the bush burned with fire, and the bush was not consumed. And Moses said, I will now turn aside, and see this great sight, why the bush is not burnt" (Exodus 3:1–3).

The flame did not consume the bush, which was a type of Israel. Moses knew and testified that God would care for and deliver His people:

"And Moses was learned in all the wisdom of the Egyptians, and was mighty in words and in deeds. And when he was full forty years old, it came into his heart to visit his brethren the children of Israel. And seeing one of them suffer wrong, he defended him, and avenged him that was oppressed, and smote the Egyptian: For he supposed his brethren would have understood how that God by his hand would deliver them: but they understood not" (Acts 7:22–25).

"By faith Moses, when he was come to years, refused to be called the son of Pharaoh's daughter; choosing rather to suffer affliction with the people of God, than to enjoy the pleasures of sin for a season; esteeming the reproach of Christ greater riches than the treasures in Egypt: for he had respect unto the recompence of the reward" (Heb. 11:24–26). Moses knew God's plan for Israel, and he knew *his part* in that plan.

God's Eternal Covenant with Israel

God made a covenant of grace with Israel, and gave that covenant to faithful Abraham. God made an unconditional promise. The covenant was wholly independent of the merits, worth, or faithfulness of the chosen people. Regardless of how unworthy that nation may be, God cannot and will not break His covenant with Abraham. Thus the picture of the burning bush sets forth the indestructible nation, Israel. Though in the fires of persecution, that nation shall not be destroyed.

"And God heard their groaning, and God remembered His covenant with Abraham, with Isaac, and with Jacob. And God looked upon the children of Israel, and God had respect unto them" (Ex. 2:24,25).

Study the second chapter of Exodus carefully and you will see the failure of Moses and the faithfulness of Jehovah God. God remembered His covenant with Abraham. The Word does not say that God remembered the virtues of Israel, nor that He remembered their faithfulness; but *God remembered HIS covenant.* He delivered Israel—not because of their goodness or merits, but because of God's faithfulness. God is faithful; He cannot break His promise.

"And when the Lord saw that (Moses) turned aside to see, God called unto him out of the midst of the bush, and said, Moses, Moses. And he said, Here am I. And He said, Draw not nigh hither: put off thy shoes from off thy feet, for the place whereon thou standest is holy ground. Moreover He said, I am the God of thy father, the God of Abraham, the God of Isaac and the God of Jacob. And Moses hid his face; for he was afraid to look upon God" (Ex. 3:4–6).

Note this: "AND THE ANGEL OF THE LORD APPEARED UNTO HIM IN A FLAME OF FIRE OUT OF THE MIDST OF A BUSH" (Ex. 3:2a).

"The angel of the Lord" in the Old Testament is the Lord Jesus Christ. This is one of many names for Jesus in the Scriptures. The One who appeared to Moses in the burning bush is the same One who appeared to the Hebrew children in the fiery furnace, the One who spent the night with Daniel in the lions' den, the One who will fight on the side of Israel in the last battle between the armies of Antichrist and the armies of God's elect.

Many preachers and teachers today are shouting long and loud that God is finished with Israel, His dealings with the Jews are over; but God clearly teaches that they will be gathered into their own land, never to be plucked up again. They will be protected by their "angel of the Lord," and they will flourish and blossom as they have never flourished since the birth of the nation Israel:

"Behold, the days come, saith the Lord, that the

plowman shall overtake the reaper, and the treader of grapes him that soweth seed; and the mountains shall drop sweet wine, and all the hills shall melt. And I will bring again the captivity of my people of Israel, and they shall build the waste cities, and inhabit them; and they shall plant vineyards, and drink the wine thereof; they shall also make gardens, and eat the fruit of them. And I will plant them upon their land, and they shall no more be pulled up out of their land which I have given them, saith the Lord thy God" (Amos 9:13–15).

"The wolf also shall dwell with the lamb, and the leopard shall lie down with the kid; and the calf and the young lion and the fatling together; and a little child shall lead them. And the cow and the bear shall feed; their young ones shall lie down together; and the lion shall eat straw like the ox. And the sucking child shall play on the hole of the asp, and the weaned child shall put his hand on the cockatrice' den. They shall not hurt nor destroy in all my holy mountain: for the earth shall be full of the knowledge of the Lord, as the waters cover the sea" (Isa. 11:6–9).

"He shall cause them that come of Jacob to take root: Israel shall blossom and bud, and fill the face of the world with fruit" (Isa. 27:6).

When Jesus comes in the Rapture, the Church will be taken up into the clouds to meet the Lord in the air. The false messiah, Antichrist, will then take over the reins of the government and of the religion of earth in the Satanic trinity–the Beast, the Antichrist, and the False Prophet. He will reign for almost seven years. In Matthew 24:22 Jesus tells us, "Except those days should be shortened, there should no flesh be saved: but for the elect's sake (Israel) those days *shall be* shortened."

For the "elect," the coming of Jesus will be a joy

at the end of the tribulation; but for the Antichrist and his followers it will be a day of wrath and fierce anger.

"And they shall go into the holes of the rocks, and into the caves of the earth, for fear of the Lord, and for the glory of His majesty, when He ariseth to shake terribly the earth" (Isa. 2:19).

"Behold, the day of the Lord cometh, cruel both with wrath and fierce anger, to lay the land desolate: and he shall destroy the sinners thereof out of it. For the stars of heaven and the constellations thereof shall not give their light: the sun shall be darkened in his going forth, and the moon shall not cause her light to shine. And I will punish the world for their evil, and the wicked for their iniquity; and I will cause the arrogancy of the proud to cease, and will lay low the haughtiness of the terrible . . . Therefore I will shake the heavens, and the earth shall remove out of her place, in the wrath of the Lord of hosts, and in the day of his fierce anger . . . Every one that is found shall be thrust through; and every one that is joined unto them shall fall by the sword. Their children also shall be dashed to pieces before their eyes; their houses shall be spoiled, and their wives ravished" (Isa. 13:9–11, 13, 15, 16).

"Come near, ye nations, to hear; and hearken, ye people: Let the earth hear, and all that is therein; the world, and all things that come forth of it. For the indignation of the Lord is upon all nations, and His fury upon all their armies: He hath utterly destroyed them, He hath delivered them to the slaughter. Their slain also shall be cast out, and their stink shall come up out of their carcases, and the mountains shall be melted with their blood. And all the host of heaven shall be dissolved, and the heavens shall be rolled together as a scroll: and all their host shall fall down, as the leaf falleth off from the vine, and as a falling fig from the fig tree. For my sword shall be bathed in heaven: Behold, it shall come down upon Idumea, and upon the people of my curse, to judgment. The sword of the Lord is filled with blood, it is made fat with fatness, and with the blood of lambs and goats, with the fat of the kidneys of rams: for the Lord hath a sacrifice in Bozrah, and a great slaughter in the land of Idumea'' (Isa. 34:1–6).

''Why do the heathen rage, and the people imagine a vain thing? The kings of the earth set themselves, and the rulers take counsel together, against the Lord, and against His anointed, saying, Let us break their bands asunder, and cast away their cords from us. He that sitteth in the heavens shall laugh: the Lord shall have them in derision. Then shall He speak unto them in His wrath, and vex them in His sore displeasure. Yet have I set my king upon my holy hill of Zion. I will declare the decree: the Lord hath said unto me, Thou art my Son; this day have I begotten thee. Ask of me, and I shall give thee the heathen for thine inheritance, and the uttermost parts of the earth for thy possession. Thou shalt break them with a rod of iron; thou shalt dash them in pieces like a potter's vessel. Be wise now therefore, O ye kings: be instructed, ye judges of the earth. Serve the Lord with fear, and rejoice with trembling. Kiss the Son, lest He be angry, and ye perish from the way, when His wrath is kindled but a little. Blessed are all they that put their trust in Him'' (Psa. 2).

CHAPTER FOUR

NEBUCHADNEZZAR'S PUNISHMENT

1. Nebuchadnezzar the king, unto all people, nations, and languages, that dwell in all the earth; Peace be multiplied unto you.

2. I thought it good to shew the signs and wonders that the high God hath wrought toward me.

3. How great are his signs! and how mighty are his wonders! his kingdom is an everlasting kingdom, and his dominion is from generation to generation.

4. I Nebuchadnezzar was at rest in mine house, and flourishing in my palace:

5. I saw a dream which made me afraid, and the thoughts upon my bed and the visions of my head troubled me.

6. Therefore made I a decree to bring in all the wise men of Babylon before me, that they might make known unto me the interpretation of the dream.

7. Then came in the magicians, the astrologers, the Chaldeans, and the soothsayers: and I told the dream before them; but they did not make known unto me the interpretation thereof.

8. But at the last Daniel came in before me, whose name was Belteshazzar, according to the name of my god, and in whom is the spirit of the holy gods: and before him I told the dream, saying,

9. O Belteshazzar, master of the magicians, because I know that the spirit of the holy gods is in thee, and no secret troubleth thee, tell me the visions of my dream that I have seen, and the interpretation thereof.

10. Thus were the visions of mine head in my bed; I saw, and behold a tree in the midst of the earth, and the height thereof was great.

11. The tree grew, and was strong, and the height thereof reached unto heaven, and the sight thereof to the end of all the earth:

12. The leaves thereof were fair, and the fruit thereof much, and in it was meat for all: the beasts of the field had shadow under it, and the fowls of the heaven dwelt in the boughs thereof, and all flesh was fed of it.

13. I saw in the visions of my head upon my bed, and, behold, a watcher and an holy one came down from heaven;

14. He cried aloud, and said thus, Hew down the tree, and cut off his branches, shake off his leaves, and scatter his fruit: let the beasts get away from under it, and the fowls from his branches:

15. Nevertheless leave the stump of his roots in the earth, even with a band of iron and brass, in the tender grass of the field; and let it be wet with the dew of heaven, and let his portion be with the beasts in the grass of the earth:

16. Let his heart be changed from man's, and let a beast's heart be given unto him; and let seven times pass over him.

17. This matter is by the decree of the watchers, and the demand by the word of the holy ones: to the intent that the living may know that the most High ruleth in the kingdom of men, and giveth it to whomsoever he will, and setteth up over it the basest of men.

18. This dream I king Nebuchadnezzar have seen. Now thou, O Belteshazzar, declare the interpretation thereof, forasmuch as all the wise men of my kingdom are not able to make known unto me the interpretation: but thou art able; for the spirit of the holy gods is in thee.

19. Then Daniel, whose name was Belteshazzar, was astonied for one hour, and his thoughts troubled him. The king spake, and said, Belteshazzar, let not the dream, or the interpretation thereof, trouble thee. Belteshazzar answered and said, My lord, the dream be to them that hate thee, and the interpretation thereof to thine enemies.

20. The tree that thou sawest, which grew, and was strong, whose height reached unto the heaven, and the sight thereof to all the earth;

21. Whose leaves were fair, and the fruit thereof much, and in it was meat for all; under which the beasts of the field dwelt, and upon whose branches the fowls of the heaven had their habitation:

22. It is thou, O king, that art grown and become strong: for thy greatness is grown, and reacheth unto heaven, and thy dominion to the end of the earth.

23. And whereas the king saw a watcher and an holy one coming down from heaven, and saying, Hew the tree down, and destroy it; yet leave the stump of the roots thereof in the earth, even with a band of iron and brass, in the tender grass of the field; and let it be wet with the dew of heaven, and let his portion be with the beasts of the field, till seven times pass over him;

24. This is the interpretation, O king, and this is the decree of the most High, which is come upon my lord the king:

25. That they shall drive thee from men, and thy dwelling shall be with the beasts of the field, and they shall make thee to eat grass as oxen, and they shall wet thee with the dew of heaven, and seven times shall pass over thee, till thou know that the most High ruleth in the kingdom of men, and giveth it to whomsoever he will.

26. And whereas they commanded to leave the stump of the tree roots; thy kingdom shall be sure unto thee, after that thou shalt have known that the heavens do rule.

27. Wherefore, O king, let my counsel be acceptable unto thee, and break off thy sins by righteousness, and thine iniquities by shewing mercy to the poor; if it may be a lengthening of thy tranquillity.

28. All this came upon the king Nebuchadnezzar.

29. At the end of twelve months he walked in the palace of the kingdom of Babylon.

30. The king spake, and said, Is not this great Babylon, that I have built for the house of the kingdom by the might of my power, and for the honour of my majesty?

31. While the word was in the king's mouth, there fell a voice from heaven, saying, O king Nebuchadnezzar, to thee it is spoken; The kingdom is departed from thee.

32. And they shall drive thee from men, and thy dwelling shall be with the beasts of the field: they shall make thee to eat grass as oxen, and seven times shall pass over thee, until thou know that the most High ruleth in the kingdom of men, and giveth it to whomsoever he will.

33. The same hour was the thing fulfilled upon Nebuchadnezzar: and he was driven from men, and did eat grass as oxen, and his body was wet with the dew of heaven, till his hairs were grown like eagles' feathers, and his nails like birds' claws.

34. And at the end of the days I Nebuchadnezzar lifted up

mine eyes unto heaven, and mine understanding returned unto me, and I blessed the most High, and I praised and honoured him that liveth for ever, whose dominion is an everlasting dominion, and his kingdom is from generation to generation:

35. And all the inhabitants of the earth are reputed as nothing: and he doeth according to his will in the army of heaven, and among the inhabitants of the earth: and none can stay his hand, or say unto him, What doest thou?

36. At the same time my reason returned unto me; and for the glory of my kingdom, mine honour and brightness returned unto me; and my counsellors and my lords sought unto me; and I was established in my kingdom, and excellent majesty was added unto me.

37. Now I Nebuchadnezzar praise and extol and honour the King of heaven, all whose works are truth, and his ways judgment: and those that walk in pride he is able to abase.

Nebuchadnezzar's Proclamation

Verse 1: "Nebuchadnezzar the king, unto all people, nations, and languages, that dwell in all the earth; Peace be multiplied unto you."

Notice that the king's proclamation was to "*all* people, *all* nations, and *all* languages that dwell *in all the earth.*" Nebuchadnezzar was the first Gentile world-king. His taking Israel into captivity marked the beginning of "the times of the Gentiles" (Luke 21:24). It is true that Nebuchadnezzar did not sway all peoples of the earth to his religion and government, but it is possible that he *could* have done so. He conquered the then known world, and its people were under his power. We know, of course, that there were many faithful servants of God, in addition to Daniel, Shadrach, Meshach, and Abed-nego.

Verses 2 and 3: "I thought it good to shew the signs and wonders that the high God hath wrought toward me. How great are His signs! and how mighty are His wonders! His kingdom is an everlasting kingdom, and His dominion is from generation to generation."

This proclamation was issued by Nebuchadnezzar after his recovery from a long period of insanity. It was issued with a view to lead men to acknowledge the true God of heaven. It was intended as a confession of his rebellion against the God of heaven, and a confession of his sin of pride. In the proclamation the king not only confesses his sin, but also gives an explanation for the cause of his insanity and the seven years during which he lived as an animal.

It states, in general, that the approach of Nebuchadnezzar's calamity was made known to him in a dream, which was interpreted by Daniel; that his own heart was lifted up with pride because of the splendid city he had built; and that the predicted madness came suddenly upon him, that he was driven from the abodes of men. It states that he recovered his reason, that he returned to his throne, and that the God who had thus humbled him and then restored him was the true God of heaven, and was worthy of universal worship and praise. The opening verses of this chapter contain Nebuchadnezzar's testimony of his conversion to the most High God–certainly a declaration in marked contrast to his previous proclamations.

The king said, "*Peace be multiplied unto you!*" These are the words of a Christian. They sound strange, coming from the lips of this mighty king who had spent his life in warfare, suppression, and making slaves of millions for the sole purpose of building a world empire to satisfy his own ego and pride. Nebuchadnezzar had learned that his kingdom was not eternal, that it could crumble–while the kingdom of the most High God would go on forever.

Verses 4 and 5: "I Nebuchadnezzar was at rest in mine house, and flourishing in my palace: I saw a dream which made me afraid, and the thoughts upon my bed and the visions of my head troubled me."

"I . . . was at rest in mine house." These significant words remind us of the rich man in Luke 16. *He* was clothed in purple and fine linen, he fared sumptuously every day, and he cared nothing for the misery of the beggar Lazarus at his gate. His thoughts were only for himself and his greatness. He, too, was resting in his palatial home–until he opened his eyes in hell, and then he changed his testimony.

Nebuchadnezzar was resting. He had conquered the known world; he had put down all of his enemies. He was familiar with the perils of the battlefield; he had faced them without fear, and he had conquered every enemy he pursued. He had even demolished the Holy City Jerusalem, destroyed the temple there and confiscated the golden vessels that belonged to the God of heaven. He had taken prisoner the princes of Israel and put them into service in his palace. Now, he was resting–but his time of rest was suddenly broken by a dream.

Nebuchadnezzar had built a wall around himself. He dwelt in a magnificent palace, a giant wall surrounded the city, and a giant moat encircled the wall, with guards patrolling night and day. He had shut out all of his enemies, and he now relaxed upon his luxurious couch–but in spite of the walls, the moat, the guards, and his great armies, he could not shut God out! God troubled the king in a dream–a dream which he could not work out in his mind, but which he knew had to do in some way with his destiny. He was very anxious to learn the interpretation of it.

Verses 6 and 7: "Therefore made I a decree to bring in all the wise men of Babylon before me, that they might make known unto me the interpretation of the dream. Then came in the magicians, the astrologers, the Chaldeans, and the soothsayers: and I told the dream before them;

but they did not make known unto me the interpretation thereof."

For some reason not made known to us, Nebuchadnezzar seemingly had forgotten about Daniel for the moment. One would think the king would have sent for Daniel above all others. However, he had *not* forgotten his dream, and he repeated it to the wise men; but they failed to give him the interpretation of it.

Verses 8 and 9: "But at the last Daniel came in before me, whose name was Belteshazzar, according to the name of my god, and in whom is the spirit of the holy gods: and before him I told the dream, saying, O Belteshazzar, master of the magicians, because I know that the spirit of the holy gods is in thee, and no secret troubleth thee, tell me the visions of my dream that I have seen, and the interpretation thereof."

What a testimony the king gave concerning Daniel! The most outstanding words in his statement were, "*No secret troubleth thee*!" After all, why *should* a child of God be troubled? It is a sin to worry. It is true that we should be concerned and alert, but concern and worry are not identical. In the presence of the king, Daniel had never displayed signs of nervousness or of a troubled spirit. He had proved to Nebuchadnezzar that his God was the God of perfect peace—"peace that passeth all understanding." And Daniel was the instrument used of God to bring this mighty king to his knees and into the knowledge of salvation. I expect to meet Nebuchadnezzar in heaven. I definitely believe he is there.

Nebuchadnezzar's Dream

Verses 10–18: "Thus were the visions of mine head in my bed; I saw, and behold a tree in the midst of the earth, and the height thereof was great. The tree grew, and was strong, and the height thereof reached unto heaven, and the sight thereof to the end of all the earth: The leaves thereof were fair, and the fruit thereof much, and in it was meat for all: the beasts of the field had shadow under it, and the fowls of the heaven dwelt in the boughs thereof, and all flesh was fed of it. I saw in the visions of my head upon my bed, and, behold, a watcher and an holy one came down from heaven; He cried aloud, and said thus, Hew down the tree, and cut off his branches, shake off his leaves, and scatter his fruit: let the beasts get away from under it, and the fowls from his branches: Nevertheless *leave the stump of his roots in the earth*, even with a band of iron and brass, in the tender grass of the field; and let it be wet with the dew of heaven, and let his portion be with the beasts in the grass of the earth: Let his heart be changed from man's, and let a beast's heart be given unto him; and let seven times pass over him. This matter is by the decree of the watchers, and the demand by the word of the holy ones: to the intent that the living may know that the most High ruleth in the kingdom of men, and giveth it to whomsoever He will, and setteth up over it the basest of men. This dream I king Nebuchadnezzar have seen. Now thou, O Belteshazzar, declare the interpretation thereof, forasmuch as all the wise men of my kingdom are not able to make known unto me the interpretation: but thou art able; for the spirit of the holy gods is in thee."

What troubled Nebuchadnezzar was not the *vision* of the tree, but the PERSONIFICATION of it by the watchers (the holy ones). If the dream had had to do only with his empire, he probably would not have feared so much; but somehow he realized that it had to do with *himself*. Through verse 12, we note that Nebuchadnezzar refers to the tree as "it." The leaves were fair, the fruit was much, "IT was meat for all . . . and all flesh was fed of IT." But where the watcher is quoted in verse 14, the pronoun changes to "HIS." The tree is hewn down and HIS branches are cut off. We read, "Shake off HIS leaves, and scatter HIS fruit . . . and the fowls from HIS branches."

When applied to the king, all of this is strikingly

significant of some awful calamity that was to befall him after he should be brought down from his throne. The idea here is that the tree is first felled, then its limbs are chopped off, and these limbs were to be stripped of their foliage. Then the fruit which it bore was to be scattered. Not only was Nebuchadnezzar to be dethroned, but humility was to be heaped upon humility.

Verse 15 instructs, "Nevertheless leave the stump of HIS roots in the earth . . . ." The word "stump" used here implies that the tree was still alive and that it would rise again. The idea is that the mighty tree would fall, yet there would remain life in its root, and this would spring up again–a most striking image of what would happen to Nebuchadnezzar after he should be cast down from his throne, and then restored to his reason and to power.

In verse 16 we read, "Let HIS heart be changed from man's, and let a beast's heart be given unto HIM; and let seven times pass over HIM."

While the king was wondering about the vision of the tree, wondering how this unusual tree concerned himself and his kingdom, he saw something else: In verse 17 we read, "This matter is by the decree of *the watchers*, and the demand by the word of *the holy ones* . . . ." According to this verse, Nebuchadnezzar's case had been turned over to the court of the watchers or holy ones of heaven, and that heavenly court had decreed that the king was to live as a beast for a period of seven years–God's perfect number. The purpose of this decree was "that the living may know that the most High ruleth in the kingdom of men, and giveth it to whomsoever He will."

The book of Daniel reveals to us, as no other book in the Bible, the extremely close connection between this earth and the spirit-world. In Daniel 8:16 and 9:21 we we read of the visit of the archangel Gabriel, and in Daniel 10:4–12 we are told of other heavenly beings. In Ephesians 6:11,12 Paul tells us of the warfare in which we are engaged–a battle, not against flesh and blood, but against principalities and powers, against *"rulers of the darkness of this world, against spiritual wickedness in high places."*

The Word of God distinctly mentions three heavens: "I knew a man in Christ above fourteen years ago, (whether in the body, I cannot tell; or whether out of the body, I cannot tell: God knoweth;) such an one *caught up to the third heaven*" (II Cor. 12:2). The *first heaven* is the air–atmosphere and clouds–just above us. The *second heaven* is where the stars and planets are–we know it as "outer space." The *third heaven* is God's house–Paradise. The atmospheric heaven just above us is the kingdom of Satan. He is prince of the power of the air; he is the god of this age.

There is only one devil, but many demons and evil spirits. Beelzebub is the prince of demons (Matt. 12:24). Daniel mentions the "prince of Persia" and the "prince of Grecia" (Dan. 10:13,20). It could be that the devil has a prince appointed by himself to supervise his affairs in every nation. These lieutenants of Satan are so powerful that it takes the power and strength of Michael the Archangel–the commander-in-chief of the armies of heaven–to cope with them: "But the prince of the kingdom of Persia withstood me one and twenty days: but, lo, Michael, one of the chief princes, came to help me; and I remained there with the kings of Persia" (Dan. 10:13).

Jude 9 tells us, "Yet Michael the archangel, when contending with the devil he disputed about the body of Moses, durst not bring against him a railing accusation, but said, The Lord rebuke thee."

"And there was war in heaven: Michael and his angels fought against the dragon; and the dragon fought and his angels, and prevailed not; neither was their place found any more in heaven. And the great dragon was cast out, the old serpent, called the Devil, and Satan, which deceiveth the whole world: he was cast out into the earth, and his angels were cast out with him" (Rev. 12:7–9).

If we could see what goes on in the atmosphere just above us, I wonder if we could live in the flesh under such a sight! The guardian angels walk beside every believer, and "*The angel of the Lord encampeth round about them that fear Him, and delivereth them*" (Psa. 34:7). We are in daily warfare with principalities, powers, and rulers of darkness and spiritual wickedness. But there is a judicial court in heaven known as the court of "the watchers," and in the case of Nebuchadnezzar, the court of watchers tried him and condemned him to the life of an animal for seven years.

Daniel was greatly troubled when he heard Nebuchadnezzar's dream, and for the space of an hour he was too astonished to speak. He understood the meaning of the dream, but he dreaded to reveal it to the king. Although King Nebuchadnezzar was ungodly, proud, and did not worship the true God, the palace had been Daniel's home for many years, and no doubt he had a warm spot in his heart for the king.

Seeing his hesitation, the king hastened to assure Daniel that he need not fear to tell the interpretation of the dream. Daniel was wise; he prepared the king for the judgment that was to come upon him. He said, "My lord, the dream be to them that hate thee, and the interpretation thereof to thine enemies!" That is, "I wish that the calamity that is to fall on you might fall upon your enemies instead." It merely implies that Daniel did not wish these things to happen to the monarch. It was the language of courtesy and respect.

Daniel's Interpretation of the Tree-Vision

Verses 19–27: "Then Daniel, whose name was Belteshazzar, was astonied for one hour, and his thoughts troubled him. The king spake, and said, Belteshazzar, let not the dream, or the interpretation thereof, trouble thee. Belteshazzar answered and said, My lord, the dream be to them that hate thee, and the interpretation thereof to thine enemies. The tree that thou sawest, which grew, and was strong, whose height reached unto the heaven, and the sight thereof to all the earth; whose leaves were fair, and the fruit thereof much, and in it was meat for all; under which the beasts of the field dwelt, and upon whose branches the fowls of the heaven had their habitation: It is thou, O king, that art grown and become strong: for thy greatness is grown, and reacheth unto heaven, and thy dominion to the end of the earth. And whereas the king saw a watcher and an holy one coming down from heaven, and saying, Hew the tree down, and destroy it; yet leave the stump of the roots thereof in the earth, even with a band of iron and brass, in the tender grass of the field; and let it be wet with the dew of heaven, and let his portion be with the beasts of the field, till seven times pass over him; This is the interpretation, O king, and this is the decree of the most High, which is come upon my lord the king: That they shall drive thee from men, and thy dwelling shall be with the beasts of the field, and they shall make thee to eat grass as oxen, and they shall wet thee with the dew of heaven, and seven times shall pass over thee, till thou know that the most High ruleth in the kingdom of men, and giveth it to whomsoever He will. And whereas they commanded to leave the stump of the tree roots; thy kingdom shall be sure unto thee, after that thou shalt have known that the heavens do rule. Wherefore, O king, let my counsel be acceptable unto thee, and break off thy sins by righteousness, and thine iniquities by shewing mercy to the poor; if it may be a lengthening of thy tranquillity."

There was no possible way for Nebuchadnezzar to miss the meaning of his dream! When Daniel finished the interpretation, he must have noted a yearning in the king's face—a longing for something stable to grasp. Faithful prophet that he was, Daniel immediately took advantage of the opportunity to witness to the king in these words: "*Wherefore, O king, let my counsel be acceptable unto thee, and break off thy sins by righteousness, and thine iniquities by shewing mercy to the poor; if it may be a lengthening of thy tranquillity!*"

Dear Daniel! Pleading, begging, inviting Nebuchadnezzar to humbly submit to Daniel's God, break off sinning, and show mercy to the poor. I do not doubt that Daniel sincerely hoped the king *would* repent and save himself from the terrible judgment that was imminent. But Nebuchadnezzar did not take the prophet's advice. Judgment fell—and now, in our present chapter, after living seven years as a beast, the king makes the humiliating confession that everything Daniel had told him about his dream had come to pass. It does seem that Nebuchadnezzar would have listened to Daniel, because God had previously dealt with him in a very definite way; but he rejected Daniel's plea that he turn from his sins, show mercy to the poor, and (in our language) surrender his heart and life to God.

Nebuchadnezzar's Dream Fulfilled

Verses 28–30: "All this came upon the king Nebuchadnezzar. At the end of twelve months he walked in the palace of the kingdom of Babylon. The king spake, and said, Is not this great Babylon, that I have built for the house of the kingdom by the might of my power, and for the honour of my majesty?"

Judgment did not fall upon Nebuchadnezzar at once; the God of grace gave him a year in which to prove himself. But during the course of that year the king did not change his mind–nor did he allow God to change his heart. Since judgment did not fall at once, perhaps Nebuchadnezzar thought Daniel was mistaken or that God had forgotten; but God's prophet, speaking under inspiration, is never wrong, and the God of Daniel never forgets. He does not always pay off on Saturday night nor at the end of the month, but He never fails to pay. *And when God pays, He always pays in full!*

Twelve months after Daniel had so clearly interpreted the king's dream and made known to him exactly what to expect, Nebuchadnezzar was walking in his palace; and as he stood on the balcony and looked out over the colossal city of Babylon, he exclaimed with pride: "IS NOT THIS GREAT BABYLON, THAT I HAVE BUILT FOR THE HOUSE OF THE KINGDOM BY THE MIGHT OF MY POWER, AND FOR THE HONOUR OF MY MAJESTY?"

That was the statement that caused the judgment of God to fall upon Nebuchadnezzar! His time of probation was finished. The warnings of God's prophet had not been heeded, and God had no alternative but to send the judgment which Daniel had declared would come.

Through the dream and Daniel's interpretation of it, God said to Nebuchadnezzar, as He said to His people, Israel: "Come now, and let us reason together . . . Though your sins be as scarlet, they shall be as white as snow; though they be red like crimson, they shall be as wool" (Isa. 1:18). In Isaiah 30:15,16 we read, "For thus saith the Lord God, the Holy One of Israel; In returning and rest shall ye be saved; in quietness and in confidence shall be your strength: and ye would not. But ye said, No; for we will flee upon horses; therefore shall ye flee: and, We will ride upon the swift; therefore shall they that pursue you be swift!" Israel thought they could outrun their enemies; Nebuchadnezzar thought he was too big for God to judge. So, like Israel, He ignored God's warning and God's mercy. His year of probation ended; he reaped what he had sown.

Verses 31 and 32: "While the word was in the king's mouth, there fell a voice from Heaven, saying, O king Nebuchadnezzar, to thee it is spoken; The kingdom is departed from thee. And they shall drive thee from men, and thy dwelling shall be with the beasts of the field: they shall make thee to eat grass as oxen, and seven times shall pass over thee, until thou know that the most High ruleth in the kingdom of men, and giveth it to whomsoever He will."

"While the word was still in the king's mouth . . . ." He did not finish his declaration that the great city of Babylon was built by his might and by his power, for his honor and for his majesty. The voice from heaven came to him in the very act of his speaking, thus showing that there could be no doubt as to the connection between the crime and the punishment. Poor, poor Nebuchadnezzar! He had forgotten that God puts up whom He will and puts down whom He will. He had forgotten that day when he had cried out, "Daniel's God is a God of gods, a Lord of kings, and a revealer of secrets!" Pride and success had swept all of this from his mind. With the words still in the king's mouth, a voice from heaven rang out:

1. *"The kingdom is departed from thee!"*
2. *"They shall drive thee from men!"*
3. *"Thy dwelling shall be with the beasts of the field!"*
4. *"They shall make thee to eat grass as oxen!"*
5. *"Seven times shall pass over thee!"*
6. *"Until thou knowest that the most High ruleth in the kingdom of men!"*
7. *"And giveth it to whomsoever He will!"*

It was a sevenfold judgment God meted out to Nebuchadnezzar; *seven*—God's perfect number! The judgment that fell upon him was directly from Jehovah God. It was not the devil who took away his kingdom; it was not the devil who cursed him with the heart of a beast; it was God Almighty—the God of all grace, the God of mercy, the longsuffering God who had given Nebuchadnezzar twelve months in which to make up his mind which god he would serve.

Verse 33: "The same hour was the thing fulfilled upon Nebuchadnezzar: and he was driven from men, and did eat grass as oxen, and his body was wet with the dew of heaven, till his hairs were grown like eagles' feathers, and his nails like birds' claws."

"*THE SAME HOUR!*" God gave Nebuchadnezzar no extended time of grace. When the sevenfold judgment was outlined by the voice from heaven, that same split second, judgment fell—and Nebuchadnezzar was driven from men. The once proud king was down on his hands and knees, eating grass like oxen. His body, no longer clothed in purple and fine linen, grew hairs like eagles' feathers. He was wet with the dew from heaven; his fingernails and toenails were like the claws of birds.

Dearly beloved, these words should shake each of us from lethargy and cause us to tremble before the God of all grace and mercy. What a monstrosity this man had become! A little while ago he had been a proud king walking in a magnificent palace. He had worn the royal robes of a king; he had looked out over a great city and claimed it as his own. Now, in a matter of only minutes, he was down on his all fours eating grass like an ox! What a species of the animal kingdom to gaze upon!

Nebuchadnezzar continued in this form for "seven times"—meaning *seven years.* This time limit is by no means accidental; it has a definite, prophetic significance:

In chapter 9 of Daniel, the "seven times" foreshadow the *seven years* of the rule of the Man of Sin, the last world dictator and last ruler of Gentile world dominion, or the seventieth week of Daniel's seventy weeks of prophecy. Later in this study we will see that sixty-nine of these weeks of prophecy have already been *literally fulfilled* and but one week remains.

Nebuchadnezzar's madness symbolizes the peoples who will be under the power of the Antichrist during the Tribulation; and the *seven years* of Nebuchadnezzar's insanity symbolizes *the period of the seventieth week*, which will be seven years—the time of which Jesus speaks in Matthew 24:22: "*And except those days should be shortened, there should no flesh be saved: but for the elect's sake those days shall be shortened.*"

During the seventieth week of Daniel's seventy weeks of prophecy, the Antichrist will reign from the temple in Jerusalem, which will have been rebuilt. The Holy Spirit will be taken out with the Church at the Rapture (II Thess. 2:7); and when the restraining power of the Holy Spirit is gone, the earth will be left to the mercy of demons. "And for this cause God shall send them strong delusion, that they should believe a lie: That they all might be damned who believed not the truth, but had pleasure in unrighteousness" (II Thess. 2:11,12).

In II Thessalonians 2:1–12 we read, "Now we beseech you, brethren, by the coming of our Lord Jesus Christ, and by our gathering together unto Him, that ye be not soon shaken in mind, or be troubled, neither by spirit, nor by word, nor by letter as from us, as that the day of Christ is at hand. Let no man deceive you by any means: for that day shall not come, except there come a falling away first, and that man of sin be revealed, the son of perdition; who opposeth and exalteth himself above all that is called God, or that is worshipped; so that he as God sitteth in the temple of God, shewing himself that he is God. Remember ye not, that, when I was yet with you, I told you these things? And now ye know what withholdeth that he might be revealed in his time. For the mystery of iniquity doth already work: only He who now letteth will let, until He be taken out of the way. And then shall that Wicked be revealed, whom the Lord shall consume with the spirit of His mouth, and shall destroy with the brightness of His coming: Even him, whose coming is after the working of Satan with all power and signs and lying wonders, and with all deceivableness of unrighteousness in them that perish; because they received not the love of the truth, that they might be saved. And for this cause God shall send them strong delusion, that they should believe a lie: That they all might be damned who believed not the truth, but had pleasure in unrighteousness." (In verse 2 of this passage, "*the day of Christ*" in the original Greek language is "*the day of the Lord,*" which is quite different from *the day of Christ*–Isaiah 2:10–12.)

During the reign of Antichrist, the Holy Spirit will not be here to suppress Satan and his demons. Men will live in a form of insanity–*madness.* They will worship the image set up by Antichrist; they will fight, murder, hunt down and kill each other like beasts. The reign of the Antichrist–especially the last part of it–will be the most inhuman, the most horrible, the bloodiest period this earth has ever known!

Proverbs 16:18 sums up the reason for the fall of Nebuchadnezzar and the judgment God poured out upon him: "*Pride goeth before destruction, and an haughty spirit before a fall.*" Pride caused Lucifer to be cast out of heaven. Pride caused Cain to slay his brother,

Abel. Pride was the undoing of Nebuchadnezzar's greatness, and pride has been the downfall of countless numbers of men and women since time began.

Nebuchadnezzar's Recovery

Verses 34 and 35: "And at the end of the days I Nebuchadnezzar lifted up mine eyes unto heaven, and mine understanding returned unto me, and I blessed the most High, and I praised and honoured Him that liveth for ever, whose dominion is an everlasting dominion, and His kingdom is from generation to generation: And all the inhabitants of the earth are reputed as nothing: and He doeth according to His will in the army of heaven, and among the inhabitants of the earth: and none can stay His hand, or say unto Him, What doest thou?"

Nebuchadnezzar served every hour of every day of his sentence. And at the end of seven years, he lifted his eyes to heaven in prayer, and acknowledged the supremacy of Jehovah God! His reason was restored, and he was capable of once more resuming his duties as king. It would do us all good to read these solemn words from Deuteronomy 32:39–43:

"See now that I, even I, am He, and there is no god with me: I kill, and I make alive; I wound, and I heal: neither is there any that can deliver out of my hand. For I lift up my hand to heaven, and say, I live for ever. If I whet my glittering sword, and mine hand take hold on judgment; I will render vengeance to mine enemies, and will reward them that hate me. I will make mine arrows drunk with blood, and my sword shall devour flesh; and that with the blood of the slain and of the captives, from the beginning of revenges upon the enemy. Rejoice, O ye nations, with His people: for He will avenge the blood of His servants, and will render vengeance to His adversaries, and will be merciful unto His land, and to His people."

Nebuchadnezzar's Kingdom Restored

Verses 36 and 37: "At the same time my reason returned unto me; and for the glory of my kingdom, mine honour and brightness returned unto me; and my counsellors and my lords sought unto me; and I was established in my kingdom, and excellent majesty was added unto me. Now I Nebuchadnezzar praise and extol and honour the King of heaven, all whose works are truth, and His ways judgment: and those that walk in pride He is able to abase."

God always keeps His promise. Nebuchadnezzar served his sentence of seven years of living the life of an animal in the fields, eating grass like an ox—and then God kept His promise of verse 26. The king's understanding returned, his kingly rights were restored, and "excellent majesty" was added unto him.

It is said that during the judgment of Nebuchadnezzar, his son Evil-Merodach occupied the throne as regent. The fact that Nebuchadnezzar was allowed by his counsellors and lords to return to his throne indicates that they looked upon his insanity as a temporary thing. It is strange that they did not confine him to the palace grounds instead of driving him out into the fields away from the palace, away from family and friends. We can only conclude that this was part of his suffering and judgment, that he should spend those years as the beasts of the field rather than with those with whom he had mingled as a king.

Nebuchadnezzar is not mentioned again in Scripture. He lived for about a year after his restoration to the throne—a year in which great honors were heaped upon him and in which he glorified the God of Daniel. He died in 561 B. C. and was succeeded by his son, Evil-Merodach.

CHAPTER FIVE

THE HISTORY OF DANIEL UNDER BELSHAZZAR AND DARIUS

1. Belshazzar the king made a great feast to a thousand of his lords, and drank wine before the thousand.

2. Belshazzar, whiles he tasted the wine, commanded to bring the golden and silver vessels which his father Nebuchadnezzar had taken out of the temple which was in Jerusalem; that the king, and his princes, his wives, and his concubines, might drink therein.

3. Then they brought the golden vessels that were taken out of the temple of the house of God which was at Jerusalem; and the king, and his princes, his wives, and his concubines, drank in them.

4. They drank wine, and praised the gods of gold, and of silver, of brass, of iron, of wood, and of stone.

5. In the same hour came forth fingers of a man's hand, and wrote over against the candlestick upon the plaister of the wall of the king's palace: and the king saw the part of the hand that wrote.

6. Then the king's countenance was changed, and his thoughts troubled him, so that the joints of his loins were loosed, and his knees smote one against another.

7. The king cried aloud to bring in the astrologers, the Chaldeans, and the soothsayers. And the king spake, and said to the wise men of Babylon, Whosoever shall read this writing, and shew me the interpretation thereof, shall be clothed with scarlet, and have a chain of gold about his neck, and shall be the third ruler in the kingdom.

8. Then came in all the king's wise men: but they could not read the writing, nor make known to the king the interpretation thereof.

9. Then was king Belshazzar greatly troubled, and his countenance was changed in him, and his lords were astonied.

10. Now the queen by reason of the words of the king and his lords came into the banquet house: and the queen spake and said, O king, live for ever: let not thy thoughts trouble thee, nor let thy countenance be changed:

11. There is a man in thy kingdom, in whom is the spirit of the holy gods; and in the days of thy father light and understanding and wisdom, like the wisdom of the gods, was found in him; whom the king Nebuchadnezzar thy father, the king, I say, thy father, made master of the magicians, astrologers, Chaldeans, and soothsayers;

12. Forasmuch as an excellent spirit, and knowledge, and understanding, interpreting of dreams, and shewing of hard sentences, and dissolving of doubts, were found in the same Daniel, whom the king named Belteshazzar: now let Daniel be called, and he will shew the interpretation.

13. Then was Daniel brought in before the king. And the king spake and said unto Daniel, Art thou that Daniel, which art of the children of the captivity of Judah, whom the king my father brought out of Jewry?

14. I have even heard of thee, that the spirit of the gods is in thee, and that light and understanding and excellent wisdom is found in thee.

15. And now the wise men, the astrologers, have been brought in before me, that they should read this writing, and make known unto me the interpretation thereof: but they could not shew the interpretation of the thing:

16. And I have heard of thee, that thou canst make interpretations, and dissolve doubts: now if thou canst read the writing, and make known to me the interpretation thereof, thou shalt be clothed with scarlet, and have a chain of gold about thy neck, and shalt be the third ruler in the kingdom.

17. Then Daniel answered and said before the king, Let thy gifts be to thyself, and give thy rewards to another; yet I will read the writing unto the king, and make known to him the interpretation.

18. O thou king, the most high God gave Nebuchadnezzar thy father a kingdom, and majesty, and glory, and honour:

19. And for the majesty that he gave him, all people, nations, and languages, trembled and feared before him: whom he would he slew; and whom he would he kept alive;

and whom he would he set up; and whom he would he put
down.
20. But when his heart was lifted up, and his mind
hardened in pride, he was deposed from his kingly throne,
and they took his glory from him:
21. And he was driven from the sons of men; and his
heart was made like the beasts, and his dwelling was
with the wild asses: they fed him with grass like oxen,
and his body was wet with the dew of heaven; till he
knew that the most high God ruled in the kingdom of men,
and that he appointeth over it whomsoever he will.
22. And thou his son, O Belshazzar, hast not humbled
thine heart, though thou knewest all this;
23. But hast lifted up thyself against the Lord of heav-
en; and they have brought the vessels of his house before
thee, and thou, and thy lords, thy wives, and thy concubines, have drunk wine in them; and thou hast praised the
gods of silver, and gold, of brass, iron, wood, and stone,
which see not, nor hear, nor know: and the God in whose
hand thy breath is, and whose are all thy ways, hast thou
not glorified:
24. Then was the part of the hand sent from him; and
this writing was written.
25. And this is the writing that was written, MENE,
MENE, TEKEL, UPHARSIN.
26. This is the interpretation of the thing: MENE;
God hath numbered thy kingdom, and finished it.
27. TEKEL; Thou art weighed in the balances, and
art found wanting.
28. PERES; Thy kingdom is divided, and given to the
Medes and Persians.
29. Then commanded Belshazzar, and they clothed
Daniel with scarlet, and put a chain of gold about his
neck, and made a proclamation concerning him, that he
should be the third ruler in the kingdom.
30. In that night was Belshazzar the king of the Chaldeans slain.
31. And Darius the Median took the kingdom, being
about threescore and two years old.

The Pride of Belshazzar and His Downfall

Chapter five records the downfall of Belshazzar, the

grandson of Nebuchadnezzar, who reigned after the death of that great king. It also records the fall of Babylon. It would be helpful if we would look at a bit of history concerning this great city before we go into a verse by verse study of the chapter.

The city of Babylon was built by Nimrod (a great-grandson of Noah) more than two thousand years before the birth of Christ:

"And Cush begat Nimrod: he began to be a mighty one in the earth. He was a mighty hunter before the Lord: wherefore it is said, Even as Nimrod the mighty hunter before the Lord. And the beginning of his kingdom was Babel (or Babylon), and Erech, and Accad, and Calneh, in the land of Shinar" (Gen. 10:8–10).

Nimrod was a forerunner of the Man of Sin. Personally, I believe the spirit that will occupy the Man of Sin also indwelt Nimrod. He was a mighty man, "a mighty hunter before the Lord"–and Hebrew authorities tell us that this means "he was a hunter of the souls of men." He wanted to bring all men into one mighty kingdom. He was a Hammite.

The great city of Nineveh, founded by Asshur, a son of Shem (Gen. 10:11,12), became the capital of Assyria. About 1270 B. C. the kings of Assyria became the masters of Chaldea (or Babylonia), of which the city of Babylon was the capital; and for centuries the history of Babylon was overshadowed by the gigantic city of Nineveh.

It was during the lifetime of Tiglath-Pileser of Assyria that Nabonassar ascended to the throne of Babylon, in 747 B. C. It was about 720 B. C. that Berodach-Baladan became king of Babylon. Study II Kings 20:12–18 and Isaiah 39:1–7. A few years later, Sargon king of Assyria led an army against Berodach-Baladan, defeated and dethroned him. Sennacherib completed the subjection of the great Babylon and annexed it to the Assyrian empire in 690 B. C. The conquest of Nineveh, combined with the overthrow of the Assyrian empire (which took place about 625 B. C. by King Cyaxeres the Mede and his ally, Nabopolassar, who at that time was the rebellious governor of Babylon), made it possible for the latter to found and begin the Babylonian empire. Nabopolassar reigned from 625 B. C. to 604 B. C. and was succeeded by his famous son, Nebuchadnezzar, who became the greatest king of ancient times. It was under the genius of Nebuchadnezzar that Babylon was rebuilt and beautified until it was the most magnificent city this world had ever seen.

I realize that so many dates and names provide reading that is not inviting; but we need to have these dates and names in mind, because secular history also testifies that these men actually lived and reigned. Archeologists from leading universities in America and England have unearthed tablets, statues, and much more evidence to prove that these men did live; and the dates of their reign in Babylon, Assyria, and Egypt have been proved from the excavation of stone tablets.

Let us look at the city of Babylon for a few minutes: According to the International Standard Bible Encyclopedia, the city was square, 14 miles on each side, making a circuit of almost 56 miles around the base of the wall which encircled it. The wall around Babylon was built of brick. According to Herodotus it was 87 feet thick and 311 feet high. Think of the amount of material and the time involved in building a wall 56 miles in length, 87 feet thick, and 311 feet high—all of which was carried out by slave labor.

On the wall were 250 towers, and the width of the wall was sufficient for six chariots to drive abreast.

Outside the great wall was a gigantic moat which surrounded the city and was kept filled with water from the Euphrates river. Drawbridges crossed the moat in front of each gate. Just inside this majestic wall was another wall, not much inferior but a bit narrower, extending around the city. Thus Babylon was encompassed by two massive walls.

The roads which ran through the city were straight, and apparently intersected each other at right angles, as do the streets in our great cities of America–which makes us realize that our super-highways and interstate roads are not so very modern, after all. These beautiful avenues crossed the city from north to south, and again at right angles from east to west, making the city a perfect 14-mile square.

A wide avenue encircled the city inside the walls and very close to them, and into this extra-wide thoroughfare all other avenues emptied. At the ends of the cross-avenues were magnificently decorated two-leaved gates of pure brass that glistened like giant leaves of flame as the gates were opened and closed at the rising and the setting of the sun.

The great river Euphrates flowed diagonally across the city, dividing it into two equal parts. The banks of the river were walled, pierced with brazen gates at each of the main avenues. Between the river walls and the river, splendid wharves lined the river on each side within the city. At the central avenue a magnificent bridge spanned the river, and ferryboats crossed the stream at each of the main avenues.

At each end of the great bridge stood a beautiful palace, and underneath the river was a passageway (or tube, like our modern tunnels) which connected these two palaces. Within the tunnel, at various intervals, were sumptuous banquet rooms which were constructed entirely of brass.

Near one of these palaces at the end of the bridge that spanned the Euphrates, stood the tower of Babel. This tower was made up of eight stages, one atop the other. The stages decreased in size from the lowest upward, but each was square in plan. The first stage was 300 feet each way, by 110 feet high, and seems to have been decorated with the usual double recesses which are a characteristic of Assyrian-Babylonian architecture. The second stage was 260 feet square by 60 feet high. The stages from the third to the fifth were all of equal height (20 feet) and were respectively 200 feet, 170 feet, and 140 feet square. The dimensions of the sixth stage were omitted, but may be restored in accordance with the others, namely, 110 feet by 20 feet high.

On this was raised the seventh stage–the upper temple or sanctuary of the god Bel-Merodach–and was 80 feet long, 60 feet wide and 50 feet high. The total height of the tower above its foundation was therefore 300 feet, the same as the breadth of its base. Outside each of the stages, a stairway wound upward to its summit.

The International Standard Bible Encyclopedia has this to say about the construction of the tower: "With this detailed description, which is quite what would be expected in a Babylonian account of such a celebrated fane, the description in Herodotus (i. 181 ff) agrees. He states that it was a temple square in form, two furlongs (1,213 ft.) each way, in the midst of which was built a solid tower a furlong square (nearly 607 ft.). This, however, must have been the platform, which, with the six stages and the chapel on the top, would make up the total of eight stages of which Herodotus speaks."

Inside the chapel atop the tower was perhaps the

most expensive furniture ever to adorn any place of worship. One golden image has been estimated by some at a value of $17,500,000, and the sacred vessels used in worship at $200,000,000. Can you think in terms of such extravagance? And all of this in a chapel approximately 410 feet above the ground!

The famous hanging gardens of Babylon were one of the seven wonders of the world. These gardens were 400 feet square, raised in terraces one above the other to the height of 350 feet. They were reached by stairways which were ten feet wide. The top of each of the terraces was covered with large stone slabs; on the slabs a bed of rushes was laid, then a very thick layer of asphalt, two courses of brick cemented together, and finally, plates of lead to make the terraces free of any leakage. This was then covered with rich earth and planted with beautiful shrubs and trees, so that from a distance the entire group of hanging gardens had the appearance of an enormous, forest-covered mountain. Certainly this was a remarkable sight in the level plains of the Euphrates valley.

These hanging gardens were built by King Nebuchadnezzar at the cost of untold millions. One might ask, "Why? Of what value were they?" They are attributed to the gallantry of Nebuchadnezzar, who constructed them in compliance with a wish of his queen, Amyitis (daughter of Cyaxeres king of Media), to possess elevated groves such as she had enjoyed on the hills around her native home. The appearance of the finished gardens, like a huge tree-covered mountain, tended to make Amyitis feel more at home and be more content with her Babylonian surroundings. The expense of building the gardens was of little concern to the king, and all of the labor was furnished by slaves.

From history we deduce that the city of Babylon in its glory and magnificence surpassed anything that had been built upon this earth. It had many beautiful parks, there were hundreds of acres of unoccupied land that could be tilled, and all kinds of vegetables and foods were grown by slave labor to support the more than a million people who inhabited the city.

Babylon was at its zenith when Belshazzar held the feast which brought his doom. Isaiah speaks of Babylon in these words: "AND BABYLON, THE GLORY OF KINGDOMS, THE BEAUTY OF THE CHALDEES' EXCELLENCY . . ." (Isa. 13:19). Please study Isaiah chapter 13 in its entirety. You will see that God is not finished with Babylon. The city which Nebuchadnezzar reconstructed, magnificent almost beyond description, has been destroyed and will never be inhabited again; but *the spirit of Babylon* (political and ecclesiastical) will be revived at the time of the Beast, and will be permanently destroyed by the Lord Jesus when He comes in the consummation of all things.

The destruction of literal Babylon typifies the *greater* destruction which will transpire upon *mystical* Babylon, as described in the seventeenth and eighteenth chapters of Revelation. Isaiah 13:1 speaks of "the burden of Babylon which Isaiah the son of Amoz did see." A "burden" means a heavy, weighty thing; and here in this oracle concerning Babylon, Assyria, and Jerusalem, Isaiah refers to the heavy burden because the wrath of God is in it—and the wrath of God is so furious and terrifying that it was a grievous and burdensome message for Isaiah to deliver. The spirit of Babylon is being revived with unbelievable rapidity today!

". . . It is appointed unto men once to die . . ." (Heb. 9:27). Regardless of how big, how powerful, or how important a person may be, he has an eventual date with death. Thus it was with Nebuchadnezzar–the grand king, the powerful monarch and world ruler, the man who designed, supervised, and financed the construction of one of the greatest (if not *the* greatest) cities ever built. Nebuchadnezzar died in 561 B. C. and his son, Evil-Merodach, took over the reins of the government of Babylon.

One of the first things the new king did was to free Jehoiachin, king of Judah, and permit him to eat from the royal table:

"And it came to pass in the seven and thirtieth year of the captivity of Jehoiachin king of Judah, in the twelfth month, on the seven and twentieth day of the month, that Evil-Merodach king of Babylon in the year that he began to reign did lift up the head of Jehoiachin king of Judah out of prison; and he spake kindly to him, and set his throne above the throne of the kings that were with him in Babylon; and changed his prison garments: and he did eat bread continually before him all the days of his life. And his allowance was a continual allowance given him of the king, a daily rate for every day, all the days of his life" (II Kings 25:27–30). (The description of this same incident is given in Jeremiah 52:31–34 in almost the same words.)

Nebuchadnezzar's son, Evil-Merodach, reigned for two years and was put to death by conspirators in his own government. These executioners were led by Neriglissar, brother-in-law of the king, who then ascended the throne of Babylon. He reigned for about four years and was killed in battle 556 B. C. Then HIS son, Laborosoarched, was king for less than a year. He was beaten to death, and the throne was seized by Nabonidus. (Some historians and Bible commentators spell his name *Nabunaid.*) He reigned from 555 B. C. to the fall of Babylon in 538 B. C.

Scripture plainly states that Belshazzar was king of Babylon at its conquest by the Medes and Persians, and that he was slain the night Darius entered the city. On the other hand, ancient historians do not mention Belshazzar, but say that Nabonidus was the last king of Babylon. They all agree that Nabonidus was absent from the city when the Persians captured it. Thus the contradiction between history and Scripture seemed absolute. Cuneiform inscriptions, however, have now solved the controversy in a most satisfactory way.

Historians who lived two and a half centuries after Daniel name Nabunaid as the father of Belshazzar, and say that he was reigning *with* Belshazzar at the time of the great feast. Be that as it may, it does not affect our salvation nor the Word of God. Tablets have been unearthed which testify that Nabunaid was the father of Belshazzar, and we know that Belshazzar was the grandson of Nebuchadnezzar. "And all nations shall serve *him*, and his *son*, and his *son's son*, until the very time of his land come: and then many nations and great kings shall serve themselves of him" (Jer. 27:7). With Nabunaid away fighting, Belshazzar was in reality the sole ruler of Babylon at the time of its fall.

Belshazzar's Feast

Verses 1–4: "Belshazzar the king made a great feast to a thousand of his lords, and drank wine before the thousand. Belshazzar, whiles he tasted the wine, commanded to bring the golden and silver vessels which his father Nebuchadnezzar had taken out of the temple which was in Jerusalem; that the king, and his princes, his wives, and his concubines, might drink therein. Then they brought the golden vessels that were taken out of the temple of the house of God which was at Jerusalem; and the king, and his princes, his wives, and his concubines, drank in them. They drank wine, and praised the gods of gold, and of silver, of brass, of iron, of wood, and of stone."

Feasts were not uncommon in the city of Babylon; but the feast of Belshazzar was no ordinary event. The only other feast we read of in the Bible that can be compared with the feast of Belshazzar was that given by Ahasuerus, king of Persia, who gave a feast to the princes of the 120 provinces of his kingdom, in 521 B. C. You can read about it in the first chapter of the book of Esther.

The feast given by Belshazzar was the turning point in the history of Babylon; it marked the end of the reign of Belshazzar and the transition from the head of gold to the arms and breast of silver in the image of Nebuchadnezzar's dream. From the death of Nebuchadnezzar until the feast of Belshazzar which immediately preceded the fall of Babylon, Daniel is not mentioned. He dropped completely out of the picture, but God did not forget him; He gave him visions of coming events.

We do not know what was in the heart of Belshazzar, but we do know that the feast he gave that night was given in the spirit of contempt and defiance toward Almighty God. At the time of the feast, the city of Babylon was in a state of siege. The armies of the Medes and the Persians were encamped outside its walls, but the king had no fear of his enemies, nor of God, nor of anything else. He felt secure within the impregnable walls of the city. The drawbridges had been raised, the brazen gates were locked. Belshazzar was confident that his soldiers on the city walls could halt any army that might storm the gates. Within the city were food and provisions for several years, as well as acres of land upon which more food could be produced. Yes, Belshazzar felt secure. ("Wherefore let him that thinketh he standeth take heed lest he fall"–I Cor. 10:12. "Be not deceived; God is not mocked: for whatsoever a man soweth, that shall he also reap. For he that soweth to his flesh shall of the flesh reap corruption; but he that soweth to the Spirit shall of the Spirit reap life everlasting"–Gal. 6:7,8.)

To show his contempt for the armies outside the walls of Babylon, and his defiance of the God who looked down from above, Belshazzar gave his feast–and need we inquire about the character of those who attended? They drank wine, they praised the gods of gold, silver, brass, iron, wood, and stone. It was a feast of drunkenness, idolatry, and licentious debauchery.

Perhaps the king tried to outdrink all his guests. Perhaps he had consumed so much wine that his brain was befuddled. Wanting to do something even more sensational and daring, he sent for the sacred vessels of gold and silver which Nebuchadnezzar had taken from the temple in Jerusalem many years before. From these vessels the drunken king and his guests drank wine; and as they drank, they praised the gods of their own making, thus desecrating the sacred vessels from the house of God–and that spelled the doom of Babylon.

The God of heaven is great in mercy and slow to anger. He is longsuffering, not willing that any should perish, but that all should come to repentance. But there is a deadline, even with the God of divine compassion. When Belshazzar and his guests poured wine into the sacred vessels and lifted those vessels to drunken lips, the cup of iniquity was filled to the brim! That second, Belshazzar stepped across God's deadline and plunged into eternal doom.

The Handwriting on the Wall

Verses 5 and 6: "In the same hour came forth fingers of a man's hand, and wrote over against the candlestick upon the plaister of the wall of the king's palace: And the king saw the part of the hand that wrote. Then the king's countenance was changed, and his thoughts troubled him, so that the joints of his loins were loosed, and his knees smote one against another."

"*In the same hour . . . .*" God is longsuffering. He gave *Nebuchadnezzar* twelve long months in which to change his ways and repent; but at the end of that twelve months, as the king stepped out on the balcony of his palace, looked out over the great city of Babylon and testified to God and to the world that it was HIS city, built by HIMSELF, FOR himself, in that same hour God sent judgment upon Nebuchadnezzar.

God could have stricken Belshazzar dumb when he asked the servants to bring the sacred vessels to the banquet room. He permitted the king to go a long way before He stopped him–but when Belshazzar finally stepped over God's deadline, "*the same hour CAME FORTH THE FINGERS OF A MAN'S HAND*!"

There was no deafening clap of thunder, no supernatural flash of lightning, no rumbling earthquake; there was only a hand, writing on the wall. "*And the king saw the part of the hand that wrote.*" The writing on the wall did not disappear, proving that it was no hallucination, no wild imagination produced by too much liquor. The hand disappeared–but the writing remained; and even though the king could not read the writing and did not know what it said, it sobered him because he knew that only the hand of God could have written those words on the palace wall.

Belshazzar was in a drunken stupor–but he had a conscience that could be sobered. He was immediately filled with fear–such overpowering fear "that *the joints of his loins were loosed, and his knees smote one against another*!" The king was frightened almost to death; and when he pulled himself together enough to speak, he cried out for the same crowd who had been unable to help his grandfather, Nebuchadnezzar.

The Wise Men Called

Verses 7–9: "The king cried aloud to bring in the astrologers, the Chaldeans, and the soothsayers. And the king spake, and said to the wise men of Babylon, Whosoever shall read this writing, and shew me the interpretation thereof, shall be clothed with scarlet, and have a chain of gold about his neck, and shall be the third ruler in the kingdom. Then came in all the king's wise men: but they could not read the writing, nor make known to the king the interpretation thereof. Then was king Belshazzar greatly troubled, and his countenance was changed in him, and his lords were astonied."

It seems that Belshazzar would have profited from his grandfather's experiences with the wise men of Babylon. He had known that one day he would reign over that empire because he was in the kingly line; he had everything the human heart could desire from the standpoint of luxury and material things; but perhaps he had let the wise men and soothsayers do his thinking and his planning. At any rate, when this emergency arose, all he knew to do was send for the wise men; and they failed him just as they had failed Nebuchadnezzar.

We know why these men could not interpret the handwriting on the wall: *The devil cannot interpret the writing of Almighty God*! Only the Spirit of God can reveal the things of God: "*But the natural man receiveth not the things of the Spirit of God: for they are foolishness unto him: neither can he know them, because they are spiritually discerned*" (I Cor. 2:14).

The wise men of Babylon could not interpret the words on the wall because those words carried a message from God Almighty that only a man of God could interpret. Belshazzar was greatly troubled because of the failure of his wise men. All hilarity left him. He had seen the hand of doom–of that he was sure–and he knew not what to do next.

If the guests at the banquet thought this was some kind of unusual entertainment the king had arranged for their pleasure, one look at the king's face convinced them that this was not part of the program. Something unexpected and supernatural was going on. The drinking ceased. The golden vessels were discarded. The boisterous laughter changed to cries of terror and shrieks of fear.

Verses 10–12: "Now the queen by reason of the words of the king and his lords came into the banquet house: and the queen spake and said, O king, live for ever: Let not thy thoughts trouble thee, nor let thy countenance be changed: There is a man in thy kingdom, in whom is the spirit of the holy gods; and in the days of thy father light and understanding and wisdom, like the wisdom of the gods, was found in him; whom the king Nebuchadnezzar thy father, the king, I say, thy father, made master of the magicians, astrologers, Chaldeans, and soothsayers; forasmuch as an excellent spirit, and knowledge, and understanding, interpreting of dreams, and shewing of hard sentences, and dissolving of doubts, were found in the same Daniel, whom the king named Belteshazzar: now let Daniel be called, and he will shew the interpretation."

Where was the queen when the hand wrote on the wall? Why was she not at the party? Bible scholars tell us that it is very unlikely that this queen was the wife of Belshazzar, for his wife would have been with him at the feast (v. 2). The only reasonable solution is that she was the Queen Mother. At any rate, she was well acquainted with Daniel and his ability to contact the God of heaven. Apparently everyone else in the kingdom had forgotten Daniel; or perhaps the wise men purposely did not mention his name. But the queen knew him, with his peculiar power and ability, and she instructed Belshazzar to send for him.

Daniel was now an old man. Many years had passed since he had interpreted Nebuchadnezzar's dream. But the dear old prophet of God answered the summons to the banquet hall where the gala affair had been so abruptly interrupted.

The King's Request

Verses 13–16: "Then was Daniel brought in before the king. And the king spake and said unto Daniel, Art thou that Daniel, which art of the children of the captivity of Judah, whom the king my father brought out of Jewry? I have even heard of thee, that the spirit of the gods is in thee, and that light and understanding and excellent wisdom is found in thee. And now the wise men, the astrologers, have been brought in before me, that they should read this writing, and make known unto me the interpretation thereof: but they could not shew the interpretation of the thing: And I have heard of thee, that thou canst make interpretations, and dissolve doubts: now if thou canst read the writing, and make known to me the interpretation thereof, thou shalt be clothed with scarlet, and have a chain of gold about thy neck, and shalt be the third ruler in the kingdom."

"*Art thou that Daniel, which art of the children of the captivity of Judah*?" This question seems to indicate that Belshazzar did not know Daniel personally. Perhaps upon the death of Nebuchadnezzar Daniel had been removed from his high position and retired to private life. But the first part of verse 13, "Then was Daniel brought in," makes it clear that he was still in Babylon—and if not actually living in the court, then certainly close by.

"*I have heard of thee, that the spirit of the gods is in thee . . . .*" Belshazzar knew nothing of the eternal God of Daniel. He spoke in terms of "gods"—*many* gods.

"*. . . Now if thou canst read the writing, and make*

known to me the interpretation thereof, thou shalt be clothed with scarlet, and have a chain of gold about thy neck, and shalt be the third ruler in the kingdom."

Why should Belshazzar offer Daniel the *third* place in the kingdom? Why not the second place? Many Bible scholars believe, as I suggested before, that Belshazzar was ruling in cooperation with, or as the prime minister of, his father, Nabonidus. Bible history and Bible antiquity seem to substantiate this—and if it be true, then that explains why the king offered to make Daniel the third ruler, himself being the second. He was willing to give Daniel the next highest place in the kingdom, clothe him with scarlet, and put a gold chain about his neck if only he would interpret the writing on the wall.

Daniel knew immediately what the writing said, and as a matter of course he knew how empty and vain Belshazzar's promises were; for the empire of Babylon was doomed, the Medes and the Persians would take the kingdom that night, the king would be slain and would have no chance to fulfill his promises. But Daniel had no ambition to be third ruler anyway, and so he answered the king:

Daniel's Answer to Belshazzar

Verses 17–21: "Then Daniel answered and said before the king, Let thy gifts be to thyself, and give thy rewards to another; yet I will read the writing unto the king, and make known to him the interpretation. O thou king, the most high God gave Nebuchadnezzar thy father a kingdom, and majesty, and glory, and honour: And for the majesty that He gave him, all people, nations, and languages, trembled and feared before him: whom he would he slew; and whom he would he kept alive; and whom he would he set up; and whom he would he put down. But when his heart was lifted up, and his mind hardened in pride, he was deposed from his kingly throne, and they took his glory from him: And he was driven from the sons of men; and his heart was made like the beasts, and his dwelling was with the wild asses: They fed him with grass like oxen, and his body was wet with the dew of heaven: till he knew that the most high God ruled in the kingdom of men, and that he appointeth over it whomsoever he will."

Daniel, God's faithful prophet, did not tremble before the king. He had no fear; he had but one duty and responsibility: To be faithful to the Word of God written on the wall, and to tell the king exactly what God had spoken. That is the responsibility of every minister, evangelist, and Bible teacher. We are responsible only to God. A minister called and ordained of God to preach the Gospel, owes his first allegiance to God, regardless of the age or dispensation. He must fear no one save God—and that includes kings, governors, and rulers. He must reprove, rebuke, and exhort. A minister need never apologize for preaching "Thus saith the Lord."

This was not a pleasant task for Daniel. He knew that in a matter of hours Belshazzar would forfeit his life and go out to meet his eternal destiny. He therefore preached a sermon to the king before he interpreted the writing on the wall:

"Let thy gifts be to thyself, and give thy rewards to another." Daniel's wisdom and understanding were not for sale. He coveted no place of power in Babylon, for he knew a King much more powerful than Belshazzar! He refused the king's proffered gifts, but assured him that he would make known the handwriting on the wall.

Daniel reminded Belshazzar that *"the most high God gave Nebuchadnezzar thy father a kingdom, and majesty, and glory, and honour."* He wanted the king to see that it was what God had given to Nebuchadnezzar which Belshazzar had been enjoying, from the standpoint of the flesh. He reminded the king that the whole world had feared Nebuchadnezzar because of the majesty and power he held: "Whom he would he slew; and whom he would he kept alive; and whom he would he set up; and whom he would he put down."

Daniel then reminded Belshazzar that his grandfather had become proud, lofty, and filled with self-importance. Because of this, God deposed him from his kingly throne and took his glory from him. Belshazzar remembered the fate that had befallen his grandfather, how he had lived as a beast for seven years, being driven from the palace into the fields to eat grass like oxen.

Verses 22 and 23: "And thou his son, O Belshazzar, hast not humbled thine heart, though thou knewest all this; but hast lifted up thyself against the Lord of heaven; and they have brought the vessels of His house before thee, and thou, and thy lords, thy wives, and thy concubines, have drunk wine in them; and thou hast praised the gods of silver, and gold, of brass, iron, wood, and stone, which see not, nor hear, nor know: and the God in whose hand thy breath is, and whose are all thy ways, hast thou not glorified."

It must have been with a sad heart that Daniel said, "Belshazzar, you knew all of this! You knew Nebuchadnezzar's punishment for pride—how he lived the life of an animal for seven years; and yet you did not humble your heart before the God who rules over all, the God who puts up whom He will, puts down whom He will, and appoints whomsoever He will as king of the kingdoms of this earth. In spite of the knowledge you had of these things, you refused to surrender to the God of kings and rulers; you lifted yourself up against the God of heaven, and it was you who sent for the holy vessels from the house of God that you might desecrate them in your idolatrous feasting! Instead of praising the God of heaven, you praised the gods of gold, silver, brass, iron, wood, and stone—gods that see not, hear not, and know not.

AND THE GOD IN WHOSE HAND THY BREATH IS, AND WHOSE ARE ALL THY WAYS, HAST THOU NOT GLORIFIED! That is the reason the hand appeared on the wall. Nebuchadnezzar made a decree, 'No gods except the God of Daniel.' But you ignored that decree; you ignored the warnings sent by the God of heaven. And now God is speaking to you in terms that you can see and which I will make you to understand."

Belshazzar definitely knew about Nebuchadnezzar and his period of punishment, and he plainly showed that he was familiar with the history of the golden vessels which Nebuchadnezzar had brought back from the temple in Jerusalem. He could not have been ignorant of the fact that there were Jews in his kingdom who were brought there as captives at the same time Nebuchadnezzar confiscated the vessels from the temple, for the first thing he asked Daniel was, "Art thou that Daniel which art of the *children of the captivity of Judah*?"

The Holy Spirit here reminds me of something that I would like to pass on to my brothers and sisters in Christ: Daniel lived in the greatest city of his day–if not the greatest city of all times–and even counting Shadrach, Meshach, Abed-nego, and other Jewish believers, the odds were definitely against this one Jew in a great city of a million idolaters. But God never lost sight of him! Daniel had long ago purposed in his heart that he would allow nothing to come between him and his God–neither kings, position, nor gold. Therefore, God watched over Daniel; and it was this faithful Hebrew whom God chose to stand before Belshazzar and announce his doom and destruction because of his life of iniquity, finally climaxed by his desecration of the sacred vessels taken from the temple of Almighty God in Jerusalem.

It was Daniel whom God chose to announce the fall

of the king and the kingdom, which fall opened the door that allowed the Jews to return to their own land two years later to build again the wall around Jerusalem and the temple of worship. If God be for us, who can be against us? If Christians today would only exercise such faith and absolute trust in God as Daniel had, we could have revival throughout the world that would sweep literally millions of souls into the kingdom of God!

When we look around us, it seems that percentage wise we are in the same position as were Daniel and his friends in Babylon. We are in the Babylon of the world, a world that has but one desire: to build a world empire, with one-world government, one-world religion, one-world language, and world currency. The rulers of today are striving to make one giant Babylon from this earth which is the Lord's, with the fullness thereof. But though it may seem that true believers are lost in the millions of unbelievers, God has not lost sight of each and every one of us—and like Daniel, He will bring us through whatever comes:

"But I would not have you to be ignorant, brethren, concerning them which are asleep, that ye sorrow not, even as others which have no hope. For if we believe that Jesus died and rose again, even so them also which sleep in Jesus will God bring with Him. For this we say unto you by the Word of the Lord, that we which are alive and remain unto the coming of the Lord shall not prevent them which are asleep. For the Lord Himself shall descend from heaven with a shout, with the voice of the archangel, and with the trump of God: and the dead in Christ shall rise first: Then we which are alive and remain shall be caught up together with them in the clouds, to meet the Lord in the air: and so shall we ever be with the Lord. Wherefore comfort one another with these words" (I Thess. 4:13–18).

Until that grand and glorious hour when we will be caught up to meet the Lord Jesus in the clouds in the air, we are admonished by David:

"Fret not thyself because of evildoers, neither be thou envious against the workers of iniquity. For they shall soon be cut down like the grass, and wither as the green herb. Trust in the Lord, and do good; so shalt thou dwell in the land, and verily thou shalt be fed. Delight thyself also in the Lord; and He shall give thee the desires of thine heart. Commit thy way unto the Lord; trust also in Him; and He shall bring it to pass. And He shall bring forth thy righteousness as the light, and thy judgment as the noonday. Rest in the Lord, and wait patiently for Him: fret not thyself because of him who prospereth in his way, because of the man who bringeth wicked devices to pass. Cease from anger, and forsake wrath: fret not thyself in any wise to do evil. For evildoers shall be cut off: but those that wait upon the Lord, they shall inherit the earth. For yet a little while, and the wicked shall not be: yea, thou shalt diligently consider his place, and it shall not be. But the meek shall inherit the earth; and shall delight themselves in the abundance of peace. The wicked plotteth against the just, and gnasheth upon him with his teeth. The Lord shall laugh at him: for He seeth that his day is coming. . . . But the salvation of the righteous is of the Lord: He is their strength in the time of trouble. And the Lord shall help them, and deliver them: He shall deliver them from the wicked, and save them, because they trust in Him" (Psalm 37:1–13, 39, 40).

The Doom of Babylon

Verses 24–31: "Then was the part of the hand sent from him; and this writing was written. And this is the writing that was written, MENE, MENE, TEKEL, UPHARSIN. This is the interpretation of the thing: MENE; God hath numbered thy kingdom, and finished it. TEKEL; Thou art weighed in the balances, and art found wanting. PERES; Thy kingdom is divided, and given to the Medes and Persians. Then commanded Belshazzar, and they clothed Daniel with scarlet, and put a chain of gold about his neck, and made a proclamation concerning him, that he should be the third ruler in the kingdom. In that night was Belshazzar the king of the Chaldeans slain. And Darius the Median took the kingdom, being about threescore and two years old."

Daniel reminded Belshazzar that he and his lords, wives, and concubines had used the sacred vessels from the temple of God for their debauchery and drunkenness, and that they had praised their false gods of gold, silver, brass, iron, wood, and stone. It was then that the hand was sent from God and the writing was placed upon the wall. Daniel then began to interpret the writing:

"MENE"—"God hath numbered thy kingdom and finished it!"

"TEKEL"—"THOU art weighed in the balances and art found wanting!" (Daniel did not need to call a name—the king knew of whom he spoke.)

"PERES"—"Thy kingdom is divided, and given to the Medes and Persians."

Perhaps some are asking why Daniel changed UPHARSIN to PERES. Scholars tell us that they are simply different forms of the same word, *peres* being singular and *upharsin* plural. Scholars tell us further that the consonants written P-R-S on the wall of the banquet hall were the same as those used for "Persians." Although it was only by divine revelation that Daniel was able to give the entire meaning, we see where he got the two words, *Medes* and *Persians*. At that time, the Medes and the Persians were a dual kingdom, and when Belshazzar was defeated and slain, the kingdom was taken by the Medes and the Persians. Thus, "*peres*" interpreted by Daniel means "Thy kingdom is divided and given to the Medes and the Persians." Babylon had been unified—one giant kingdom under Nebuchadnezzar and down through the reign of Belshazzar; but now it was to be divided and become a dual kingdom under the rule of the Medes and Persians.

Belshazzar Did Not Expect So Sudden Destruction

The king commanded that Daniel be clothed in scarlet, that a chain of gold be placed around his neck, and that he be the third ruler in the kingdom, thus indicating that he expected the kingdom to continue for awhile. Certainly he did not expect it to fall within a matter of hours and himself to be slain that very night. But even while Daniel was interpreting the writing on the wall, God had already given the kingdom to the Medes and the Persians. And that very night Darius the Mede took the kingdom, "*being about threescore and two years old.*" (The city and kingdom were actually taken by Cyrus, acting in the name and by authority of Darius.)

The order in which the kings reigned in Daniel's time and during the period of the captivity and restoration of Judah is as follows:

1. *Nebuchadnezzar.* This was the greatest king of all. He reigned from 606 B. C. to 561 B. C. His reign marked the captivity of Judah and the beginning of "the times of the Gentiles" (Luke 21:24). He was the founder of the first of the four world empires (Dan. 2:37, 38; 7:4). Nebuchadnezzar was one of the most powerful kings who ever lived, and under his leadership was built the greatest city of all time—Babylon.

2. *Belshazzar.* His reign began very probably in 541 B. C. History bears out the fact that he was the grandson of Nebuchadnezzar and the son of Nabonidus, a powerful general who was victorious in many great battles.

3. *Darius the Mede* (Dan. 5:31; 6:1–27; 9:1). Concerning Darius, secular history awaits further discoveries. He was the son of an Ahasuerus, he was of the lineage of the Medes, and he was made king over the kingdom of the Chaldeans (Dan. 9:1). The name *Ahasuerus* (which is more of a title than a name) in modern language means *majesty.* It is used in the Scriptures in connection with at least four persons, and is Persian, rather than Median. Since Darius the Mede was the son (or the grandson) of an Ahasuerus, we know that he was of royal seed (probably through his mother) not only of Media, but also of Persia. He would therefore have been in line for the throne from the standpoint of either the Medes OR the Persians. Only one King Darius is mentioned in the book of Daniel (Dan. 9:1).

4. *Cyrus.* With his rise to power, the Media-Persian empire (which was the second of the world empires—Dan. 2:39; 7:5) came fully into existence. In Daniel's vision of this empire in the third year of the reign of King Belshazzar (Dan. 8:1–4), the Median power of Darius is seen as the lesser of the two horns of the ram which Daniel saw in the vision. The Persian power of Cyrus, under whom the Media-Persian power was consolidated, is the higher, more powerful of the two horns—and the higher horn came up last. Cyrus was prophetically named more than a century before his birth:

"That saith of Cyrus, He is my shepherd, and shall perform all my pleasure: even saying to Jerusalem, Thou shalt be built; and to the temple, Thy foundation shall be laid. Thus saith the Lord to His anointed, to Cyrus, whose right hand I have holden, to subdue nations before him; and I will loose the loins of kings, to open before him the two leaved gates; and the gates shall not be shut; I will go before thee, and make the crooked places straight: I will break in pieces the gates of brass, and cut in sunder the bars of iron: And I will give thee the treasures of darkness, and hidden riches of secret places, that thou mayest know that I, the Lord, which call thee by thy name, am the God of Israel. For Jacob my servant's sake, and Israel mine elect, I have even called thee by thy name. I have surnamed thee, though thou hast not known me" (Isa. 44:28–45:4).

It was under the rule of Cyrus that the decree was made which allowed the Jews to return to Palestine to rebuild their temple and their city Jerusalem:

"Now in the first year of Cyrus king of Persia, that the word of the Lord by the mouth of Jeremiah might be fulfilled, the Lord stirred up the spirit of Cyrus king of Persia, that he made a proclamation throughout all his kingdom, and put it also in writing, saying, Thus saith Cyrus king of Persia, The Lord God of heaven hath given me all the kingdoms of the earth; and He hath charged me to build Him an house at Jerusalem, which is in Judah. Who is there among you of all His people? his God be with him, and let him go up to Jerusalem, which is in Judah, and build the house of the Lord God of Israel, (He is the God,) which is in Jerusalem. And whosoever remaineth in any place where he sojourneth, let the men of his place help him with silver, and with gold, and with goods, and with beasts, beside the freewill-offering for the house of God that is in Jerusalem" (Ezra 1:1–4).

"And now will I shew thee the truth. Behold, there shall stand up yet three kings in Persia; and the fourth shall be far richer than they all: and by his strength through his riches he shall stir up all against the realm of Grecia" (Dan. 11:2).

The great kingdom of Babylon was founded and built by the great king Nebuchadnezzar. God gave him power, wealth, and great dominion. But Nebuchadnezzar forgot the God of gods and Lord of kings, as did his grandson Belshazzar, who met a violent, shameful death. It is impossible to ignore God, insult Him, tempt Him . . . and get away with it. The wages of sin is death. When sin is finished, it brings forth death.

The God of heaven holds the scales on which the destinies of kings and peasants are weighed, and the only possible way for the scales to balance is for the one being weighed to know the Lord Jesus Christ and be in the yoke with Him. Christ is the only One who can balance the scales of destiny. The only way anyone–king or peasant–can please God is in God's Christ, His only begotten Son.

"For what is a man profited, if he shall gain the whole world, and lose his own soul?" (Matt. 16:26a).

Why Did Babylon Fall?

In our previous studies we have seen that Babylon was fortified in every way possible. The city was protected by two giant walls encircled by great moats, towers atop the walls, gates that closed and locked at night, and a patrol on duty twenty-four hours a day. How could a city so well protected fall?

Romans 8:31 says: "If God be for us, who can be against us?" But it is just as true that if God writes "*Finished*" across our record and "*Doomed*" across our destiny, we cannot win, no matter how well fortified and protected we may be. God and one believer are a majority over any army; but regardless of how large an army may be, if God is against it, it cannot win. "Except the Lord build the house, they labour in vain that build it: except the Lord keep the city, the watchman waketh but in vain" (Psalm 127:1).

Two years after the death of Nebuchadnezzar, war broke out between the Babylonians and the Medes. This war continued, off and on, for more than twenty years. Finally, Cyaxeres king of the Medes (the same person called Darius in Daniel 5:31) called upon his nephew Cyrus, who was a Persian, to come to his aid; and in the seventeenth year of Nabonidus and the third year of Belshazzar, Cyrus laid siege to the city of Babylon. The soldiers in Babylon entrenched themselves behind the giant, impregnable walls of the city. They had enough foodstuffs and provisions to last for years, and they scoffed at Cyrus, making fun of his poor little army. The Babylonians had no fear. They lost no sleep in worrying about the army outside their walls. They were just waiting for the opportune time to destroy the enemy.

But this was a false security–because Almighty God had already decreed, one hundred and seventy-five years before, that the city would be taken by a man not even born at that time, a man who would be named Cyrus (Isa. 44:28; 45:1–4). The man whom God appointed to besiege the city of Babylon and take it was at that very time standing at its gates, waiting. And when the time was ripe, the God of heaven would open those gates. When God decrees judgment upon a fortress, a city, or a king, that judgment *will fall.*

Cyrus was a thinking man, as are all men truly called of God to do a task for Him. God has never called a lazy person into service. Cyrus decided that the only way to take the city was to drain the river and march his soldiers into Babylon through the dry riverbed. Historians tell us that Cyrus dug a new channel far up the river, out of sight of the guards in the towers on top of the walls of Babylon; and when this new channel was finished, the waters of the Euphrates were directed into it. When the waters had been diverted, the original riverbed ran dry. Cyrus then waited for a suitable occasion to move against the city–and that occasion was the feast of Belshazzar!

How Cyrus received news of the feast is not known; but he knew that those in the city would be so wrapped up in pleasure that night, and would be so drunk that they would not be thinking of the danger from without the city walls. Cyrus divided his army into three divisions. One group was to divert the waters of the Euphrates at the proper time, into the new channel which had been prepared for this night. The second division was stationed where the river entered the city on the north side. The third division of the army was stationed where the river left the city on the south. These second and third groups were instructed to enter the channel of the river as soon as the waters subsided, and march until they met in the center of the city where the king's palace was located.

The plan of Cyrus worked perfectly. However, it would have failed had not the city been engaged in a gala, drunken party. The guards were careless. The brass gates in the walls that lined the banks of the Euphrates were left unbolted, thus giving easy entrance to the soldiers who quickly seized Babylon. Had not the gates been unbolted, the soldiers of Cyrus' army would have been trapped and would have had to march out again. But the hand of God was in it. God had said that Cyrus would take the city, and the time had come for God's plan to be worked out. The plan of Cyrus was

God-ordained, and therefore blessed. God saw to it that the gates of the city were left unbolted along the river banks so the soldiers of the enemy could take the city. Had the guards been alert while on duty, they would have noticed the water subsiding in the river, they could have given the alarm and saved the city; but God took care of that, also. Probably most of the guards were at the party, and those who remained on duty were careless.

The soldiers of Cyrus took possession of the city, stormed the palace, slew Belshazzar and brought the drunken affair to an abrupt close. This ended the sinful reign of Belshazzar, and Babylon fell that night. I repeat: Isaiah prophesied this event, even to naming Cyrus as the one who would bring it to pass; and that prophecy was given one hundred and seventy-five years before it took place. Who would dare doubt the inspiration of the Word of God?

It is altogether possible that Cyrus was not a believer in God when he besieged the city of Babylon. It is altogether possible that he was unaware of being chosen and used of God to bring about the downfall of that great city. God has a plan and a program. Since God is the creator of all things, He has a right to carry out His plan as He foreordained it to be. From the statement in the Scripture, "*I have surnamed thee, though thou hast not known me*," we see that Cyrus was foreordained of God and named by Him more than a hundred years before he was born; and he was appointed and ordained of God to do two things: To take Babylon, and to allow the Jews to return to Jerusalem to rebuild the Holy City. He was in power at the end of the seventy years of captivity.

CHAPTER SIX

THE HISTORY OF DANIEL TO THE RULE OF CYRUS

1. It pleased Darius to set over the kingdom an hundred and twenty princes, which should be over the whole kingdom;

2. And over these three presidents; of whom Daniel was first: that the princes might give accounts unto them, and the king should have no damage.

3. Then this Daniel was preferred above the presidents and princes, because an excellent spirit was in him; and the king thought to set him over the whole realm.

4. Then the presidents and princes sought to find occasion against Daniel concerning the kingdom; but they could find none occasion nor fault; forasmuch as he was faithful, neither was there any error or fault found in him.

5. Then said these men, We shall not find any occasion against this Daniel, except we find it against him concerning the law of his God.

6. Then these presidents and princes assembled together to the king, and said thus unto him, King Darius, live for ever.

7. All the presidents of the kingdom, the governors, and the princes, the counsellors, and the captains, have consulted together to establish a royal statute, and to make a firm decree, that whosoever shall ask a petition of any God or man for thirty days, save of thee, O king, he shall be cast into the den of lions.

8. Now, O king, establish the decree, and sign the writing, that it be not changed, according to the law of the Medes and Persians, which altereth not.

9. Wherefore king Darius signed the writing and the decree.

10. Now when Daniel knew that the writing was signed, he went into his house; and his windows being open in his chamber toward Jerusalem, he kneeled upon his knees three times a day, and prayed, and gave thanks before his God, as he did aforetime.

11. Then these men assembled, and found Daniel praying and making supplication before his God.

12. Then they came near, and spake before the king concerning the king's decree; Hast thou not signed a decree, that every man that shall ask a petition of any God or man within thirty days, save of thee, O king, shall be cast into the den of lions? The king answered and said, The thing is true, according to the law of the Medes and Persians, which altereth not.

13. Then answered they and said before the king, That Daniel, which is of the children of the captivity of Judah, regardeth not thee, O king, nor the decree that thou hast signed, but maketh his petition three times a day.

14. Then the king, when he heard these words, was sore displeased with himself, and set his heart on Daniel to deliver him: and he laboured till the going down of the sun to deliver him.

15. Then these men assembled unto the king, and said unto the king, Know, O king, that the law of the Medes and Persians is, That no decree nor statute which the king establisheth may be changed.

16. Then the king commanded, and they brought Daniel, and cast him into the den of lions. Now the king spake and said unto Daniel, Thy God whom thou servest continually, he will deliver thee.

17. And a stone was brought, and laid upon the mouth of the den; and the king sealed it with his own signet, and with the signet of his lords; that the purpose might not be changed concerning Daniel.

18. Then the king went to his palace, and passed the night fasting: neither were instruments of musick brought before him: and his sleep went from him.

19. Then the king arose very early in the morning, and went in haste unto the den of lions.

20. And when he came to the den, he cried with a lamentable voice unto Daniel: and the king spake and said to Daniel, O Daniel, servant of the living God, is thy God, whom thou servest continually, able to deliver thee from the lions?

21. Then said Daniel unto the king, O king, live for ever.

22. My God hath sent his angel, and hath shut the lions' mouths, that they have not hurt me: forasmuch as before him innocency was found in me; and also before thee, O king, have I done no hurt.

23. Then was the king exceeding glad for him, and commanded that they should take Daniel up out of the den. So

Daniel was taken up out of the den, and no manner of hurt was found upon him, because he believed in his God.

24. And the king commanded, and they brought those men which had accused Daniel, and they cast them into the den of lions, them, their children, and their wives; and the lions had the mastery of them, and brake all their bones in pieces or ever they came at the bottom of the den.

25. Then king Darius wrote unto all people, nations, and languages, that dwell in all the earth; Peace be multiplied unto you.

26. I make a decree, That in every dominion of my kingdom men tremble and fear before the God of Daniel: for he is the living God, and stedfast for ever, and his kingdom that which shall not be destroyed, and his dominion shall be even unto the end.

27. He delivereth and rescueth, and he worketh signs and wonders in heaven and in earth, who hath delivered Daniel from the power of the lions.

28. So this Daniel prospered in the reign of Darius, and in the reign of Cyrus the Persian.

Daniel Highly Favored by the New King

Verses 1–3: "It pleased Darius to set over the kingdom an hundred and twenty princes, which should be over the whole kingdom; and over these three presidents; of whom Daniel was first: that the princes might give accounts unto them, and the king should have no damage. Then this Daniel was preferred above the presidents and princes, because an excellent spirit was in him; and the king thought to set him over the whole realm."

This chapter introduces Media-Persia, the second world empire of the "times of the Gentiles." After sixty-seven years of powerful rule over the known world, the head of gold at last gave way to the arms and breast of silver. The events in this chapter must have occurred during the two-year period that Darius was king. Babylon fell in 538 B. C. King Darius immediately took the throne and reigned until his death in 536 B. C.

Daniel was almost ninety years old at this time, and it is remarkable that he was equal to the strenuous task

King Darius placed upon him. The king made Daniel not just ONE of THREE presidents; he made him CHIEF of the presidents. There is no record as to what prompted Darius to so honor Daniel, but undoubtedly the king had become acquainted with the prophet in some way. At least he must have learned of Daniel's integrity, his superior statesmanship, his unusual wisdom, and his devotion to God.

This second world empire was not an absolute monarchy as Babylon had been. Nebuchadnezzar had been the final word in government. . . he put up whom he would, he put down whom he would; he slew whom he would, and whom he would he kept alive. But the presidents and princes under King Darius made up what we would call congress or parliament today, and they had a definite voice in making laws, which laws must then be ratified by the king. The laws of the Medes and the Persians were unalterable; once a decree was signed, it could not be altered or set aside.

When Darius became better acquainted with Daniel, he realized that here was a much greater man than he had supposed; and before long he preferred Daniel above all the other presidents and princes. Because of his "excellent spirit" the king "thought to set him *over the whole realm*"—a position second in power only to that of the king himself.

This promotion brought real trouble to Daniel, for the other presidents and princes were filled with jealousy, envy, and fear. They knew Daniel would not tolerate graft or dishonesty in the administration of the affairs of the empire, and thus much of their anticipated gain and profit would be in jeopardy. They did not want to lose their present opportunities for gain through graft and governmental corruption; so when they learned that this

God-fearing, upright man of Judah had been promoted to the highest office in the land apart from that of the king, they immediately set about to get rid of him—either by destroying him, or having the king demote him. Since Daniel was, in the words of Paul, "blameless" and they could find nothing against him, they had to manufacture some accusation. They therefore laid plans which they felt would, without fail, destroy this old saint of God.

The Plot to Destroy Daniel

Verses 4–9: "Then the presidents and princes sought to find occasion against Daniel concerning the kingdom; but they could find none occasion nor fault; forasmuch as he was faithful, neither was there any error or fault found in him. Then said these men, We shall not find any occasion against this Daniel, except we find it against him concerning the law of his God. Then these presidents and princes assembled together to the king, and said thus unto him, King Darius, live for ever. All the presidents of the kingdom, the governors, and the princes, the counsellors, and the captains, have consulted together to establish a royal statute, and to make a firm decree, that whosoever shall ask a petition of any God or man for thirty days, save of thee, O king, he shall be cast into the den of lions. Now, O king, establish the decree, and sign the writing, that it be not changed, according to the law of the Medes and Persians, which altereth not. Wherefore king Darius signed the writing and the decree."

The same old devil who walked in the Garden of Eden attended the first meeting of the presidents and princes as they came together to devise a plan whereby they could destroy Daniel, and their plot was as cunning as the devil himself. They knew the old prophet was devoted to God and that nothing would cause him to be *disloyal* to his God. They also knew that the king loved and respected him very highly; but to them, this old Jew was narrow and foolish.

These men had no doubt observed Daniel's life and

habits over a period of time, but had found no fault in him. He was faithful to the king; he was honest and upright, a man of character and integrity. They knew that if they carried out their plan to be rid of him they must find some way to trap him; and the surest way to do that would be through his devotion to his God.

So the presidents and princes assembled together before the king, and by words of flattery and praise they presented their petition to him: "*King Darius, live for ever*! All the presidents of the kingdom, the governors, and the princes, the counsellors, and the captains, have consulted together to establish a royal statute, and to make a firm decree, *that whosoever shall ask a petition of any God or man for thirty days, save of thee, O king, he shall be cast into the den of lions*!"

These crafty cabinet members knew that it would not be safe to give the king time to consider this proposal and think it through. They hastened him on to a decision: "Now, O king, establish the decree, and sign the writing, that it be not changed, according to the law of the Medes and Persians, which altereth not."

On first consideration, the decree sounded good to the king. He did not see the hand of Satan in it nor the diabolical scheme behind it. He accepted the plot, and unwittingly signed the decree that was designed to destroy the best friend he had in the entire kingdom. He considered the drafting of the statute as an honor to him, proffered by his presidents, princes, and counsellors, not realizing the grief and heartache it would bring to him.

The conspirators did not tell the king that Daniel had not been consulted in the matter. He took at face value their statement that ALL of the presidents and leaders had agreed upon it, and was swept off his feet by such a unanimous vote to honor him by directing all prayers and petitions to him for a period of thirty days. It was not uncommon for the subjects of kingdoms in those days to look upon their kings as gods and pray to them, making all requests to them. It was only human for Darius to think that these men really revered and loved him, and perhaps it would have been an insult to them not to place the royal seal upon the decree. Thus it became a law, under the unalterable seal of the Medes and Persians.

I imagine that as the presidents and princes left the meeting, they thought their troubles would soon be over Their scheme had worked perfectly (so they thought), and Daniel would soon be dead. But they reckoned without considering that they were dealing with God's prophet, and God had said, "*Touch not mine anointed, and do my prophets no harm*" (I Chr. 16:22). These men were not dealing with an ordinary man; they were dealing with one whom God had chosen and appointed to carry out a part of His eternal plan and purpose.

This Is the Same Daniel Who "Purposed in His Heart" (Dan. 1:8)

Verse 10: "Now when Daniel knew that the writing was signed, he went into his house; and his windows being open in his chamber toward Jerusalem, he kneeled upon his knees three times a day, and prayed, and gave thanks before his God, as he did aforetime."

Daniel knew that this royal decree was aimed directly at him. He also knew that if he continued his practice of praying to his God he would break the law of the Medes and Persians and bring about his own destruction. He must therefore choose between his loyalty to God and his loyalty to the king. He respected the king–but *he worshipped God*! To be faithful to the king would preserve his life, but to be faithful to the king also meant to be faithless to God; and if he denied his God *now*, he would not only acknowledge spiritual defeat and shame in the face of the king's decree, but he would also deny the faithfulness he had demonstrated since the day he was brought captive to Babylon and purposed in his heart that he would not defile himself with the king's meat and wine.

If he tried to keep his faith toward God by praying in secret, he would dishonor both himself AND God. I doubt that Daniel wasted any time considering the pro's and con's of the matter. I think he knew immediately what he must do. He had known his God too long, had served Him too well, and God had been too good to him for him to prove faithless now to the God who had walked with him throughout his life. He entertained no thought of praying to the king instead of to Jehovah God. If these men thought they would frighten Daniel, they were mistaken. "There is no fear in love; but perfect love casteth out fear. . . He that feareth is not made perfect in love" (I John 4:18).

So–"When Daniel knew that the writing was signed, *he went into his house. . . he kneeled upon his knees . . . and prayed, and gave thanks before his God, as he did aforetime!*" The king's decree, signed with the royal seal of the Medes and Persians which made it an unalterable law of the land, did not change Daniel's mind nor alter his actions toward God.

Daniel and His Open Window

Let us look at this prophet who stands taller than any other man in the Word of God save possibly the Apostle Paul. To me, Daniel is the *Paul* of the Old Testament, and Paul is the *Daniel* of the New Testament.

It was dawn over the great old city of Babylon. The light of early morning painted the eastern sky. It would not be long until thousands of Babylonians would be walking up and down the boulevards, crossing the river on ferryboats, or hurrying to fertile fields within the city walls. A cool breeze blew across the river Euphrates. From what we know of Daniel's character and habits, we must conclude that he arose at an early hour; and we can almost see him standing in the open window of his house, looking out over the city in early morning–this dear old prophet with the eyes of a Seer and the face of a Saint.

Many years ago as I studied the great book of Daniel, a question came to my mind: "*When* did Daniel first open his window toward the Holy City, *and why*?" Nothing is said about other Hebrews opening their windows toward Jerusalem, yet we know that this act on Daniel's part was no accident. It was planned and it was visionary. "Where there is no vision, the people perish" (Prov. 29:18), and Daniel saw more through his window with the eye of faith than most people see with a high-powered telescope!

We know that Daniel did not have the Bible as we have it today, but we may well suppose that before his session of prayer he spent some time in the Word. We are not told whether Daniel was taught by the elders, or whether he discovered the truth of the Old Testament Scriptures by himself; but he was steeped in history, and when his people were carried captive into Babylon they took the Word of God with them–*in their hearts*, if not in written form; and when they were in the city of Babylon they remembered the words of I Kings 8:45–49:

"Then hear thou in heaven their prayer and their supplication, and maintain their cause. If they sin against thee, (for there is no man that sinneth not,) and thou be angry with them, and deliver them to the enemy, so that they carry them away captives unto the land of the enemy, far or near; yet if they shall bethink themselves in the land whither they were carried captives, and repent, and make supplication unto thee in the land of them that carried them captives, saying, We have sinned, and have done perversely, we have committed wickedness; and so return unto thee with all their heart, and with all their soul, in the land of their enemies, which led them away captive, *and pray unto thee toward their land,* which thou gavest unto their fathers, the city which thou hast chosen, and the house which I have built for thy name: Then hear thou their prayer and their supplication in heaven thy dwelling place, and maintain their cause."

Note the words, "*And pray unto thee toward their land.*" I sincerely believe that Daniel was familiar with this passage, and that his knowledge of the Word of God is the reason he opened his windows. He knew and believed the promises of God concerning His people. He believed in an open Bible, he hid the Word of God in his heart, and as he fed his soul upon the open Bible, his soul was opened also.

Hear these words again: "Yet if they . . . repent and make supplication unto thee in the land of them that carried them captives, saying, WE HAVE SINNED, AND HAVE DONE PERVERSELY, WE HAVE COMMITTED WICKEDNESS; and so return unto thee with all their heart, and with all their soul, in the land of their enemies . . . and pray unto thee toward their land . . . then hear thou their prayer . . . ." Through the open window of his house in Babylon, Daniel looked toward the Holy City; and as he prayed he thought of his people, captives in Babylon—and he poured out his heart and soul to God in behalf of his people.

Perhaps when Daniel had learned the ancient account of the Hebrew Scriptures concerning his people—

their sin and their captivity–he thought of Solomon's prayer. Perhaps with his face toward Jerusalem, bowed upon his knees before the open window in his chambers, he prayed as Solomon prayed:

"And it was so, that when Solomon had made an end of praying all this prayer and supplication unto the Lord, he arose from before the altar of the Lord, from kneeling on his knees with his hands spread up to heaven. And he stood, and blessed all the congregation of Israel with a loud voice, saying, Blessed be the Lord, that hath given rest unto His people Israel, according to all that He promised: There hath not failed one word of all His good promise, which He promised by the hand of Moses His servant. The Lord our God be with us, as He was with our fathers: let Him not leave us, nor forsake us: That He may incline our hearts unto Him, to walk in all His ways, and to keep His commandments, and His statutes, and His judgments, which He commanded our fathers. And let these my words, wherewith I have made supplication before the Lord, be nigh unto the Lord our God day and night, that He maintain the cause of His servant, and the cause of His people Israel at all times, as the matter shall require: That all the people of the earth may know that the Lord is God, and that there is none else" (I Kings 8:54–60).

The Scriptures are a searchlight. David said, "Thy Word is a lamp unto my feet, and a light unto my path. . . The entrance of thy words giveth light; it giveth understanding unto the simple" (Psalm 119:105, 130). The Scriptures search the heart, revealing the need of man and at the same time revealing the sufficiency of God. Daniel had an open heart to confess his own sin and his own need of God, and he believed with all of his heart that God was sufficient. He opened his windows, knelt before them, and with his face lifted toward heaven his soul yearned for the blessings of God upon his people—blessings they should and would receive if they would only repent. (They were in Babylon because of sin.)

With an open heart and soul, bowed upon his knees before his open windows, *Daniel also opened heaven*! God said, "PROVE ME . . . . if I will not open you the windows of heaven, and pour you out a blessing, that there shall not be room enough to receive it. And I will rebuke the devourer for your sakes, and he shall not destroy the fruits of your ground; neither shall your vine cast her fruit before the time in the field, saith the Lord of hosts" (Mal. 3:10,11). This is the promise of God—but there IS a condition, and Daniel was willing to meet it. He did not count his life dear; he was willing to die, if need be, to meet God's condition.

When Daniel opened his windows toward Jerusalem, he well knew that it could cost him his life; but he also knew that if he were faithful to God, if he refused to compromise with the law of the Medes and Persians, his faithfulness could be the means of God's opening the windows of heaven and saving Daniel's people from bondage.

In Romans 9:1–3 Paul said, "I say the truth in Christ, I lie not, my conscience also bearing me witness in the Holy Ghost, that I have great heaviness and continual sorrow in my heart. For I could wish that myself were accursed from Christ for my brethren, my kinsmen according to the flesh." Paul and Daniel had kindred hearts—hearts that beat in unison for Israel.

Daniel believed that if we open the windows of our hearts toward God, God will open the windows of heaven toward US. He put Jehovah to the test that day; he proved the Word to be true. He was penitent; he confessed sin.

He was prayerful; he prayed three times a day. He was powerful; he refused to compromise. He "purposed in his heart"–and the "devourers" were indeed rebuked:

"And the king commanded, and they brought those men which had accused Daniel, and they cast them into the den of lions, them, their children, and their wives; and the lions had the mastery of them, and brake all their bones in pieces or ever they came at the bottom of the den" (Dan. 6:24).

God does what He says He will do. He promises to honor those who honor Him. Daniel opened the windows of his house and of his soul; God opened the windows of heaven to him–and through it all, *Daniel opened the prophecy of future events to US:*

"Now I am come to make thee understand what shall befall thy people in the latter days: for yet the vision is for many days" (Dan. 10:14). Daniel was the instrument through whom God has given instruction to the world concerning future events that are still out in front of us who live today. God said to Daniel, "But go thou thy way till the end be: for thou shalt rest, and stand in thy lot at the end of the days" (Dan. 12:13).

The religious leaders of today, such as the Ecclesiastical Committee of the World Council of Churches, would have voted that Daniel was making a sad mistake when he refused to honor the king's decree. When he deliberately went to his house, knelt before his open windows and prayed where he could be seen and heard, he would definitely have been branded as a crackpot, a fanatic, and "off on a tangent." But Daniel lives today in the hearts and lives of spiritually minded people who believe the Bible and take God's Word literally, as it *should* be taken.

As the royal princes left the palace of King Darius,

they felt that they were assured of three things: They knew the king could not and would not break the seal on the decree that was to cost Daniel his life. He had signed the law, and once signed, it could not be set aside. They also knew that Daniel would never deny his faith in God, no matter what the cost. They undoubtedly knew him well enough to know that he would die before he would renounce his faith or offer his prayers to any person other than his God. They believed, therefore, that their plan could not fail; it was flawless. It would not now be long until the old prophet would be "prophet chops" for hungry lions, and the path to promotion would be open to his enemies.

True to what they expected of him, *Daniel prayed "as he did aforetime."* He could have panicked. He could have questioned God. After all, why should God let this happen to HIM, a faithful prophet, now old, with not much time left to live? He could have protested to the king when he learned of the decree. He could have presented his case in a very pathetic light before the king. But he did not panic; he did not reproach God; he did not try to gain the sympathy of the king nor of his friends. Instead, he prayed, he sought God's face, he used wisdom: "But of Him are ye in Christ Jesus, who of God is made unto us wisdom, and righteousness, and sanctification, and redemption: That, according as it is written, He that glorieth, let him glory in the Lord" (I Cor. 1:30,31).

Daniel was a man of extraordinary courage. He could have reasoned thus: "God understands; He knows my heart. I will therefore go into my house, close the windows or enter into my closet—and pray in secret." He could have listened to the voice of the devil whispering, "Daniel, do not be foolish! You can pray silently, you can pray behind closed doors and windows. God will hear you just the same–and if your enemies see you praying, that will mean the end for you."

It is not hard to imagine that Daniel would have met such temptation as *Jesus* met all that Satan hurled at *Him* on the Mount of Temptation, when He said, "*Get thee hence, Satan*!" Daniel knew God, and he knew the devil. If he *had* gone into his house, closed his windows and prayed in secret, he would have ruined his testimony in Babylon, and all that he had stood for in that city would have been destroyed. In addition to a lost testimony, he would have been tormented in his mind for the rest of his life, he would have grieved the great heart of God, and his prayer would not have been heard. This man believed that it was better to die in the sunshine than to live in the shadows of disgrace. Like Paul, he gloried only in his God, and he counted all things loss–even his life–that he might gain God's approval and respect, that he not "become a castaway."

I am sure there were other windows in Daniel's house–he could have opened another window. But he knelt before the windows facing Jerusalem–the city of the temple, the city of his fathers. That was his home; it was the city of God, and God had promised that one day His chosen people would return there. Therefore, it was before the windows facing the city of worship that Daniel knelt, humbly, and prayed to his God in defiance of the king's decree.

He had not knelt before Nebuchadnezzar; he had not knelt before Belshazzar. As chief advisor to the king, he had been in company of the greatest dignitaries of his day–but he had knelt in homage to none save his God. Why should he now kneel to Darius and pray to him? Great saints have become great upon their knees–not with their names heading the list of religious dignitaries. The way *up*, with God, is *down*; and the reason we have so few Daniels, so few Pauls, is simply because so few people are willing to pay the price. It does not require grace to accept promotions in the religious world; but to be *demoted* by man and *promoted only by God* requires the faith of one like Daniel!

We know from the Scriptures that Daniel believed in consistent and persistent prayer, for he prayed *three times a day*. He believed in bombarding the throne of God with fervent prayer. In Daniel 10:1–13 we learn that on one occasion he prayed for twenty-one days—and if the answer had not come then, I do not doubt but that he would have prayed for twenty-one more! Prayer was a habit with him. He believed in prayer, and he believed that God could intervene in this crucial moment if only he remained true to his faith and prayed as he had prayed before the decree was issued under the unalterable seal of the Medes and the Persians.

You will note that Daniel was a man of gratitude. He prayed *"and gave thanks before his God."* In this dark hour when his life hung in the balance and from the human standpoint death seemed imminent, he could have been despondent and discouraged. It is easy to thank God for answered prayer—but Daniel thanked God BEFORE the answer came. He undoubtedly hoped that God would hear his prayer and fight his battle in this matter, intervening on his behalf; but it seems sure that his attitude was the same as that of the three Hebrew children when they said, "If God *does not* deliver us from the fiery furnace, we have already made up our minds that *we will not* worship the golden image." Daniel had already made up his mind that whether God answered in the affirmative or not, he would pray as had been his custom, and he had the assurance that God would do that which was best.

Therefore, he gave thanks to God for whatever happened. Perhaps he gave thanks for past mercies God had extended to him. Perhaps he gave thanks for the peace that ruled in his heart: "Thou wilt keep him in perfect peace, whose mind is stayed on thee: because he trusteth in thee" (Isa. 26:3). Most assuredly, he must have thanked God for future deliverance–if not from the lions, then from everlasting destruction. (Daniel knew where he would spend eternity.) Like Paul, he could have said, "In everything give thanks: for this is the will of God in Christ Jesus concerning you" (I Thess. 5:18).

Daniel Has Visitors

Verse 11: "Then these men assembled, and found Daniel praying and making supplication before his God."

Daniel's enemies had figured correctly. They felt sure the end of the old prophet was at hand. They gathered on the Jerusalem side of his house where he was accustomed to pray before his open windows–and just as they had expected, when his hour of prayer arrived Daniel faced toward the city of God, bowed before his open windows, and began to pray.

The words of Daniel's prayer are not recorded here; for some reason God did not see fit to put that mighty prayer into the Scriptures. I would love to know just how he prayed, and what supplication he made before God that day; but of one thing we may rest assured: As he prayed, he knew that he was being watched and that it was only a matter of moments until he would be arrested and taken before the king; but that did not stop him. He prayed with the peace of God in his heart, calm and unafraid.

A Sad King

Verses 12–15: "Then they came near, and spake before the king concerning the king's decree; Hast thou not signed a decree, that every man that shall ask a petition of any God or man within thirty days, save of thee, O king, shall be cast into the den of lions? The king answered and said, The thing is true, according to the law of the Medes and Persians, which altereth not. Then answered they and said before the king, That Daniel, which is of the children of the captivity of Judah, regardeth not thee, O king, nor the decree that thou hast signed, but maketh his petition three times a day. Then the king, when he heard these words, was sore displeased with himself, and set his heart on Daniel to deliver him: and he laboured till the going down of the sun to deliver him. Then these men assembled unto the king, and said unto the king, Know, O king, that the law of the Medes and Persians is, That no decree nor statute which the king establisheth may be changed."

I wonder if the king realized what he had done before Daniel's enemies came to him with their report? Somehow I feel that even a few minutes after the king had sealed the law with his royal seal, his conscience reminded him that he had made a grave mistake. However, if he did not realize it immediately, it could not have been long until the enemies of Daniel reminded him. Note the utter contempt and disrespect with which the conspirators made the announcement to the king: "*THAT DANIEL, which is of the children of the captivity of Judah* . . . ."—as if to say: "That old foreigner, that Jew, who is no more than a captive and a slave and who is in a position of prominence because of you, is very ungrateful for the power you gave him and the position to which you promoted him. He certainly does not appreciate the favors you bestowed upon him. He has willingly, knowingly, and deliberately disregarded your decree—the law of the Medes and the Persians; and he has shown his disrespect by going to his house, opening his windows toward Jerusalem, and praying to his God."

However, in spite of the way Daniel's enemies

approached the king, in spite of the evident disrespect they held for the prophet and the slander they heaped upon him, they did not succeed in making the king angry with Daniel. On the contrary, he was angry with himself for signing the decree, and brokenhearted because of the results.

It humiliated the king to be forced to admit that he had been led into a trap. He realized that his pride had overpowered his better judgment, that he should have been suspicious when his cabinet reported to him that "*all* the presidents" had agreed to the decree. Had he considered for one moment, he would have known that Daniel would never have agreed to such a law; but he signed the decree before thinking the matter through thoroughly.

The king was now helpless in regard to the fate of Daniel. He loved the old Hebrew, and the uppermost thing in his mind was to save him from the lions' den. He "*set his heart on Daniel to deliver him: and he laboured till the going down of the sun to deliver him*"; but there was no way to bypass the unalterable law of the Medes and the Persians. At sundown, the enemies of God's prophet assembled at the king's palace and demanded that the penalty of the law be carried out and that Daniel be thrown into the den of lions. The king had no alternative but to carry out the decree.

Daniel in the Lions' Den

Verses 16 and 17: "Then the king commanded, and they brought Daniel, and cast him into the den of lions. Now the king spake and said unto Daniel, Thy God whom thou servest continually, He will deliver thee. And a stone was brought, and laid upon the mouth of the den; and the king sealed it with his own signet, and with the signet of his lords; that the purpose might not be changed concerning Daniel."

It seems that Daniel was brought before the king at the setting of the sun. There is something touching about this incident. Daniel was an old man–probably ninety–but I picture him as tall and straight, walking toward the king's palace as the sun set in the western sky. It was not only sundown in Babylon–but from the human standpoint, it was sunset in Daniel's life.

You will note that his enemies were not allowed to take him directly to the den of lions; they were commanded to first bring him before the king–and this is the king's testimony:

"THY GOD WHOM THOU SERVEST CONTINUALLY, HE WILL DELIVER THEE!" He did not say, "Your God is ABLE to deliver you," nor did he say, "If it is God's WILL He will deliver you." He assured Daniel emphatically that his God WOULD DELIVER him. The king then went with Daniel to the lions' den, the old prophet was lowered into the den, a stone was placed over the mouth of the den, and the king then sealed the stone *"with his own signet, and with the signet of his lords, that the purpose might not be changed concerning Daniel."* The king had carried out the letter of the law!

In my mind I picture Darius as he hastened back to the palace; and I fancy the enemies of Daniel tarried close by the lions' den, listening intently to hear the old prophet's last cry, mingled with the roar of the lions as they tore the life from him. But if they expected to hear a shriek of pain and terror from Daniel (or even the roar of the lions as they tore into their prey) they were sadly disappointed; for the God of Daniel was and still is seated on His throne in the highest heavens.

With the old prophet of God sealed in the den of lions, the brokenhearted king in the palace, fasting and waiting, and with the enemies of Daniel gathered eagerly around the mouth of the lions' den, what will happen?

God Delivers Daniel

Verses 18–23: "Then the king went to his palace, and passed the night fasting: neither were instruments of musick brought before him: and his sleep went from him. Then the king arose very early in the morning, and went in haste unto the den of lions. And when he came to the den, he cried with a lamentable voice unto Daniel: and the king spake and said to Daniel, O Daniel, servant of the living God, is thy God, whom thou servest continually, able to deliver thee from the lions? Then said Daniel unto the king, O king, live for ever. My God hath sent His angel, and hath shut the lions' mouths, that they have not hurt me: forasmuch as before Him innocency was found in me; and also before thee, O king, have I done no hurt. Then was the king exceeding glad for him, and commanded that they should take Daniel up out of the den. So Daniel was taken up out of the den, and no manner of hurt was found upon him, because he believed in his God."

The king returned to his palace; but he could not sleep. Neither did he eat, and no music was heard in the palace. According to the Scriptures, "*His sleep went from him,*" which would indicate that he was awake all night. Early in the morning he hastened to the lions' den. He forgot his dignity; he forgot his position as head of the kingdom; he forgot everything—*except Daniel in the den of lions*!

We note that Darius did not send his officers or counsellors to check on the prophet to see if he were dead or alive. The dignified king of Babylon hastened in person to the mouth of the lions' den, and with a sound of weeping in his voice he called, "O Daniel, servant of the living God, is thy God, whom thou servest continually, able to deliver thee from the lions?"

We note that when the stone was rolled away from

the entrance to the lions' den it was not Daniel who spoke first. He did not plead, "Get me out of here! I have spent a terrifying night!" No; Daniel was resting peacefully when the king called to him asking if God had delivered him from the mouths of the lions. Daniel answered, "O KING, LIVE FOR EVER!" Then Daniel gave honor and praise to God for deliverance:

"My God hath sent His angel," (that angel, I believe, was none other than the Lord Jesus Christ) "and hath shut the lions' mouths, that they have not hurt me: forasmuch as before Him innocency was found in me; and also before thee, O king, have I done no hurt!"

This is a repetition of the miracle God performed in the fiery furnace when He delivered Shadrach, Meshach, and Abed-nego without even a hair of their heads being singed and without the smell of smoke upon them; for Daniel was delivered from the den of lions without a scratch upon him! God took care of him and delivered him with "no manner of hurt." God's prophet was innocent; he had not sinned against either God or the king; he was under the protecting hand of God, and the lions could not touch him.

Many light and humorous statements have been made as to why the lions did not devour Daniel. It has been said that they knew they could not digest the old prophet because he was "all backbone and gristle." It may not be sinful to speak lightly of Daniel in such words, but we know the real reason the lions did not devour him: *God worked a miracle*! The natural thing for such beasts to do would be to immediately pounce upon the person cast among them and tear him to shreds; but God preserved Daniel. He closed the lions' mouths, and they did not touch him!

Personally–and this is neither sarcasm nor jest–I do

not doubt that Daniel had the best night's rest he had had since he was brought to Babylon. I believe he spent a peaceful night and that he was sound asleep the next morning when the stone was rolled from the mouth of the lions' den!

There is a deep spiritual lesson in the deliverance of Daniel from the lions' den. Here is a picture of the preservation of Israel through the lions' den of the tribulation period under the reign of Antichrist; and it is also a beautiful spiritual picture of the Lord Jesus Christ, who was placed in the tomb of Joseph of Arimathaea. As in Daniel's case, a stone was rolled against the entrance of the tomb and sealed with the king's signet.

Daniel was placed in the den of lions because of a law that could not be altered or set aside, for it was physically impossible to change a law of the Medes and Persians once it had been sealed with the king's signet. Daniel had broken that law, and he must pay the penalty.

By way of parallel, God thundered out, "THE SOUL THAT SINNETH, IT SHALL DIE!" (Ezek. 18:4). Under God's law, sin demands death—and though heaven and earth will pass away, not one jot or one tittle of God's law will pass away or be altered. Man has sinned—"ALL have sinned, and come short of the glory of God" (Rom. 3:23). But Jesus took our place. He satisfied the law that demands death—the unalterable law of God. The Son of God was placed in a tomb, a stone was placed over the mouth of the tomb, and it was securely sealed; but the same God who delivered Daniel from the lions' den also brought forth Jesus from the tomb, alive forevermore!

After Daniel had served his sentence in the den of lions, even though he was taken out the next morning without harm, he could not be executed in any other way;

the unalterable law of the Medes and Persians had been satisfied. Daniel had paid the penalty for breaking that law, and but for the grace of God his life would have been forfeited; but when he came forth from the lions' den he was a free man—the law could not touch him, his enemies could not cast him again into the den of lions.

The same is true concerning Jesus. (Read the tenth chapter of Hebrews.) He suffered once, for all, forever; He paid sin's debt in full, and there can be no repetition of His sacrifice. He suffered, He died, He was buried—but He was delivered from the tomb. God raised Him for our justification. The tomb could not hold Him, and death can never again claim Him. He paid the sin-debt *once*, never to be repeated: "Who being the brightness of His glory, and the express image of His person, and upholding all things by the word of His power, when He had by Himself purged our sins, sat down on the right hand of the Majesty on high" (Heb. 1:3). Daniel came out of the lions' den and returned to his position in the king's government, and no one could touch him; he had paid his debt to the law of the Medes and the Persians.

When we trust Jesus and accept His death, burial, and resurrection, when we exercise faith in His finished work and rely upon His shed blood for the remission of sin, death cannot claim us, sin cannot damn us, the devil cannot point the finger of accusation at us. We are free: "Ye shall know the truth, and the truth shall make you free. . . If the Son therefore shall make you free, ye shall be free indeed" (John 8:32 and 36). Daniel, in the den of lions, delivered by God's miracle, foreshadows Jesus in the tomb of Joseph of Arimathaea. The same God—the God of gods, the Lord of kings, the revealer of secrets—delivered Daniel from the den of lions and delivered Jesus from the death that sin demanded.

The God of Daniel Versus the Gods of the Presidents and Princes

Verse 24: "And the king commanded, and they brought those men which had accused Daniel, and they cast them into the den of lions, them, their children, and their wives; and the lions had the mastery of them, and brake all their bones in pieces or ever they came at the bottom of the den."

The king was not willing to let things drop with the deliverance of Daniel from the lions' den; he felt that those who had conspired against the prophet in such a selfish and inhuman way in order to profit from his death, should undergo the same punishment. But you will notice that the enemies of Daniel did not reach the bottom of the lions' den before they were broken to pieces by the beasts—and the news spread across the city that *the God of Daniel was certainly more powerful than the gods of Babylon.*

There is another tremendous lesson to be learned here: Not only were those who had conspired against Daniel cast into the den of lions, but "their children and their wives" were cast in also. God declared that the iniquity of the fathers should be visited upon the children unto the third and fourth generation. Parents should be careful how they live and how they conduct themselves before their children—as well as how they feel toward the God of all creation.

Paul said to the Philippian jailer, "Believe on the Lord Jesus Christ, and thou shalt be saved—and thy house!" The God whose Word cannot be broken or altered promises household salvation if the head of the home will believe on the Lord Jesus Christ and set the example before his family. I firmly believe that parents who are truly born again will see their family saved if they themselves will live right and pray right. If parents honor God as they should, the family circle will not be broken in the great judgment day. It is not true that wicked men harm only themselves, as so many of them say: *they also bring sorrow, heartache, and death upon their families.*

Critics have suggested that the reason the lions did not devour Daniel was because the king had previously filled their den with choice meats and they were so gorged that they were not hungry when Daniel was cast in among them; but these claimants fail to explain why the lions so quickly devoured the group of men and their families who were cast into the den for conspiring against Daniel. We know, of course, that they do not explain that part of the story because they *have* no explanation! If you want a Bible answer to the question, "Why did the lions refrain from devouring Daniel?" the answer is found in verse 23–my favorite verse in this chapter:

"Then was the king exceeding glad for him, and commanded that they should take Daniel up out of the den. So Daniel was taken up out of the den, and no manner of hurt was found upon him, BECAUSE HE BELIEVED IN HIS GOD!"

The Decree of Darius

Verses 25–28: "Then king Darius wrote unto all people, nations, and languages, that dwell in all the earth; Peace be multiplied unto you. I make a decree, That in every dominion of my kingdom men tremble and fear before the God of Daniel: for He is the living God, and stedfast for ever, and His kingdom that which shall not be destroyed, and His dominion shall be even unto the end. He delivereth and rescueth, and He worketh signs and wonders in heaven and in earth, who hath delivered Daniel from the power of the lions. So this Daniel prospered in the reign of Darius, and in the reign of Cyrus the Persian."

After the "Daniel in the lions' den" episode, King

Darius wrote another law (quite different from the first) and signed it with the royal signet. He declared that all people, all nations, and all languages that dwell upon the face of the earth should tremble and fear before God—(the God of Daniel, not the gods of Babylon). King Darius declared that the God of Daniel "is the living God, and stedfast for ever, and His kingdom that which shall not be destroyed, and His dominion shall be even unto the end."

Darius decreed that the God of Daniel is the living God—everlasting, all-powerful; and he signed a law that all people must recognize this fact. He declared that the living, everlasting God is able to deliver, rescue, work miracles and wonders in heaven and in earth; and he gave God full credit for delivering Daniel from death in the lions' den.

The decree of Darius did not exactly make the worship of Jehovah a state religion, but it did bring about religious tolerance, and permitted the Jews to worship without fear of being molested by the king and martyred for their faith in worshipping the true God rather than the gods of Babylon. Daniel's faithfulness had again rewarded him, gained another promotion for him, and "*So this Daniel prospered in the reign of Darius and in the reign of Cyrus the Persian.*"

God miraculously delivered Daniel from the lions' den in order that he might be the advisor of Darius and Cyrus, the first two monarchs representing the Media-Persian world empire. These two were rulers in the dual kingdom, representing the arms and breast of silver seen in Nebuchadnezzar's colossal image. God had other work for Daniel to do, and He preserved him for that purpose.

I have always believed and preached that God's people are indestructible until God is finished with them on this earth. If a minister lives right, fears God, trusts and obeys God's Word, all hell cannot destroy his life until he has finished the work God gives him to do. The Old Testament bears out this truth, and in the New Testament we read of the deliverance of Peter, Paul, and others when such deliverance could have been nothing less than the hand of a miracle-working God.

"If God be for us, who can be against us?" (Rom. 8:31b).

". . . For He hath said, I will never leave thee, nor forsake thee. So that we may boldly say, The Lord is my helper, and I will not fear what man shall do unto me" (Heb. 13:5,6).

"And we KNOW that all things work together for good to them that love God, to them who are the called according to His purpose" (Rom. 8:28).

Daniel loved God. The three Hebrew children loved God. Joseph loved God. The Apostle Paul loved God. Do I love God? Do YOU love God? If we love and honor God as these men did, He will do for us all that He did for them. The God of Daniel is still able to do exceedingly abundant above all that we think or ask!

PART II

Chapters 7 through 12

STRICTLY PROPHETIC

CHAPTER SEVEN

THE BEAST VISIONS

1. In the first year of Belshazzar king of Babylon Daniel had a dream and visions of his head upon his bed: then he wrote the dream, and told the sum of the matters.

2. Daniel spake and said, I saw in my vision by night, and, behold, the four winds of the heaven strove upon the great sea.

3. And four great beasts came up from the sea, diverse one from another.

4. The first was like a lion, and had eagle's wings: I beheld till the wings thereof were plucked, and it was lifted up from the earth, and made stand upon the feet as a man, and a man's heart was given to it.

5. And behold another beast, a second, like to a bear, and it raised up itself on one side, and it had three ribs in the mouth of it between the teeth of it: and they said thus unto it, Arise, devour much flesh.

6. After this I beheld, and lo another, like a leopard, which had upon the back of it four wings of a fowl; the beast had also four heads; and dominion was given to it.

7. After this I saw in the night visions, and behold a fourth beast, dreadful and terrible, and strong exceedingly; and it had great iron teeth: it devoured and brake in pieces, and stamped the residue with the feet of it: and it was diverse from all the beasts that were before it; and it had ten horns.

8. I considered the horns, and, behold, there came up among them another little horn, before whom there were three of the first horns plucked up by the roots: and, behold, in this horn were eyes like the eyes of man, and a mouth speaking great things.

9. I beheld till the thrones were cast down, and the Ancient of days did sit, whose garment was white as snow, and the hair of his head like the pure wool: his throne was like the fiery flame, and his wheels as burning fire.

10. A fiery stream issued and came forth from before him: thousand thousands ministered unto him, and ten thousand times ten thousand stood before him: the judgment was set, and the books were opened.

11. I beheld then because of the voice of the great words which the horn spake: I beheld even till the beast was slain, and his body destroyed, and given to the burning flame.

12. As concerning the rest of the beasts, they had their dominion taken away: yet their lives were prolonged for a season and time.

13. I saw in the night visions, and, behold, one like the Son of man came with the clouds of heaven, and came to the Ancient of days, and they brought him near before him.

14. And there was given him dominion, and glory, and a kingdom, that all people, nations, and languages, should serve him: his dominion is an everlasting dominion, which shall not pass away, and his kingdom that which shall not be destroyed.

15. I Daniel was grieved in my spirit in the midst of my body, and the visions of my head troubled me.

16. I came near unto one of them that stood by, and asked him the truth of all this. So he told me, and made me know the interpretation of the things.

17. These great beasts, which are four, are four kings, which shall arise out of the earth.

18. But the saints of the most High shall take the kingdom, and possess the kingdom for ever, even for ever and ever.

19. Then I would know the truth of the fourth beast, which was diverse from all the others, exceeding dreadful, whose teeth were of iron, and his nails of brass; which devoured, brake in pieces, and stamped the residue with his feet;

20. And of the ten horns that were in his head, and of the other which came up, and before whom three fell; even of that horn that had eyes, and a mouth that spake very great things, whose look was more stout than his fellows.

21. I beheld, and the same horn made war with the saints, and prevailed against them;

22. Until the Ancient of days came, and judgment was given to the saints of the most High; and the time came that the saints possessed the kingdom.

23. Thus he said, The fourth beast shall be the fourth kingdom upon earth, which shall be diverse from all kingdoms, and shall devour the whole earth, and shall tread it down, and break it in pieces.

24. And the ten horns out of this kingdom are ten kings that shall arise: and another shall rise after them; and he shall be diverse from the first, and he shall subdue three kings.
25. And he shall speak great words against the most High, and shall wear out the saints of the most High, and think to change times and laws: and they shall be given into his hand until a time and times and the dividing of time.
26. But the judgment shall sit, and they shall take away his dominion, to consume and to destroy it unto the end.
27. And the kingdom and dominion, and the greatness of the kingdom under the whole heaven, shall be given to the people of the saints of the most High, whose kingdom is an everlasting kingdom, and all dominions shall serve and obey him.
28. Hitherto is the end of the matter. As for me Daniel, my cogitations much troubled me, and my countenance changed in me: but I kept the matter in my heart.

The book of Daniel contains 12 chapters, and these 12 chapters are evenly divided into two sections. The first six chapters have to do with Daniel's personal history as God's prophet during the reign of Nebuchadnezzar, Belshazzar, Darius the Mede, and Cyrus the Persian. Daniel was an old man when Darius became king of Babylon along with Cyrus in the dual kingdom of Media-Persia.

Chapter seven marks the beginning of the second and closing section of Daniel's prophecy. In these chapters we have the account of a series of visions which God gave to Daniel at various times, under various conditions. These visions are definitely prophetic, and contain in their entirety a moving, most graphic and comprehensive picture of the history of man from the time of Daniel until the setting up of the Kingdom of Heaven on earth at the return of Jesus in the Revelation at the close of the reign of the Antichrist. Chapter 7 records the first in this series of visions:

The First Vision

Verses 1–3: "In the first year of Belshazzar king of

Babylon Daniel had a dream and visions of his head upon his bed: then he wrote the dream, and told the sum of the matters. Daniel spake and said, I saw in my vision by night, and, behold, the four winds of the heaven strove upon the great sea. And four great beasts came up from the sea, diverse one from another."

This vision came to Daniel a few years after the death of Nebuchadnezzar, soon after the beginning of the reign of Belshazzar, who led Babylon to her doom and himself to an untimely death, and goes back beyond the sixth chapter, which we have just completed. Daniel recorded the vision and exactly what God revealed to him through it:

"*I saw in my vision by night, and, behold, the four winds of the heaven strove upon the great sea.*" Thus we have the setting for this particular vision. The "four winds of the heaven" are referred to again in Revelation 7:1,2, where John tells us that an angel commanded the four winds to be held back from destroying the earth until the faithful remnant of the elect of God had been sealed in their foreheads–referring to the 144,000 who will deliver God's message during the reign of Antichrist, Daniel's seventieth week of the seventy weeks of prophecy. We will study this a bit later in these messages.

I personally believe that these four winds are the same four winds we read of in Revelation as having to do with God's dealings with the Gentiles versus Israel in the consummation of all things. God's care for His people through the storms of Babylon points to the day when He will care for His own through the storm of great tribulation under the persecution of Antichrist–the devil in flesh. God will seal and protect His own elect–and all hell cannot destroy them!

The Four Winds – The Great Sea:

Daniel said, "I saw . . . and behold, *the four winds*

of heaven strove upon the great sea." In Scripture, *the sea* symbolizes the nations of the world in turmoil; but "*the GREAT sea*" in the Word of God always has but one meaning–literally, *the Mediterranean Sea.*

In Scripture we read of three seas:

1. The Sea of Galilee, around which much of the ministry of Jesus was carried on, and which is actually not a sea, but a lake.

2. The Dead Sea.

3. The Great Sea–which always refers to the Mediterranean. The Babylonian and Medo-Persian empires were not located on the Mediterranean, as were the Grecian and the Roman, but they were greatly indebted for their wealth and power to their Mediterranean coast line which they had conquered. Therefore, the setting for the four nations described in the seventh chapter of Daniel centers around the Mediterranean Sea, at the eastern end of which lies the land of Palestine–the center of all human history and the center of God's government upon earth when the Lord Jesus returns with His Church to reign in the Millennium. Prophetically speaking, Palestine is the center of the earth. God deals with Palestine particularly, and His dealings with all other nations and countries are mentioned only in their relationship to Palestine. Therefore, the directions mentioned in the Bible are always with reference to the center of the earth prophetically–that is, Palestine.

When the Word of God speaks of the north country, it means *north of Palestine*; when it speaks of the west, it means *west of Palestine.* When we read of the armies of the south or the armies of the north, we may know that these armies will be located south or north of *Palestine.* The Holy City of Jerusalem is the center of the world in the program of Almighty God in dealing with Israel and the nations.

In chapter 13 of Revelation we read of the beast coming up out of the sea. The sands of the sea represent multitudes; the sea itself represents unrest and turmoil among the masses. Almost without exception Bible scholars agree that this beast is the revived Roman empire (with its dictator). The second beast in Revelation 13 comes up out of the land–and this, of course, refers to the land of Palestine. Thus we are given the two great leaders of the end time–one arising out of the countries around the Mediterranean Sea and the other arising out of Palestine–the center of God's dealings with the nations.

In our present chapter we see the four winds striving upon the great sea. The number *four* points out the direction of the winds, as coming from the four points of the compass, and denotes their universality. Ephesians 6:12 says, "For we wrestle not against flesh and blood, but against principalities, against powers, against the rulers of the darkness of this world, against spiritual wickedness in high places." As the winds of heaven stir up the seas, so these "winds" representing the "powers of the air" cause unrest among the nations of the earth. This is the introduction to the vision of Daniel which is to follow immediately. The great conflict–the greatest battle of all ages–centers around the Mediterranean Sea and the countries that border on that "great sea."

"*And four great beasts came up from the sea, diverse one from another.*" It is most interesting to read today concerning the political and religious unrest of Palestine, Trans-Jordan, the Arab countries of Egypt, and the drastic changes that are being brought about in Rome and in Roman Catholicism. The stage is being set and the spirit of Babylon is on the rise. The Babylonian system of world power and dominion is in the making again. "Only He (the Holy Spirit) who now letteth will let until He be taken out of the way" (II Thess. 2:7). Then Antichrist will take over the reins of government and religion of this world, and two beasts—one political, one religious—will reign over the peoples of earth.

As we study the four beasts that Daniel saw in his vision, we will find that they correspond to the *four metals* of the image that Nebuchadnezzar saw in his dream (chapter 2). This vision was given to Daniel that he might have more light on the "times of the Gentiles"—light which God was not willing to give to a heathen king like Nebuchadnezzar.

The First Beast:

Verse 4: "The first was like a lion, and had eagle's wings: I beheld till the wings thereof were plucked, and it was lifted up from the earth, and made stand upon the feet as a man, and a man's heart was given to it."

This verse describes the first beast Daniel saw coming up out of the great sea. The beast was like a lion, but it had the wings of an eagle—*until the wings were plucked.* The beast was then lifted up from the earth and made to stand upon its feet like a man, "and a man's heart was given to it."

The lion is king of beasts, and the description of this beast could point to none other than Nebuchadnezzar—the most powerful of the Gentile world rulers. In this first beast we see a combination of "the king of beasts" and "the king of birds," which is typical of absolute monarchy and therefore belongs to Nebuchadnezzar and his kingdom of Babylon—the most powerful of the four world empires. As Daniel gazed upon this beastly monstrosity, its wings disappeared; they were "plucked."

After Nebuchadnezzar had conquered the known world

in his day, he gave himself over to building the magnificent city of Babylon—and from that time on, his powerful kingdom began to crumble.

Then Daniel saw the beast lifted up, and instead of walking on all fours like a lion, it walked on two feet like a man—and "a man's heart was given to it." But apart from walking like a man and possessing the heart of a man, it was still a beast.

The plucking of the wings may also refer to the insanity of Nebuchadnezzar when he had feathers like an eagle; and the standing upright on two feet could refer to his recovery from insanity, when he returned to his kingdom and no longer ate grass like an ox in the fields.

The Second Beast:

Verse 5: "And behold another beast, a second, like to a bear, and it raised up itself on one side, and it had three ribs in the mouth of it between the teeth of it: and they said thus unto it, Arise, devour much flesh."

". . . And THEY said thus unto it . . . ." To whom does this statement refer? I believe it refers to the heavenly watchers mentioned in Daniel 4:17. The court in session in heaven said to this beast, "*ARISE, devour much flesh*!"

The second beast was like a bear—which is second in power to the lion. The lion is the most powerful of the beasts, the most majestic in its movements and actions. By contrast, the bear is slow, awkward, depending upon brute force to conquer its enemies. These were certainly the characteristics of the Media-Persian empire, for she gained her victories by hurling masses of troops against her enemies. Xerxes went against Greece with 2,500,000 fighting men—and *now* we understand the statement, "Arise, devour much flesh." Certainly an army of 2,500,000 *would* "devour much flesh."

In the vision, Daniel saw the bear "raise up itself on one side," making ready to attack the enemy–and this side of the bear represented Persia, the stronger and more aggressive of the dual empire of Media-Persia. Persia corresponded to the right shoulder and arm, which, generally speaking, are much stronger than the left arm and shoulder.

When the bear raised itself up on one side, Daniel saw that it had three ribs in its mouth, between its teeth. These three ribs represented three kingdoms–Lydia, Babylon, and Egypt–which formed a triple alliance in an effort to check the Media-Persian power; but they were destroyed by Media-Persia.

Just as the bear is inferior to the lion, so was Media-Persia inferior to Babylon–not so much in power, but in wealth, in magnificence, and in government. Thus, the four wild beasts of Daniel's vision correspond to the image seen by Nebuchadnezzar in his dream, with each succeeding beast weaker and inferior to the one that precedes it.

The Third Beast:

Verse 6: "After this I beheld, and lo another, like a leopard, which had upon the back of it four wings of a fowl; the beast had also four heads; and dominion was given to it."

This beast was like a leopard–the most agile and most graceful of the wild beasts. The leopard is slight, slender in frame and body, but very powerful and swift–and extremely fierce. These characteristics of the leopard are a very fitting symbol of the speed with which the Greeks, under the leadership of Alexander the Great, overthrew the forces of Persia and conquered Media-Persia. Thus, the third world Gentile empire was that of Greece. Led by Alexander the Great, the Greeks conquered the entire civilized world of that day.

This beast had "*four wings of a fowl.*" The Holy Spirit was careful to reveal to us that these four wings were those of a *fowl*–not the wings of an eagle. This third beast moved swiftly–but not so swiftly and with such power as had Nebuchadnezzar, symbolized by eagles' wings.

The leopard had four heads, which represent the four kingdoms into which the empire of Alexander was divided after he had conquered the known world of his day. These kingdoms were Thrace, Macedonia, Syria, and Egypt.

There is no doubt that Daniel thoroughly understood that the four beasts of his vision corresponded to the image in Nebuchadnezzar's dream. There was no question in his mind about the lion; he fully understood the bear, and he understood the leopard–but the *four heads* of the leopard troubled him. In the great image of gold, silver, brass, iron, and mixture of iron and clay, there had been no fourfold division of any kingdom. Therefore the indication in his vision that the Grecian empire was to be divided into four kingdoms troubled Daniel:

"I Daniel was grieved in my spirit in the midst of my body, and the visions of my head troubled me. . . Hitherto is the end of the matter. As for me Daniel, my cogitations much troubled me, and my countenance changed in me: *but I kept the matter in my heart*" (Dan. 7:15, 28). Daniel waited two years longer, until he saw the vision of the ram and the he-goat, which gave him the solution to the difficulty that troubled him. We will study the vision of the ram and the he-goat in the next chapter.

The Fourth Beast:

Verses 7 and 8: "After this I saw in the night visions,

and behold a fourth beast, dreadful and terrible, and strong exceedingly; and it had great iron teeth: it devoured and brake in pieces, and stamped the residue with the feet of it: and it was diverse from all the beasts that were before it; and it had ten horns. I considered the horns, and, behold, there came up among them another little horn, before whom there were three of the first horns plucked up by the roots: and, behold, in this horn were eyes like the eyes of man, and a mouth speaking great things."

This fourth beast was "dreadful and terrible . . . *exceedingly* strong." It had great iron teeth with which it "devoured," nails of brass with which it "brake in pieces," and it "stamped upon the residue" with its feet. It was different from all the beasts that were before it (verse 19).

This beast had ten horns, and out of the ten horns there came up a "little horn, before whom there were three of the first horns plucked up by the roots: and, behold, in this horn were eyes like the eyes of a man, and a mouth speaking great things." *This "little horn" is the Antichrist described in Revelation 13.*

The words "after this" do not imply that the vision of this fourth wild beast was separate in time from the vision of the three preceding beasts, for we note that the vision of the third beast in verse 6 begins with the same words. Verses 3 and 4 tell us that Daniel saw the four beasts come up out of the great sea; and while they did not all come up at once, they DID emerge from the sea one after the other. Daniel saw them all in one vision–they did not come up weeks, months, or years apart.

Inspired of God, Daniel points out here that this fourth beast was singular. No other beast was like it, ever on this earth. It was hideous to behold, powerful in its movements, and it had what no natural beast has: *teeth of iron and nails of brass* (verse 19). Daniel had no trouble in identifying this beast in relation to the image of Nebuchadnezzar's dream, for the teeth of iron corresponded to the iron legs, and the ten horns corresponded to the ten toes of the image. The fourth beast represented the Roman empire—but there was one thing that mystified Daniel, and that was *the little horn* which sprang up in the midst of the ten horns.

As Daniel gazed upon this horrible beast, a little horn began to appear, growing out of the ten large horns. Daniel well remembered the ten toes of Nebuchadnezzar's image, but there was no "little toe" among the ten. There was something else unusual about the little horn: it had eyes like a man and a mouth like a man—a mouth "*speaking great things.*" Daniel knew that God was showing him something in addition to the teaching of the colossal image of Nebuchadnezzar's dream; God was revealing something that He had not hitherto seen fit to reveal relative to that image. God had reserved this special revelation for Daniel and for His people, Israel.

The revelations given to Daniel in the last six chapters of this prophecy primarily concern Israel—the Jewish people—in the latter days. If Daniel wanted to call on God and plead for an explanation of this little horn, he did not have a chance; because before he could bow upon his knees in prayer, God gave him a second vision.

The Second Vision

Verses 9–12: "I beheld till the thrones were cast down, and the Ancient of days did sit, whose garment was white as snow, and the hair of His head like the pure wool: His throne was like the fiery flame, and His wheels as burning fire. A fiery stream issued and came forth from before Him: thousand thousands ministered unto Him, and ten thousand times ten thousand stood before Him: the judgment was set, and the books were opened. I beheld then because of the voice of the great words which the horn spake: I beheld even till the beast was slain, and his body destroyed, and given to the burning flame. As concerning the rest of the beasts, they had their dominion taken away: yet their lives were prolonged for a season and time."

The scene here is one of judgment. As Daniel gazed upon the *little horn* in utter amazement, God gave him a second vision. *He saw thrones cast down*—meaning that he saw thrones *placed.* No doubt he saw these thrones descend out of heaven and come to rest, either in the air or upon the earth; and the judgment was set. Then Daniel saw "the Ancient of days" sit upon the throne. (It may be that Daniel saw the thrones in the air; but we know that the throne upon which Jesus will sit in judgment will be both here on earth AND in the air, because there is no such thing as a *general judgment.* There are several judgments yet in the future.)

The Scriptures anticipate coming judgment by God, the Righteous Judge, upon all men. The Psalmist believed in coming judgments: ". . . For He cometh, for He cometh TO JUDGE THE EARTH: He shall judge the world with righteousness, and the people with His truth" (Psalm 96:13).

In the New Testament we read, "Because He hath appointed a day, in the which He will judge the world in righteousness by that man whom He hath ordained; whereof He hath given assurance unto all men, in that He hath raised Him from the dead" (Acts 17:31).

The subject of judgment is tremendous; it is a large subject in God's Holy Word. To help you to better understand what I mean, I point out some of the judgments:

First, *the judgment of the cross.* Study carefully John 5:24; Romans 5:9; 8:1; II Corinthians 5:21; Galatians 3:13; Hebrews 9:26–28; 10:10, 14–17.

Second, *the judgment concerning the believer in chastening.* Study I Corinthians 11:31,32; Hebrews 12:5–11.

Third, the Bible speaks of *self-judgment* on the part of believers. Study I John 1:9; I Corinthians 11:31; Psalm 32:5; Psalm 51.

Fourth, *judgment of believers' works–or stewardship.* This will take place at the judgment seat of Christ. Study carefully Romans 14:10; I Corinthians 3:11–15; 4:5; II Corinthians 5:10.

With the exception of the last judgment mentioned, these judgments have taken place (and will take place) here upon earth; but the judgment seat where believers will be rewarded will be in the clouds in the air when Jesus comes in the Rapture. Now let me point out four other tremendous judgments which are yet to occur:

First, *the judgment of the nation Israel.* Study carefully Ezekiel 20:37,38; Zechariah 13:8,9.

Second, *the judgment of the nations.* Study Matthew 25:31–46; Isaiah 34:1,2; Joel 3:11–16.

Third, *the judgment of the fallen angels.* Study Jude 6.

Fourth, *the great White Throne judgment.* At this judgment only the wicked and the ungodly will appear. Study carefully Revelation 20:11–15.

I would stress the Bible fact that Scripture nowhere teaches a general judgment–a time when all peoples of all ages will be gathered around the throne of God to be judged. This is man-made dogma; it is not Bible doctrine.

The Judgment of the Nation Israel

The next judgment in the program of Almighty God, having to do with prophecy and the second coming of Jesus Christ, will be the judgment of the nation Israel.

The Word of God teaches clearly that the future judgment program of Almighty God will begin with judgment upon Israel, God's chosen nation through much of the Old Testament era. The Gospel was presented to the Jew first. He rejected his Messiah and desired Barabbas instead, requesting that the blood of Jesus be upon him and upon his children.

However, God made an everlasting covenant with Abraham, and He will fulfill every minute detail of His promise. Through the covenants, God promised Israel a kingdom over which the Messiah, son of David, should reign. Before this promised kingdom can become a reality, Jesus must personally return to this earth, and there must be a definite judgment upon Israel to determine those who will enter into the kingdom on earth. The New Testament clearly reveals this truth: "THEY ARE NOT ALL ISRAEL, WHICH ARE OF ISRAEL" (Rom. 9:6b).

The time of Israel's judgment is given in the chronology of prophesied events laid down in Matthew chapters 24 and 25. In Matthew 24:4–12 we are given a description of the events that will occur just before the end of this age; and in Matthew 24:13–26 we are given the description of the tribulation period, at which time the Antichrist will announce to the world that he is God and terrible tribulation will engulf the earth–such terrible tribulation that "except those days should be shortened, there should no flesh be saved": but for the sake of the elect (Israel) those days shall be shortened.

Matthew 24:27–31 describes the Lord's coming "as the lightning cometh out of the east" and shining unto the west. This is not the Rapture of the Church, but *the Revelation of Jesus* when every eye shall see Him (Rev. 1:7).

Matthew 24:31 tells of the regathering of Israel "from

the four winds, from one end of heaven to the other." That is, Israel will be gathered from the whole wide world, wherever there is an Israelite, and they will be brought to their own land for this judgment. And in Matthew 25:1–30 we are given the description of the judgment *upon* Israel.

In Matthew 25:31–46 we have the judgment on the Gentiles; and then the kingdom on earth when King Jesus will sit on the throne of King David, and we (the bride) will reign with Him here upon this earth for one thousand glorious years of peace on earth, good will toward men.

In these two chapters we see clearly that the judgment upon Israel will follow the second coming of the Lord Jesus Christ to the earth, and the regathering of Israel as a nation. We know that the fig tree is budding today, and there are many Jews in the land of Israel; but the judgment upon Israel will not occur until they are gathered from every square foot of this universe, and that will take place AFTER the Rapture of the Church.

The Bible clearly teaches that Israel is an earthly people with earthly promises. Do not misunderstand . . . Jews can be saved in this dispensation exactly as Gentiles are saved: by grace, through faith in the shed blood of Jesus. But as a nation, Israel is an earthly people, and this last judgment having to do with Israel will take place here on this earth, after the Lord personally returns TO the earth.

"And His feet shall stand in that day upon the mount of Olives, which is before Jerusalem on the east, and the mount of Olives shall cleave in the midst thereof toward the east and toward the west, and there shall be a very great valley; and half of the mountain shall remove toward the north, and half of it toward the south" (Zech. 14:4).

Some teachers and ministers spiritualize Israel and the judgment; they teach that this judgment has to do with the soul at death; but this is not rightly dividing the word of truth. It is wrongly handling God's holy Word. This judgment is not spiritual. It will not take place in heaven or in the heavens; it will take place right here upon this earth.

"And I will bring you out from the people, and will gather you out of the countries wherein ye are scattered, with a mighty hand, and with a stretched out arm, and with fury poured out. And I will bring you into the wilderness of the people, and there will I plead with you face to face. Like as I pleaded with your fathers in the wilderness of the land of Egypt, so will I plead with you, saith the Lord God. And I will cause you to pass under the rod, and I will bring you into the bond of the covenant: And I will purge out from among you the rebels, and them that transgress against me: I will bring them forth out of the country where they sojourn, and they shall not enter into the land of Israel: and ye shall know that I am the Lord" (Ezek. 20:34–38).

This passage and other passages which deal with Israel's restoration clearly teach that this judgment will be upon *all living Israel*. They will be gathered into their own land–the land that God promised Abraham–and they will be judged as a nation. Study carefully Matthew 25: 1–30, and you will plainly see that this judgment has to do with the entire nation. You will also see that God is judging Israel in order to separate the saved from the unsaved. The works of the individual will be brought into judgment. This is made very clear in Ezekiel 20:37,38:

"And I will cause you to pass under the rod, and I will bring you into the bond of the covenant: And I will purge out from among you the rebels, and them that

transgress against me . . . ."

"But who may abide the day of His coming? and who shall stand when He appeareth? for He is like a refiner's fire, and like fullers' soap: And He shall sit as a refiner and purifier of silver: and He shall purify the sons of Levi, and purge them as gold and silver, that they may offer unto the Lord an offering in righteousness. Then shall the offering of Judah and Jerusalem be pleasant unto the Lord, as in the days of old, and as in former years. And I will come near to you to judgment; and I will be a swift witness against the sorcerers, and against the adulterers, and against false swearers, and against those that oppress the hireling in his wages, the widow, and the fatherless, and that turn aside the stranger from his right, and fear not me, saith the Lord of hosts" (Malachi 3:2–5).

The result of this judgment will be twofold: *First*, the unsaved will be cut off from the land: ". . . I will bring them forth out of the country where they sojourn, AND THEY SHALL NOT ENTER INTO THE LAND OF ISRAEL: and ye shall know that I am the Lord" (Ezek. 20:38b). "And cast ye the unprofitable servant into outer darkness: there shall be weeping and gnashing of teeth" (Matt. 25:30).

Through these Scriptures we learn that the unsaved will be cast into hell-fire before the Millennium begins (the one thousand years of Christ's reign on earth).

Second, the saved will be taken into the Millennium to share the blessings of the thousand years of peace on earth, good will toward men, when Jesus reigns from the throne of David: ". . . And I will bring you into the bond of the covenant" (Ezek. 20:37b).

Paul enlightens us concerning this judgment upon

Israel: "*And so all Israel shall be saved: as it is written, There shall come out of Sion the Deliverer, and shall turn away ungodliness from Jacob: For this is my covenant unto them, when I shall take away their sins*" (Rom. 11:26,27).

Yes, God will regather the nation Israel at the second coming of Christ. He will divide the saved from the unsaved. The saved will be taken into the kingdom prepared for them from the foundation of the world; the unsaved will be cut off and cast into hell-fire. God will keep His promise to Abraham and to His chosen people, Israel.

It is spiritual robbery to take the promises God made to Abraham and spiritualize them, giving them to the Church. Israel is an earthly people with earthly promises; the Church of the living God is a heavenly people with heavenly blessings.

The Judgment of the Nations

The second future judgment which will occur after the Rapture of the Church is the judgment upon the Gentiles. The time of this judgment, as recorded in Matthew 24 and 25, follows the judgment upon the nation Israel. Joel describes it in these words: "For, behold, in those days, and in that time, when I shall bring again the captivity of Judah and Jerusalem, I will also gather all nations, and will bring them down into the valley of Jehoshaphat, and will plead with them there for my people and for my heritage Israel, whom they have scattered among the nations, and parted my land" (Joel 3:1,2).

The prophet Joel revealed to us that the judgment on the Gentiles will take place at the same time the Lord restores Israel to the land given to them for an everlasting possession when God made His covenant with faithful Abraham. The restoration of the land to Israel will take place at the second advent. Therefore the judgment on the Gentile nations must fall at the time of the second advent, after the regathering of and judgment on Israel. The judgment of the Gentiles must precede the Millennium, for those accepted in this judgment will enter the kingdom: "Then shall the King say unto them on His right hand, Come, ye blessed of my Father, inherit the kingdom prepared for you from the foundation of the world" (Matt. 25:34).

The judgment of the Gentiles will take place right here upon this earth. There is not one iota of Scripture that suggests that any of these nations will come back from the dead. Nor is there Scripture to suggest that any of them will descend from heaven to be judged. The language used clearly pin-points the judgment (and the nations) here on earth. In Joel 3:2 it is clearly stated that the judgment will take place in the valley of Jehoshaphat. ("Jehoshaphat" means *Jehovah judges.*)

The judgment upon the Gentiles will be on living individuals, not those who have died. The resurrection of all the wicked dead will take place later. There is a definite judgment concerning the wicked dead, and we will study it a little later. The Gentiles will be judged on the basis of their treatment of a group whom the King calls "my brethren." This, of course, refers to the nation Israel:

"And the King shall answer and say unto them, Verily I say unto you, Inasmuch as ye have done it unto one of the least of these my brethren, ye have done it unto me. . . Then shall He answer them, saying, Verily I say unto you, Inasmuch as ye did it not to one of the least of these, ye did it not to me" (Matt. 25:40,45). This definitely refers to the Jews who will be gathered in their own land during the time preceding this judgment.

Notice that in Joel 3:2 Israel is the center of the

entire judgment program of Almighty God: "I will also gather all nations . . . and will plead with them there for my people and for my heritage Israel, whom they have scattered among the nations, and parted my land."

Note what Isaiah has to say concerning the people of Israel who will be believing witnesses and will no doubt preach the Gospel of the kingdom. We read of such a group in Revelation 7:4–8, where 12,000 from every tribe of Israel will be sealed with God's seal in their foreheads. In Isaiah 66:19 and 20 we read, "And I will set a sign among them, and I will send those that escape of them unto the nations, to Tarshish, Pul, and Lud, that draw the bow, to Tubal, and Javan, to the isles afar off, that have not heard my fame, neither have seen my glory; and they shall declare my glory among the Gentiles. And they shall bring all your brethren for an offering unto the Lord out of all nations upon horses, and in chariots, and in litters, and upon mules, and upon swift beasts, to my holy mountain Jerusalem, saith the Lord, as the children of Israel bring an offering in a clean vessel into the house of the Lord."

This judgment upon the Gentiles must be a judgment to determine the spiritual condition of the Gentiles who will be judged. This judgment is to determine whether the one being judged is saved or unsaved. Those who casually look at God's Word would have you believe that the outcome of the judgment depends upon the *works* of the individual; but when we *study* the Word of God, comparing spiritual things with spiritual and rightly dividing the Word of truth, the Scripture does not support this conclusion.

In the first place, the Word of God does not teach–in any book, chapter, or verse–that man is saved by works. Nowhere in Scripture is salvation offered on the basis of works. In Matthew 25:46 we read, "And these shall go away into everlasting punishment: but the righteous into life eternal." Here we clearly see that the eternal destiny of those appearing before the Judge in this judgment is to be decided. Certainly this could not be a judgment of works, for eternal destiny is never decided according to works, but on the basis of whether the one judged accepts or rejects the finished work of Christ in our behalf.

Notice that those who had fed, clothed, given drink to, and visited the "brethren" were called "righteous." The only way for one to become righteous, either in the Old Testament era or in this day of grace–or even during the tribulation–is through the righteousness of God. Apart from God there IS no righteousness. All men of all times are sinners by nature, and the only way anyone can become righteous is by receiving the righteousness of God. It is definitely contrary to the teaching of the Word of God to suggest that these people will enter the kingdom because of their righteous works. They will perform righteous works toward Israel because they have been made righteous in their hearts by hearing the Gospel of the kingdom and receiving the Christ who will be the King.

During this period the "brethren" will preach the Gospel of the kingdom: "And this Gospel of the kingdom shall be preached in all the world for a witness unto all nations" (Matt. 24:14). The Gospel of the kingdom which will be preached to all nations by the faithful, righteous Israelites (the sealed ones) will require personal faith in the sacrifice of Jesus, the finished work accomplished in His death, burial, and resurrection. Before the Cross the Old Testament saints were saved by faith, *looking forward to the Cross* (Heb. 11:4). Since the Cross–even after the Rapture–all who are saved are saved by faith in *the finished work of Jesus on the cross.* There has never been, nor will there ever be, salvation apart from the sacrificial death of the Lamb of God.

Jesus said, "Except ye be converted, and become as little children, ye shall not enter into the kingdom of heaven" (Matt. 18:3). You may rest assured that Jesus has not revoked this clear command. It is imperative that the individual exercise faith in the finished work of Jesus in order to enter the Kingdom of Heaven.

Many ask, "Does this judgment have to do with individuals, or with nations? Will it be on a national basis, or on an individual basis?" In Revelation 7:9–17 we read of a great multitude who will come out of great tribulation, who will wash their robes and make them white in the blood of the Lamb. These were saved only as individuals, because they came out of every nation, every tongue, every tribe and kindred. If this judgment were on a national basis, then whole nations would be permitted to enter the Millennium. Certainly no nation on earth is made up entirely of saved people, and we know that unsaved people will not enter the Millennium. Study carefully Matthew 18:3; 25:31–46; Jeremiah 31:33,34; Ezekiel 20:37,38; and Zechariah 13:9.

Yes, this will be an individual judgment to determine whether the individual is saved or lost, whether the individual has received or rejected the message of the kingdom. All other judgments in the program of Almighty God have to do with individuals–not with groups, families, or nations. No other part of God's program is interpreted other than having to do with the *individual* when that individual stands before God to be judged. Other passages having to do with the judgment at the end of the age, in connection with the second coming of Christ, certainly teach individual judgment:

"Let both grow together until the harvest: and in the time of harvest I will say to the reapers, Gather ye together first the tares, and bind them in bundles to burn them: but gather the wheat into my barn. . . Again, the kingdom of heaven is like unto a net, that was cast into the sea, and gathered of every kind: Which, when it was full, they drew to shore, and sat down, and gathered the good into vessels, but cast the bad away. So shall it be at the end of the world: the angels shall come forth, and sever the wicked from among the just, and shall cast them into the furnace of fire: there shall be wailing and gnashing of teeth" (Matt. 13:30, 47–50).

"And Enoch also, the seventh from Adam, prophesied of these, saying, Behold, the Lord cometh with ten thousands of His saints, to execute judgment upon all, and to convince all that are ungodly among them of all their ungodly deeds which they have ungodly committed, and of all their hard speeches which ungodly sinners have spoken against Him" (Jude 14 and 15).

The result of the judgment of the Gentile nations will be twofold: Those who have been appointed to the King's right hand will hear the invitation, "Come, ye blessed of my Father, inherit the kingdom prepared for you from the foundation of the world" (Matt. 25:34). In the second place, those who are commanded to sit on the King's left hand will hear the solemn words of doom: "Depart from me, ye cursed, into everlasting fire, prepared for the devil and his angels" (Matt. 25:41). From these passages we see that one group is taken into the kingdom, thereby becoming subjects of the King to reign with Him, while the other group is excluded from the kingdom and consigned to hell-fire. THUS WE HAVE FULFILLED DANIEL 7:14, ISAIAH 55:5, and MICAH 4:2 in this group of Gentiles taken into the kingdom:

"And there was given Him dominion, and glory, and a kingdom, that all people, nations, and languages, should serve Him: His dominion is an everlasting dominion, which shall not pass away, and His kingdom that which shall not be destroyed" (Dan. 7:14).

"Behold, thou shalt call a nation that thou knowest not, and nations that knew not thee shall run unto thee because of the Lord thy God, and for the Holy One of Israel; for He hath glorified thee" (Isa. 55:5).

"And many nations shall come, and say, Come, and let us go up to the mountain of the Lord, and to the house of the God of Jacob; and He will teach us of His ways, and we will walk in His paths: for the law shall go forth of Zion, and the word of the Lord from Jerusalem" (Micah 4:2).

The kingdom will be Israel's kingdom—but there will be a great number of Gentiles brought into the kingdom who will share under the King's reign during the Millennium, the time of which nations and politicians have talked a great deal, but which they have done but little to bring about.

The Judgment of the Fallen Angels

The third judgment in line after the Rapture of the Church will be the judgment of the fallen angels. Jude reveals to us the solemn fact that angels will be brought into judgment: "And the angels which kept not their first estate, but left their own habitation, He hath reserved in everlasting chains under darkness unto the judgment of the great day" (Jude 6). The time of this judgment will be "the great day," which undoubtedly refers to the Day of the Lord—the day in which all judgment is to be fulfilled.

The judgment of these fallen angels is evidently associated with the judgment of Satan, which precedes the great White Throne judgment: "And the devil that deceived them was cast into the lake of fire and brimstone, where the beast and the false prophet are, and shall be tormented day and night for ever and ever" (Rev. 20:10). We therefore conclude that these fallen angels will be judged after the Millennium, but before the great White Throne judgment. As to the place of the judgment of these angels, the Word of God does not enlighten us; however, since the judgment has to do with angels, it is logical to suppose that it will take place in the angelic realm. Since the Judge is the King, and since these are fallen angels, having rebelled against the God of heaven and attempted to overthrow His throne, it might be suggested that they will be brought back to the very place where their rebellion took place, and there they will be judged.

Only fallen angels will be present at this judgment: "For if God spared not the angels that sinned, but cast them down to hell, and delivered them into chains of darkness, to be reserved unto judgment" (II Pet. 2:4). The basis of this judgment is their one sin of following Satan in his rebellion against God. Satan was an angel in his original state. He was "the anointed cherub . . . the shining one." He was no doubt the chief archangel; but he became jealous and envious of God, brainwashed some of the angels and led them to believe that he, with their support, could overthrow God and take the throne, thus no longer being subordinate to God but superior to Him. But since Satan and the angels are created beings, and the Creator is greater than the created, God cast them out. These fallen angels will be judged on the basis of their sin against God, their Creator; and the result will be that they will be cast into the lake of fire forever.

Sin is synonymous with eternal destruction. Sin brings death—whether it be a heavenly creature or a creature of earth. "The wages of sin is death," and nothing that defiles will be permitted to enter into God's presence or into the new creation: "And there shall in no wise enter into it any thing that defileth, neither whatsoever worketh abomination, or maketh a lie: but they which are written in the Lamb's book of life" (Rev. 21:27).

The Great White Throne Judgment

And now we come to the final judgment: *The great White Throne judgment.* "And I saw a great white throne, and Him that sat on it, from whose face the earth and the heaven fled away; and there was found no place for them. And I saw the dead, small and great, stand before God; and the books were opened: and another book was opened, which is the book of life: and the dead were judged out of those things which were written in the books, according to their works. And the sea gave up the dead which were in it; and death and hell delivered up the dead which were in them: and they were judged every man according to their works. And death and hell were cast into the lake of fire. This is the second death. And whosoever was not found written in the book of life was cast into the lake of fire" (Rev. 20:11–15).

The great White Throne judgment can be rightly called "the final judgment." It constitutes the termination of God's resurrection and His judgment program. It is the last judgment. The time of the great White Throne judgment is clearly pointed out: It will take place AFTER the Millennium:

"But the rest of the dead lived not again until the thousand years were finished. . . And I saw the dead, small and great, stand before God; and the books were opened: and another book was opened, which is the book of life: and the dead were judged out of those things which were written in the books, according to their works.

And the sea gave up the dead which were in it; and death and hell delivered up the dead which were in them: and they were judged every man according to their works" (Rev. 20:5, 12, 13).

The place where this judgment will take place is not in heaven or on earth, but somewhere *between* heaven and earth: "And I saw a great white throne, and Him that sat on it, from whose face the earth and the heaven fled away; and there was found no place for them" (Rev. 20:11). This verse is self-explanatory.

Those who will be judged at the great White Throne judgment are referred to as "the dead." The bodies of all believers who die before the Rapture will be raised when Jesus descends in the air to call the Church up to meet Him in the clouds in the air. The only ones left unresurrected are the unsaved dead; therefore, all unbelievers who have died or who will die after the Rapture will be the subjects of the great White Throne judgment.

There is not one suggestion that this judgment has anything to do with any living person. All the living have been judged, and only the wicked dead remain to be judged when the great White Throne is set.

The basis for the White Throne judgment is not whether those to be judged are saved or lost. ALL who appear at the great White Throne judgment are already lost. The saved have already been rewarded for their stewardship and are already entered into their eternal state. The great White Throne judgment will have to do with the evil works of the ungodly. The sentence passed upon them is "the second death": "And death and hell were cast into the lake of fire. This is the second death" (Rev. 20:14).

The wicked dead will be judged according to their wicked works. That there will be degrees of punishment in the lake of fire is clearly taught in this passage, and in other passages as well:

"And that servant, which knew his lord's will, and prepared not himself, neither did according to his will, shall be beaten with many stripes. But he that knew not, and did commit things worthy of stripes, shall be beaten with few stripes. For unto whomsoever much is given, of him shall be much required: and to whom men have committed much, of him they will ask the more" (Luke 12:47,48).

However, the sentence of "second death" will be passed upon all who appear at the great White Throne judgment. Those who have been extremely wicked will be punished according to the degree of their wickedness.

The *first death* was that spiritual death which was suffered in Adam. Paul tells us, "In Adam all die." David declared that we are born in sin and shapen in iniquity. We inherit spiritual death from Adam. This "second death" is the confirmation—and making eternal—of that separation from God which the first death entailed. All who refuse to believe on the Lord Jesus Christ will die eternally. All who hear the Gospel and believe on the Lord Jesus Christ have everlasting life.

The result of the great White Throne judgment is clearly stated in these words: *"And whosoever was not found written in the book of life was cast into the lake of fire."* All who are at the White Throne judgment will be eternally separated from God and confined to the lake of fire—the destiny of all unbelievers.

General Judgment Unscriptural

It is almost unbelievable that anyone could study the Word of God and still believe in a general resurrection and a general judgment. There are no less than eight different judgments mentioned in Scripture, each of which occurs at a different time and a different place; each judgment concerns different subjects and is on a different basis. Each produces a different result.

Many Bible teachers suggest that Matthew 25:31–46 and Revelation 20:11–15 are one and the same; but there are many distinctions between these two judgments. If we study and rightly divide the Word of truth, it is impossible to make these two passages of Scripture refer to the same judgment. For instance, in Matthew there is no resurrection before the judgment, but a *gathering of His elect* (Matt. 24:31). In John's account in Revelation, there is definitely a resurrection of all unbelievers. In Matthew the judgment has to do with living nations; but in Revelation it has to do with "*the dead.*" In Matthew, *nations* are judged; but in Revelation, it could not be a judgment of nations, but only of *individuals*, for they are judged after heaven and earth flee away. Nations are certainly confined to the earth, and if the earth is to "flee away" then there certainly could be no nations present.

In Matthew, the judgment takes place here on earth; but in Revelation, heaven and earth are fled away. Therefore, the judgment in Revelation must be somewhere in God's great "outer space." In Matthew no BOOKS are mentioned, but in Revelation THE BOOKS WILL BE OPENED. The book of life will be brought forth, and those who are judged will be judged out of the things written in the books. Those who do not have their names in the book of life will be cast into the fire.

In Matthew the judgment occurs at the return of Christ to this earth; but in Revelation it takes place a thousand years AFTER Jesus returns to the earth. In Matthew we have two classes of people–the righteous and the wicked; but in Revelation we have only one class–*the wicked.* In

Matthew we learn that some will enter the kingdom, and some will go into everlasting punishment; but in Revelation at the great White Throne judgment there is no blessing, no eternal life: *There is only eternal punishment in the lake of fire.*

In Matthew we see the Judge seated on the throne of His glory (Matt. 25:31). But in Revelation He is seated on the great White Throne. In Matthew the basis of the judgment is the treatment shown the "brethren"; and the reason some will treat the "brethren" with love, compassion and pity is because they will have obeyed the Gospel of the kingdom. Others will persecute the "brethren" because they will reject the message. However, in Revelation the judgment is based on evil works only—there is no mention of good works.

In Matthew the coming of Christ precedes the judgment; but in Revelation there is no coming of Christ mentioned. His coming occurred more than a thousand years previously. In Matthew sheep, goats, and brethren are named; but in Revelation one class only is named—*the wicked.*

In Matthew the sentence is pronounced and the result is declared before the cause of the judgment is spelled out; but there is no judgment in Revelation until after a careful examination of the record in the books. Those to be judged in Revelation are judged carefully according to the record and the books written against them because of their wickedness.

In Matthew there has been no one thousand years of peace on earth and good will toward men. We find that there were those who hungered and thirsted, they were naked, they were strangers, they were sick and in prison, they were destitute; but in Revelation a thousand years of peace on earth and good will toward men precede the great White Throne judgment: "But the rest of the dead lived not again until the thousand years were finished. . ." (Rev. 20:5).

It seems to me that the facts stated here are sufficient to support the declaration that there is no such thing as a general judgment, and that the judgments in Matthew 25 and Revelation 20 are not one and the same, but are two separate parts of the judgment program of Almighty God.

I have taken this time and used this space to point out God's judgment program in order to make this declaration, and it is from my heart. It is my own personal belief. In our present section of verses 9 through 12 of Daniel 7, there is more than one judgment. I stated earlier that there are no less than eight judgments mentioned in Scripture. Notice in Daniel 7:9: "I beheld till the *thrones* (plural) were cast down"—not "*throne*" (singular). ". . . And the Ancient of days did sit, whose garment was white as snow, and the hair of His head like the pure wool." Then the Holy Spirit points out, "*His throne was like the fiery flame, and His wheels as burning fire.*" This seems to point to the great White Throne judgment. When the nations are judged we do not read about fire, or flame, or the blazing whiteness of Shekinah glory. Neither do we read of fire or flame in the judgment of Israel nor in the judgment of the fallen angels—but *only when the wicked dead are raised* at the great White Throne (or the final) judgment.

We notice in verse 10 of our present chapter, "*A fiery stream issued and came forth from before Him: thousand thousands ministered unto Him, and ten thousand times ten thousand stood before Him: the judgment was set, and the books were opened.*" Nowhere in the Word of God do we read of books being opened except at the great White Throne judgment, where the record of every wicked person will be there to face the unbeliever. There are no books mentioned concerning the judgment of Israel as a nation, nor concerning the Gentiles, nor the fallen angels. The fallen angels are simply "reserved in chains," and they will be brought forth and consigned to the lake of fire; but here in our present verse there is a "fiery stream" issuing–and we notice that only one out of a hundred are ministering, while ninety-nine stand to be judged! This seems to point to the great White Throne judgment.

In verse 11 we notice that Daniel declares that "because of the voice of the great words which the horn spake," he stopped to look and listen; and here is what we find: "I beheld even till the beast was slain, and his body destroyed, and given to the burning flame." In Revelation 19:20 we read, "And the beast was taken, and with him the false prophet that wrought miracles before him, with which he deceived them that had received the mark of the beast, and them that worshipped his image.' These both were cast alive into a lake of fire burning with brimstone." And this occurs immediately after the "Alleluias" in heaven (Rev. 19:1–6), the marriage supper of the Lamb (Rev. 19:7–9), and the appearing of Christ in glory (Rev. 19:11–16):

"And I saw heaven opened, and behold a white horse; and He that sat upon him was called Faithful and True, and in righteousness He doth judge and make war. His eyes were as a flame of fire, and on His head were many crowns; and He had a name written, that no man knew, but He Himself. And He was clothed with a vesture dipped in blood: and His name is called The Word of God. And the armies which were in heaven followed Him upon white horses, clothed in fine linen, white and clean. And out of His mouth goeth a sharp sword, that with it

He should smite the nations: and He shall rule them with a rod of iron: and He treadeth the winepress of the fierceness and wrath of Almighty God. And He hath on His vesture and on His thigh a name written, KING OF KINGS, AND LORD OF LORDS" (Rev. 19:11–16).

Immediately following this gripping description of the second coming of Christ with the saints riding upon white horses, we are given a moving account of the Battle of Armageddon. An angel is seen standing in the sun, crying with a loud voice, calling the fowls of the air to come to the supper of the great God. They are called to devour the flesh of kings, captains, mighty men and horses, soldiers, men both bond and free, small and great. And in verse 19 we read, *"And I saw the beast, and the kings of the earth, and their armies, gathered together to make war against Him that sat on the horse, and against His army."* We know, of course, that He who is seated on the beautiful white horse is none other than the Lord Jesus Christ, "the Ancient of days."

It is at this time that Jesus defeats the beast and the false prophet, and they are both cast alive into the lake burning with fire and brimstone. This occurs at the end of the tribulation, immediately preceding the Millennium. Therefore, I say in my humble and limited opinion, after much study and prayer, *I see more than one judgment set forth in Daniel 7:9–12.* I believe that verse 10 deals with the great White Throne judgment, while verse 11 has to do with the judgment of the beast, the false prophet, and the armies that are gathered around Jerusalem with the desire to wipe out God's people Israel and the saved nations who will be in the land of Israel when Jesus comes in the Revelation with His saints to set up the kingdom.

Verses 13 and 14 of this chapter set forth and describe

the coming of the Lord Jesus to set up the kingdom here on earth. The kingdom is given to Jesus; glory, power, and majesty are given to Him; and entering that kingdom are all people, nations, and languages who are saved. They will serve Him in His dominion. His kingdom is everlasting; it shall not pass away; it shall not be destroyed.

Isaiah describes the King in these words: "For unto us a Child is born, unto us a Son is given: and the government shall be upon His shoulder: and His name shall be called Wonderful, Counsellor, The mighty God, The everlasting Father, The Prince of Peace. Of the increase of His government and peace there shall be no end, upon the throne of David, and upon His kingdom, to order it, and to establish it with judgment and with justice from henceforth even for ever. The zeal of the Lord of hosts will perform this" (Isa. 9:6,7).

Gabriel said to the virgin Mary, "And, behold, thou shalt conceive in thy womb, and bring forth a Son, and shalt call His name JESUS. He shall be great, and shall be called the Son of the Highest: and the Lord God shall give unto Him the throne of His father David: AND HE SHALL REIGN OVER THE HOUSE OF JACOB FOR EVER; AND OF HIS KINGDOM THERE SHALL BE NO END" (Luke 1:31–33).

Perhaps someone is asking, "What about the one thousand years–the Millennium–if He shall reign over the house of Jacob forever and His kingdom is to be an everlasting kingdom that shall never be destroyed?" The answer is simple to all who live by faith:

There will be one thousand years of peace on earth and good will toward men. That time is described in Isaiah 11:6–9. It will be a time when the cow and the bear shall feed, their young ones shall lie down together.

"The lion shall eat straw like the ox. And the sucking child shall play on the hole of the asp, and the weaned child shall put his hand on the cockatrice' den." There will be no killing or hurting in all the earth, because the earth will be "full of the knowledge of the Lord, as the waters cover the sea."

Thus we have the description of the Millennium—the one thousand years of the reign of Christ here upon earth. However, the Millennium will give way to the *everlasting kingdom* of God. Jesus will be King, and this is described in Isaiah 65:17–25 and also parts of Isaiah 66. Isaiah declares that there will be new heavens and a new earth, "and the former shall not be remembered, nor come into mind." Jerusalem will be a city of rejoicing; there will be no more weeping, no more "infant of days," no old people who have filled their days or come to the end of their years. "And they shall build houses, and inhabit them; and they shall plant vineyards, and eat the fruit of them." They will not build for someone else to inhabit their homes, nor plant for another to eat of their fruit. They shall not labour in vain, nor shall they "bring forth for trouble." They are the seed of the blessed of the Lord. "And it shall come to pass, that before they call, I will answer; and while they are yet speaking, I will hear. The wolf and the lamb shall feed together, and the lion shall eat straw like the bullock: and dust shall be the serpent's meat. *They shall not hurt nor destroy in all my holy mountain, saith the Lord.*"

I repeat: God made an everlasting covenant with Abraham. God gave the land of Palestine to Abraham for an everlasting possession. By the establishment of the kingdom on earth for one thousand years under the Messianic King, God will have accomplished His purpose. There will be a new heaven and a new earth. At this time Christ will hand over the mediatorial kingdom to God, to be merged into the *eternal kingdom*—so that the mediatorial kingdom is perpetuated forever, but no longer having a separate identity (I Cor. 15:24,28). The Millennium will just move into the new earth, and the kingdom over which Jesus will reign will last throughout the eternal ages. There will be no end to the reign of righteousness with King Jesus sitting on the throne.

The Third Vision

Verses 13 and 14: "I saw in the night visions, and, behold, one like the Son of man came with the clouds of heaven, and came to the Ancient of days, and they brought Him near before Him. And there was given Him dominion, and glory, and a kingdom, that all people, nations, and languages, should serve Him: His dominion is an everlasting dominion, which shall not pass away, and His kingdom that which shall not be destroyed."

In these verses we see the scene in heaven before the coming of the Lord Jesus to receive His kingdom. Daniel saw this vision at night time, and he beheld one "like the Son of man," who came with the clouds of heaven. He came to the Ancient of days (God the Father), and to Him was given "dominion, and glory, and a kingdom, that all people, nations, and languages should serve Him." This sounds like the great multitude which no man could number, in Revelation 7:9–15. The dominion of the King of kings is an everlasting dominion; it shall never pass away nor be destroyed (Isa. 9:6,7).

Yes, there is a day coming when the nations will beat their swords into plowshares and their spears into pruning hooks, and man will study war no more. Peace on earth and good will toward men will prevail on earth—but only when Jesus sits on the throne in Jerusalem.

The Scriptures teach that Jesus will receive the kingdom from the Father (Luke 1:32,33; 22:29). Therefore, the "Ancient of days" in this vision must represent *God the Father.* Pilate asked Jesus, "Art thou the king of the Jews?" Jesus did not say, "Yes, I am king of the Jews." He simply said, "To this end I was born. . . My kingdom is not of this world." That is to say, "My kingdom is not here, *now*; my Father will give me the kingdom, and it will come from heaven." Study carefully John 18:33–37.

"And as they heard these things, He added and spake a parable, because He was nigh to Jerusalem, and because they thought that the kingdom of God should immediately appear. He said therefore, A certain nobleman went into a far country to receive for himself a kingdom, and to return" (Luke 19:11,12). We learn from this parable that Jesus is that "certain nobleman" who has gone into a far country–*Heaven*–to receive the kingdom. When He has received it He will return to this earth, and *the Kingdom of Heaven will BE on earth.* Jesus has not yet received the kingdom, and He will not receive it until all His enemies are made His footstool and the knowledge of the Lord covers the earth as the waters cover the sea. We will have new heavens and a new earth wherein dwelleth righteousness:

"And the seventh angel sounded; and there were great voices in heaven, saying, THE KINGDOMS OF THIS WORLD ARE BECOME THE KINGDOMS OF OUR LORD, AND OF HIS CHRIST; AND HE SHALL REIGN FOR EVER AND EVER" (Rev. 11:15).

Daniel Troubled because of the Visions

Verse 15: "I Daniel was grieved in my spirit in the midst of my body, and the visions of my head troubled me."

These three visions which Daniel saw in succession troubled him exceedingly. He knew from Nebuchadnezzar's dream-vision of the great image of gold, silver, brass, iron, iron-and-clay, that there were to be four great world empires to succeed each other before the times of the Gentiles would come to a close and the stone "cut out of the mountain without hands" would fill the whole earth. Daniel knew that the first empire–Babylon–was still in existence, with no signs at that time of a speedy ending of her far-reaching power; and if the three empires to follow should each last as long as Babylon had, the end of "the times of the Gentiles" would be a great way off in the future. To Daniel, this meant that the setting up of the stone kingdom–the kingdom of God on earth–was far, far away; but what troubled him most of all was the *character* of the four wild beasts and the meaning of the little horn that came up out of the ten horns of the last beast of his vision.

Verse 16: "I came near unto one of them that stood by, and asked him the truth of all this. So he told me, and made me know the interpretation of the things."

The one whom Daniel approached was certainly not a human being. When Daniel "came near to one of them that stood by," he was still in the vision–and certainly no *human* could have revealed himself to Daniel in the visions, to make known the meaning of them. The one approached by Daniel was a heavenly messenger like the messenger sent to him later; and this messenger was waiting to interpret the visions and make known the meaning thereof.

The Three Visions Interpreted

Verses 17 and 18: "These great beasts, which are four, are four kings, which shall arise out of the earth. But the saints of the most High shall take the kingdom, and possess the kingdom for ever, even for ever and ever."

This heavenly bystander to whom Daniel came near

informed him that the four wild beasts of the visions represented four kings–four world empires which should rise in the earth–thus identifying them with the four empires represented by the metals in the image seen in Nebuchadnezzar's dream.

The vision also revealed to Daniel that the power of these world empires would be taken from them by "THE SAINTS OF THE MOST HIGH," and that the kingdom of the saints of the most High would last forever. Who ARE these "saints of the most High"? Some would have us believe that these are the believers of today who make up the Church; but the saints who make up the New Testament Church will be caught out before the tribulation begins, before Antichrist takes over *and makes war with the saints*: "I beheld, and the same horn made war with the saints, and prevailed against them" (verse 21). The location of the war between the little horn and the saints of the most High will be here upon the earth during the reign of the Antichrist, and according to verse 25 is to last for three and one-half years: "And he shall speak great words against the most High, *and shall wear out the saints of the most High*, and think to change times and laws: and they shall be given into his hand until a time and times and the dividing of time."

"*A time, and times, and the dividing of time*" is three and one-half years–the last half of Daniel's seventieth week of the seventy weeks of prophecy–or the time of the Great Tribulation here upon this earth. Therefore, "*the saints of the most High*" must refer to Daniel's people, the Jews. "*The most High*" is definitely the Son of man, the Messiah. The Jews were looking for their Messiah–yet they did not recognize Him when He came, and they nailed Him to a cross! But when He comes the second time, they will recognize the scars in His hands; they will know Him and receive Him, and He will be their *Messiah* in the end time. They are the people who will suffer the most severe torment and terror during the reign of the Antichrist, the false messiah.

In verse 27 of our present chapter we read: "And the kingdom and dominion, and the greatness of the kingdom under the whole heaven, shall be given to the people of the saints of the most High, whose kingdom is an everlasting kingdom, and all dominions shall serve and obey Him." God will save the tents of Judah first, and the Jews will be the head of the nations during the Millennium: "And the Lord shall make thee the head, and not the tail; and thou shalt be above only, and thou shalt not be beneath; if that thou hearken unto the commandments of the Lord thy God, which I command thee this day, to observe and to do them" (Deut. 28:13).

It seems that Daniel did not fully understand the fourth wild beast (the little horn) and this little horn making war on the saints of the most High.

Daniel Desires to Know More

Verses 19 and 20: "Then I would know the truth of the fourth beast, which was diverse from all the others, exceeding dreadful, whose teeth were of iron, and his nails of brass; which devoured, brake in pieces, and stamped the residue with his feet; and of the ten horns that were in his head, and of the other which came up, and before whom three fell; even of that horn that had eyes, and a mouth that spake very great things, whose look was more stout than his fellows."

This beast was "exceeding dreadful," with teeth of iron and nails of brass. He "devoured, and brake in pieces, and stamped the residue with his feet." Daniel marveled at the unusual sight of ten horns, with the little horn coming up out of these ten horns. This horn had a mouth and eyes, and was speaking great swelling words. Daniel wanted to know the meaning of this unusual creature.

Verses 21 and 22: "I beheld, and the same horn made war with the saints, and prevailed against them; until the Ancient of days came, and judgment was given to the saints of the most High; and the time came that the saints possessed the kingdom."

Daniel was perplexed and extremely concerned that the little horn made war against the saints and prevailed against them. The little horn was winning the victory over the people of Daniel until "the Ancient of days" came to the rescue and judgment was given to the saints of the most High; *and then the saints possessed the kingdom.*

The Explanation of the Fourth Beast

Verses 23–28: "Thus he said, The fourth beast shall be the fourth kingdom upon earth, which shall be diverse from all kingdoms, and shall devour the whole earth, and shall tread it down, and break it in pieces. And the ten horns out of this kingdom are ten kings that shall arise: and another shall rise after them; and he shall be diverse from the first, and he shall subdue three kings. And he shall speak great words against the most High, and shall wear out the saints of the most High, and think to change times and laws: and they shall be given into his hand until a time and times and the dividing of time. But the judgment shall sit, and they shall take away his dominion, to consume and to destroy it unto the end. And the kingdom and dominion, and the greatness of the kingdom under the whole heaven, shall be given to the people of the saints of the most High, whose kingdom is an everlasting kingdom, and all dominions shall serve and obey him. Hitherto is the end of the matter. As for me Daniel, my cogitations much troubled me, and my countenance changed in me: but I kept the matter in my heart."

We have here two figures that demand our strict attention: The first is *the beast*; the second is *the little horn.* If we are to understand the fourth beast, the horns, and the "*little horn,*" we must distinguish between them.

The little horn shall "*think to change times and laws: and they shall be given into his hand until a time and times and the dividing of time*" (Dan. 7:25). Prophetically, "time" is one year, "times" is two years, and "the dividing of time" is one-half year. Therefore the little horn will be at the zenith of his power for three and one-half years.

The people of Israel understood what was meant by "times and laws." To the Jewish rabbi, "times and laws" referred to the Hebrew Sabbaths and festivals, and the "law" (Levitical) which regulated them. These set times and laws will be re-established when the Jews return to Palestine to rebuild the temple, and will be in force when Antichrist (the little horn) makes a covenant with the Jews for one week (a period of seven years). In the middle of this "one week" the Antichrist will break the covenant: "He shall confirm the covenant with many for one week: and in the midst of the week he shall cause the sacrifice and the oblation to cease, and for the overspreading of abominations he shall make it desolate, even until the consummation, and that determined shall be poured upon the desolate" (Dan. 9:27).

He will forbid the Jews to worship God any longer and will substitute himself as God. He will cause the Jewish sacrifices and oblations to cease—and in his fanatical desire to annihilate all the Jewish people and institutions he will think to change all Jewish rituals, ceremonies, laws, commandments, and anything else that has to do with Jewish worship, referred to here as "times and laws." He will carry out this strict order during the last half of Daniel's seventieth week of the seventy weeks of prophecy—the last three and one-half years of the tribulation.

In Revelation 6:2 the Antichrist rides out on a white horse. He will be carrying a bow, but he will not have an arrow—the deadly part of the weapon; and he will go forth conquering, and to conquer. He will gain the respect of the world through flatteries, promising peace; and for three and one-half years there will BE peace; but after three and one-half years he will take away all the times and laws having to do with the Jews, who will then be back in their own country, and all hell will break out upon this earth. The white horse is followed by the RED horse—the horse of blood; and by the BLACK horse of famine and the PALE horse of death. Blood will run in the streets like water after a summer rain.

The Fourth Beast

"The fourth beast shall be the fourth kingdom upon the earth, which shall be diverse from all kingdoms, and shall devour the whole earth, and shall tread it down, and break it in pieces" (Dan. 7:23). Note that this beast has iron teeth, which characteristic identifies it with the iron legs of the image Nebuchadnezzar saw in his dream; and the ten horns on the head of the fourth beast correspond to the ten toes of the image, or the last stage of the Roman empire. So we see that this fourth beast represents the Roman empire in its first stage, and also in its last stage, under the rule of the "little horn."

In this beast, however, is not revealed what happens to the Gentile dominions and powers between the first and last stages of Gentile world dominion; but we *do have* the revelation of what takes place during the last days of Gentile power:

In Revelation, chapters 6 through 19, we find the details of what will take place during Daniel's seventieth week (the period covered by the ten toes of the image and also represented here in Daniel by the fourth wild beast). John gives us this reign of terror in heart-rending, soul-searching description, and the Revelation sheds much light on the fourth beast.

Daniel's Beast Compared with John's Beast

Daniel 7:7,8: "After this I saw in the night visions, and behold a fourth beast, dreadful and terrible, and strong exceedingly; and it had great iron teeth: it devoured and brake in pieces, and stamped the residue with the feet of it: and it was diverse from all the beasts that were before it; and it had ten horns. I considered the horns, and, behold, there came up among them another little horn, before whom there were three of the first horns plucked up by the roots: and, behold, in this horn were eyes like the eyes of man, and a mouth speaking great things."

Notice again: "Thus he said, The fourth beast shall be the fourth kingdom upon earth, which shall be diverse from all kingdoms, and shall devour the whole earth, and shall tread it down, and break it in pieces. And the ten horns out of this kingdom are ten kings that shall arise: and another shall rise after them; and he shall be diverse from the first, and he shall subdue three kings. And he shall speak great words against the most High, and shall wear out the saints of the most High, and think to change times and laws: and they shall be given into his hand until a time and times and the dividing of time" (Dan. 7:23–25).

In these verses we have a description of Daniel's fourth beast. Now let us look at John's beast who will come up out of the sea:

"And I stood upon the sand of the sea, and saw a beast rise up out of the sea, having seven heads and ten horns, and upon his horns ten crowns, and upon his heads the name of blasphemy. And the beast which I saw was like unto a leopard, and his feet were as the feet of a bear, and his mouth as the mouth of a lion: and the dragon gave him his power, and his seat, and great authority. And I saw one of his heads as it were wounded to death; and his deadly wound was healed: and all the world wondered after the beast. And they worshipped the dragon which gave power unto the beast: and they worshipped the beast, saying, Who is like unto the beast? who is able to make war with him? And there was given unto him a mouth speaking great things and blasphemies; and power was given unto him to continue forty and two months. And he opened his mouth in blasphemy against God, to blaspheme His name, and His tabernacle, and them that dwell in heaven. And it was given unto him to make war with the saints, and to overcome them: and power was given him over all kindreds, and tongues, and nations'' (Rev. 13:1–7).

We find that these beasts are identical in origin–they both came up out of the sea. Daniel's beast came up out of ''the great sea'' (the Mediterranean), as explained in Daniel 7:2,3. John was in exile on the isle of Patmos when God gave him the Revelation; so we see that both beasts came up from the same locality–the ''great sea,'' or the *Mediterranean.*

We further learn that both of these beasts were unlike any other of which we have ever heard. They could both be described in one word: ''*monstrosity.*'' The beast described by Daniel was ''dreadful, terrible, and exceedingly strong,'' with great iron teeth and nails of brass. John's beast was like a leopard, but its feet were like those of a bear and its mouth was like the mouth of a lion.

We learned that Daniel's beast represented the fourth kingdom, which was the Roman empire; and the characteristics given to this empire pin-point it as *the OLD Roman empire.* The characteristics of the beast described by John point to *the FUTURE Roman empire*—the world empire which will be revived immediately after the Rapture and over which the beast will rule. We know from history that the old Roman empire was worldwide in power and exceedingly strong. In traveling throughout Bible lands—Rome, Greece, Egypt, Assyria, Trans-Jordan, Israel—I have seen the ruins of Roman buildings. On every road we traveled and in every village where we visited, we saw the marks left by Rome. She held an iron grip on the world—(thus the great iron teeth of Daniel's beast)—and she certainly displayed claws of brass.

When we study the description of John's beast we learn that the *future* Roman empire which will be set up immediately after the Rapture will embody all the characteristics of the four world empires as seen in the beast with the leopard body, with feet like a bear and mouth like a lion. The Roman empire which will be revived after the Rapture will incorporate all of the power and terror of the empires that have existed and have fallen.

In comparison, we notice that both of these beasts have ten horns, which point to the ten toes of Nebuchadnezzar's image; and the ten toes (representing a kingdom of ten satellites) will exist just before the setting up of the "stone kingdom," when Jesus will sit on the throne of David in Jerusalem and reign right here on earth.

In Daniel 7:7 we are clearly told that Daniel's beast had ten horns, and that the ten horns represent *ten kings* (Dan. 7:24). In Revelation 17:12 we read, "And the ten horns which thou sawest are *ten kings,* which have received no kingdom as yet; but receive power as kings one hour with the beast." Thus it is clear that both beasts represent the Roman empire and in the end time this great empire will be divided into ten federated kingdoms, whose kings will be puppets, giving their power and authority to the Antichrist.

As we read our newspapers, magazines, and periodicals and keep abreast of current events, we know that such a kingdom is in the making today. There are many little Communist satellites who look to the head of Communism, and when it becomes to their advantage they will give their power and homage to the head of Communism.

We note that the two beasts differ in that John's beast had *seven* heads, while Daniel's beast had only ONE head. But Daniel tells us of ten horns on the head of the beast, and out of the ten horns, Daniel saw a *little horn* come up. This little horn is not seen amid the ten horns of the beast in Revelation.

We must get this fixed in our minds thoroughly: The beast *Daniel* saw had ONE head and ten horns, and out of the ten horns a *little* horn rose up. *John's* beast had SEVEN heads and ten horns; but John does not refer to the "little horn." We see features that point to the LAST STAGE of the beast, and we cannot hope to understand that last stage without carefully comparing the beast of Daniel with the beast of the Revelation. *Why do I say this*?

The LITTLE HORN that Daniel saw rise up amid the ten horns, *plucks up THREE of the ten horns and destroys them*! The little horn takes away their kingdoms; but John does not mention this at all.

The "little horn" of Daniel is definitely anti-worship (anti-Christian), because he changes the times and the laws having to do with Israel's worship. The anti-Christian character of Daniel's beast and the conduct of the "little horn" corresponds in every detail with the beast John saw in the Revelation. And they both carry out this anti-

Christian conduct for the same length of time–three and one-half years (Dan. 7:25 and Rev. 13:5). (John describes the length of time as "forty-two months," while Daniel refers to it as "time and times and the dividing of time," which in either case is three and one-half years.)

Both beasts make war against "the saints of the most High" and both blaspheme the name of Jehovah God. Certainly anyone with an open mind, desiring to know spiritual truth, can readily see from this comparison that these two beasts are identical; and we cannot understand Daniel without looking into Revelation. This is why God told Daniel to go his way and rest until the time of the end, and when the end time should come the book would be opened, knowledge would be increased, the wise would understand–but *none of the wicked would understand.* We will study this tremendous truth when we near the end of our series.

There is no portion of God's holy Word that seems difficult but what another portion somewhere in the sixty-six books sheds light on that which seems hard to understand. We will never understand everything about these beasts–and other symbols in prophecy–but we CAN understand all that we need to understand in order to know where we are, *according to God's great time-clock.* We can understand enough to enable us to instruct others that surely the day of the Lord is at hand, and we who are born again should lift up our eyes–*because our redemption draweth nigh*!

The Little Horn

Believers are not looking for Antichrist: *we are looking for Christ*! All believers do not agree on *all details* of the second coming, but all born again people DO BELIEVE that Jesus is coming the second time. Those who deny the return of Jesus to this earth testify that they have never been saved. Bible truth for this statement is found in these words from Titus 2:11–13:

"For the grace of God that bringeth salvation hath appeared to all men, teaching us that, denying ungodliness and worldly lusts, we should live soberly, righteously, and godly, in this present world; looking for that blessed hope, and the glorious appearing of the great God and our Saviour Jesus Christ."

Apart from grace there is no salvation. We are saved by grace through faith (Eph. 2:8). Any person who claims to be a child of God and denies that he *possesses the grace of God* is certainly scripturally ignorant concerning salvation. The grace of God saves us–and then sets up a classroom in our heart and teaches us:

1 – to deny ungodliness and worldly lusts,

2 – to live soberly, righteously, and godly in this present world,

3 – to look for that blessed hope and the glorious appearing of the great God and our Saviour, Jesus Christ.

The grace of God teaches us to look for Jesus, and Christians are not looking for Antichrist. There are those who teach that Antichrist will be revealed before the Rapture, but such doctrine is man-made and is foreign to the Word of God. Antichrist will not be unveiled until the Church is raptured and the Holy Ghost is taken out of the earth:

"For the mystery of iniquity doth already work: only He (the Holy Spirit) who now letteth will let, until He be taken out of the way. And then shall that Wicked be revealed, whom the Lord shall consume with the spirit of His mouth, and shall destroy with the brightness of His coming: Even him, whose coming is after the working of Satan with all power and signs and lying wonders, and with all deceivableness of unrighteousness in them that perish; because they received not the love of the truth, that they might be saved. And for this cause God shall send them strong delusion, that they should believe a lie: that they all might be damned who believed not the truth, but had pleasure in unrighteousness" (II Thess. 2:7–12).

The devil has a cheap counterfeit for everything God is and has that is good. The devil has counterfeited the Trinity: We believe in ONE God manifested in three Persons: God the Father, God the Son, and God the Holy Ghost. Satan also has a trinity: The Antichrist, the Beast, and the False Prophet. These three will be revealed after the Rapture, during the time of great tribulation.

In the Old Testament as well as in the New, we read much concerning a mysterious and terrible person who shall be revealed in the last times . . . that is, after the Rapture of the Church, at the beginning of the tribulation period known in the Old Testament as "the time of Jacob's trouble." This mysterious and terrible person is known by many names. *Jesus* had many names–for example, "Wonderful, Counsellor, Mighty God, Everlasting Father, Prince of Peace . . . the Rose of Sharon, the Lily of the Valley, the Bright and Morning Star . . . the Way, the Truth, the Life; the Door, the Good Shepherd; the Bread of Life, the Water of Life, the Alpha, the Omega," and others. The *counterfeit messiah* (and that is exactly what he will be) has many names–both in the Old Testament and in the New. I will list a few of them here:

Old Testament Names

In our present study in the book of Daniel we find this mysterious person called "the little horn" (Dan.

7:8; 8:9). In Daniel 8:23 he is called "a king of fierce countenance." In Daniel 9:26 he is called "the prince that shall come." In Daniel 11:36 he is referred to as the willful king. In Isaiah 14:25; 10:5; and 30:31 he is called "the Assyrian." In Isaiah 11:4 he is referred to as "the wicked," and in Isaiah 14:4 he is called "king of Babylon." In Ezekiel 28:11–19 we read of the devil himself as "king of Tyrus," and in Isaiah 14:12 he is called "Lucifer."

The Antichrist will be the devil in flesh. There is ONE devil, but he can take many forms; he can employ any guise that will best accomplish his purpose—as he has done in the past, and will do in the future.

New Testament Names

Writing to believers at Thessalonica, Paul referred to this mysterious personality as "the man of sin . . . the son of perdition . . . that Wicked" (II Thess. 2:3–8). John refers to him simply as "antichrist" (I John 2:18) and again as "the beast" (Rev. 13:1–8).

These Scriptures in both the Old and New Testaments refer to the same person. Not everyone will agree with me, but I personally believe that this mysterious person has been on earth many times since God created Adam. I believe that his spirit first appeared in Nimrod, and that the same spirit dwelt in the bosom of Pharaoh. There is a statement in God's Word concerning Pharaoh that is not made about any other person who ever dwelt upon the face of this earth. Concerning kings and rulers, God said that He puts up whom He will, and puts down whom He will. In Romans 9:17 Paul said, "For the Scripture saith unto Pharaoh, Even for this same purpose have I raised thee up, that I might shew my power in thee, and that my name might be declared throughout all the earth."

That settles it! God raised up Pharaoh to do what

he did, and then God destroyed him. Since God is the Creator of the earth and all things therein, and of heaven and all things therein, then from the standpoint of common sense God has the right to run His universe as He ordains.

I believe the spirit of Antichrist dwelt in the bosom of Judas Iscariot. Jesus clearly said to His disciples, "Have not I chosen you twelve, and one of you is a devil?" (John 6:70). Greek authorities declare that the "*a*" is not in the original and is not used in connection with the Greek. Therefore, Jesus said, "Have I not chosen you twelve, *and one of you is DEVIL*?" I believe that the spirit which will abide in the body of Antichrist is the same spirit that dwelt in Judas Iscariot.

There are other Scriptures to substantiate what I have just said. In His intercessory prayer, recorded in John 17, Jesus prayed to the Father, "While I was with them in the world, I kept them in thy name: those that thou gavest me I have kept, and none of them is lost, *but the son of perdition*; that the Scripture might be fulfilled" (John 17:12). In other words, Jesus is saying to the Father, "You gave me *all twelve*—including Judas." God had a purpose in choosing Judas among the disciples, and that purpose was "THAT THE SCRIPTURE MIGHT BE FULFILLED."

Writing to the troubled saints at Thessalonica, Paul said, "Now we beseech you, brethren, by the coming of our Lord Jesus Christ, and by our gathering together unto Him (in the Rapture), that ye be not soon shaken in mind, or be troubled, neither by spirit, nor by word, nor by letter as from us, as that the day of Christ is at hand. Let no man deceive you by any means: for that day shall not come, except there come a falling away first, AND THAT MAN OF SIN be revealed, THE SON OF PERDITION"

(II Thess. 2:1–3). Please note: Paul says, "THAT man of sin," not just *any* man of sin–but a specific individual. Paul is not referring to the Rapture in these verses, but to the day of the Lord as described in Isaiah 2:12.

Judas betrayed the Lord–and then went out and hanged himself. The disciples were electing one to take his place, and we read in Acts 1:25: "That he may take part of this ministry and apostleship, from which Judas by transgression fell, THAT HE MIGHT GO TO HIS OWN PLACE." This certainly suggests that Judas HAS his own specific place (or cell) where he has been before, and where he is now in prison, in chains–just as the angels who left their first estate are chained in darkness, waiting the day of judgment. The Word tells us that Judas went "to his own place," wherever his own place may be; and in whatever body or condition he may be at this present time, he is waiting the day when he will be revealed after the Rapture of the Church. He will be Antichrist in flesh–in the body of a man–and he will present himself to the Jews as their Messiah. He will be the false messiah . . . "anti"–opposite the Christ. He is the son of Satan as Jesus is the Son of God.

CHAPTER EIGHT

THE RAM AND THE HE GOAT

1. In the third year of the reign of king Belshazzar a vision appeared unto me, even unto me Daniel, after that which appeared unto me at the first.

2. And I saw in a vision; and it came to pass, when I saw, that I was at Shushan in the palace, which is in the province of Elam; and I saw in a vision, and I was by the river of Ulai.

3. Then I lifted up mine eyes, and saw, and, behold, there stood before the river a ram which had two horns: and the two horns were high; but one was higher than the other, and the higher came up last.

4. I saw the ram pushing westward, and northward, and southward; so that no beasts might stand before him, neither was there any that could deliver out of his hand; but he did according to his will, and became great.

5. And as I was considering, behold, an he goat came from the west on the face of the whole earth, and touched not the ground: and the goat had a notable horn between his eyes.

6. And he came to the ram that had two horns, which I had seen standing before the river, and ran unto him in the fury of his power.

7. And I saw him come close unto the ram, and he was moved with choler against him, and smote the ram, and brake his two horns: and there was no power in the ram to stand before him, but he cast him down to the ground, and stamped upon him: and there was none that could deliver the ram out of his hand.

8. Therefore the he goat waxed very great: and when he was strong, the great horn was broken; and for it came up four notable ones toward the four winds of heaven.

9. And out of one of them came forth a little horn, which waxed exceeding great, toward the south, and toward the east, and toward the pleasant land.

10. And it waxed great, even to the host of heaven; and it

cast down some of the host and of the stars to the ground, and stamped upon them.

11. Yea, he magnified himself even to the prince of the host, and by him the daily sacrifice was taken away, and the place of his sanctuary was cast down.

12. And an host was given him against the daily sacrifice by reason of transgression, and it cast down the truth to the ground; and it practised, and prospered.

13. Then I heard one saint speaking, and another saint said unto that certain saint which spake, How long shall be the vision concerning the daily sacrifice, and the transgression of desolation, to give both the sanctuary and the host to be trodden under foot?

14. And he said unto me, Unto two thousand and three hundred days; then shall the sanctuary be cleansed.

15. And it came to pass, when I, even I Daniel, had seen the vision, and sought for the meaning, then, behold, there stood before me as the appearance of a man.

16. And I heard a man's voice between the banks of Ulai, which called, and said, Gabriel, make this man to understand the vision.

17. So he came near where I stood: and when he came, I was afraid, and fell upon my face: but he said unto me, Understand, O son of man: for at the time of the end shall be the vision.

18. Now as he was speaking with me, I was in a deep sleep on my face toward the ground: but he touched me, and set me upright.

19. And he said, Behold, I will make thee know what shall be in the last end of the indignation: for at the time appointed the end shall be.

20. The ram which thou sawest having two horns are the kings of Media and Persia.

21. And the rough goat is the king of Grecia: and the great horn that is between his eyes is the first king.

22. Now that being broken, whereas four stood up for it, four kingdoms shall stand up out of the nation, but not in his power.

23. And in the latter time of their kingdom, when the transgressors are come to the full, a king of fierce countenance, and understanding dark sentences, shall stand up.

24. And his power shall be mighty, but not by his own power: and he shall destroy wonderfully, and shall prosper, and practise,

and shall destroy the mighty and the holy people.

25. And through his policy also he shall cause craft to prosper in his hand; and he shall magnify himself in his heart, and by peace shall destroy many: he shall also stand up against the Prince of princes; but he shall be broken without hand.

26. And the vision of the evening and the morning which was told is true: wherefore shut thou up the vision; for it shall be for many days.

27. And I Daniel fainted, and was sick certain days; afterward I rose up, and did the king's business; and I was astonished at the vision, but none understood it.

The Time and Place of Daniel's Vision

Verses 1 and 2: "In the third year of the reign of king Belshazzar a vision appeared unto me, even unto me Daniel, after that which appeared unto me at the first. And I saw in a vision; and it came to pass, when I saw, that I was at Shushan in the palace, which is in the province of Elam; and I saw in a vision, and I was by the river of Ulai."

Beginning with this chapter, the remainder of the book of Daniel is written in Hebrew. The first chapter and the first three verses of the second chapter are also written in Hebrew. The reason: This section of Daniel gives the account of the fall of Jerusalem when God's chosen people Israel were taken captive by Nebuchadnezzar and carried into Babylon, where they spent seventy years as slaves.

From verse 4 of chapter 2 to the end of chapter 7, Daniel is written in Aramaic, because this portion of the book has to do with the four world-wide Gentile powers. Chapter 8 through the rest of the book is in Hebrew because it deals directly with the Jews—Jerusalem, the temple, and the Antichrist who will desecrate the temple and persecute the Jews during the Great Tribulation period. The purpose of chapter 8 through the remainder of the book is to reveal to Daniel the things that shall befall Israel in "the latter days."

The vision of the ram and the he-goat recorded here occurred in the third year of Belshazzar's reign, 538 B. C. Thus, Daniel had the vision two years *after* the vision of the four wild beasts and in the same year as the fall of the Babylonian empire. Through this vision Daniel was to learn the kingdoms that would succeed the Babylonian empire, and the purpose of the vision was to make known unto him the prophecy concerning the "little horn" in relation to Israel in the latter days.

Although Daniel was in Babylon when he received the vision, he was transported *in spirit* to Shushan, the capital of Persia, located in the province of Elam. As Daniel stood beside the river Ulai, he saw a wonderful sight–a tremendous vision given to him by the God of his fathers, the God to whom he had been faithful through all the years of his captivity in a strange land.

The Vision of the Ram

Verses 3 and 4: "Then I lifted up mine eyes, and saw, and, behold, there stood before the river a ram which had two horns: and the two horns were high; but one was higher than the other, and the higher came up last. I saw the ram pushing westward, and northward, and southward; so that no beasts might stand before him, neither was there any that could deliver out of his hand; but he did according to his will, and became great."

When Daniel was carried in the spirit to the side of the river Ulai, he lifted up his eyes and saw a ram which had two horns–one horn a little higher than the other; and the horn that was the higher of the two came up last. As Daniel continued to gaze at the ram, he saw it push westward, northward, and southward; and as it advanced there was no beast that could stop it or stand before it, and no power "that could deliver out of his hand." This ram did according to his own will, and he became very great and powerful.

Daniel Sees the He-Goat

Verses 5–7: "And as I was considering, behold, an he goat came from the west on the face of the whole earth, and touched not the ground: and the goat had a notable horn between his eyes. And he came to the ram that had two horns, which I had seen standing before the river, and ran unto him in the fury of his power. And I saw him come close unto the ram, and he was moved with choler against him, and smote the ram, and brake his two horns: and there was no power in the ram to stand before him, but he cast him down to the ground, and stamped upon him: and there was none that could deliver the ram out of his hand."

In amazement Daniel beheld this powerful ram pushing forward with such irresistible force that nothing could stop him; and as Daniel considered that vision, wondering who and what the ram was and what was taking place, another sight appeared: *a he-goat came from the west.* This he-goat appeared *on the face of the whole earth*, he filled the horizon looking westward–and "he touched not the ground." He had a "notable horn" between his eyes–certainly an unusual sight–and he came directly to the ram that had the two horns and ran unto the ram "in the fury of his power."

Daniel saw him come close to the ram, moved with "choler" (bitter anger or terror) against him. The goat smote the ram and broke his two horns, and thus the ram stood powerless before the he-goat, which then crushed the ram to the ground and stamped upon him with his feet, "and there was none that could deliver the ram out of his hand."

Certainly *GOATS do not have hands*. This monstrosity of Daniel's vision was in the *form* of a goat, and it had a horn–but it points to a man, not an animal. The ram is down, the he-goat is now in power.

Four Horns Appear on the He-Goat

Verse 8: "Therefore the he goat waxed very great:

and when he was strong, the great horn was broken; and for it came up four notable ones toward the four winds of heaven."

Daniel beheld the he-goat, now the most powerful personage on earth. Daniel saw "the great horn" (referred to in verse 5 as the "notable horn"); and this great horn was broken. Then Daniel saw four "notable horns" come up out of the place where the one great horn had been. These four notable horns pointed toward the four winds of heaven–which, of course, point to the four directions of the compass–North, South, East, and West–denoting the entire earth.

Daniel Continues to See the Unusual

Verses 9–12: "And out of one of them came forth a little horn, which waxed exceeding great, toward the south, and toward the east, and toward the pleasant land. And it waxed great, even to the host of heaven; and it cast down some of the host and of the stars to the ground, and stamped upon them. Yea, he magnified himself even to the prince of the host, and by him the daily sacrifice was taken away, and the place of his sanctuary was cast down. And an host was given him against the daily sacrifice by reason of transgression, and it cast down the truth to the ground; and it practised, and prospered."

There has been much discussion and disagreement among scholars concerning the "little horn" which came out of one of the four "notable horns." It is my personal opinion that the verses following verse 9 identify the person represented by this little horn; however, I agree with Dr. Scofield and others that the prophecy set forth here was fulfilled in part (but NOT in its entirety) by Antiochus Epiphanes in 175 B. C. It is true that he profaned the temple and persecuted the Jews in a most terrible way, and he is a remarkable type of the beast (the "little horn") of the last days; but I believe that the real person pointed to here in Daniel 8:9 is the *same* person as that of Daniel 7:8.

I confess that there are many things I do not fully understand about the books of Daniel and Revelation; but I see no reason to speculate or follow what others have taught if there is Scripture to tell us clearly *who the little horn is* in Daniel 8:9. Antiochus Epiphanes did desecrate the temple at Jerusalem by erecting an idol altar there. He actually built an altar to an idol *on the altar in God's temple*, and history bears out the fact that he literally offered a PIG in sacrifice on that altar; but the description and conduct of this "little horn" do not fit the description and conduct of Antiochus Epiphanes, although they DO apply perfectly to the description of the "little horn" of the fourth wild beast.

For instance–Antiochus Epiphanes never cast down any of "the host of heaven"; he never "magnified himself even to the Prince of the host" (which is none other than Jesus Christ). Neither did he stand up against "the Prince of princes"–which is definitely the Lord Jesus Christ. Nor was Antiochus Epiphanes "broken without hand." History records the fact that he died a natural death, at Tabae, in 164 B. C.

Gabriel distinctly tells us that this vision belongs–not to a king named Antiochus Epiphanes–but to "THE TIME OF THE END" (Dan. 8:17). The "time of the end" points to *the end of the times of the Gentiles*, and that time is still in the future. Gabriel also explained that his mission was to make known to Daniel what shall come to pass "IN THE LAST END OF THE INDIGNATION" (Dan. 8:19)–and this refers to the New Testament time of the Great Tribulation.

Therefore we see that the little horn of Daniel 8:9–12, 23–25 synchronizes with "the time of the end"; it also synchronizes with the little horn of the fourth wild beast described in Daniel 7:7,8. It is my belief that they both refer to the same person—"the Man of Sin . . . the king of fierce countenance . . . the Antichrist . . . the son of perdition," who are all one and the same.

I would not break fellowship with any brother who declares that this little horn in Daniel 8:9 was fulfilled in the day of Antiochus Epiphanes, because certainly that has nothing to do with our salvation nor with our fellowshipping together. I could not fellowship with one who denies the virgin birth or the blood atonement; but I can fellowship with brethren who do not agree with me on every specific point of prophecy. I do not claim to understand all there is to know about the book of Daniel—and any minister who makes such a claim is certainly presumptuous! I believe that Antiochus Epiphanes was a forerunner (or type and shadow) of the "little horn" of the end time, but I do not believe that he fulfilled all that is said about this "little horn" in our present verse. I point out these facts in support of my belief:

The "little horn" which Daniel saw come up out of one of the four "notable" horns "waxed exceeding great toward the south, the east, and toward the pleasant land." This could not have been said of Antiochus Epiphanes. He was great—but not *exceeding* great. The "little horn" also waxed great "even to the host of heaven; and it cast down some of the host and of the stars to the ground, and stamped upon them." To me, this does not refer to Israel, for we know that throughout Scripture Israel is an earthly people with earthly promises; they are not the stars, and they are never referred to AS stars. In the book of Revelation we read of a star coming down from heaven, and this sometimes points to special messengers, and on other occasions points to the Lord Jesus Christ Himself. But this powerful "little horn" waxed great "*even to the host of heaven,*" and even to the casting down of some of the stars, and stamping upon them.

We notice that he also "*magnified himself even to the prince of the host,* and by him the daily sacrifice was taken away, and the place of his sanctuary was cast down." This little horn will take away the daily sacrifice by reason of transgression, and we know that when the Antichrist rides out on a white horse with a bow in his hand (Revelation 6) he will make peace on earth—a peace which will continue for three and one-half years. He will permit the Jews to rebuild their temple, set up their worship, and go through their daily routine of the rituals of Judaism and offering of daily sacrifices. This will continue during the first three and one-half years of Antichrist's reign, and then after this brief time of peace he will break the covenant and take away every privilege. All hell will break loose right here on earth, truth will be cast down by Antichrist, and he will "practice and prosper." Paul tells us clearly that in that day God will send the people strong delusion and they will believe THE LIE (Antichrist—the one opposite Christ, who is The Truth).

The people will follow him as God. In II Thessalonians 2:8–12 Paul refers to him as "that Wicked," and tells us that the Lord will "consume him with the spirit of His mouth and destroy him with the brightness of His coming." When Antichrist comes, he will come "AFTER THE WORKING OF SATAN, with all power and signs and lying wonders, and with all deceivableness of unrighteousness in them that perish; because they received not the love of the truth, that they might be saved." And because these peoples on earth during the reign of the Antichrist who received the mark of the beast or the number of his name *would not receive* The Truth (Jesus),

God will send them strong delusion that they should believe The Lie (Antichrist); and all will be damned who believed not the truth but had pleasure in unrighteousness (in the *unrighteous one*, The Lie).

It is Antichrist, not Antiochus Epiphanes, who will put down truth and prosper in the lie. I therefore maintain that there are not TWO little horns in Daniel, but only ONE; and each time we read of the "little horn" it points to the same terrible person—the Antichrist, who is the devil in flesh. Jesus was The Truth, God in flesh; and the last world ruler will be anti-God—opposite Christ.

I repeat: I will accept what many outstanding Bible scholars say about this "little horn" insofar as it was a double prophecy and was partially (but not entirely) fulfilled in the time of Antiochus Epiphanes. However, I believe the main prophecy of the horn points—not to Antiochus Epiphanes—but to the "Man of Sin" who will come on the scene immediately after the Rapture.

An Angel Speaks to Daniel

Verses 13 and 14: "Then I heard one saint speaking, and another saint said unto that certain saint which spake, How long shall be the vision concerning the daily sacrifice, and the transgression of desolation, to give both the sanctuary and the host to be trodden under foot? And he said unto me, Unto two thousand and three hundred days; then shall the sanctuary be cleansed."

While Daniel stood beside the river Ulai, pondering, wondering and amazed at what he had seen and wanting to know the meaning of the vision of the ram and the he-goat, he overheard a conversation between two "*saints*" —or two heavenly creatures. Notice that the Holy Spirit does not name the saint who is speaking: "Then I heard *one saint* speaking, and another saint said unto that *CERTAIN saint* which spake . . . ." It would be interesting to know the name of that saint, but the Holy Spirit did not see fit to reveal it to us. It is possible that had Scripture given the name, some religions would have deified or made an idol to that saint and worshipped at the feet of the idol.

The conversation between the two saints concerned "how long shall be the vision concerning the daily sacrifice, and the transgression of desolation, to give both the sanctuary and the host to be trodden under foot?" In other words, "*How long will the little horn exercise such power as to take away the daily sacrifice, stop all temple worship, stamp the truth to the ground and prosper in the lie that he IS? How long will it be?*" And then "that certain saint" said to Daniel, "*Unto two thousand and three hundred days; then shall the sanctuary be cleansed.*"

What is the meaning of "two thousand and three hundred days"? Hebrew scholars tell us that in the original language this reads "two thousand and three hundred evenings and mornings." That is, 2300 evening and morning sacrifices would be taken away. They would not be permitted to offer any morning or evening sacrifice for 2300 days. So we know that the meaning here is *24-hour* days—not 2300 years, months, or weeks—but *2300 days* as WE know days; and they will extend from the time when the daily sacrifice is taken away by the little horn (Antichrist) in the middle of Daniel's seventieth week of prophecy (Dan. 9:27), until the end of the tribulation period. These 2300 days begin in the middle of the week (and the "week" is not *days*, but *prophetic years*). Therefore it would be during the last three and one-half years (42 months) or the last half of the tribulation period.

However, prophetic months are 30 days. Three and one-half years would be forty-two months, and 42 months of 30 days would be 1260 days. This would be 1040 days more than three and one-half years. According to the vision, the "sanctuary" is not to be cleansed nor will the "daily sacrifice" be allowed until the 2300 days have run their course. This would appear as if the temple will not be cleansed and the services IN the temple will not be re-established until the future temple described by Ezekiel has been built. Study carefully Ezekiel 41–43. Space will not permit me to give you this text here, but please read it and study it carefully. This temple described by Ezekiel will be built after the tribulation period.

As Daniel stood, wondering and thinking, trying to imagine the meaning of the vision he had just seen and the words he had just heard, he was startled by the appearing of one who was in "the appearance of a man."

Interpreter Appears

Verses 15 and 16: "And it came to pass, when I, even I Daniel, had seen the vision, and sought for the meaning, then, behold, there stood before me as the appearance of a man. And I heard a man's voice between the banks of Ulai, which called, and said, Gabriel, make this man to understand the vision."

Daniel had seen the vision; he had sought the meaning of it. Then suddenly there stood before him a being in "the appearance of a man," and Daniel heard a man's voice "between the banks of Ulai," and the voice said, "*Gabriel, make this man to understand the vision.*"

This voice probably came from a cloud hanging over the river between the two banks. Heaven wanted Daniel to fully understand what he had just seen in the vision; therefore an interpreter (the angel Gabriel) was sent from heaven. It was imperative that Daniel understand the vision, and the things which it foretold must be made perfectly clear to him. (These things will also be clear to US if we let the Word of God speak and keep religious ideas and man's interpretations out of it.)

What had disturbed Daniel in his former vision had not been so much the four wild beasts. What had troubled him was "the little horn." And now, in this vision of the ram and the he-goat, there is *another* "little horn." Daniel was indeed perplexed. Could it be that these two little horns were one and the same? or were they two *different* little horns pointing to two different *persons*? God gave these visions to Daniel one by one, and each succeeding vision was given to add light to those previously given. Thus the ram and the he-goat shed more light on the "little horn" which had appeared in the vision of the four beasts. Step by step God was making known to Daniel His dealings with the Gentiles, as the age of grace (or "the times of the Gentiles") comes to a close, making ready for the Millennium—the reign of righteousness God promised Israel through Abraham.

Gabriel Comes Near to Daniel

Verses 17–19: "So he came near where I stood: and when he came, I was afraid, and fell upon my face: but he said unto me, Understand, O son of man: for at the time of the end shall be the vision. Now as he was speaking with me, I was in a deep sleep on my face toward the ground: but he touched me, and set me upright. And he said, Behold, I will make thee know what shall be in the last end of the indignation: for at the time appointed the end shall be."

Gabriel came to where the prophet stood on the banks of the Ulai river, and when he came near, Daniel was afraid and fell upon his face. Gabriel spoke and said, "Understand, O son of man: for at the time of the end shall be the vision."

These are clear words; there is no reason why anyone should misunderstand them. As Gabriel was speaking to Daniel, God's prophet was in a deep sleep lying on his face on the ground. Gabriel touched him, set him upright, and said to him, "*Behold, I will make thee know what shall be in the last end of the indignation: for at the time appointed the end shall be.*"

The statement, "in the last end of the indignation" refers to the last days of the Great Tribulation–the end of the reign of the Gentile powers. The key that unlocks this vision has to do with "*the time of the end.*" This is a definite period of time referred to in Scripture many times, and it points to the end of "the times of the Gentiles." The vision of the little horn that Daniel had just seen had nothing to do with the times in which he lived. It pointed to the last days of the Great Tribulation period ("the time of Jacob's trouble"); not to the time in which Daniel saw the vision.

Gabriel touched Daniel, set him upright, and explained to him that this terrible thing would not happen in HIS day, but in the end of the times of the Gentiles. Then Daniel was instructed to shut up the vision because it would not be fulfilled for "many days."

The Interpretation of the Vision

Verses 20–25: "The ram which thou sawest having two horns are the kings of Media and Persia. And the rough goat is the king of Grecia: and the great horn that is between his eyes is the first king. Now that being broken, whereas four stood up for it, four kingdoms shall stand up out of the nation, but not in his power. And in the latter time of their kingdom, when the transgressors are come to the full, a king of fierce countenance, and understanding dark sentences, shall stand up. And his power shall be mighty, but not by his own power: and he shall destroy wonderfully, and shall prosper, and practise, and shall destroy the mighty and the holy people. And through his policy also he shall cause craft to prosper in his hand; and he shall magnify himself in his heart, and by peace shall destroy many: he shall also stand up against the Prince of princes; but he shall be broken without hand."

Gabriel begins the interpretation of the vision to Daniel. He makes it very clear–and it will be clear to US if we will just read, and let the Holy Spirit speak to us as we read God's Word. Gabriel said to Daniel, "The ram which thou sawest, having two horns are the kings of Media-Persia"–the dual kingdom which came into power after Nebuchadnezzar. "The rough goat is the king of Grecia; and the great horn that is between his eyes is the first king." *That "great horn" was Alexander the Great,* and history bears this out. But the "great horn" was broken and then *four horns* stood up where the ONE horn had stood, indicating that *four kingdoms* should stand up out of the nation–"but not in his power"–that is, *not in the power of the great horn* (Alexander the Great).

"*And in THE LATTER TIME*" (that is, at the very end of the four kingdoms into which the Grecian empire was divided at the death of Alexander the Great), "*when the transgressors are come to the full, a king of fierce countenance, and understanding dark sentences, shall stand up.*" The "king of fierce countenance" will be mighty, "*but not by his own power.*" He will not himself be the powerful one; he will be only a tool controlled by Satanic power–"*and he shall destroy wonderfully.*"

In Revelation 6:2 this same personage rides forth on a beautiful white horse, carrying a bow in his hand–no deadly arrow, just a harmless bow. Thus he "destroys wonderfully": *through flatteries, vain promises, and starvation* he shall "prosper and practise, and shall destroy the mighty and the holy people." This refers to Israel, back in their own land at that particular time. "*And through his policy also he shall cause craft to prosper in his hand.*" He will be the spirit of the master of all evil–Satan himself. He will be the same spirit who so cunningly led Eve into sin and spiritual death. "*He shall magnify himself in his heart.*"

You will remember that in Ezekiel 28 and Isaiah 14 we are told that "Lucifer, the shining one. . . the anointed cherub that covereth" became the loathsome devil because of pride. He wanted to ascend above the stars and exalt his throne above the throne of the Almighty. God threw Lucifer out of heaven, and he became the devil. This is the same spirit to which Daniel is referring. At this time the devil will occupy the body of "the king of fierce countenance . . . the Antichrist . . . the son of perdition."

"*And by peace (he) shall destroy many.*" In Revelation 6:2 the Antichrist rides out in peace; and the first three and one-half years of Daniel's seventieth week of prophecy WILL be peaceful. Then after three and one-half years, Satan's forces will be unleashed in full fury upon the earth and blood will run like water in the streets!

"*He shall also stand up against the Prince of princes,*" referring here to Jesus Christ–for the Prince of princes could be none other than He. But the king of fierce countenance "*shall be broken without hand.*" This points to the time when Jesus Christ Himself will personally put the Antichrist into the lake that burns with fire and brimstone:

"And I saw heaven opened, and behold a white horse; and He that sat upon him was called Faithful and True, and in righteousness He doth judge and make war. His eyes were as a flame of fire, and on His head were many crowns; and He had a name written, that no man knew, but He Himself. And He was clothed with a vesture dipped in blood: and His name is called The Word of God.

And the armies which were in heaven followed Him upon white horses, clothed in fine linen, white and clean. And out of His mouth goeth a sharp sword, that with it He should smite the nations: and He shall rule them with a rod of iron: and He treadeth the winepress of the fierceness and wrath of Almighty God. And He hath on His vesture and on His thigh a name written, KING OF KINGS, AND LORD OF LORDS. And I saw an Angel standing in the sun; and He cried with a loud voice, saying to all the fowls that fly in the midst of heaven, Come and gather yourselves together unto the supper of the great God; that ye may eat the flesh of kings, and the flesh of captains, and the flesh of mighty men, and the flesh of horses, and of them that sit on them, and the flesh of all men, both free and bond, both small and great. And I saw the beast, and the kings of the earth, and their armies, gathered together to make war against Him that sat on the horse, and against His army. And the beast was taken, and with him the false prophet that wrought miracles before him, with which he deceived them that had received the mark of the beast, and them that worshipped his image. *These both were cast alive into a lake of fire burning with brimstone.* And the remnant were slain with the sword of Him that sat upon the horse, which sword proceeded out of His mouth: and all the fowls were filled with their flesh. And I saw an Angel come down from heaven, having the key of the bottomless pit and a great chain in His hand. And He laid hold on the dragon, that old serpent, which is the Devil, and Satan, and bound him a thousand years. And cast him into the bottomless pit, and shut him up, and set a seal upon him, that he should deceive the nations no more, till the thousand years should be fulfilled: and after that he must be loosed a little season" (Rev. 19: 11–20:3).

The *counterfeit* Christ rides out on a white horse in Revelation 6:2, but Revelation 19:11 refers to the Lamb of God. There is no mistaking the identity of the rider of this white horse. In Revelation 19:17 we read, "I saw an angel standing in the sun." That angel is Jesus Christ, and He personally puts the beast and the false prophet into the lake that burns with fire and brimstone (Rev. 19:20); and in Revelation 20:1 the angel who comes down from heaven is also Jesus in angelic form. In the Old Testament on many occasions Jesus appeared as the angel of Jehovah.

Daniel Was God's Prophet

Daniel knew from the dream-image of Nebuchadnezzar that there would be four world empires; he knew that they were to succeed each other, and he knew that the gold, silver, brass, and iron of the image represented these empires. God did not name these kingdoms, except for the first one–Babylon. Again, the kingdoms are not named in the vision of the four wild beasts in chapter 7. However, in the ram and the he-goat vision in chapter 8, we have the *names* of the kingdoms represented by the silver and the brass of the image, and their corresponding beasts–the bear and the leopard.

That is just one more reason why we know the Bible is inspired. The names of these kingdoms had been withheld until the time came for Babylon to fall. Since Babylon was still a world power and Nebuchadnezzar was a world ruler, Daniel did not need to know the names of the kingdoms that would follow; but when the time came that he needed to be informed of the names of those kingdoms, God gave him the vision in which He named the Medes and the Persians who were to conquer Babylon. This information was given to Daniel just before the fall of Babylon; and the knowledge helped him to interpret the handwriting on the wall.

In Daniel's vision of the four wild beasts, Media-Persia and Greece are represented by a bear and a leopard; but in this second vision, they are represented by a ram and a he-goat. It is a historical fact that the emblem of Persia was a ram. Archeologists have unearthed coins which display a ram's head on one side, and a ram recumbent on the other. We also read in history of a Persian king riding in front of his army, wearing a golden figure of a ram's head, set with precious gems.

It is also a historical fact that the national emblem of Macedonia (Greece) was a goat. Coins unearthed by archeologists in Greece bore the likeness of a goat, and the capital of Greece was Aegae–which means "the goat city." Adjacent to Greece was the Aegean Sea, which means "the goat sea," and the son of Alexander the Great (the son given to him by Roxana) was called *Aegus*, meaning "son of a goat."

Daniel immediately recognized the meaning of the ram and the he-goat in his vision, knowing that they corresponded to the leopard and the bear in his vision of the four beasts, and to the arms and breast of silver and the abdomen of brass seen in Nebuchadnezzar's dream. The ram, the bear, the arms and breast of silver, pointed to Media-Persia. The he-goat, the leopard, and the abdomen of brass pointed to Greece.

As Daniel closely compared the beasts of the two visions, the *one side* that was raised up on the bear corresponded to the *horn* that was higher on the ram. The ribs in the mouth of the bear stood for three kingdoms–Lydia, Babylon, and Egypt. These three kingdoms formed a triple alliance to check the Media-Persian power, but were finally destroyed by it–which corresponds to the powerful action of the ram, pushing westward toward Lydia, northward toward Babylon, and southward toward Egypt.

As Daniel compared the leopard and the he-goat, he saw that the four heads of the leopard corresponded with the four horns that came up in place of the great horn on the head of the he-goat. Up to this point, the vision was clear to Daniel; but what troubled him was the meaning of the little horn that came out of one of the four horns of the he-goat. This was a mystery to him. He had seen nothing on the leopard to correspond to the little horn. There was no beast in this vision to compare with the fourth wild beast of the previous vision, on whose head he had seen ten horns, with a little horn appearing out of the ten. What mystified and troubled him was the relationship, if any, of these little horns to each other. Bible teachers have done much speculating on Daniel and the book of Revelation, but we will not speculate. We will compare Scripture with Scripture and take the interpretation of the angel Gabriel.

Gabriel Identifies the Little Horn

Gabriel told Daniel that the great horn between the eyes of the he-goat represented the first powerful king of Greece, and history tells us that the name of that king was Alexander the Great, who was born in 356 B. C. and lived till 323 B. C. He was the son of Philip, king of Macedon. He became king of Greece when he was twenty years old, ascending the throne in 336 B. C. Two years later, in 334 B. C., like a giant goat he leaped over the Hellespont and with his army of 30,000 infantry and 5,000 cavalry he completely crushed a Persian army on the banks of the Granicus. He then swiftly advanced eastward and a year later defeated a Persian army of 600,000 men led by King Darius in a battle at Issus.

Following this tremendous victory Alexander had only minor conquests in Egypt and Phoenicia, after which he returned to Syria where, in 331 B. C., on the banks of the Tigris river, he defeated an enormous army which was personally led by King Darius. This great battle is known in history as the battle of Arbela.

Between the years 330 B. C. and 327 B. C., Alexander the Great captured the outlying provinces of the Persian empire in what we might call his "mopping up" campaign. He conquered all the small villages, then returned to Babylon where he climaxed his reign of glory. At the very early age of 33 years he died of marsh fever which was aggravated by his intemperate living.

When Alexander the Great died (June 323 B. C.), there arose much dissension among the people as to who should be his successor, and this dissension climaxed in the appointing of four of his generals, who divided among themselves the territory he had conquered. The names of the generals were *Gassander*, who laid claim to Macedonia and the western part of the empire; *Lysimachus*, who claimed Thrace and the northern part of the empire; *Seleucus*, who laid claim to Syria and the eastern part of the empire; and *Ptolemy*, who took what was left–Egypt and the southern part of the empire. These four kingdoms were later completely absorbed by the Roman empire, the last one (Egypt) conquered by Rome in 30 B. C. This fact is proved by history, although we do not need history to prove what God says (if we read it in the Word of God, it is a fact); but history and the spade of the archeologist *have proved* that Daniel was a prophet and that his book is inspired beyond a shadow of a doubt.

Daniel learned through Nebuchadnezzar's dream of the great image that there would be *four great world empires*; but neither the image nor the vision of the four wild beasts made known the fact that they would not succeed each other without a break. This fact is first made known in the vision of the he-goat, which showed a break between the four kingdoms and the little horn: "And in the latter time of their kingdom, when the transgressors are come to the full, a king of fierce countenance, and understanding dark sentences, shall stand up" (verse 23).

Having laid the foundation by explaining the meaning of the ram and the he-goat, and the meaning of the four horns that came up where the great horn was broken off, the angel then explained to Daniel the meaning of the one thing that troubled him most—the *"little horn."* Had Gabriel not given Daniel the interpretation of the little horn, we might have believed that he was a ruler who would come forth out of one of the four minor kingdoms, and we might be led to agree that this prophecy was fulfilled in Antiochus Epiphanes. Many Bible scholars who are truly men of God have declared that the little horn pointed to this wicked king who completely desecrated the temple of God.

I repeat, I agree that he was definitely a forerunner of the one to whom the little horn points, but *he was not the fulfillment* of that prophecy. Gabriel clearly tells us in verse 23 that this person is not to make his appearance until *"the latter time of their kingdom, when the transgressors are come to the full."*

Paul tells us that the only way to understand the things of God is to compare spiritual things with spiritual (I Cor. 2:13). We are to study and rightly divide the Word (II Tim. 2:15). In the Bible, terms always mean the same; they do not change. For example, *"Millennium"* always refers to the reign of Christ on earth; *"the kingdom of God"* always means the kingdom within us ("the kingdom of God is not meat and drink"); and *"the kingdom of Heaven"* will be on earth, as pointed out in the model prayer given by Jesus to His disciples. *"The latter times"* used in our present Scripture refers to the time of Great

Tribulation—or, as stated in verse 23, the time "when the transgressors are come to the full." That will be the ultimate of demon-control and power here on earth—a control so fierce that except those days be shortened, there would no flesh be saved (Matt. 24:22). But for the sake of the elect (Israel) God will shorten those days, in order that the elect of God and the Gentiles who have befriended Israel during "the time of Jacob's trouble" may be preserved.

This "little horn" is to make his appearance "in the latter time . . . when the transgressors are come to the full," thus distinguishing between the "*former*" time of these four kingdoms and "*the latter time*" when these four kingdoms will be part of the TEN kingdoms referred to in Revelation 17 and 18. The Roman empire under the shrewd and powerful leadership of the Antichrist will be revived after the Rapture, and it will be divided into ten kingdoms. We see this in the making today—even in the daily newspapers we read more about Greece and Egypt day by day, and no one knows just how soon we will be reading about Thrace and Syria. It is not a hard thing for Jehovah God to raise powerful kingdoms of yesteryear from the dead. God's plan will be worked out in every detail, according to His own blueprint.

Here we see further proof that Antiochus Epiphanes could not have been the powerful ruler to whom the "little horn" points. It would not do to say that the "latter time of their kingdom" means the latter time of the four kingdoms before they were swallowed up by the fourth world empire (Rome), for they were not all swallowed up at one time. Neither would it do to say that Antiochus Epiphanes is the "little horn" in the "latter times"—for he did not live in the latter time of the four kingdoms; he was not ruling when they were destroyed, neither were the four kingdoms all destroyed at one time. Egypt was the last to succumb to Rome, but *"in the latter time"* all ten kingdoms over which the Antichrist reigns in power will fall at the same moment. *The kingdoms of this earth will become the kingdoms of our God in one split second*!

Antiochus Epiphanes was one of twenty-six kings who ruled over Syria. He died in 164 B. C.–134 years before Egypt fell and ceased to be a kingdom. History proves that he desecrated the temple of God; but in Matthew 24:15 when Jesus refers to Daniel's prophecy that "the abomination of desolation" will stand in the holy place, He was not talking about a past occurrence; He was referring to a future event–and at the time Jesus gave this discourse Antiochus Epiphanes had been dead for 200 years.

It is certainly not consistent to say that verses 9 through 12 refer to Antiochus Epiphanes and then say that verses 23 through 25 point to the Antichrist who will reign in the end time. The truth of the matter is, verses 23 through 25 are the *interpretation* of verses 9 through 12. ALL of these verses refer to one and the same person. There is definitely a gap between the "former" four kingdoms which were absorbed by Rome, and the "latter time" of the four kingdoms which are a part of the revived Roman empire; and that gap corresponds to the gap between Daniel's sixty-ninth and seventieth week (which is the Church Age), as revealed to him in our next chapter of this prophecy.

Let us take a closer look at the "little horn." In the seventh chapter, Daniel describes the little horn as *plucking up three of the TEN horns.* He also describes him as having "eyes like the eyes of a man, and a mouth speaking great things." The holy one who interprets the vision repeats that the little horn will conquer three kings, and "he shall speak great words against the most High, and shall wear out the saints of the most High, and think to change times and laws: and they shall be given into his hand until a time and times and the dividing of time" (Dan. 7:25).

In chapter 8 Daniel describes the little horn as waxing "exceedingly great toward the south, and toward the east, and toward the pleasant land (Palestine). And it waxed great, even to the host of heaven; and it cast down some of the host and of the stars to the ground, and stamped upon them. Yea, he magnified himself even to the prince of the host, and by him the daily sacrifice was taken away, and the place of His sanctuary was cast down. And an host was given him against the daily sacrifice by reason of transgression, and it (the little horn) cast down the truth to the ground; and it practised and prospered" (Dan. 8:9–12). (The *sanctuary* here refers to the sanctuary of Christ, not Antichrist.)

The angel Gabriel gives us in minute detail the interpretation of this little horn. Gabriel said to Daniel, ". . . In the latter time of their kingdom, when the transgressors are come to the full, a king of fierce countenance, and understanding dark sentences, shall stand up. And his power shall be mighty, but not by his own power: and he shall destroy wonderfully, and shall prosper, and practise, and shall destroy the mighty and the holy people. And through his policy also he shall cause craft to prosper in his hand; and he shall magnify himself in his heart, and by peace shall destroy many: he shall also stand up against the Prince of princes; but he shall be broken without hand" (Dan. 8:23–25).

However, these two passages do not complete the picture of the little horn. There is more.

He Is Called The Willful King

"And the king shall do according to his will"; (This

is the king of the North.) "and he shall exalt himself, and magnify himself above every god, and shall speak marvellous things against the God of gods, and shall prosper till the indignation (the Great Tribulation) be accomplished: for that that is determined shall be done." (What God has ordained will be.) "Neither shall he regard the God of his fathers, nor the desire of women, nor regard any god; for he shall magnify himself above all. But in his estate shall he honour the God of forces; and a god whom his fathers knew not shall he honour with gold, and silver, and with precious stones, and pleasant things. Thus shall he do in the most strong holds with a strange god, whom he shall acknowledge and increase with glory: and he shall cause them to rule over many, and shall divide the land for gain" (Dan. 11:36–39).

In this passage, the Holy Spirit puts the finishing touches on the picture of the Antichrist set forth in Daniel by "the little horn."

This Much We Know

From what we have seen thus far in our study of the "little horn," we know that he is to rise amid the TEN horns of the fourth wild beast, we know that the fourth beast is the Roman empire, and that of those ten horns (ten kingdoms), four shall be the four kingdoms into which the empire of Alexander the Great was divided: Macedonia (Greece), Thrace (Asia-Minor), Syria (Assyria), and Egypt. We also know that the little horn is to rise out of one of these four kingdoms, which kingdom will be revealed to us in chapter 11:36–45.

We are told that the king represented by the little horn will be "a king of fierce countenance," a king who understands "dark sentences." By that, we know that he will be a revealer of secret things, possessing the power and wisdom of the devil himself. In Ezekiel 28 we learn that "the anointed cherub that covereth" was *perfect* in wisdom, and he is still very wise; he knows much, much more than we give him credit for knowing, and is much more powerful than we have ever realized. This little horn (the "king of fierce countenance") will stand up against Jesus Christ (referred to here as the "Prince of princes"), and will bring his transgression to the full. Then he "shall be broken without hand." He will drink the cup of indignation to the last bitter dregs; he will fill to its fullness the cup of ungodliness, unrighteousness, and debauchery; *but he will be broken and destroyed without the assistance of man*! Jesus Christ will personally take care of the destruction of the "little horn" of Daniel–the Antichrist of the New Testament. In II Thessalonians 2:8 we learn that the Lord Jesus will consume him with the spirit of His mouth, and destroy him by the brightness of His coming. (Read also Revelation 19:11–20.)

Daniel's vision was interpreted and he was told that the *fulfillment* of the vision would not be for "many days"–not until "*the latter time.*" This refers to the latter time of the four kingdoms, and is still future.

Then Daniel–the prophet of God–the same extraordinary man who could face Nebuchadnezzar and tell him the truth about his approaching downfall, the same man who could stand before Belshazzar and read to him the message of doom in the handwriting on the wall, the same Daniel who had faced a den of hungry lions rather than deny his God, "FAINTED AND WAS SICK CERTAIN DAYS" when he saw the "king of fierce countenance," *the Antichrist*!

Daniel had the same concern for his people that Paul had. In Romans 9:1–3 Paul testified, "I say the truth in Christ, I lie not, my conscience also bearing me witness in the Holy Ghost, that I have great heaviness and continual sorrow in my heart. For I could wish that myself were accursed from Christ for my brethren, my kinsmen according to the flesh." In other words, Paul said that he would be willing to burn in hell if by so doing he could save his people. He had a burning passion and a heavy burden for Israel.

Daniel had that same spirit when he saw the Antichrist–the king who, but for the mercy of God in shortening the days, would destroy all flesh. When Daniel saw this horrible person and the things he would do to God's chosen people, it was more than he could bear: He fainted "*and was sick certain days.*"

A Word-Picture of the King of Fierce Countenance

Verses 24–27: "And his power shall be mighty, but not by his own power: and he shall destroy wonderfully, and shall prosper, and practise, and shall destroy the mighty and the holy people. And through his policy also he shall cause craft to prosper in his hand; and he shall magnify himself in his heart, and by peace shall destroy many: he shall also stand up against the Prince of princes; but he shall be broken without hand. And the vision of the evening and the morning which was told is true; wherefore shut thou up the vision; for it shall be for many days. And I Daniel fainted, and was sick certain days; afterward I rose up, and did the king's business; and I was astonished at the vision, but none understood it."

The power of this king of fierce countenance shall be mighty–but it will not be his own power; *he will be energized by Satan.* In the same manner that Jesus was God in flesh, this king of fierce countenance will be *the devil in flesh.* In the same way that the power of God was embodied in Christ, the power of the devil will be embodied in the Antichrist and he shall "destroy wonderfully." He will be the opposite of Jesus: Jesus *healed* wonderfully, *blessed* wonderfully, He was the most wonderful Person who ever lived . . . His very name was called "*Wonderful*" (Isa. 9:6). By contrast, *Antichrist* will DESTROY wonderfully. He shall "prosper and practice," he shall "destroy the mighty and the holy people"–and were it not for the mercies of God in shortening his reign of terror, he would destroy all flesh (Matt. 24:22).

During the reign of Antichrist, craft will prosper exceedingly in his hand. He will be the proudest person who ever lived–he will "magnify himself in his heart"; he will announce that he is God–and the world will fall at his feet (with the exception of the remnant of Israel, those who have heard the message of the kingdom, and those who are sealed in their foreheads). The multitudes will worship at his feet and call him God.

This king will come upon the scene of action riding a beautiful white horse, and he will have a bow in his hand–but no arrow. This is the symbol of peace–and he will announce himself as the saviour of the world. He will make his appearance just after the Rapture. All believers will be missing then, and there will be a state of chaos and shock. The business world will be paralyzed for a brief period, and this superman will offer a solution. He will bring peace for a period of three and one-half years–but through that peace he will destroy many in that he will draw them to himself through his miracle-working power; and when they believe him (The Lie) they will be sent strong delusion and they will be damned. Study the entire second chapter of II Thessalonians.

The Antichrist will be so proud, so mighty, and so powerful that he will even stand against "The Prince of princes" (The Lord Jesus Christ); but he will meet his match in the Son of God! He will be broken, and the "Prince of princes" will be the One to crush him: "And I (God) will put enmity between thee and the woman, and between thy seed and her seed; it shall bruise thy head, and thou shalt bruise His heel" (Gen. 3:15).

It seems today that believers are in the minority and on the losing side–but not so. *If God be for us, who can be against us? Who shall separate us from the love of God?* There is nothing in earth or in hell that can destroy us if we are in Christ Jesus. In Him we are definitely on the winning side! One day this earth will be turned over to the devil, his demons, and the forces of hell; but the Church will be comfortably seated at the marriage supper in the sky while this horrible siege of hell transpires on earth.

I believe in speaking in clear, understandable words, so please do not misunderstand the following statement: Today the masses seem by their actions and habits of life to be saying, "We want sin; we want the devil; we want lust. We want the Bible taken out of our schools; we want no religion in our schools; we want churches to be forced to pay taxes and do homage to the government, and we want Sunday abolished as a holy day."

The world and the masses of humanity seem to be asking for what the devil can give–and one day (surely it will be very, very soon) God will remove the Church from the earth. Then, with every born again believer caught up into the clouds to meet Jesus in the air, God will give the remaining peoples on earth the hell, misery, and destruction they are asking for!

God's Word promises that if we sow to the flesh we will reap corruption. I ask you, *What is America sowing today?* Check the statistics on liquor, wine, beer–strong drink in all of its forms. Check the statistics on dope and other forms of lust; and I think you will agree that in general America and the world are sowing to the flesh. But dear believer, "Fret not thyself because of evildoers, neither be thou envious against the workers of iniquity. For they shall soon be cut down like the grass, and wither as the green herb" (Psalm 37:1,2).

Daniel had this vision in the evening and the morning; and when the vision was complete, he was told to shut it up because it would not take place for "many days." Then it was that Daniel fainted and was sick for several days. After that, he was able to again take care of the king's business.

Daniel was astonished at the vision–BUT NONE UNDERSTOOD IT. That simply means that none of the people understood why Daniel was so astonished at what he had seen, and why it made him so sick that he was not able to work in the king's court for many days.

I give praise and thanksgiving to God that I will not be here when "the king of fierce countenance" takes over the reins of the government of earth; neither will YOU be here if you are born again. However, if you are not a believer, you MAY be here, because no one knows the day or the hour when Jesus will come–and He may come today! If the Rapture should take place and you are not saved, you would find yourself in a world without a Christian in it–and then you would realize that you are in the kingdom of Antichrist!

If you are a believer you have nothing to fret about, nothing to worry about; but if you are an *unbeliever* you have nothing to be at ease about, because within the next sixty seconds you could find yourself left on earth when the "king of fierce countenance" takes over!

CHAPTER NINE

THE VISION OF THE SEVENTY WEEKS

1. In the first year of Darius the son of Ahasuerus, of the seed of the Medes, which was made king over the realm of the Chaldeans;

2. In the first year of his reign I Daniel understood by books the number of the years, whereof the word of the Lord came to Jeremiah the prophet, that he would accomplish seventy years in the desolations of Jerusalem.

3. And I set my face unto the Lord God, to seek by prayer and supplications, with fasting, and sackcloth, and ashes:

4. And I prayed unto the Lord my God, and made my confession, and said, O Lord, the great and dreadful God, keeping the covenant and mercy to them that love him, and to them that keep his commandments;

5. We have sinned, and have committed iniquity, and have done wickedly, and have rebelled, even by departing from thy precepts and from thy judgments:

6. Neither have we hearkened unto thy servants the prophets, which spake in thy name to our kings, our princes, and our fathers, and to all the people of the land.

7. O Lord, righteousness belongeth unto thee, but unto us confusion of faces, as at this day; to the men of Judah, and to the inhabitants of Jerusalem, and unto all Israel, that are near, and that are far off, through all the countries whither thou hast driven them, because of their trespass that they have trespassed against thee.

8. O Lord, to us belongeth confusion of face, to our kings, to our princes, and to our fathers, because we have sinned against thee.

9. To the Lord our God belong mercies and forgivenesses, though we have rebelled against him;

10. Neither have we obeyed the voice of the Lord our God, to walk in his laws, which he set before us by his servants the prophets.

11. Yea, all Israel have transgressed thy law, even by departing, that they might not obey thy voice; therefore the curse is poured upon us, and the oath that is written in the law of Moses the servant of God, because we have sinned against him.

12. And he hath confirmed his words, which he spake against us, and against our judges that judged us, by bringing upon us a great evil: for under the whole heaven hath not been done as hath been done upon Jerusalem.

13. As it is written in the law of Moses, all this evil is come upon us: yet made we not our prayer before the Lord our God, that we might turn from our iniquities, and understand thy truth.

14. Therefore hath the Lord watched upon the evil, and brought it upon us: for the Lord our God is righteous in all his works which he doeth: for we obeyed not his voice.

15. And now, O Lord our God, that hast brought thy people forth out of the land of Egypt with a mighty hand, and hast gotten thee renown, as at this day; we have sinned, we have done wickedly.

16. O Lord, according to all thy righteousness, I beseech thee, let thine anger and thy fury be turned away from thy city Jerusalem, thy holy mountain: because for our sins, and for the iniquities of our fathers, Jerusalem and thy people are become a reproach to all that are about us.

17. Now therefore, O our God, hear the prayer of thy servant, and his supplications, and cause thy face to shine upon thy sanctuary that is desolate, for the Lord's sake.

18. O my God, incline thine ear, and hear; open thine eyes, and behold our desolations, and the city which is called by thy name: for we do not present our supplications before thee for our righteousnesses, but for thy great mercies.

19. O Lord, hear; O Lord, forgive; O Lord, hearken and do; defer not, for thine own sake, O my God: for thy city and thy people are called by thy name.

20. And whiles I was speaking, and praying, and confessing my sin and the sin of my people Israel, and presenting my supplication before the Lord my God for the holy mountain of my God;

21. Yea, whiles I was speaking in prayer, even the man Gabriel, whom I had seen in the vision at the beginning, being caused to fly swiftly, touched me about the time of the evening oblation.

22. And he informed me, and talked with me, and said, O Dan-

iel, I am now come forth to give thee skill and understanding.
23. At the beginning of thy supplications the commandment came forth, and I am come to shew thee; for thou art greatly beloved: therefore understand the matter, and consider the vision.
24. Seventy weeks are determined upon thy people and upon thy holy city, to finish the transgression, and to make an end of sins, and to make reconciliation for iniquity, and to bring in everlasting righteousness, and to seal up the vision and prophecy, and to anoint the most Holy.
25. Know therefore and understand, that from the going forth of the commandment to restore and to build Jerusalem unto the Messiah the Prince shall be seven weeks, and threescore and two weeks: the street shall be built again, and the wall, even in troublous times.
26. And after threescore and two weeks shall Messiah be cut off, but not for himself: and the people of the prince that shall come shall destroy the city and the sanctuary; and the end thereof shall be with a flood, and unto the end of the war desolations are determined.
27. And he shall confirm the covenant with many for one week: and in the midst of the week he shall cause the sacrifice and the oblation to cease, and for the overspreading of abominations he shall make it desolate, even until the consummation, and that determined shall be poured upon the desolate.

The Time of the Vision

Verses 1 and 2: "In the *first year* of Darius the son of Ahasuerus, of the seed of the Medes, which was made king over the realm of the Chaldeans; in the first year of his reign I Daniel understood by books the number of the years, whereof the Word of the Lord came to Jeremiah the prophet, that He (Jehovah) would accomplish *seventy years in the desolations of Jerusalem.*"

This is one of the most important chapters in the book of Daniel. In the very outset of the chapter we learn the time (or the date) of the vision of the seventy weeks which were determined upon Israel and the Holy City, and it is very important to see this. Daniel tells us that it was *in the first year* of the reign of Darius the Mede over the Babylonian empire, and this was 538 B. C.

It was an extremely critical time, and Daniel's mind was perplexed. After seeing the vision of the "king of fierce countenance" in chapter 8, he was astonished beyond measure and was sick for several days. He had understood the vision of the four wild beasts, and he had understood the vision of the ram and the he-goat. These visions foretold a prolonged period of dispersion for the people of Israel—that they would be dispersed to every corner of the earth. But while Daniel believed what he had understood and learned as revealed to him in the visions, he found it extremely hard to reconcile what he had learned *through the visions* with what he had learned *through the books* (the books of Moses and the prophets). It is interesting to note that though a captive in Babylon, Daniel was a student of God's Word and had studied much concerning the captivity of Israel. From the book of Jeremiah he had learned that the Babylonian captivity was to last only 70 years:

"*And this whole land shall be a desolation, and an astonishment; and these nations shall serve the king of Babylon SEVENTY YEARS*" (Jer. 25:11).

In the days of Jeremiah there were false prophets, and they taught Israel to believe that their captivity in Babylon would be very brief. To give the truth to the people and thus counteract this lie, Jeremiah wrote to the captives in Babylon and instructed them to prepare for a *long captivity* in that heathen land.

Jeremiah's Message to Israel

Jeremiah 29:4–10: "Thus saith the Lord of hosts, the God of Israel, unto all that are carried away captives, whom I have caused to be carried away from Jerusalem unto Babylon; Build ye houses, and dwell in them; and plant gardens, and eat the fruit of them; Take ye wives, and beget sons and daughters; and take wives for your sons, and give your daughters to husbands, that they may bear sons and daughters; that ye may be increased there, and not diminished. And seek the peace of the city whither I have caused you to be carried away captives, and pray unto the Lord for it: for in the peace thereof shall ye have peace. For thus saith the Lord of hosts, the God of Israel; Let not your prophets and your diviners, that be in the midst of you, deceive you, neither hearken to your dreams which ye cause to be dreamed. For they prophesy falsely unto you in my name: I have not sent them, saith the Lord. For thus saith the Lord, *That after seventy years* be accomplished at Babylon I will visit you, and perform my good word toward you, in causing you to return to this place."

(It is interesting and instructive to seek a reason why the captivity was seventy years in duration . . . just that and no more. The answer is in II Chronicles 36:21: "To fulfil the word of the Lord by the mouth of Jeremiah, until the land had enjoyed her sabbaths: for as long as she lay desolate she kept sabbath, to fulfil threescore and ten years." According to the instructions of Moses, as given in the twenty-fifth chapter of Leviticus, the Israelites were to observe every seventh year as a sabbath year, allowing the ground to rest without raising a crop. The Israelites did not obey this command and did not let the land rest. They owed God 70 years–and God took it by taking them into Babylon. While they were there the land had her sabbaths of rest.)

Daniel did not have II Timothy 2:15: "Study to shew thyself approved unto God, a workman that needeth not to be ashamed, rightly dividing the word of truth." But even though he did not have these inspired words of Paul in an epistle, he had them in his heart. He was a student of the Word of God; he studied prophecy; and he believed what he read in the Word.

Jeremiah was recognized as a divinely inspired prophet of God. Daniel accepted the message of "the books" (including the book of Jeremiah) as God's inspired Word. He believed in searching the Scriptures.

Daniel was a man of wisdom. In studying the Word of God he knew that the Babylonian captivity began in 606 B. C., and therefore, 68 years of the seventy had already passed. He also knew that Cyrus, of whom Isaiah spoke, would issue an edict allowing Israel to return to their land:

"That saith of Cyrus, He is my shepherd, and shall perform all my pleasure: even saying to Jerusalem, Thou shalt be built; and to the temple, Thy foundation shall be laid" (Isa. 44:28). According to Daniel's reasoning and the prophecies of Jeremiah and Isaiah, the captivity should climax in about two years; but what astonished Daniel was how to reconcile that fact with the visions he had just had. How was he to reconcile the fact that only two of the seventy years remained, and yet *four world empires* were to come and go before the children of Israel would be restored to their homeland of Palestine? At the time of his visions, only Babylon had risen and fallen. There were only two years left in which the other three might come into existence and be destroyed.

Daniel was sorely perplexed. The thing that he must learn before he could fully understand what he had seen concerning his people, was that the seventy years' captivity in Babylon was only a *type* of a longer dispersion that would last seven times as long as the seventy years. Daniel was to learn this in his vision of the seventy weeks recorded in our present chapter. Daniel believed in prayer. Having studied the books just referred to, he believed with all of his heart that if his people would repent and forsake their wicked ways, God would hear their cry, forgive their sins, and allow them to return to their homeland.

"If they shall confess their iniquity, and the iniquity of their fathers, with their trespass which they trespassed against me, and that also they have walked contrary unto me; and that I also have walked contrary unto them, and have brought them into the land of their enemies; if then their uncircumcised hearts be humbled, and they then accept of the punishment of their iniquity: Then will I remember my covenant with Jacob, and also my covenant with Isaac, and also my covenant with Abraham will I remember; and I will remember the land. The land also shall be left of them, and *shall enjoy her sabbaths*, while she lieth desolate without them: and they shall accept of the punishment of their iniquity: because, even because they despised my judgments, and because their soul abhorred my statutes. And yet for all that, when they be in the land of their enemies, I will not cast them away, neither will I abhor them, to destroy them utterly, and to break my covenant with them: for I am the Lord their God. But I will for their sakes remember the covenant of their ancestors, whom I brought forth out of the land of Egypt in the sight of the heathen, that I might be their God: I am the Lord" (Lev. 26:40–45).

"And it shall come to pass, when all these things are come upon thee, the blessing and the curse, which I have set before thee, and thou shalt call them to mind among all the nations, whither the Lord thy God hath driven thee, and shalt return unto the Lord thy God, and shalt obey His voice according to all that I command thee this day, thou and thy children, with all thine heart, and with all thy soul; That then the Lord thy God will turn thy captivity, and have compassion upon thee, and will return and gather thee from all the nations, whither the Lord thy God hath scattered thee. If any of thine be driven out unto the outmost parts of heaven, from thence will the Lord thy God gather thee, and from thence will He fetch thee: And the Lord thy God will bring thee into the land which thy fathers possessed, and thou shalt possess it; and He will do thee good, and multiply thee above thy fathers. And the Lord thy God will circumcise thine heart, and the heart of thy seed, to love the Lord thy God with all thine heart, and with all thy soul, that thou mayest live. And the Lord thy God will put all these curses upon thine enemies, and on them that hate thee, which persecuted thee. And thou shalt return and obey the voice of the Lord, and do all His commandments which I command thee this day. And the Lord thy God will make thee plenteous in every work of thine hand, in the fruit of thy body, and in the fruit of thy cattle, and in the fruit of thy land, for good: for the Lord will again rejoice over thee for good, as He rejoiced over thy fathers: If thou shalt hearken unto the voice of the Lord thy God, to keep His commandments and His statutes which are written in this book of the law, and if thou turn unto the Lord thy God with all thine heart, and with all thy soul" (Deut. 30:1–10).

Knowing the truth of these Scriptures given to Moses by divine inspiration, Daniel poured out his heart to God in behalf of his people.

Daniel's Confession to God in Behalf of Israel

Verses 3–19: "And I set my face unto the Lord God, to seek by prayer and supplications, with fasting, and sackcloth, and ashes: And I prayed unto the Lord my God, and made my confession, and said, O Lord, the great and dreadful God, keeping the covenant and mercy to them that love Him, and to them that keep His commandments; We have sinned, and have committed iniquity, and have done wickedly, and have rebelled, even by departing from thy precepts and from thy judgments: Neither have we hearkened unto thy servants the prophets, which spake in thy name to our kings, our princes, and our fathers, and to all the people of the land. O Lord, righteousness belongeth unto thee, but unto us confusion of faces, as at this day; to the men of Judah, and to the inhabitants of Jerusalem, and unto all Israel, that are near, and that are far off, through all the countries whither thou hast driven them, because of their trespass that they have trespassed against thee. O Lord, to us belongeth confusion of face, to our kings, to our princes, and to our fathers, because we have sinned against thee. To the Lord our God belong mercies and forgivenesses, though we have rebelled against Him; Neither have we obeyed the voice of the Lord our God, to walk in His laws, which He set before us by His servants the prophets. Yea, all Israel have transgressed thy law, even by departing, that they might not obey thy voice; therefore the curse is poured upon us, and the oath that is written in the law of Moses the servant of God, because we have sinned against Him. And He hath confirmed His words, which He spake against us, and against our judges that judged us, by bringing upon us a great evil: for under the whole heaven hath not been done as hath been done upon Jerusalem. As it is written in the law of Moses, all this evil is come upon us: yet made we not our prayer before the Lord our God, that we might turn from our iniquities, and understand thy truth. Therefore hath the Lord watched upon the evil, and brought it upon us: for the Lord our God is righteous in all His works which He doeth: for we obeyed not His voice. And now, O Lord our God, that hast brought thy people forth out of the land of Egypt with a mighty hand, and hast gotten thee renown, as at this day; we have sinned, we have done wickedly. O Lord, according to all thy righteousness, I beseech thee, let thine anger and thy fury be turned away from thy city Jerusalem, thy holy mountain: because for our sins, and for the iniquities of our fathers, Jerusalem and thy people are become a reproach to all that are about us. Now therefore, O our God, hear the prayer of thy servant, and his supplications, and cause thy face to shine upon thy sanctuary that is desolate, for the Lord's sake. O my God, incline thine ear, and hear; open thine eyes, and behold our desolations, and the city which is called by thy name: for we do not present our supplications before thee for our righteousnesses, but for thy great mercies. O Lord, hear; O Lord, forgive; O Lord, hearken and do; defer not, for thine own sake, O my God: for thy city and thy people are called by thy name."

The prayer recorded here is one of the most sublime, one of the most touching, burning prayers in all of the Word of God. The disciples asked of Jesus, "*Lord, teach us to pray.*" And Jesus gave them the model prayer recorded in the sixth chapter of Matthew. In this prayer of Daniel's, we have another model prayer—a model of true confession, true supplication, true intercession. In this prayer, Daniel—the purest, most spotless character aside from the Lord Jesus Christ—readily and willingly classed himself as a poor sinner in association with his people. He did not exalt himself and say, "Lord, *I* have not sinned, *I* have not forsaken thee for other gods." He came to God along with his people, putting himself in their midst as their representative, confessing and interceding to the only One who could help Israel.

According to verse 1, it was in the first year of the reign of Darius that Daniel had his vision of the seventy weeks. Accordingly, he prayed this prayer the same year he was cast into the den of lions for praying to his God (chapter 6). Could it be that in the chapter before us now, we are informed of the nature and subject of the Prophet's prayers at that time . . . where he received his inspiration to pray (from reading the Word—verse 2), the language he used, the intensity with which he pursued the desired object, and the answer he received? I am not saying that Daniel was praying this prayer recorded here when his enemies conceived the idea for their diabolical decree which forbade him to pray to his God—but if this *was* the prayer that caused Daniel to be cast into the den of lions, we can understand why he had no fear, why he was strengthened and willing to sacrifice his life, if need be, rather than forsake his God who had been so gracious in revealing to him the fate of his people, as well as the glorious promises that lay ahead for them.

In verse 3 we notice the preparation of Daniel for his prayer. He set his face to God and with fasting, sackcloth, and ashes (a token of humility), made his supplication known. I am not advocating that we have sackcloth around the altars in our churches and ashes on the floor, but I am saying that this world is much more in need of humble men who know how to pray, than it is in need of men who know how to preach. Our churches today have become largely places of dress parades, banquets, robed choirs, carpeted floors, cushioned pews, and beautiful stained glass windows.

I am not against comfortable, inviting churches. I believe that Christianity will cause its converts to wash their faces, comb their hair, and shine their shoes. I believe according to Paul that a man who will not provide for his own household is worse than an infidel; but when the disciples could not cast the demon out of the boy, Jesus told them, "This kind goeth not out but by prayer and fasting" (Matt. 17:21). To the moneychangers in the temple, He said, "My house shall be a house of prayer, but ye have made it a den of thieves." Then He took cords, made a whip, and drove them out of the temple.

Today most spiritual leaders are appointed or elected; only a few are *called.* The average church spends more money on interior decorating than it gives to missions. Some churches can seat more people in the church cafeteria than can be seated in the sanctuary.

Daniel fasted, he replaced his royal garments with sackcloth (we would call it "burlap"), and in ashes he prayed unto his God. He knew God personally; he had the same assurance Paul had when that great apostle said, "*I know whom I have believed, and am persuaded that HE is able . . . .*" Daniel did not pray to a historical God. He prayed to his own personal God. He made his confession, and in the very outset of his prayer he said, "*O Lord, the great and dreadful God.*" Daniel would not fit in with the average ministerial association of today. He would be called fanatical and narrow, talking about a "dreadful God." Today we are hearing about "the Fatherhood of God, the brotherhood of man, God is love, God is good, God is kind." I am glad that God is love (I am what I am by the grace of God); but while God is love, He is also *a consuming fire*!

Daniel confessed, "O Lord . . . WE have sinned, and have committed iniquity, and have done wickedly . . . ." Daniel did not say, "*THEY* have sinned . . . *my fathers* have committed iniquity." He did not pray like the Pharisee in the temple who said, "I thank thee, Lord, that I am not as other men are." Such words come from the lips and the heart of a hypocrite. Daniel took his place with his sinning people.

Disobedience to God was prevalent. In Daniel's prayer we read the words *sin*, *iniquity*—or the equivalent of these two words—no less than twenty-nine times:

"We have *sinned* . . . (verse 5)

We have committed *iniquity* . . . (verse 5)

We have *done wickedly* . . . (verse 5)

We have *rebelled* . . . (verse 5)

Even by *departing from thy precepts and thy judgments* . . . (verse 5)

Neither have we hearkened unto thy servants the prophets (thus the sin of disobedience) . . . (verse 6)

Unto us confusion of faces because of our *sin* . . . (verses 7 and 8)

Because of their *trespasses* . . . (verse 7)

They have *trespassed* against thee . . . (verse 7)

Because we have *sinned* against thee . . . (verse 8)

We have *rebelled* . . . (verse 9)

Neither have we obeyed the voice of the Lord our God . . . (verse 10)

The *curse* is poured upon us . . . (verse 11)

Because we have *sinned* against (Jehovah) . . . (verse 11)

We have *transgressed* thy law . . . (verse 11)

Not obey thy voice . . . (verse 11)

By bringing upon us a great *evil* (the captivity in Babylon) . . . (verse 12)

All this *evil* is come upon us . . . (verse 13)

That we might turn from our *iniquities* . . . (verse 13)

The Lord watched upon the *evil* (the God of Israel neither slumbers nor sleeps. Nothing misses His eye.) . . . (verse 14)

We *obeyed not* His voice . . . (verse 14)

We have *sinned* . . . (verse 15)

We have done *wickedly* . . . (verse 15)

Because of our *sins* . . . (verse 16)

For the *iniquities* . . . thy people are become a reproach . . . (verse 16)

Is *desolate* (Desolation is the result of sin–of a person, a city, or a nation.) . . . (verse 17)

Behold our *desolations* . . . (verse 18)

Confessing my *sin* . . . (verse 20)

The *sin* of my people, Israel" (verse 20).

Because of the sins and rebellion of Daniel's people, confusion reigned among them. The kings and princes of Israel were confused because they had trespassed against Jehovah, they had not sought His face nor had they hearkened to His voice. They had departed from His law and had rebelled against Him. Therefore the curse of God was poured out upon His chosen people. They had sinned–and sin brings judgment. God brought great evil upon His people *that they might come to themselves* and return unto Him.

Daniel closes his prayer in words aflame with deep desire and longing for God to have mercy upon His people: *"O my God, incline thine ear, and hear; open thine eyes, and behold our desolations, and the city which is called by thy name: for we do not present our supplications before thee for our righteousnesses, but for thy great mercies. O LORD, HEAR; O LORD, FORGIVE; O LORD, HEARKEN AND DO; defer not, for thine own sake, O my God: for thy city and thy people are called by thy name!"* (verses 18 and 19).

Daniel did not beg for mercy because of righteousness on the part of his people. He said in essence, "O my God–we throw ourselves at thy feet! In sackcloth and ashes we beg for thy mercy. O dear God, because of the misery that is upon us, the deplorable conditions that reign in the Holy City, we beseech thee to move with compassion and tenderness. O Lord, our God, hear and forgive! Do not put it off, Lord, but hear me NOW. Forgive our sins NOW. Deliver us NOW. O Lord, thou art able. Hearken to my cry. Perform for us that which I beg. Accomplish it now; do it speedily. Have mercy upon us."

Notice the last words of Daniel's prayer: "O Lord, hear. O Lord, forgive. O Lord, hearken and do. Defer not, *for thine own sake.*" In other words, "Dear God, I know from studying the sacred books of Jeremiah, Isaiah, and Ezekiel, that Judah and Israel are thy people. I know that the Holy City is thy city. I know that the temple was thy temple. But the heathen have made desolate thy temple and thy city. Dear God, for the sake of thy temple, for the sake of thy people—but most of all, FOR THY NAME'S SAKE, hear my prayer and speedily deliver thy people." What a prayer!!!

God Interrupts Daniel's Prayer

Verses 20–23: "And whiles I was speaking, and praying, and confessing my sin and the sin of my people Israel, and presenting my supplication before the Lord my God for the holy mountain of my God; Yea, whiles I was speaking in prayer, even the man Gabriel, whom I had seen in the vision at the beginning, being caused to fly swiftly, touched me about the time of the evening oblation. And he informed me, and talked with me, and said, O Daniel, I am now come forth to give thee skill and understanding. At the beginning of thy supplications the commandment came forth, and I am come to shew thee; for thou art greatly beloved: therefore understand the matter, and consider the vision."

It is not often that God breaks into our prayers, but He sent Gabriel to interrupt the prayer of Daniel. While the prophet was praying and confessing the sins of Israel, laying his supplication before God, even while he yet spoke, Gabriel appeared—about the time of the evening oblation, which would be about 3:00 P. M.

Gabriel swiftly approached Daniel, touched him, and told him that God greatly loved and honored him. "And I am come to show thee. Therefore understand the matter, and consider the vision." Note the swiftness with which Gabriel appeared—the urgency of his mission. When he appeared to Daniel, he spoke as a man. When God sends angels to make known to His prophets what He would have them know, those angels always assume the form of a man.

In Genesis 18:1,2 we read, "And the Lord appeared unto (Abraham) in the plains of Mamre: and he sat in the tent door in the heat of the day; and he lift up his eyes and looked, and, lo, three men stood by him: and when he saw them, he ran to meet them from the tent door, and bowed himself toward the ground."

The first thing of which Gabriel assured Daniel was that he was greatly beloved in heaven. Certainly Daniel was respected by heaven's host–God the Father, God the Son, God the Holy Ghost; cherubim, seraphim, and angels had such high regard for Daniel that Gabriel was appointed to make a swift journey to earth to help him in his extreme suffering of soul and spirit, and to give him skill and understanding.

The Seventy Weeks

Verses 24–27: "Seventy weeks are determined upon thy people and upon thy holy city, to finish the transgression, and to make an end of sins, and to make reconciliation for iniquity, and to bring in everlasting righteousness, and to seal up the vision and prophecy, and to anoint the most Holy. Know therefore and understand, that from the going forth of the commandment to restore and to build Jerusalem unto the Messiah the Prince shall be seven weeks, and threescore and two weeks: the street shall be built again, and the wall, even in troublous times. And after threescore and two weeks shall Messiah be cut off, but not for Himself: and the people of the prince that shall come shall destroy the city and the sanctuary; and the end thereof shall be with a flood, and unto the end of the war desolations are determined. And he shall confirm the covenant with many for one week: and in the midst of the week he shall cause the sacrifice and the oblation to cease, and for the overspreading of abominations he shall make it desolate, even until the consummation, and that determined shall be poured out upon the desolate."

Gabriel reveals to Daniel that a period seven times as long as the one mentioned by Jeremiah, which he has just been studying, is yet to pass before God's plan for Israel will be consummated.

In many ways, the vision of the seventy weeks is the most important revelation in all Scripture because it gives the interpretation of prophetic chronology, it is the key that unlocks the Scriptures of truth, and it discloses that the seventy weeks cover the period *when the Jews are dwelling in their own land.* It has nothing to do with the period of time when the Jews are NOT in their land. It does not cover this dispensation–the period of their dispersion–but it will again take up their history when they return to their own land immediately after the Rapture, when the decree is given to restore and rebuild Jerusalem.

The time marked off by the seventy weeks of prophecy has to do with Israel–but only while they dwell in their own land. It is utterly impossible for anyone to understand the Word of God without understanding the purpcse and the prophecy set forth in the vision of the seventy weeks. Verse 24 reveals that the purpose of the seventy weeks is sixfold:

1. To finish the transgression,
2. To make an end of sin,
3. To make reconciliation for iniquity,
4. To bring in everlasting righteousness,
5. To seal up the vision and prophecy, and
6. To anoint the most Holy.

Now let us look at each of these individually and see just what we have:

1. To Finish the Transgression:

It is extremely important to keep in mind that these six things have to do only with Daniel's people, the Jews, and that the events will take place in the Holy City, Jerusalem. Since these seventy weeks have to do only with the Jews and Jerusalem, we know that they do not concern the Gentiles or the Church. To take the promises God gave to Abraham and apply them to the Church is nothing short of spiritual robbery. To spiritualize Israel and teach that the Church has taken the place of God's chosen people is to wrongly divide the Word of Truth. We know that Messiah the Prince (the Lord Jesus Christ) on the cross made an end to sin: "But this man, after He had offered one sacrifice for sins for ever, sat down on the right hand of God" (Heb. 10:12).

We know that the Lord Jesus Christ brought about reconciliation from iniquity: "For when we were yet without strength, in due time Christ died for the ungodly. For scarcely for a righteous man will one die: yet peradventure for a good man some would even dare to die. But God commendeth His love toward us, in that, while we were yet sinners, Christ died for us. Much more then, being now justified by His blood, we shall be saved from wrath through Him. For if, when we were enemies, we were reconciled to God by the death of His Son, much more, being reconciled, we shall be saved by His life" (Rom. 5:6–10).

But the atonement and the reconciliation purchased by Jesus for the whole world, through His shed blood on the cross, is not in view here, for here we read of the *putting away* or the *finishing* of the transgression, and this refers to one distinct class of people–*the Jews.*

To this very day and hour, the Jews are still cut off and the "wild olive branch" is still grafted in. The transgression of the Jew will not be finished until they as a nation repent and turn to God. This will take place after the Rapture at the end of the Great Tribulation period when Israel sees Him whom they pierced and recognize Him by the nailprints in His hands:

"And one shall say unto Him, What are these wounds in thine hands? Then He shall answer, Those with which I was wounded in the house of my friends. Awake, O sword, against my shepherd, and against the man that is my fellow, saith the Lord of hosts: smite the shepherd, and the sheep shall be scattered: and I will turn mine hand upon the little ones. And it shall come to pass, that in all the land, saith the Lord, two parts therein shall be cut off and die; but the third shall be left therein. And I will bring the third part through the fire, and will refine them as silver is refined, and will try them as gold is tried: they shall call on my name, and I will hear them: I will say, It is my people: and they shall say, The Lord is my God" (Zech. 13:6–9).

The eleventh chapter of Romans tells us plainly that God has not cast away His people. True, they are cut off for a season; but the nation of Israel will be saved in a day, and God will fulfill to them every word of the promises made to Abraham. Always keep in mind that Israel is an earthly people with earthly blessings, while the Church is a heavenly people with heavenly blessings. Our citizenship is in heaven; we sit together in heavenly places in Christ Jesus. We are strangers in a strange land; we are traveling to a city whose builder and maker is God.

2. To Make an End of Sin:

Again the statement has to do with a specific people (Israel) at a specific time. Paul describes the time: "And so all Israel shall be saved: as it is written, There shall come out of Sion the Deliverer, and shall turn away ungodliness from Jacob: For this is my covenant unto them, when I shall take away their sins'' (Rom. 11:26, 27).

This will not take place until the Lord Jesus Christ comes in the Revelation at the end of the Great Tribulation period. This does not refer to the Rapture when the Church will be caught out of the earth to meet the Lord in the clouds in the air. The *Rapture* takes place before the Tribulation period, but in the *Revelation*, Jesus will come and every eye shall see Him, all the kindreds of the earth shall wail because of Him, and He will then deliver Israel and make an end of sin.

3. To Make Reconciliation for Iniquity:

Here, the Holy Spirit is speaking of *the iniquity of Israel.* The word *iniquity* means "unrighteousness, wickedness, ungodliness." Isaiah speaks of iniquity in his memorable chapter that tells of the Lamb without spot and without blemish: "All we like sheep have gone astray; we have turned every one to his own way; and the Lord hath laid on Him the iniquity of us all'' (Isa. 53:6).

It is true that Jehovah God laid on Jesus the iniquity of us all. Peter describes this glorious truth in I Peter 2:24: "Who His own self bare our sins in His own body on the tree, that we, being dead to sins, should live unto righteousness: by whose stripes ye were healed.'' But this does not apply to the Jew as a nation. In this dispensation of grace, the Jew is saved exactly as the Gentile is saved. If a Jew desires to become a Christian, he must believe on the Lord Jesus Christ, trust in the shed blood of His cross, receive Him by faith–and then he becomes a member of the body of Christ where there is neither Jew nor Gentile.

"For ye are all the children of God by faith in Christ Jesus. For as many of you as have been baptized into

Christ have put on Christ. There is neither Jew nor Greek, there is neither bond nor free, there is neither male nor female: for ye are all one in Christ Jesus" (Gal. 3:26–28).

"And have put on the new man, which is renewed in knowledge after the image of Him that created him: Where there is neither Greek nor Jew, circumcision nor uncircumcision, Barbarian, Scythian, bond nor free: but Christ is all, and in all" (Col. 3:10,11).

During this dispensation, "whosoever will" is invited–regardless of race, color, or whatsoever. ANY person–Jew or Gentile, can become a member of the body of Christ, the New Testament Church; and when that body is complete, it will be caught out. Then the Jews–not as individuals, but *as a nation*–will look upon Him whom they pierced: "Behold, He cometh with clouds; and every eye shall see Him, and they also which pierced Him: and all kindreds of the earth shall wail because of Him. Even so, Amen" (Rev. 1:7).

The Jewish nation will be converted when they see Him–yea, a nation will be converted in a day: "Who hath heard such a thing? Who hath seen such things? Shall the earth be made to bring forth in one day? or shall a nation be born at once? For as soon as Zion travailed, she brought forth her children" (Isa. 66:8).

"In that day there shall be a fountain opened to the house of David and to the inhabitants of Jerusalem for sin and for uncleanness" (Zech. 13:1).

There are many people across this great land today who teach that the English-speaking peoples are Israel, and that the Church has replaced Israel in the program of God; but this is definitely wrong. These are not rightly dividing the word of truth; they are robbing Abraham and the nation of God's covenant people of their promises. But regardless of what these spiritual thieves teach, *God will fulfill every promise He made to His chosen people.*

4. To Bring in Everlasting Righteousness:

The night Jesus was born, a heavenly host appeared in the sky, "praising God, and saying, Glory to God in the highest, and on earth peace, good will toward men!" Isaiah tells us that there will be a day when men will beat their swords into plowshares, they will beat their spears into pruning hooks, and will study war no more. Governments, kings, and presidents have talked much about the Utopia they plan to bring to this earth, but in spite of their promises and plans, evil men and seducers wax worse and worse, as the Holy Spirit dictated to Paul in II Timothy 3:13.

If kings, presidents, and rulers would study the Bible, they would know that there can be no "everlasting righteousness" as long as the devil is loose on this earth. There can be no everlasting righteousness until King Jesus sits on the throne of David in Jerusalem, when the knowledge of the Lord will cover the earth. *Then* we will have peace on earth and good will toward men. *Then* men will beat their swords into plowshares and their spears into pruning hooks—and war will be forever removed from this earth. But these things *will not* come to pass until Jesus comes to reign on this earth. When the Lord comes with His Church and the kingdom is set up on earth, He will make a new Covenant with the house of Israel, He will be their God, and they will be His people.

"But this shall be the covenant that I will make with the house of Israel; After those days, saith the Lord, I will put my law in their inward parts, and write it in their hearts; and will be their God, and they shall be my people.

And they shall teach no more every man his neighbour, and every man his brother, saying, Know the Lord: for they shall all know me, from the least of them unto the greatest of them, saith the Lord: for I will forgive their iniquity, and I will remember their sin no more" (Jer. 31:33,34).

5. *To Seal Up the Vision and Prophecy:*

When Jesus comes and sets up His kingdom on earth, there will be no further need for visions or prophecy: "Charity never faileth: but whether there be prophecies, they shall fail; whether there be tongues, they shall cease; whether there be knowledge, it shall vanish away. For we know in part, and we prophesy in part. But when that which is perfect is come, then that which is in part shall be done away" (I Cor. 13:8–10).

Visions and prophecy will be no more, because since God will be with His people and they will commune one with another, there will be no need for a prophet and no need for visions. "For I would not, brethren, that ye should be ignorant of this mystery, lest ye should be wise in your own conceits; that blindness in part is happened to Israel, until the fulness of the Gentiles be come in" (Rom. 11:25).

It is singular that visions and prophecies have been confined to the nation Israel, and when all visions and all prophecies have been fulfilled there will be no further need for them. They will be sealed up for preservation in God's unending ages of ages. Revelation 5:8 mentions "golden vials full of odours, which are the prayers of saints." God will seal and preserve the visions and the prophecies given to His covenant people.

6. *To Anoint the Most Holy:*

I would like for you to read and study the entire

forty-first and forty-second chapters of Ezekiel. Time and space will not permit me to give the text and discuss it here. In those passages we learn that there will be a new temple–the Millennial temple. It will be erected in Jerusalem on the very spot where Solomon's temple was built. The Mosque of Omar stands there today, but with the exception of this one building the entire temple area is now open. After the Rapture–probably during the very first part of the tribulation period, when Antichrist brings peace--the temple will be rebuilt.

The first appearance of Shekinah glory was at the Exodus when the Lord God Almighty went before the children of Israel in a pillar of cloud by day and a pillar of fire by night: "And the Lord went before them by day in a pillar of a cloud, to lead them the way; and by night in a pillar of fire, to give them light; to go by day and night: He took not away the pillar of the cloud by day, nor the pillar of fire by night, from before the people" (Ex. 13:21,22).

When the tabernacle was erected, Shekinah glory took possession of the most holy place in the tabernacle and dwelt between the cherubim on the ark of the covenant: "Then a cloud covered the tent of the congregation, and the glory of the Lord filled the tabernacle. And Moses was not able to enter into the tent of the congregation, because the cloud abode thereon, and the glory of the Lord filled the tabernacle" (Ex. 40:34,35). "And there I will meet with thee, and I will commune with thee from above the mercy seat, from between the two cherubims which are upon the ark of the testimony, of all things which I will give thee in commandment unto the children of Israel" (Ex. 25:22).

"And when Moses was gone into the tabernacle of the congregation to speak with him, then he heard the voice of one speaking unto him from off the mercy seat that was upon the ark of testimony, from between the two cherubims: and he spake unto him'' (Num. 7:89).

When the temple of Solomon was dedicated, the Shekinah cloud filled the holy place so that the priest of Jehovah could not stand up to minister in the temple: ''And it came to pass, when the priests were come out of the holy place, that the cloud filled the house of the Lord, so that the priests could not stand to minister because of the cloud: for the glory of the Lord had filled the house of the Lord'' (I Kings 8:10,11).

Ezekiel 9:3 refers to Shekinah glory: ''And the glory of the God of Israel was gone up from the cherub, whereupon he was, to the threshold of the house. And he called to the man clothed with linen, which had the writer's inkhorn by his side.'' In Ezekiel 11:23 we read: ''And the glory of the Lord went up from the midst of the city, and stood upon the mountain which is on the east side of the city.''

Ezekiel chapters 41 and 42 describe the prophet's vision of the temple, and in Ezekiel 43:1–6 he again sees Shekinah glory return from the east: ''Afterward he brought me to the gate, even the gate that looketh toward the east: And, behold, the glory of the God of Israel came from the way of the east: and His voice was like a noise of many waters: and the earth shined with His glory. And it was according to the appearance of the vision which I saw, even according to the vision that I saw when I came to destroy the city: and the visions were like the vision that I saw by the river Chebar; and I fell upon my face. And the glory of the Lord came into the house by the way of the gate whose prospect is toward the east. So the Spirit took me up, and brought me into the inner court; and, behold, the glory of the Lord filled the house. And I heard Him speaking unto me out of the house; and the man stood by me."

From these Scriptures we learn that when Jesus returns to this earth and the Millennial temple is built, Shekinah glory will return and anoint the most holy place. Thus we clearly see that the time-space between the departure of Shekinah glory from the earth, and its return to earth, is the duration of "the times of the Gentiles." The Shekinah glory of God has to do with God's covenant people *when they are in their rightful position here upon this earth.*

Seventy Sevens

The Hebrew words translated "seventy weeks" in our authorized King James version of the Bible read "*seventy sevens.*" The word "week" is used because we have no word in the English language that is the exact equivalent of the Hebrew word which signifies *seven*, and the translators of our King James version used "week" instead of "sevens." Thus, the vision Daniel saw was really seventy SEVENS.

In the Word of God we find the law of sevens–both in this world and in the spirit world. We read that God created the earth and all things therein in six days, and rested on the *seventh* day. All through the Scripture, seven is a basic number. Our week is a week of seven days. The Scripture speaks of the week of *weeks*, the week of *months*, the week of *years*, and the week of *weeks of years.*

In Revelation we read of seven churches, seven seals, seven trumpets, seven personages, seven vials, seven dooms and seven NEW THINGS. Seven is God's perfect number. It is made up of the divine number of *three* (Father, Son, and Holy Spirit) and the number of the earth, which is *four*: Spring, Summer, Autumn, Winter; North, South, East, and West. The earth is the Lord's and the fulness thereof, God is the Creator of heaven and earth and all things therein; therefore, the Trinity plus the number of the earth make seven–God's number for perfection.

The Key to Bible Understanding

Spiritual truths are not discovered by human wisdom or through human understanding. God cannot be explained in a test tube in the laboratory. Paul explains, "But as it is written, Eye hath not seen, nor ear heard, neither have entered into the heart of man, the things which God hath prepared for them that love Him. But God hath revealed them unto us by His SPIRIT: for the Spirit searcheth all things, yea, the deep things of God. For what man knoweth the things of a man, save the spirit of man which is in him? Even so the things of God knoweth no man, but *the Spirit of God.* Now we have received, not the spirit of the world, but the Spirit which is of God; that we might know the things that are freely given to us of God" (I Cor. 2:9–12).

Now notice the tremendous truth and revelation in verse 13 of this same passage: *"Which things also we speak, not in the words which man's wisdom teacheth, but which the Holy Ghost teacheth; comparing spiritual things with spiritual."* This is the key to spiritual understanding. The reason the Bible is a riddle instead of a revelation to many church people is that they have never been born of the Spirit. The natural man cannot receive the things of the Spirit of God. They are foolishness to him. Neither can he know them, because they are spiritually discerned.

It is true that we will never know ALL there is to know about the Bible; but we can *believe* it because it is

God's Word, verbally inspired—the mind of God, the wisdom of God, yea, *very God* (John 1:1). However, by studying and rightly dividing the Word of truth, by comparing Scripture with Scripture and spiritual things with spiritual, we can understand much—yes, we can understand ALL that God would have us to know about His Word and coming events while we are in this body of flesh. We could not endure the real depth of spiritual truths. Such knowledge is too glorious, too marvelous, for flesh. God reveals all that we need to know; it is impossible for us to know some of the things that have to do with the Almighty and divine dealings.

God has, in the language of man, a plan, a timetable. We are faced with "the law of sevens." Does it not seem reasonable that there is a time element set forth in this law? And if God deals in "the law of sevens," is it not reasonable that He is making known His plan and His purpose as having to do with this earth and man during these days in which we live, and the dispensations that lie ahead?

The disciples asked of Jesus, "Lord, wilt thou at this time restore again the kingdom to Israel?" For forty days the risen Lord walked and talked with His disciples, instructing them in things pertaining to the kingdom of God. According to His custom (Luke 24:27, 32, 44, 45) He had probably been instructing them directly out of the Scriptures. But one point He had not touched upon was that time when He would restore the kingdom to Israel, and Himself sit on the throne of David in Jerusalem.

The disciples questioned Him concerning this earthly kingdom which was to be set up. Jesus answered that the time of the kingdom on earth (at which time He would sit on the throne of David and reign) was God's secret. No man knows the day or the hour. God has the times and the seasons set according to His sovereign will (Matt. 24:36, 42, 44: 25:13).

Notice the words of Jesus in Acts 1:6,7. He pointed out to the disciples that it was not for them to know "the times and the seasons" which are in God's plan for the ages. That plan must and WILL run according to the foreknowledge of Him who planned it, and all hell cannot stop the program of the sovereign God of heaven and earth.

In Genesis 3:15 God promised the seed of the woman, and Paul declares, "When the fulness of the time was come, God sent forth His Son, made of a woman, made under the law, to redeem them that were under the law, that we might receive the adoption of sons" (Gal. 4:4,5).

If you are familiar with the years preceding and following the birth of Jesus, you know that all hell allied together to prevent His birth. There is a literal stream of blood flowing from Genesis to Malachi; and when Jesus was born and His birth was announced, King Herod had all the babies under three years of age slaughtered in an attempt to destroy the seed of the woman. Jesus came at the God-appointed time—"the fulness of the time." Everything moves on schedule in heaven, in earth—and throughout the universal systems, all of which were created by God and for Him.

In studying the Old Testament, we learn that according to the prophecies already fulfilled, nothing has failed; all has been accomplished on time according to schedule in spite of "principalities and powers and rulers of wickedness in high places." If everything in the past has been accomplished and fulfilled according to schedule, why should we not expect all *future events* prophetically set forth in Scripture to be fulfilled with the same accuracy?

In studying prophecy we read of hours, weeks, months,

and years. We also read of "time, times, and an half time." If we are to understand the meaning of these terms we must interpret them according to the scriptural rule for Bible interpretation. Notice these enlightening words: "After the number of the days in which ye searched the land, even FORTY DAYS, each day for a year, shall ye bear your iniquities, even FORTY YEARS, and ye shall know my breach of promise" (Num. 14:34). Certainly we know this judgment was literally fulfilled to the very day and hour. God's chosen people wandered in the wilderness for exactly forty years—a year for each and every day the spies spent in searching out the land of Canaan: "And when thou hast accomplished them, lie again on thy right side, and thou shalt bear the iniquity of the house of Judah forty days: I have appointed thee each day for a year" (Ezek. 4:6).

The divine scale for measuring prophetic time is "A DAY STANDS FOR A YEAR." When we see this, the mist begins to disappear; and when we apply the divine scale for measuring prophetic time, to the seventy weeks, we find that seventy weeks add up to 490 years. "That from the going forth of the commandment to restore and to build Jerusalem unto Messiah the Prince shall be seven weeks, and threescore and two weeks." What do we have here? *Seven plus threescore and two.* ONE score is twenty; threescore is 60; plus two makes 62. Seven plus 62 adds up to 69 weeks—or, according to the prophetic scale, *483 years.* But there is one week missing, and we will point out later why this is true.

The Starting Point of the Seventy Weeks

In the interpretation of this important and well known prophecy, Gabriel gave Daniel not only the starting point, but the stopping place as well. The starting point dates from the giving of the commandment to *restore and build*

Jerusalem, and from then unto "Messiah the Prince" shall be 69 sevens–or, *69 weeks*–divided in the twenty-fourth verse as *7 weeks and 62 weeks.* Bible scholars have not agreed as to the date that marks the starting point of the "seventy weeks."

There were four decrees given concerning the restoration of Jerusalem and the rebuilding of the temple, and all four decrees were issued after the Babylonian captivity.

The First Decree:

This was given by King Cyrus in 536 B. C. (Ezra 1:1–4). II Chronicles 36:22,23 is another passage which confirms this proclamation: "Now in the first year of Cyrus king of Persia, that the word of the Lord spoken by the mouth of Jeremiah might be accomplished, the Lord stirred up the spirit of Cyrus king of Persia, that he made a proclamation throughout all his kingdom, and put it also in writing, saying, Thus saith Cyrus king of Persia, All the kingdoms of the earth hath the Lord God of heaven given me; and He hath charged me to build Him an *house in Jerusalem*, which is in Judah. Who is there among you of all His people? The Lord his God be with him, and let him go up."

In these passages, not one word is said about restoring and rebuilding the city of Jerusalem. All that is mentioned in this proclamation is the house of the Lord–the temple.

Cyrus was a heathen king and we might well ask what prompted him to make his decree. Could it be that Daniel had read Jeremiah 25:11–14 to him? Or perhaps Isaiah 44:28: "That saith of Cyrus, He is my shepherd, and shall perform all my pleasure: even saying to Jerusalem, Thou shalt be built; and to the temple, Thy foundation shall be laid." Did Daniel *ask* Cyrus to free his people, or remind him that the 70 years of their prophesied captivity were almost ended? Could it be that the Holy Spirit used this tremendous prophecy to soften the heart of the king and lead him to grant freedom to the Jews and allow them to return to Jerusalem to rebuild their temple? He even allowed them to carry back to their temple the gold and silver vessels which Nebuchadnezzar had confiscated when he overran Jerusalem.

The Holy Spirit did not see fit to reveal to us just what prompted Cyrus to issue his decree; but we know that as a result of that decree, approximately 50,000 Israelite captives returned to Jerusalem:

"The whole congregation together was forty and two thousand three hundred and threescore, beside their servants and their maids, of whom there were seven thousand three hundred thirty and seven: and there were among them two hundred singing men and singing women" (Ezra 2:64,65). They set up an altar; they renewed their offerings, their feasts, their sacrifices–and they began to rebuild their temple; but the work dragged because of many, many adversaries.

The Second Decree:

In 519 B. C., after the Jews appealed to King Darius, he issued a decree to make a search in the king's treasure house in Babylon. The search was made–and revealed the decree that had been given by Cyrus. The decree given by Darius was therefore simply a renewing of that issued by Cyrus–but penalties were attached. Notice in the Scripture that nothing is said of the city–just the temple:

"Then the prophets, Haggai the prophet, and Zechariah the son of Iddo, prophesied unto the Jews that were in Judah and Jerusalem in the name of the God of Israel, even unto them. Then rose up Zerubbabel the son of

Shealtiel, and Jeshua the son of Jozadak, and began to *build the house of God* which is at Jerusalem: and with them were the prophets of God helping them.

"At the same time came to them Tatnai, governor on this side the river, and Shetharboznai, and their companions, and said thus unto them, Who hath commanded you to build this house, and to make up this wall? Then said we unto them after this manner, What are the names of the men that make this building? But the eye of their God was upon the elders of the Jews, that they could not cause them to cease, till the matter came to Darius: and then they returned answer by letter concerning this matter.

"The copy of the letter that Tatnai, governor on this side the river, and Shetharboznai, and his companions the Apharsachites, which were on this side the river, sent unto Darius the king: They sent a letter unto him, wherein was written thus; Unto Darius the king, all peace. Be it known unto the king, that we went into the province of Judea, to the house of the great God, which is builded with great stones, and timber is laid in the walls, and this work goeth fast on, and prospereth in their hands. Then asked we those elders, and said unto them thus, Who commanded you to build this house, and to make up these walls? We asked their names also, to certify thee, that we might write the names of the men that were the chief of them. And thus they returned us answer, saying, We are the servants of the God of heaven and earth, and build the house that was builded these many years ago, which a great king of Israel builded and set up. But after that our fathers had provoked the God of heaven unto wrath, He gave them into the hand of Nebuchadnezzar the king of Babylon, the Chaldean, who destroyed this house, and carried the people away into Babylon.

"But in the first year of Cyrus the king of Babylon the same king Cyrus made a decree to build this house of God. And the vessels also of gold and silver of the house of God, which Nebuchadnezzar took out of the temple that was in Jerusalem, and brought them into the temple of Babylon, those did Cyrus the king take out of the temple of Babylon, and they were delivered unto one, whose name was Sheshbazzar, whom he had made governor; And said unto him, Take these vessels, go, carry them into the temple that is in Jerusalem, and let the house of God be builded in his place. Then came the same Sheshbazzar, and laid the foundation of the house of God which is in Jerusalem: and since that time even until now hath it been in building, and yet *it is not finished.* Now therefore, if it seem good to the king, let there be search made in the king's treasure house, which is there at Babylon, whether it be so, that a decree was made of Cyrus the king to build this house of God at Jerusalem, and let the king send his pleasure to us concerning this matter.

"Then Darius the king made a decree, and search was made in the house of the rolls, where the treasures were laid up in Babylon. And there was found at Achmetha, in the palace that is in the province of the Medes, a roll, and therein was a record thus written:

"In the first year of Cyrus the king the same Cyrus the king made a decree concerning the house of God at Jerusalem, *Let the house be builded*, the place where they offered sacrifices, and let the foundations thereof be strongly laid; the height thereof threescore cubits, and the breadth thereof threescore cubits; with three rows of great stones, and a row of new timber: and let the expenses be given out of the king's house: And also let the golden and silver vessels of the house of God, which Nebuchadnezzar took forth out of the temple which is at Jerusalem, and brought unto Babylon, be restored, and brought again unto the temple which is at Jerusalem, every one to his place, and place them in the house of God.

"Now therefore, Tatnai, governor beyond the river, Shetharboznai, and your companions the Apharsachites, which are beyond the river, be ye far from thence: Let the work of this house of God alone; let the governor of the Jews and the elders of the Jews build this house of God in his place. Moreover I make a decree what ye shall do to the elders of these Jews for the building of this house of God: that of the king's goods, even of the tribute beyond the river, forthwith expenses be given unto these men, that they be not hindered. And that which they have need of, both young bullocks, and rams, and lambs, for the burnt-offerings of the God of heaven, wheat, salt, wine, and oil, according to the appointment of the priests which are at Jerusalem, let it be given them day by day without fail: That they may offer sacrifices of sweet savours unto the God of heaven, and pray for the life of the king, and of his sons.

"Also I have made a decree, that whosoever shall alter this word, let timber be pulled down from his house, and being set up, let him be hanged thereon; and let his house be made a dunghill for this. And the God that hath caused His name to dwell there destroy all kings and people, that shall put to their hand to alter and to destroy this house of God which is at Jerusalem. I Darius have made a decree; let it be done with speed" (Ezra 5:1 – 6:12).

The Third Decree:

In 458 B. C. Artaxerxes king of Persia gave Ezra a letter granting him permission to go to Jerusalem and take priests and levites with him. Ezra was given authority to collect gold and silver, purchase bullocks, rams, and lambs for offerings in the temple; and, should it become necessary, draw on the king's treasury for "whatsoever more shall be needful" for the house of God:

"Now this is the copy of the letter that the king Artaxerxes gave unto Ezra the priest, the scribe, even a scribe of the words of the commandments of the Lord, and of His statutes to Israel. Artaxerxes, king of kings, unto Ezra the priest, a scribe of the law of the God of heaven, perfect peace, and at such a time. I make a decree, that all they of the people of Israel, and of his priests and levites, in my realm, which are minded of their own freewill to go up to Jerusalem, go with thee. Forasmuch as thou art sent of the king, and of his seven counsellors, to enquire concerning Judah and Jerusalem, according to the law of thy God which is in thine hand; And to carry the silver and gold, which the king and his counsellors have freely offered unto the God of Israel, whose habitation is in Jerusalem, and all the silver and gold that thou canst find in all the province of Babylon, with the freewill offering of the people, and of the priests, offering willingly for the house of their God which is in Jerusalem: That thou mayest buy speedily with this money bullocks, rams, lambs, with their meat offerings and their drink offerings, and offer them upon the altar of the house of your God which is in Jerusalem. And whatsoever shall seem good to thee, and to thy brethren, to do with the rest of the silver and the gold, that do after the will of your God. The vessels also that are given thee for the service of the house of thy God, those deliver thou before the God of Jerusalem. And whatsoever more shall be needful for the house of thy God, which thou shalt have occasion to bestow, bestow it out of the king's treasure house. And I, even I Artaxerxes the king, do make a decree to all the treasurers which are beyond the river, that whatsoever Ezra the priest, the scribe of the law of the God of heaven, shall require of you, it be done speedily, unto an hundred talents of silver, and to an hundred measures of wheat, and to an hundred baths of wine, and to an hundred baths of oil, and salt without prescribing how much" (Ezra 7:11–22).

There is nothing in this decree concerning the restoration of the Holy City Jerusalem.

The Fourth Decree:

In 445 B. C. in the twentieth year of the reign of Artaxerxes Longimanus, Nehemiah appeared before the king with a sad heart. His countenance told the king that something was drastically wrong and that Nehemiah was a man under a heavy burden and much sorrow. The king asked him, "Why is thy countenance sad, seeing thou art not sick? This is nothing else but sorrow of heart" (Neh. 2:2). Nehemiah made his request known to the king and asked permission to return to Jerusalem to rebuild it. He said to the king, ". . . Why should not my countenance be sad, *when the city*, the place of my fathers' sepulchres, lieth waste, and the gates thereof are consumed with fire?" (Neh. 2:3).

When Nehemiah made this statement to the king, he inquired how long the prophet desired to be away, and just what he wanted the king to do concerning the rebuilding of the city of Jerusalem. Nehemiah was allowed to return to the Holy City, and his mission was not only religious; it was also political in the eyes of the enemies of the Jews, because such outsiders as Sanballat and Tobiah opposed the mission, saying that the building of the walls and restoration of the city would be an act of rebellion and a danger to the king's empire.

Nehemiah and the group who returned with him repaired the walls in 52 days (Neh. 6:15), but it took 12 years to complete the rebuilding and restoration of the city of Jerusalem, re-establish the law and ordinances of worship in the temple. Nehemiah's rebuilding of the wall and the city is definitely a fulfillment of the prophecy in Daniel 9:25: ". . . *The street shall be built again, and the wall, even in troublous times.*"

Nehemiah's mission was not only to re-establish Jerusalem as a city of worship (the city of the temple) but as a political capital also—the capital of the Jewish nation:

"And it came to pass in the month Nisan, in the twentieth year of Artaxerxes the king, that wine was before him: and I took up the wine, and gave it unto the king. Now I had not been beforetime sad in his presence. Wherefore the king said unto me, Why is thy countenance sad, seeing thou art not sick? This is nothing else but sorrow of heart. Then I was very sore afraid, and said unto the king, Let the king live for ever: why should not my countenance be sad, when the city, the place of my fathers' sepulchres, lieth waste, and the gates thereof are consumed with fire? Then the king said unto me, For what dost thou make request? So I prayed to the God of heaven. And I said unto the king, If it please the king, and if thy servant have found favour in thy sight, that thou wouldest send me unto Judah, unto the city of my fathers' sepulchres, that I may build it.

"And the king said unto me, (the queen also sitting by him,) For how long shall thy journey be? and when wilt thou return? So it pleased the king to send me; and I set him a time. Moreover I said unto the king, If it please the king, let letters be given me to the governors beyond the river, that they may convey me over till I come into Judah; and a letter unto Asaph the keeper of the king's forest, that he may give me timber to make beams for the gates of the palace which appertained to the house, and for the wall of the city, and for the house that I shall enter into. And the king granted me, according to the good hand of my God upon me.

"Then I came to the governors beyond the river, and gave them the king's letters. Now the king had sent captains of the army and horsemen with me. When Sanballat the Horonite, and Tobiah the servant, the Ammonite, heard of it, it grieved them exceedingly that there was come a man to seek the welfare of the children of Israel. So I came to Jerusalem, and was there three days.

"And I arose in the night, I and some few men with me; neither told I any man what my God had put in my heart to do at Jerusalem: neither was there any beast with me, save the beast that I rode upon. And I went out by night by the gate of the valley, even before the dragon well, and to the dung port, and viewed the walls of Jerusalem, which were broken down, and the gates thereof were consumed with fire.

"Then I went on to the gate of the fountain, and to the king's pool: but there was no place for the beast that was under me to pass. Then went I up in the night by the brook, and viewed the wall, and turned back, and entered by the gate of the valley, and so returned. And the rulers knew not whither I went, or what I did; neither had I as yet told it to the Jews, nor to the priests, nor to the nobles, nor to the rulers, nor to the rest that did the work.

"Then said I unto them, Ye see the distress that we are in, how Jerusalem lieth waste, and the gates thereof are burned with fire: come, and let us build up the wall of Jerusalem, that we be no more a reproach. Then I told them of the hand of my God which was good upon me; as also the king's words that he had spoken unto me. And they said, Let us rise up and build. So they strengthened their hands for this good work. But when Sanballat the Horonite, and Tobiah the servant, the Ammonite, and Geshem the Arabian, heard it, they laughed us to scorn, and despised us, and said, What is this thing that ye do? Will ye rebel against the king? Then answered I them, and said unto them, The God of heaven, He will prosper us; therefore we His servants will arise and build: but ye have no portion, nor right, nor memorial, in Jerusalem" (Neh. 2:1–20).

In the second chapter of Nehemiah, there is no decree in words, but the king undoubtedly gave the prophet some form of document or letters giving him the authority to *repair the walls and rebuild the city*—for had not Nehemiah had some form of legal document, the enemies of the restoration of the Holy City would certainly have stopped him from repairing the walls. The decree given to Nehemiah by Artaxerxes is the only one which has to do with rebuilding the city; therefore, it must be the same decree referred to by Gabriel as having to do with the beginning of the seventy weeks of prophecy.

By using literal arithmetic, it will be found that the yardstick of 483 years (7 weeks and 62 weeks . . . 69 weeks) will not fit into any of these spaces. We can see that the decree of Cyrus in 536 B. C. could not have been the starting point of the seventy weeks, because according to the scale of *a day representing a year*, counting from the time Cyrus issued his decree until "Messiah the Prince," the time would have run out in 53 B. C.—49 years before the birth of Christ (which Bible authorities agree was 4 B. C.).

Then, if we should take the second decree (given by King Darius in 519 B. C.) the 483 years of the 69 weeks would have run out in 36 B. C., 32 years before the birth of Christ.

If we should take the third decree (given by Artaxerxes in 458 B. C.) the 69 weeks of years – 483 years – would run OVER to the year 25 A. D.–29 years AFTER the birth of Christ.

If we take the fourth decree (given by Artaxerxes in 445 B. C.) the 483 years would carry us to 38 A. D., which would be *after the crucifixion of Christ.*

We have seen four suggested beginning points of the 69 weeks. Now let us consider points of ending for those weeks. Certainly we know that "Messiah the Prince" (Dan. 9:25) refers to the Lord Jesus Christ – it could mean none other; but what particular period or event in the life of the Lord Jesus does the prophecy point out? Does it refer to His birth? His baptism? His triumphal entry? or to some other incident?

According to authorities, the life of Jesus on earth was 33 years. Was the birth of Christ the point where the 69 weeks climaxed? Many Bible scholars teach that the birth of Christ was the termination of the 69 weeks of prophecy. Remember, it was Gabriel who announced the 69 weeks to Daniel, and it was the same Gabriel who announced to Mary that she would be the mother of *Messiah the Prince*: "And the angel said unto her, Fear not, Mary: for thou hast found favour with God. And, behold, thou shalt conceive in thy womb, and bring forth a son, and shalt call His name JESUS. He shall be great, and shall be called the Son of the Highest: and the Lord God shall give unto Him the throne of His father David: And He shall reign over the house of Jacob for ever; and of His kingdom there shall be no end" (Luke 1:30–33).

It is true that Gabriel did not, in so many words,

tell Mary that Jesus was *Messiah the Prince*, but he did announce to her that Jesus would have the throne of David–and He was born a prince of the house of David. The wise men in Matthew 2:1,2 referred to Jesus as King, in John 18:33–37 Pilate asked Him if He were a king, and He was crucified *"King of the Jews."* Yet He was never crowned king, He never occupied the throne of David; but He was a *Prince*, a prince is a king in the making–and a king must be a prince in the house of his father before he is crowned king. To date Jesus has not been crowned king, He has not received His kingdom; but *He will be crowned King*, He will sit on the throne of His father David in Jerusalem and reign over this earth during the Millennium. Jesus is now our High Priest; He is at the right hand of God making intercession for believers (Heb. 1:1–3; I Tim. 2:5).

In the fulness of time Jesus came, born of a virgin, born Jesus the Saviour–born to die on the cross to satisfy the holiness of God and make possible the salvation of sinners in that His death made it possible for God the Father to be just, and yet justify the ungodly on the merit of the shed blood of His Son. Jesus was not king while here upon this earth–He was *Saviour.* He came, born of a woman, born under the law–not to reign, but to *redeem* those who were under the law (Gal. 4:4).

After the custom of the law, Jesus went with His parents to the temple at the age of twelve; but with that one exception, His first public appearance was at the age of thirty when He came to John to be baptized in Jordan. John knew who He was and refused to baptize Him, saying, "I have need to be baptized of thee, and comest thou to me?" But Jesus said, "Suffer it to be so now: for thus it becometh us to fulfil all righteousness" (Matt. 3:13–17 in part). John baptized Jesus, "and, lo, the heavens were opened unto Him, and He saw the Spirit of God descending like a dove and lighting upon Him." Jesus was anointed by the Holy Ghost. ("Messiah" means "anointed one.")

When Jesus was baptized, God the Father announced, "*This is my beloved Son, in whom I am well pleased.*" He did not announce, "This is my King who shall reign over all the earth." God the Father–sovereign God–knows the end in the beginning; He knows all that will occur *between* the beginning and the ending. Jesus was to wear the crown of thorns before He was to wear a crown as King of kings and reign over the earth. The baptism of Jesus announced His entrance into His public ministry, which ministry announced the kingdom; but the Jews rejected the kingdom. They cried out, "We will not have this man to reign over us! Give us Barabbas! Crucify the Christ! Let His blood be upon us, and upon our children!"

The third outstanding event in the life of Jesus here on earth was His *triumphal entry* into the Holy City. Christ was omniscient, knowing all things. He knew who He was, He knew why He came into the world. He said, "I came not to be ministered unto, but to minister, and to give my life a ransom for many. No man taketh my life from me–I lay it down of myself. I have come that they might have life and have it more abundantly."

Jesus knew that His crucifixion was near, and that He was soon to be "cut off" (Dan. 9:26). His Messiahship must be publicly declared and publicly recognized before He was nailed to the cross. He therefore set the stage and took the proper steps toward the public declaration of His Messiahship:

"Rejoice greatly, O daughter of Zion; shout, O daughter of Jerusalem: behold, thy King cometh unto thee: He is just, and having salvation; lowly, and riding upon an ass, and upon a colt the foal of an ass" (Zech. 9:9).

At the time of the yearly Passover, people flocked to the city by the hundreds. On that memorable day Jesus descended the Mount of Olives, riding upon an ass, "the foal of an ass" (as was prophesied centuries before). The people shouted, "*Hosanna to the Son of David: Blessed is He that cometh in the name of the Lord!*"

Since Jesus was omniscient (He was God in flesh), why did He permit the people to refer to Him as King of Israel when He knew that in a few days He would be nailed to a cross, to die the most shameful death any criminal could die in His day? The answer is simple: *To fulfill the Word of God.* Jesus not only allowed it—He encouraged it and set the stage for it. He instructed His disciples to bring a donkey which they would find tied at the entrance to the city (Matt. 21:1–3; Luke 19:28–40). He even told them what to say if the owners of the donkey asked why they were taking him. They were to answer, "The Master hath need of him."

As the people shouted, "*Hosanna! Blessed be the King that cometh in the name of the Lord!*" the Pharisees said to Jesus, "Master, rebuke thy disciples." Jesus answered, "I tell you that, *if these should hold their peace, THE STONES WOULD IMMEDIATELY CRY OUT!*" (Luke 19:40).

Earlier in the ministry of Jesus this same crowd had attempted to force Him to become their King—they would have crowned Him by force; but He rejected their attempt. Now He is consenting and contributing to it. He accepted their calling Him King and gave aid in bringing it about, thus proving that the triumphal entry certainly had prophetic significance. The people spread their garments in His path, strewed His way with palm branches and cried, "Hosanna!" Jesus did not allow this just in order to put Himself in the limelight, to put on a "dress parade" or to make the headlines. This was definitely a fulfillment of prophecy.

Many Bible scholars agree (and so does this author) that the triumphal entry is the end of Daniel's 69th week and marks the point of the coming of Messiah the Prince. It was the only time in His earthly ministry when Jesus assumed the attitude of a king. Those who accepted Jesus as King accepted Him as *Messiah the Prince*, and there is no reason why the prophecies recorded in Zechariah 9:9 and Daniel 9:25 should not refer to this event.

The first time Jesus rode into Jerusalem, He was riding on an humble little donkey as prophesied in Zechariah 9:9. When He comes to Jerusalem a second time, He will be riding on a magnificent white stallion and He will be followed by the armies of heaven riding on white horses (Rev. 19:11–16). When He rides into Jerusalem from the air, followed by His armies on white horses, that will mark the end of the 70th week of Daniel's prophecy–the end of the reign of Antichrist, the time when Jesus will *destroy the armies of Antichrist* and annihilate the enemies of God's chosen people, Israel.

It seems reasonable that when Jesus rode into Jerusalem upon a little colt, His humble entry into the Holy City should mark the ending of the 69 weeks of troublesome times; and when He comes with the armies of heaven as recorded in Revelation 19, this tremendous event will mark the climax of the reign of the false messiah, Antichrist.

Scripture's Calendar

How many days are in a year according to the Scriptures? The answer is found in Genesis 7:11–24 and 8:3,4.

"In the six hundredth year of Noah's life, in the second month, the seventeenth day of the month, the same day were all the fountains of the great deep broken up, and the windows of heaven were opened" (Gen. 7:11).

"And the waters prevailed upon the earth an hundred and fifty days" (Gen. 7:24).

"And the ark rested *in the seventh month, on the seventeenth day of the month,* upon the mountains of Ararat" (Gen. 8:4).

Here is what we have in these verses: The waters were upon the earth for 150 days. According to Genesis 7:11 the flood began in the second month, the seventeenth day of that month; and according to Genesis 8:4 the ark rested the seventh month, the seventeenth day. From the seventeenth day of the second month to the seventeenth day of the seventh month is exactly five months; and five months of 30 days each add up to 150 days. According to Genesis 7:24, *the waters prevailed upon the earth for 150 days.* Thus, the calendar of Scripture gives us a month of 30 days, a year of 360 days.

It is true that in our day we use a year of 365¼ days; but according to Genesis, God determines time by 30 days to the month, 360 days to the year. So in prophetical chronology we use the calendar year of 360 days, and we have learned that God measures prophetic time *a day for a year.* Therefore, 30 days to a month would apply to 30 years–(7 weeks plus 62 weeks would be 483 years)–and by reckoning from the edict granted by Artaxerxes in 445 B. C. as the starting point of the 69 weeks, and the triumphal entry as the climax of the 69 weeks, we have the 483 years represented by the 69 weeks pointed out in Daniel 9:25, plus 6 to 8 years not accounted for.

So it seems that there is a small gap between the

seven weeks and the sixty-two weeks, in which there are years not accounted for, just as there is a gap between the sixty-ninth and the seventieth weeks.

One Bible scholar says: "In order to show that in sacred history and prophecy it is no unusual thing to skip years during which God's people are not especially concerned, it may be helpful to look at other dates.

"In I Kings 6:1 it is stated that it was in the four hundred and eightieth year after the children of Israel came out of Egypt that Solomon began building the temple. If we will take the chronological Bible dates and follow them through from the Exodus to the 4th year of Solomon, we will find it is 611 years, or 131 years more than what is stated in I Kings 6:1. But by carefully going through the book of Judges and taking out the years when Israel was under the domination of foreign kings, and adding to it the 20-year period in I Samuel when the ark was out of its accustomed place, we will find that they amount to just exactly 131 years.

1. In Judges 3:8 we learn that the children of Israel served Chushanrishathaim *eight years.*
2. Judges 3:12–14 tells us that they were in servitude to the Moabites for a period of *eighteen years.*
3. In Judges 4:2,3 we learn that Israel was in servitude to the Canaanites for *twenty years.*
4. In Judges 6:1 they served the Midianites for *seven years.*
5. In Judges 10:7,8 they were in servitude to the Philistines for *eighteen years.*
6. In Judges 13:1 we read, 'And the children of Israel did evil again in the sight of the Lord; and the Lord delivered them into the hands of the Philistines for *forty years.*'

7. In I Samuel 7:2 the ark was out of its accustomed place.

So it seems evident that the 480 years of I Kings 6:1 is a sacred cycle in which the years of foreign domination are not counted."

Sir Robert Anderson, a converted English lawyer, worked out the problem in his book called *The Coming Prince*, and used the date 445 as the one to coincide with the prediction of Daniel 9:25. He shows that according to Jewish reckoning, the 483 years would involve a total of 173,880 days. I quote from his book:

> The 1st Nisan in the twentieth year of Artaxerxes (the edict to rebuild Jerusalem) was 14th March, B. C. 445.
>
> The 10th Nisan in Passion Week (Christ's entry into Jerusalem) was 6th April, A. D. 32.
>
> The intervening period was 476 years and 24 days (the days being reckoned inclusively, as required by the language of the prophecy, and in accordance with the Jewish practice).
>
> | | |
> |---|---|
> | But 476 X 365 equals– | 173,740 days |
> | Add (14th March to 6th April, both inclusive) | 24 days |
> | Add for leap years | 116 days |
> | | 173,880 days |
>
> And 69 weeks of prophetic years of 360 days (or 69 x 7 x 360) equals 173,880 days.
>
> It may be well to offer here two explanatory remarks. First: in reckoning years from B. C. to A. D., one year must always be omitted; for it is obvious, ex. gr., that from B. C. 1 to A. D. 1 was not TWO years, but one year. B. C. 1 ought to be described as B. C. 0, and it is so reckoned by astronomers.

Regardless of whose calculations we use, there seems to be a year or two difference. We can count on one thing, however: The Bible is not wrong and God's calculations are not wrong. Any error that may occur is in profane chronology or could easily be in the time space not counted in God's timetable between the "7 weeks and the 62 weeks." The fact is, however, the difference in time in the calculations we have given is so small as to indicate that the "69 weeks" cover the time between the edict of Artaxerxes in B. C. 445 and the triumphal entry of Jesus into Jerusalem.

Then we read, "And after threescore and two weeks shall Messiah be cut off, but not for Himself: and the people of the prince that shall come shall destroy the city and the sanctuary; and the end thereof shall be with a flood, and unto the end of the war desolations are determined" (Dan. 9:26). We know that shortly after Jesus rode into Jerusalem on the little donkey, He was nailed to the cross; *He was "cut off."*

Now this is the question to which we must find an answer: *Is there a time-space between the 69th and 70th weeks of Daniel's seventy weeks of prophecy*? The only place to find the answer is in the textbook of the Christian, the Word of God.

Daniel 9:26 clearly tells us that between the 69th and 70th weeks, Messiah the Prince (the Lord Jesus Christ) should be cut off. *That was fulfilled in the crucifixion of the Lord Jesus on Golgotha.*

In the second place, Daniel 9:26 tells us that Jerusalem and the temple will be destroyed: *This occurred in 70 A. D.* when Titus the Roman overran the city, butchered 5,000,000 Jews and left not one stone upon another.

In the third place, we learn in this verse that after the destruction of the Holy City, there will be a long period of wars and rumors of wars, which period Jesus spoke of as *the times of the Gentiles*: "Jerusalem shall be trodden down of the Gentiles until the times of the

Gentiles be fulfilled" (Luke 21:24). We are still in *the times of the Gentiles* and Gentile rulers still dominate world power throughout the earth. It is true that *the fig tree* (Israel) is budding and putting forth leaves, and by that sign we know that summer is near. Certainly we are living in the closing days of this age of grace–the period of time between the 69th and 70th weeks of Daniel's prophecy.

The Olivet Discourse recorded in Matthew 24, Mark 13, and Luke 21 is the key to the interpretation of Daniel 9:26,27. In Matthew 24, the disciples came to Jesus and showed Him the buildings of the temple–tremendous buildings of stone; and Jesus said to them, "Verily I say unto you, There shall not be left here one stone upon another, that shall not be thrown down." This literally happened in 70 A. D. *Every stone was thrown down and the city was utterly destroyed.*

Later, on the Mount of Olives, the disciples asked Jesus, "Tell us, when shall these things be? and what shall be the sign of thy coming, AND OF THE END OF THE WORLD?"

In reply, Jesus gave the disciples a list of things that will take place before His coming again. He warned, "Take heed that no man deceive you. For many shall come in my name, saying, I am Christ; and shall deceive many." This is the age of religious deception.

There will be "wars and rumours of wars." These things must come to pass–"but the end is not yet. For nation shall rise against nation, and kingdom against kingdom: and there shall be famines, and pestilences, and earthquakes, in divers places. *All these are the beginning of sorrows.* Then shall they deliver you (the Jews) up to be afflicted, and shall kill you; and ye shall be hated of all nations for my name's sake." (*We are living in that hour of which Jesus spoke.* Jews have been butchered by the millions in the last few years.)

"And then shall many be offended, and shall betray one another, and shall hate one another. And many false prophets shall rise, and shall deceive many. And because iniquity shall abound, the love of many shall wax cold. . . and this Gospel of the Kingdom shall be preached in all the world for a witness unto all nations; AND THEN SHALL THE END COME" (Matt. 24:1–14 in part).

The "END" is the time when Jesus will return–not FOR the Church in the Rapture, but WITH the Church in the Revelation–to destroy Antichrist. Notice in the very next verse: "When ye therefore shall see the abomination of desolation, spoken of by Daniel the prophet, stand in the holy place, (whoso readeth, let him understand:) Then let them which be in Judaea flee into the mountains."

Here Jesus specifically names four things: (1) Daniel; (2) the "abomination of desolation"; (3) the temple; (4) Judaea. In other words, Jesus points out a specific place and specific events that will transpire just before all hell breaks out on earth, and these things will occur in the middle of the *seventieth week.* After three and one-half years of peace, Antichrist will break his covenant with the Jews and make one last, desperate attempt to annihilate Israel from the face of the earth.

The following verses describe *the Revelation*–not the Rapture. Then in verse 32 of the same chapter, Jesus gives the parable of the fig tree–and the fig tree is definitely Judah. (Study Jeremiah 24 in connection with this.) In this parable we are clearly instructed, "So likewise ye, when ye shall see all these things, know that (the Revelation) is near, even at the doors."

In the true sense of the word, there are no *"signs"*

of the Rapture; the signs given point to the Revelation—the time when Jesus will come in judgment to make His enemies His footstool. The Rapture is the time when Jesus will come to make up His jewels. At that time He will come as a thief in the night, and in a moment, "in the twinkling of an eye," all believers will be translated to meet the Lord in the clouds in the air. Daniel's seventieth week separates the Rapture from the Revelation. The Rapture will take place before the beginning of the reign of Antichrist; the Revelation will come *at the close* of the reign of Antichrist. There is definitely a time space between the 69th and 70th weeks of Daniel, and that space has already run through more than 1900 years.

We clearly see from the Scriptures we have studied in detail that *Daniel's seventieth week* (as described in Daniel 9:24–27); *the Olivet discourse* (given by Jesus and recorded in Matthew 24:1–35); and *the revelation given to John* on the Isle of Patmos (the message contained in the seals, the trumpets and the vials—Rev. 6:1 through 18:24), all cover exactly the same period. This period has to do with the Jews here on earth; it has no reference whatsoever to the Church of the living God. We of the Church will not be here when these events take place; we will be with Jesus at the marriage supper in the sky, being rewarded for our stewardship.

God gave Daniel the blueprint of the seventieth week. In the Olivet discourse, Jesus gave His disciples a much *fuller* picture of Daniel's seventieth week. John the Beloved, in exile, was given a minutely detailed report on Daniel's seventieth week, and what Daniel said in *one verse*, John enlarged to a grand total of thirteen tremendous chapters!

This proves to me beyond the shadow of a doubt

that the Bible is not the product of man, but that it is God's infallible, verbally inspired Word. There was no need for Daniel to write 13 chapters describing the Great Tribulation period; there was no need for Jesus to give the disciples 13 chapters in Matthew; but in this day and hour there IS a drastic need for the preaching of these 13 chapters that describe the judgment which will fall upon this earth immediately following the Rapture of the Church, when the Antichrist will reign supreme and blood will run like water in the streets.

The Second Coming of Christ

In studying the book of Daniel we must keep in mind the fact that the book has to do with *"the times of the Gentiles."* Therefore the visions of Daniel cover the entire period of that time. The dream of Nebuchadnezzar (the first vision recorded in Daniel) covers the whole time of the Gentiles, and the image IN the vision was not to be totally destroyed until the stone cut out of the mountain without hands destroyed the colossal kingdom of Babylon. This will take place at the second coming of Jesus Christ. He is the stone that will crumble, crush, and grind Babylon into powder.

The beast visions seen by Daniel cover the entire "times of the Gentiles," even to the end when the counterfeit Christ (the "little horn") will be destroyed. This will take place at the time when Christ comes as described by Jude, with tens of thousands of His saints.

Is the vision of the seventy weeks (seventy sevens) an exception to all other visions in the book of Daniel? Do the seventy weeks extend only to the *first* coming–the *birth of Christ*? And does the seventy-week period end with the destruction of Jerusalem? It stands to reason that the vision of the seventy weeks also covers the entire period of the "times of the Gentiles." The visions of Daniel are not separated; they are one and the same–each adding light and understanding to the others. Therefore, the visions in Daniel–from the beginning of the book to the end–cover the entire period known as "the times of the Gentiles," and this period has already lasted for more than 25 centuries.

It is perhaps a few years–a few weeks, months, days, or even moments–until the Rapture; and then the reign of Antichrist will bring *the times of the Gentiles* to a climax. Jehovah God gave Daniel these visions by way of instructing him as to what would take place concerning the Jews and the Holy City of Jerusalem, until the transgressions of the Jews were finished. Their transgressions are *not yet finished,* and they are still scattered all over the world. It is true that the fig tree is now budding, but the Jews are still hated above all peoples of earth, and by no means are they all back in their own land; only a percentage of them have returned. Daniel learned through these visions that his people would be scattered all over the world and would be trodden down of the Gentiles until *the times of the Gentiles* shall come to an end. The seventy weeks are distinctly Jewish; they concern the dealings of God with His chosen nation and people, and have nothing whatsoever to do with the Church.

It is very significant that Daniel, in one great leap, moves from "the cutting off" of the Prince (the crucifixion of Christ) *all the way to the destruction of Jerusalem*–which we know happened in 70 A. D. when Titus overran and destroyed the city; and then he moves on from the destruction of Jerusalem in 70 A. D. to the Antichrist (verse 27) and his covenant with the Jews for three and one-half years. This will take place immediately after the Rapture, so we see that in these two verses (26 and 27) Daniel covers a period of more than 1900 years thus far.

The Church had no place in the prophecy concerning Daniel's people and city. Daniel did not see the Church. He knew nothing of the Church, and the period of time from the crucifixion to the Rapture was completely blank to him. The mystery of the Church was not revealed to Daniel (nor to any of the Old Testament prophets); it was revealed to the Apostle Paul at the appointed time. The gap between Daniel's 69th and 70th weeks is as wide as the Dispensation of the Church–the period of time in which we now are, and which is rapidly headed toward the climax–the end of the Dispensation of Grace.

In Daniel's seventy weeks of prophecy we have seen that 69 weeks (483 years according to the prophetic scale of a day representing a year) have elapsed, and they closed with the triumphal entry of Jesus into Jerusalem. It is true that Jerusalem was not destroyed until 70 A. D., but the sentence was passed when the Jews crucified Jesus.

As Jesus looked out over Jerusalem and wept, He said, "O Jerusalem, Jerusalem, which killest the prophets, and stonest them that are sent unto thee; how often would I have gathered thy children together, as a hen doth gather her brood under her wings, and ye would not! Behold, *your house is left unto you desolate*: and verily I say unto you, Ye shall not see me, until the time come when ye shall say, Blessed is He that cometh in the name of the Lord" (Luke 13:34,35).

Notice the words, ". . . *Your house IS left unto you desolate.*" Jesus did not say, "Your house WILL BE left desolate at some future date." Titus did not destroy the city and its houses until 70 A. D., and these words were spoken in 33 A. D.; but at that very moment they had crossed God's deadline and sentence had been passed! God does not always pay off on Saturday night–but He always pays *for sure.*

We clearly see that 483 years of Daniel's seventy weeks have already passed. Only one week of years remains to be fulfilled. For 1900 years the Jews have been scattered to the ends of the earth and to every island of the sea; but they have never been assimilated by other nations. They have kept their identity: anywhere, under any circumstance, Jews are clearly recognized as Jews. They have never lost their national peculiarities; they are the same today as when Jesus walked upon this earth. Everything that has ever happened to the Jews and to their land of Palestine was prophesied and is clearly laid down in God's Word:

"For the children of Israel shall abide many days without a king, and without a prince, and without a sacrifice, and without an image, and without an ephod, and without teraphim: Afterward shall the children of Israel return, and seek the Lord their God, and David their king; and shall fear the Lord and His goodness in the latter days" (Hos. 3:4,5).

There are teachers and preachers today who would have us believe that God has cast away His people, but He has not: Paul says, "I say then, Hath God cast away His people? God forbid. For I also am an Israelite, of the seed of Abraham, of the tribe of Benjamin. God hath not cast away His people which He foreknew. Wot ye not what the Scripture saith of Elias? how he maketh intercession to God against Israel. . . For I would not, brethren, that ye should be ignorant of this mystery, lest ye should be wise in your own conceits; that *blindness IN PART is happened to Israel, until the fulness of the Gentiles be come in*" (Rom. 11:1,2,25).

God has preserved His people, and in the latter days they will return to their own land. They are returning in this very hour just as rapidly as they can possibly return to the new state of Israel. In May 1948 the fig tree began to bud. The buds are swelling, the leaves are growing. The stage is now set and one day Israel will be restored to their land. Time will not permit me to give the text of all these Scriptures, but please read and study Jeremiah 30:10,11; 16:14,15; 24:6. Then study Isaiah 11:11,12; 43:5–7; Amos 9:14,15. These Scriptures given to us by God's holy prophets prove beyond the shadow of a doubt that the Jews will be restored to their own land *as a nation*–not just a handful of them. To the student of God's Word it is crystal-clear that the Jew is God's timepiece in relation to prophecy; and as far as the Jew is concerned, God's timeclock stopped at the end of the 69th week of Daniel's seventy weeks of prophecy. It stopped when the Jews crucified the Lord of glory:

"Ye men of Israel, hear these words; Jesus of Nazareth, a man approved of God among you by miracles and wonders and signs, which God did by Him in the midst of you, as ye yourselves also know: Him, being delivered by the determinate counsel and foreknowledge of God, ye have taken, and by wicked hands have crucified and slain" (Acts 2:22,23).

The Period Between the 69th and 70th Weeks

"And after threescore and two weeks shall Messiah be cut off, but not for Himself: and the people of the prince that shall come shall destroy the city and the sanctuary; and the end thereof shall be with a flood, and unto the end of the war desolations are determined" (Dan. 9:26).

Four things are named in this verse that will occur between the 69th and the ending of the 70th week:

1. Messiah, the Lord Jesus Christ, should be "cut off–but not for Himself."
2. The Holy City and the temple of God will be destroyed.

3. A prince will come who will destroy the city and the sanctuary.
4. Palestine, the home of Israel, will be desolate until the consummation of the seventy weeks, which will end in the second coming of Christ in the Revelation with tens of thousands of His saints to destroy the desolator, the man of sin, the Antichrist.

Messiah WAS cut off; Jesus DID die . . . but not for Himself: He died for others. He bore our sins on the tree in His own body: "Who His own self bare our sins in His own body on the tree, that we, being dead to sins, should live unto righteousness: by whose stripes ye were healed" (I Pet. 2:24).

Gabriel announced to Mary that her Son Jesus would sit on the throne of His father David—but instead of receiving the kingdom and reigning from the throne of David, Jesus was rejected, denied, arrested, and crucified. He was "cut off" for no reason of His own . . . there was no guile in Him, He was spotless, not one of His enemies could convince Him of sin. False witnesses were called to *lie*, in order that He might be condemned and sentenced to die on the cross.

Jesus (whom they thought would be the Saviour of Israel, the great King to lead them to victory over the Romans) displayed none of the earthly glories and dignities to which Israel's promised Messiah was entitled, according to the prophecies of the Old Testament. Jesus of Nazareth was not crowned with a king's crown: He was crowned with a crown of thorns. He did not sit on a throne: He was nailed to a cross. But the fact that *He would be cut off* was prophesied by Daniel centuries before it happened.

History teaches that soon after the Jews rejected

their Messiah and requested Barabbas in His stead, God refused to recognize them any longer as a nation, and the temple was no longer recognized as God's house. Jesus said, "*It is written, My house shall be called the house of prayer; but ye have made it a den of thieves*" (Matt. 21:13). And from that time forward, Jesus no longer recognized the temple as God's house. He said, "Behold, your house is left unto you desolate (meaning God-forsaken)" (Matt. 23:38).

Jesus sat on the Mount of Olives overlooking the city He so loved and over which He wept, and foretold the destruction of that city and its inhabitants: "And they shall fall by the edge of the sword, and shall be led away captive into all nations: and Jerusalem shall be trodden down of the Gentiles, until *the times of the Gentiles* be fulfilled" (Luke 21:24). We know that in 70 A. D. the city was leveled and millions of Jews were slaughtered.

It is clearly set forth in Daniel 9:25 that "the prince that shall come" (Antichrist, not the Lord Jesus Christ) shall arise after the Rapture of the Church, when the Roman empire will be revived and the ten kings ally themselves for one purpose, and the "little horn" rises out of the revived Roman empire. The Antichrist (the little horn), the last Gentile ruler, is described in Daniel 7:8, 24, 25 and various other verses.

We must not forget in the study of Daniel that it has to do with "the times of the Gentiles," and its purpose is to disclose in *the "little horn"* the last great Gentile world ruler—*the Antichrist.*

The prophecy of the seventy weeks of necessity includes this prince who will arise in the end time and will rule over this earth in the latter days. The prince referred to in verse 26 is "the king of fierce countenance," the devil in flesh–*Antichrist.*

Also in this verse we learn that Palestine and the Holy City will be desolated until the consummation of the seventy weeks, at which time the Lord Jesus will come and destroy the desolator and restore the land. There will then be peace on earth and good will toward men.

From Deuteronomy 8:7–9 we learn that when the children of Israel moved into the land of Palestine under Joshua, they found it a land flowing with milk and honey and "all manner of fruits":

"For the Lord thy God bringeth thee into a good land, a land of brooks of water, of fountains and depths that spring out of valleys and hills; a land of wheat, and barley, and vines, and fig trees, and pomegranates; a land of oil olive, and honey; a land wherein thou shalt eat bread without scarceness, thou shalt not lack any thing in it; a land whose stones are iron, and out of whose hills thou mayest dig brass."

(The soil in Palestine brought forth abundantly and will do so again during the Millennium.) This land of milk and honey continued as long as God's people obeyed His laws and kept His sabbaths; but God warned Israel that if they did not obey Him, if they turned to other gods, He would punish them. He would shut up the heavens and the fields would not yield a harvest:

"And it shall come to pass, if ye shall hearken diligently unto my commandments which I command you this day, to love the Lord your God, and to serve Him with all your heart and with all your soul, That I will give you the rain of your land in his due season, the first rain and the latter rain, that thou mayest gather in thy corn, and thy wine, and thine oil. And I will send grass in thy fields for thy cattle, that thou mayest eat and be full. Take heed to yourselves, that your heart be not deceived, and ye turn aside, and serve other gods, and worship them; and then the Lord's wrath be kindled against you, and He shut up the heaven, that there be no rain, and that the land yield not her fruit; and lest ye perish quickly from off the good land which the Lord giveth you" (Deut. 11:13–17).

It is true that the Jews who are now in Israel are working miracles through irrigation, but only to a small degree compared with the time when Jesus will restore the land to the descendants of Abraham: "The wilderness and the solitary place shall be glad for them; and the desert shall rejoice, and blossom as the rose" (Isaiah 35:1).

"Instead of the thorn shall come up the fir tree, and instead of the brier shall come up the myrtle tree: and it shall be to the Lord for a name, for an everlasting sign that shall not be cut off" (Isaiah 55:13).

"Then shall the earth yield her increase; and God, even our own God, shall bless us" (Psalm 67:6).

"And the floors shall be full of wheat, and the fats shall overflow with wine and oil. And I will restore to you the years that the locust hath eaten, the cankerworm, and the caterpiller, and the palmerworm, my great army which I sent among you. And ye shall eat in plenty, and be satisfied, and praise the name of the Lord your God, that hath dealt wondrously with you: and my people shall never be ashamed" (Joel 2:24–26).

From the Scriptures we have considered under each of these four headings, we see that of these things prophesied in Daniel 9:26 (to occur after the 69th week), *two* have been fulfilled, one is *now in the process* of fulfillment, and the fourth is definitely future: this is the appearing of the prince–the Antichrist:

"And he (Antichrist) shall confirm the covenant with many for one week: and in the midst of the week he shall cause the sacrifice and the oblation to cease, and for the overspreading of abominations he shall make it desolate, even until the consummation, and that determined shall be poured upon the desolate" (verse 27).

Some will suggest that the personal pronoun in this verse refers to the Prince of princes, the Lord Jesus–but not so. The covenant of Christ is everlasting:

"Now the God of peace, that brought again from the dead our Lord Jesus, that great shepherd of the sheep, through the blood of the *everlasting covenant*" (Heb. 13:20).

By contrast, the Antichrist–the same personage who rides out on a white horse, bearing a bow (the symbol of peace) in Revelation 6:2–will *bring* peace for about three and one-half years – and then *he will break the covenant* "in the midst of the week," and all hell will be loosed here upon earth. Here is the picture:

The Jews will be gathered back in their own land, and they will become a great nation. In Jeremiah 16:14,15; 30:10,11; Amos 9:14,15 and Isaiah 43:5–7 we read concerning the great nation that will be revived in the land of Palestine. When the Rapture takes place and the Church is taken out of the earth, every born again person will be gone. The Antichrist will then offer peace to the Jews in their own land. He will permit them to build their temple; and, of course, when he offers them this covenant of peace and permits them to rebuild their temple and set up their worship, they will receive it gladly. (While on a missionary tour in Palestine, I heard that the Jews already have the stones cut, ready to build their temple when they possess the land where the Mosque of Omar now stands–the very spot where Solomon's temple once stood.)

They will enjoy peace for a space of three and one-half years, and then in the midst of the week the Antichrist will break the covenant, take away the freedom he has given Israel, and if Jesus did not intervene and shorten those days there would not be one person left alive!

But God has always had a faithful remnant—and He always will. In I Kings 19:18 we read of the seven thousand who had not bowed their knees to Baal, and in Revelation 7:2–10 we read of the 144,000 sealed in their foreheads with the seal of God. These 144,000 are all children of Israel, and the devil cannot kill them. They will live through the reign of terror and will lead many to believe in the coming kingdom. There will be a great number converted under their preaching . . . a great host that no man can number.

A New Covenant

After the reign of terror and the destruction of the Antichrist and his armies, there will be *a new covenant.* When Jesus comes in the Revelation with His saints, there will be a great national repentance on the part of Israel and they will see Messiah the King. They will recognize Him by the scars in His hands and they will fall at His feet to worship:

"Behold, the days will come, saith the Lord, that I will make a new covenant with the house of Israel, and with the house of Judah: Not according to the covenant that I made with their fathers in the day that I took them by the hand to bring them out of the land of Egypt; which my covenant they brake, although I was an husband unto them, saith the Lord: But this shall be the covenant that I will make with the house of Israel; After those days, saith the Lord, I will put my law in their inward parts, and write it in their hearts; and will be their God, and they shall be my people. And they shall teach no more every man his neighbour, and every man his brother, saying, Know the Lord: for they shall all know me, from the least of them unto the greatest of them, saith the Lord: for I will forgive their iniquity, and I will remember their sin no more'' (Jer. 31:31–34).

In Hebrews 8:7–13 Paul gives the same truth. Please study this passage carefully in connection with that just quoted from Jeremiah. Paul here declares the promise of the new covenant, and makes it very clear that this is for the Jews, not for the Church. The Church will share in it, in that we will reign with Christ; but the NEW covenant is definitely to the seed of Abraham and it will be made with the Jews when they repent nationally and accept Christ as King. Their sins and iniquities will be forgiven and put away, God will again be their God, and Jesus will reign from the throne of David in the Holy City, Jerusalem.

CHAPTER TEN

THE VISION OF THE GLORY OF GOD

1. In the third year of Cyrus king of Persia a thing was revealed unto Daniel, whose name was called Belteshazzar; and the thing was true, but the time appointed was long: and he understood the thing, and had understanding of the vision.

2. In those days I Daniel was mourning three full weeks.

3. I ate no pleasant bread, neither came flesh nor wine in my mouth, neither did I anoint myself at all, till three whole weeks were fulfilled.

4. And in the four and twentieth day of the first month, as I was by the side of the great river, which is Hiddekel;

5. Then I lifted up mine eyes, and looked, and behold a certain man clothed in linen, whose loins were girded with fine gold of Uphaz:

6. His body also was like the beryl, and his face as the appearance of lightning, and his eyes as lamps of fire, and his arms and his feet like in colour to polished brass, and the voice of his words like the voice of a multitude.

7. And I Daniel alone saw the vision: for the men that were with me saw not the vision; but a great quaking fell upon them, so that they fled to hide themselves.

8. Therefore I was left alone, and saw this great vision, and there remained no strength in me: for my comeliness was turned in me into corruption, and I retained no strength.

9. Yet heard I the voice of his words: and when I heard the voice of his words, then was I in a deep sleep on my face, and my face toward the ground.

10. And, behold, an hand touched me, which set me upon my knees and upon the palms of my hands.

11. And he said unto me, O Daniel, a man greatly beloved, understand the words that I speak unto thee, and stand upright: for unto thee am I now sent. And when he had spoken this word unto me, I stood trembling.

12. Then said he unto me, Fear not, Daniel: for from the first day that thou didst set thine heart to understand, and to chasten thyself before thy God, thy words were heard, and I am come for thy words.
13. But the prince of the kingdom of Persia withstood me one and twenty days: but, lo, Michael, one of the chief princes, came to help me; and I remained there with the kings of Persia.
14. Now I am come to make thee understand what shall befall thy people in the latter days: for yet the vision is for many days.
15. And when he had spoken such words unto me, I set my face toward the ground, and I became dumb.
16. And, behold, one like the similitude of the sons of men touched my lips: then I opened my mouth, and spake, and said unto him that stood before me, O my lord, by the vision my sorrows are turned upon me, and I have retained no strength.
17. For how can the servant of this my lord talk with this my lord? for as for me, straightway there remained no strength in me, neither is there breath left in me.
18. Then there came again and touched me one like the appearance of a man, and he strengthened me,
19. And said, O man greatly beloved, fear not: peace be unto thee, be strong, yea, be strong. And when he had spoken unto me, I was strengthened, and said, Let my lord speak; for thou hast strengthened me.
20. Then said he, Knowest thou wherefore I come unto thee? and now will I return to fight with the prince of Persia: and when I am gone forth, lo, the prince of Grecia shall come.
21. But I will shew thee that which is noted in the scripture of truth: and there is none that holdeth with me in these things, but Michael your prince.

The Time of the Vision

Verse 1: "In the third year of Cyrus king of Persia a thing was revealed unto Daniel, whose name was called Belteshazzar; and the thing was true, but the time appointed was long: and he understood the thing, and had understanding of the vision."

This is the last in the series of visions God gave Daniel. The time of the vision was "*in the third year of Cyrus, king of Persia.*" Daniel was an old man at this time, past ninety. Possibly he was not nearly so active in public affairs as when he was younger. Why he did not return to the Holy City three years previous to this when Cyrus allowed others to return, we do not know, but in Daniel 1:21 we learn that Daniel "continued even unto the first year of king Cyrus."

"Now in the first year of Cyrus king of Persia, that the word of the Lord by the mouth of Jeremiah might be fulfilled, the Lord stirred up the spirit of Cyrus king of Persia, that he made a proclamation throughout all his kingdom, and put it also in writing, saying, Thus saith Cyrus king of Persia, The Lord God of heaven hath given me all the kingdoms of the earth; and He hath charged me to build Him an house at Jerusalem, which is in Judah. Who is there among you of all His people? his God be with him, and let him go up to Jerusalem, which is in Judah, and build the house of the Lord God of Israel, (He is the God,) which is in Jerusalem. And whosoever remaineth in any place where he sojourneth, let the men of his place help him with silver, and with gold, and with goods, and with beasts, beside the freewill-offering for the house of God that is in Jerusalem.

"Then rose up the chief of the fathers of Judah and Benjamin, and the priests, and the Levites, with all them whose spirit God had raised, to go up to build the house of the Lord which is in Jerusalem. And all they that were about them strengthened their hands with vessels of silver, with gold, with goods, and with beasts, and with precious things, beside all that was willingly offered.

"Also Cyrus the king brought forth the vessels of the house of the Lord, which Nebuchadnezzar had brought forth out of Jerusalem, and had put them in the house of his gods; Even those did Cyrus king of Persia bring forth by the hand of Mithredath the treasurer, and numbered them unto Sheshbazzar, the prince of Judah. And this is the number of them: thirty chargers of gold, a thousand chargers of silver, nine and twenty knives, thirty basons of gold, silver basons of a second sort four hundred and ten, and other vessels a thousand. All the vessels of gold and of silver were five thousand and four hundred. All these did Sheshbazzar bring up with them of the captivity that were brought up from Babylon unto Jerusalem" (Ezra chapter 1).

It could well be that when these returned to Palestine, God revealed to Daniel that He did not want him to return, that He had at least one more vision for him in order that he might finish his work as God's prophet. There is no doubt that Daniel was extremely interested in the group that returned to his homeland, and in their success in rebuilding the wall and the temple; but he could have been disappointed that so few returned. In Ezra 2:64 and 65 we read, "The whole congregation together was forty and two thousand three hundred and threescore, beside their servants and their maids, of whom there were seven thousand three hundred thirty and seven: and there were among them two hundred singing men and singing women."

Probably many of the priests and leaders had their own homes and were comfortably situated in Babylon and they did not care to pull up stakes and return to a land that was desolate and troubled by the enemies who dwelt there.

From Ezra 2:61–63 we learn an enlightening thing: "And of the children of the priests: the children of Habaiah, the children of Koz, the children of Barzillai; which took a wife of the daughters of Barzillai the Gileadite, and was called after their name: These sought their register among those that were reckoned by genealogy, but they were not found: therefore were they, as polluted, put from the priesthood. And the Tirshatha said unto them, that they should not eat of the most holy things, till there stood up a priest with Urim and with Thummim."

Some of the children of the priests had failed to register among those who were reckoned by genealogy, and they were polluted and put from the priesthood. How it must have saddened the heart of Daniel, that the priests of God should be so careless when he and his three Hebrew friends had been so faithful.

In Ezra 4:1–6 we learn that the adversaries of God hindered the work severely. The people who were in the land hindered the work of the returning Israelites in three ways: First, they sought to draw the Jews away from their pure worship of Jehovah and get them to incorporate their true worship with the religion of the adversaries, thus bringing about a union which God could not and would not recognize.

In the second place, they sought to weaken the hands of the people of Judah by withholding supplies which were an absolute necessity in building the wall and the temple. In the third place, they brought accusations against the people to Ahasuerus and Darius; and the combination of these things disheartened many of those in Babylon who would probably have gone back if all had gone smoothly. It is no wonder Daniel had a sad, heavy heart and his appetite departed from him.

Verses 2 and 3: "In those days I Daniel was mourning three full weeks. I ate no pleasant bread, neither came flesh nor wine in my mouth, neither did I anoint myself at all, till three whole weeks were fulfilled."

Daniel fasted for 21 days. This does not mean that

he did not eat at all. His statement is clear: *"I ate no pleasant bread."* That is, no dainties. We might say that he ate no sweets or fine foods. He ate the bare necessities of life . . . perhaps he ate only bread and water. At any rate, he ate the simplest articles of food for 21 days.

It is interesting to observe the time of year when Daniel had this season of prayer. He records that it was "in the four and twentieth day of the first month." The Passover came on the fourteenth day of the first month, and the following day began the Feast of Unleavened Bread, continuing for seven days. Therefore Daniel's 21 days of prayer and fasting included the days of the Passover, the celebration of the deliverance from Egypt.

It is not unlikely that other Jews ate unleavened bread and kept the Passover as a matter of form, to whom it may have been a relief when the days were over and their conscience relieved with the thought that they had done what the law required.

On the other hand Daniel, while keeping the days required, was after far more than just keeping a ceremony. So he continued praying and fasting, seeking an answer concerning his people. There is no doubt that he would have continued to fast had not God sent an angelic being to bring relief to the old prophet.

God Gives Daniel a Tremendous Vision

Verses 4–6: "And in the four and twentieth day of the first month, as I was by the side of the great river, which is Hiddekel; Then I lifted up mine eyes, and looked, and behold a certain man clothed in linen, whose loins were girded with fine gold of Uphaz: His body also was like the beryl, and his face as the appearance of lightning, and his eyes as lamps of fire, and his arms and his feet like in colour to polished brass, and the voice of his words like the voice of a multitude."

The twenty-fourth day of the first month, Daniel was by the river Hiddekel (which we know as the Tigris). He lifted his eyes and looked toward heaven, and beheld "a certain man clothed in linen, whose loins were girded with fine gold." The description Daniel gives of this Personage is the same as that given of the Lord Jesus Christ by John the Beloved in Revelation 1:9–18:

"I John, who also am your brother, and companion in tribulation, and in the kingdom and patience of Jesus Christ, was in the isle that is called Patmos, for the Word of God, and for the testimony of Jesus Christ. I was in the Spirit on the Lord's day, and heard behind me a great voice, as of a trumpet, saying, I am Alpha and Omega, the first and the last: and, What thou seest, write in a book, and send it unto the seven churches which are in Asia; unto Ephesus, and unto Smyrna, and unto Pergamos, and unto Thyatira, and unto Sardis, and unto Philadelphia, and unto Laodicea. And I turned to see the voice that spake with me. And being turned, I saw seven golden candlesticks; and in the midst of the seven candlesticks one like unto the Son of man, clothed with a garment down to the foot, and girt about the paps with a golden girdle. His head and His hairs were white like wool, as white as snow; and His eyes were as a flame of fire; and His feet like unto fine brass, as if they burned in a furnace; and His voice as the sound of many waters. And He had in His right hand seven stars: and out of His mouth went a sharp twoedged sword: and His countenance was as the sun shineth in his strength. And when I saw Him, I fell at His feet as dead. And He laid His right hand upon me, saying unto me, Fear not; I am the first and the last: I am He that liveth, and was dead; and, behold, I am alive for evermore, Amen; and have the keys of hell and of death."

In the vision of the seventy weeks, Daniel had been

told that Messiah, when He came, would be "cut off"—that is, Jesus would be crucified. It is true that John saw Him *after* the crucifixion and thus describes the glorified Christ; but that does not mean that Jesus could not have appeared to Daniel in like form even before His crucifixion. We must remember that God the Son is co-equal with God the Father—omniscient, omnipotent, omnipresent. So to make the statement that this Person in Daniel's vision is the same Person described in Revelation is not to strain the Scriptures nor wrongly divide the Word.

When Daniel saw this "certain man" he said, "There remained no strength in me, for my comeliness was turned in me into corruption. . . *Then was I in a deep sleep on my face toward the ground.*" John the Beloved said, "*When I saw Him, I fell at His feet as dead*" (Rev. 1:17). I personally believe that John and Daniel saw the same Person—the Son of God.

Daniel Alone Saw the Lord of Glory

Verses 7–9: "And I Daniel alone saw the vision: for the men that were with me saw not the vision; but a great quaking fell upon them, so that they fled to hide themselves. Therefore I was left alone, and saw this great vision, and there remained no strength in me: for my comeliness was turned in me into corruption, and I retained no strength. Yet heard I the voice of His words: and when I heard the voice of His words, then was I in a deep sleep on my face, and my face toward the ground."

The men who were with Daniel did not see the vision of the Lord; but a great quaking fell upon them. They trembled, they fled to hide—and Daniel was left alone to witness this great vision. His strength left him, he fell to the ground, and he tells us, "Yet heard I the voice of His words."

When Daniel heard the words spoken by the Lord

of glory, He was in a deep sleep on his face toward the ground. This reminds us of the experience of Saul of Tarsus recorded in Acts 9:1–9:

"And Saul, yet breathing out threatenings and slaughter against the disciples of the Lord, went unto the high priest, and desired of him letters to Damascus to the synagogues, that if he found any of this way, whether they were men or women, he might bring them bound unto Jerusalem. And as he journeyed, he came near Damascus: and suddenly there shined round about him a light from heaven: And he fell to the earth, and heard a voice saying unto him, Saul, Saul, why persecutest thou me? And he said, Who art thou, Lord? And the Lord said, I am Jesus whom thou persecutest: it is hard for thee to kick against the pricks. And he trembling and astonished said, Lord, what wilt thou have me to do? And the Lord said unto him, Arise, and go into the city, and it shall be told thee what thou must do. And the men which journeyed with him stood speechless, hearing a voice, but seeing no man. And Saul arose from the earth; and when his eyes were opened, he saw no man: but they led him by the hand, and brought him into Damascus. And he was three days without sight, and neither did eat nor drink."

This is a familiar passage to most believers. As Saul traveled to Damascus to persecute the Christians, God simply rolled back the sky and Jesus looked down. The brightness of His face blinded Saul, he fell to the ground–and heard the voice of Jesus speaking to him. He listened, he obeyed, and he was converted . . . to become Paul, the great prince of apostles.

We note that the men with Paul, like those with Daniel, did not see the vision–nor did they hear the message Paul heard. They trembled and quaked. They saw a light, but they did not have the experience Saul of Tarsus had. There is no doubt in my mind that Paul and Daniel saw the same Person–they saw the Lord of glory.

Daniel had this glorious experience *after 21 days of fasting and prayer.* One reason we in the church today have no more results than we have is that we do not have the burden Daniel had. (We do not have the burden Paul had as recorded in Romans 9:1–3, where he clearly states that he would be willing to be cut off from Jesus and burn in hell if it would save his people.) Daniel was crushed and broken on behalf of his people. Today we have fashionable churches with elaborate cafeterias in them, and many feasts are spread there–but very few FASTS are called and few prayer meetings are attended. *The power has departed.*

In Matthew 17:14–21 we read that when Jesus, with Peter, James, and John, came down from the Mount of Transfiguration, "there came to Him a certain man" whose son was a lunatic, so sorely vexed with a devil that he fell into the fire and into the water. Jesus rebuked the demon and he departed out of the boy immediately. The disciples asked why THEY had not been able to cast out the demon, and Jesus replied, "*Because of your unbelief. . . This kind goeth not out BUT BY PRAYER AND FASTING.*"

Daniel Has a Heavenly Visitor

Verses 10 and 11: **"And, behold, an hand touched me, which set me upon my knees and upon the palms of my hands. And He said unto me, O Daniel, a man greatly beloved, understand the words that I speak unto thee, and stand upright: for unto thee am I now sent. And when He had spoken this word unto me, I stood trembling."**

Verse 10 introduces an angel. While Daniel was on the ground with his face toward the ground in a deep sleep, a hand touched him, and he found himself upon his knees and the palms of his hands. The heavenly visitor had a message for Daniel, and He began to talk to him. He said, "O Daniel, *a man greatly beloved . . .*" thus assuring Daniel that he was not forgotten nor left alone. Then the heavenly messenger said to Daniel, "Understand the words that I speak unto thee, and stand upright: for unto thee am I now sent."

Daniel stood trembling. He was astonished in the same manner as Saul of Tarsus had been astonished on the Damascus road. In the same manner, he trembled before God. While the "certain Man" was assuredly the Lord Jesus Christ, He was not alone; it was an angel (Bible authorities suggest *Gabriel*) who touched Daniel and caused him to stand upright, and then gave him the understanding of the words. It seems reasonable that Jesus was not the one who touched Daniel and told him to stand upright, because later in the chapter we learn that the prince of the kingdom of Persia hindered the answer to Daniel's prayer for 21 days. It is absolutely unreasonable to suggest that the devil could have kept *Jesus* from reaching Daniel for 21 days. Jesus would have smitten him with the "twoedged sword of His mouth" (Rev. 1:16) and would not have needed to call upon Michael for help. Therefore, it must have been Gabriel whom the prince of Persia withstood and held back for so long.

If we compare this vision with that of the ram and he-goat in Daniel 8:15–19, it seems only logical that the angel was Gabriel. In Daniel 8 we are told that as Daniel was by the river Ulai he heard a man's voice between the banks of Ulai, which called and said, "Gabriel, make this man to understand the vision." While Daniel did not describe this "certain man" between the banks of Ulai, it no doubt was the Lord of glory. So in the eighth chapter the Lord calls on Gabriel to explain the vision to Daniel.

Then in the vision of the seventy weeks while Daniel was speaking, praying, and confessing the sins of his people, Gabriel was sent to him again. In his speech to Daniel in chapter 9 verse 23, he says, "Thou art greatly beloved." In this vision in our present chapter notice that twice the angel used the same words . . . "a man greatly beloved" (verses 11 and 19). Surely from comparing this chapter with the other two where Gabriel was named, this angel could be no other than Gabriel.

The Prince of Persia

Verses 12–14: "Then said he unto me, Fear not, Daniel: for from the first day that thou didst set thine heart to understand, and to chasten thyself before thy God, thy words were heard, and I am come for thy words. But the prince of the kingdom of Persia withstood me one and twenty days: but, lo, Michael, one of the chief princes, came to help me; and I remained there with the kings of Persia. Now I am come to make thee understand what shall befall thy people in the latter days: for yet the vision is for many days."

This is a very enlightening portion of Daniel concerning the relationship between the spirits of the underworld and this world. The heavenly messenger's first words were words of explanation as to why Daniel's prayer had not been answered immediately: The one who finally brought the answer was hindered for 21 days—the same length of time Daniel had been fasting and praying. The one who had hindered the answer to prayer was "the prince of Persia," and had not Michael the archangel come to assist the messenger, he would not have arrived even at the end of 21 days. But Michael helped Gabriel to free himself from the power of the prince of

Persia, and thus Gabriel arrived on the river bank, touched Daniel, and made known the interpretation of his vision.

Certainly the prince of Persia was not Cyrus (who was king of Persia at that time). We would not suggest that Cyrus could withstand a supernatural being such as Gabriel—or any other one of the angels who might have been sent to answer Daniel's prayer; and this prince of Persia HAD hindered God's messenger, even for 21 days. Certainly this prince of Persia was none other than the devil himself—or one of his top emissaries.

Satan's Kingdom

Very few believers have ever given the devil credit for being the powerful creature that he really is. He reigns as king over a tremendous kingdom:

"But when the Pharisees heard it, they said, This fellow (Jesus) doth not cast out devils, but by Beelzebub the prince of the devils. And Jesus knew their thoughts, and said unto them, Every kingdom divided against itself shall not stand: And if Satan cast out Satan, he is divided against himself; how shall then his kingdom stand? And if I by Beelzebub cast out devils, by whom do your children cast them out? therefore they shall be your judges. But if I cast out devils by the Spirit of God, then the kingdom of God is come unto you. Or else how can one enter into a strong man's house, and spoil his goods, except he first bind the strong man? and then he will spoil his house. He that is not with me is against me; and he that gathereth not with me scattereth abroad" (Matt. 12:24–30).

The kingdom of Satan is made up of principalities, powers, rulers of spiritual darkness, wicked spirits: "For we wrestle not against flesh and blood, but against principalities, against powers, against the rulers of the darkness of this world, against spiritual wickedness in high places'' (Eph. 6:12). In Ephesians 2:2 Paul refers to Satan as ''the prince of the power of the air,'' and in II Corinthians 4:4 he calls him ''the god of this world.'' If the very Son of God was faced by a personal devil on the Mount of Temptation, never entertain the idea that the devil fears YOU. You are no match for Satan.

Immediately after the baptism of Jesus, recorded in Matthew 3, He was led of the Holy Spirit into the wilderness to be tempted of the devil; and a personal Jesus met a personal devil on the Mount of Temptation:

''Then was Jesus led up of the Spirit into the wilderness to be tempted of the devil. And when He had fasted forty days and forty nights, He was afterward an hungred. And when the tempter came to Him, he said, If thou be the Son of God, command that these stones be made bread. But He answered and said, It is written, Man shall not live by bread alone, but by every word that proceedeth out of the mouth of God. Then the devil taketh Him up into the Holy City, and setteth Him on a pinnacle of the temple, and saith unto Him, If thou be the Son of God, cast thyself down: for it is written, He shall give His angels charge concerning thee: and in their hands they shall bear thee up, lest at any time thou dash thy foot against a stone. Jesus said unto him, It is written again, Thou shalt not tempt the Lord thy God. Again, the devil taketh Him up into an exceeding high mountain, and sheweth Him all the kingdoms of the world, and the glory of them; and saith unto Him, All these things will I give thee, if thou wilt fall down and worship me. Then saith Jesus unto him, Get thee hence, Satan: for it is written, Thou shalt worship the Lord thy God, and Him only shalt thou serve. Then the devil leaveth Him, and, behold, angels came and ministered unto Him'' (Matt. 4:1–11).

In Luke 4:5,6 we read, "And the devil, taking Him up into an high mountain, shewed unto Him all the kingdoms of the world in a moment of time. And the devil said unto Him, ALL THIS POWER WILL I GIVE THEE, AND THE GLORY OF THEM: FOR THAT IS DELIVERED UNTO ME; AND TO WHOMSOEVER I WILL I GIVE IT."

Certainly these two passages enlighten us concerning the tremendous power of Satan and the kingdom over which he is king. Could it be that Satan has a special demon who heads his program in every nation on earth? He had a "prince of Persia," and he also had a "prince of Grecia." Then does it not stand to reason that he has appointed a chief demon to lead in his attack on the peoples of every nation on the face of the earth?

In chapter 12 of Revelation and also in Jude 9 we learn that Michael has at least two run-ins with Satan. In the book of Jude he did not rebuke the devil, but said, "The LORD rebuke thee!" Michael knew that Satan was a powerful personality. I personally believe that Lucifer in his original state was one of the archangels. I believe there were three archangels–Gabriel, Michael, and Lucifer–and that Lucifer was the leader of the trio.

But Lucifer, "the shining one," decided that he would overthrow God, take God's throne and exalt HIS throne above the throne of God. Therefore God cast him out of heaven, and he became the devil. I believe that is the reason Michael would not rebuke him when contending with Satan about the body of Moses, because Michael knew what a powerful creature Lucifer was.

We read in Revelation 12:7–9 that there will be war in heaven–war to be fought between Michael and his angels, and Satan and *his* angels. Michael will win the victory, and Satan and his angels will be cast out of heaven, down to the earth. In Daniel 12:1 we learn that Michael is *the guardian angel* of the children of Israel; he stands for God's chosen nation.

The Messenger Makes Known the Meaning of the Vision

In verse 14 we learn the purpose of Gabriel's visit. He had come to Daniel to make him understand and know what would come upon the Jews in the latter days, during the reign of the Antichrist. However, the vision pointed to a future date: "FOR YET THE VISION IS FOR MANY DAYS." We have here the key to the understanding of *the remainder of the book of Daniel*; but before the heavenly messenger outlines in detail the things that are to happen to his people in the latter days during the reign of Antichrist, he makes known what will happen during a period of time *before* the latter days. There is a prelude which describes in detail the wars that will be fought by two of the four kingdoms into which the empire of Alexander the Great was to be divided, and which are spoken of here as the wars between "the king of the north and the king of the south."

These wars carry us down to the end of the reign of Antiochus Epiphanes, 164 B. C. The prelude described here ends with Daniel 11:31, which we will study as we go along. The rest of the chapter (verses 32 through 35) covers the entire period from the reign of the Maccabees (166 B. C.) down to "the time of the end."

Then verse 36 in chapter 11 points out "the willful king"—and we know that this person is the Antichrist, otherwise known as "the king of fierce countenance . . . the little horn . . . the Man of Sin"—*the devil incarnate*, who will reign over the earth until Jesus comes and destroys him with the sword of His mouth.

Daniel 11:36 through the remainder of the book records

in detail the account of what shall befall the Jews in the latter days–the closing days of the reign of Antichrist, days that will be shortened in order that there be some flesh saved.

Daniel Strengthened

Verses 15–17: "And when he had spoken such words unto me, I set my face toward the ground, and I became dumb. And, behold, one like the similitude of the sons of men touched my lips: then I opened my mouth, and spake, and said unto him that stood before me, O my lord, by the vision my sorrows are turned upon me, and I have retained no strength. For how can the servant of this my lord talk with this my lord? For as for me, straightway there remained no strength in me, neither is there breath left in me."

The tremendous import of Gabriel's words struck Daniel dumb, and he remained in that state until One like "the similitude of the sons of men" touched his lips. Daniel then began to speak. He said, "O my lord, by the vision my sorrows are turned upon me, and I have retained no strength." This reminds us of another great prophet, who cried out, "Woe is me! for I am undone; because I am a man of unclean lips, and I dwell in the midst of a people of unclean lips: for mine eyes have seen the King, the Lord of hosts. Then flew one of the seraphims unto me, having a live coal in his hand, which he had taken with the tongs from off the altar: And he laid it upon my mouth, and said, Lo, this hath touched thy lips; and thine iniquity is taken away, and thy sin purged" (Isa. 6:5–7).

In verse 16 Daniel addresses the angelic visitor as "lord"; but the word is not capitalized, and therefore we know that this is not Jesus, Lord of glory. This could be the same seraph who visited Isaiah when he saw the Lord, high and lifted up. Paul tells us in the first chapter of Hebrews that the angels are "ministering spirits to the heirs of salvation." The angels are the servants of the sons of God–not just when we reach heaven, but while we are here on earth. I personally believe that if we could see with spiritual eyes, we would see that our surroundings are literally filled with angels. "The angel of the Lord encampeth round about them that fear God," and angels do minister to us who love, fear, and serve God as Lord.

Daniel confessed to this heavenly visitor that his strength was gone, he had no breath, and therefore how could he speak? Think of that! Daniel had spent the night with lions, he had faced Nebuchadnezzar, Belshazzar, and all the others without fear and trembling; but now the vision he had seen struck him dumb and took away all of his strength. After the heavenly being restored Daniel's speech, verse 18 says, "Then there came *again* and touched me one like the appearance of a man . . . ." From the word "again" we know it was the same one who touched him in verse 10. By this we know that it was Gabriel who again approached him, strengthened him, and began to talk with him once more; and then Daniel requested that the interpretation be continued:

Verses 18–21: "Then there came again and touched me one like the appearance of a man, and he strengthened me, and said, O man greatly beloved, fear not: peace be unto thee, be strong, yea, be strong. And when he had spoken unto me, I was strengthened, and said, Let my lord speak; for thou hast strengthened me. Then said he, Knowest thou wherefore I come unto thee? and now will I return to fight with the prince of Persia: and when I am gone forth, lo, the prince of Grecia shall come. But I will shew thee that which is noted in the Scripture of truth: and there is none that holdeth with me in these things, but Michael your prince."

In verse 20, Gabriel asked Daniel a question: "Knowest thou wherefore I come unto thee?" Then he announced,

"I return to fight with the prince of Persia," and told Daniel that after he had gone, the prince of Grecia would come. But in spite of the prince of Persia, the prince of Grecia, and all the demons and the devil himself, Gabriel declared, "I will show thee that which is noted in the Scripture of truth, and there is none that holdeth with me in these things, BUT MICHAEL YOUR PRINCE." So you see, Daniel had a very capable guardian angel.

To me, there is a tremendous truth set forth in verse 21 which we do not see simply by scanning or reading lightly the Word of God. It is no wonder that in this day and hour the devil is doing all in his power to discredit and destroy the Scripture of truth. You will notice in Daniel 9:2, "In the first year of his reign, I, Daniel understood by books the number of the years, whereof the Word of the Lord came to Jeremiah the prophet, that He would accomplish seventy years in the desolations of Jerusalem." Now, Gabriel is saying to Daniel, "I will show thee that which is noted in the Scripture of truth." God could speak new Scripture, He could declare new statements; but He stands by His Word. The Word of God is forever settled in heaven: It is fixed, final, and it is filed. Yes, God has the original Word, the original plan, and Gabriel showed Daniel things "noted in the Scripture of truth." Heaven and earth will pass away; we will have a new heaven and a new earth. But Jesus said, "Heaven and earth shall pass away, but my words shall not pass away" (Matt. 24:35).

God's Word will never fail nor be destroyed. All hell cannot discredit the Word of God, regardless of what the modernists, liberals, atheists, free-thinkers, or anyone else may say about the Word of God, regardless of what they write about it, regardless of what they do to it. God has "the Scripture of truth" reserved and protected in heaven, and it cannot be destroyed or discredited. God has a record, eternally protected in heaven, of everything He said to Daniel, and all that He made known to him through Gabriel.

CHAPTER ELEVEN

PROPHECIES PAST AND FUTURE

1. Also I in the first year of Darius the Mede, even I, stood to confirm and to strengthen him.

2. And now will I shew thee the truth. Behold, there shall stand up yet three kings in Persia; and the fourth shall be far richer than they all: and by his strength through his riches he shall stir up all against the realm of Grecia.

3. And a mighty king shall stand up, that shall rule with great dominion, and do according to his will.

4. And when he shall stand up, his kingdom shall be broken, and shall be divided toward the four winds of heaven; and not to his posterity, nor according to his dominion which he ruled: for his kingdom shall be plucked up, even for others beside those.

5. And the king of the south shall be strong, and one of his princes; and he shall be strong above him, and have dominion; his dominion shall be a great dominion.

6. And in the end of years they shall join themselves together; for the king's daughter of the south shall come to the king of the north to make an agreement: but she shall not retain the power of the arm; neither shall he stand, nor his arm: but she shall be given up, and they that brought her, and he that begat her, and he that strengthened her in these times.

7. But out of a branch of her roots shall one stand up in his estate, which shall come with an army, and shall enter into the fortress of the king of the north, and shall deal against them, and shall prevail:

8. And shall also carry captives into Egypt their gods, with their princes, and with their precious vessels of silver and of gold; and he shall continue more years than the king of the north.

9. So the king of the south shall come into his kingdom, and shall return into his own land.

10. But his sons shall be stirred up, and shall assemble a multitude of great forces: and one shall certainly come, and

overflow, and pass through: then shall he return, and be stirred up, even to his fortress.

11. And the king of the south shall be moved with choler, and shall come forth and fight with him, even with the king of the north: and he shall set forth a great multitude; but the multitude shall be given into his hand.

12. And when he hath taken away the multitude, his heart shall be lifted up; and he shall cast down many ten thousands: but he shall not be strengthened by it.

13. For the king of the north shall return, and shall set forth a multitude greater than the former, and shall certainly come after certain years with a great army and with much riches.

14. And in those times there shall many stand up against the king of the south: also the robbers of thy people shall exalt themselves to establish the vision; but they shall fall.

15. So the king of the north shall come, and cast up a mount, and take the most fenced cities: and the arms of the south shall not withstand, neither his chosen people, neither shall there be any strength to withstand.

16. But he that cometh against him shall do according to his own will, and none shall stand before him: and he shall stand in the glorious land, which by his hand shall be consumed.

17. He shall also set his face to enter with the strength of his whole kingdom, and upright ones with him; thus shall he do: and he shall give him the daughter of women, corrupting her: but she shall not stand on his side, neither be for him.

18. After this shall he turn his face unto the isles, and shall take many: but a prince for his own behalf shall cause the reproach offered by him to cease; without his own reproach he shall cause it to turn upon him.

19. Then he shall turn his face toward the fort of his own land: but he shall stumble and fall, and not be found.

20. Then shall stand up in his estate a raiser of taxes in the glory of the kingdom: but within few days he shall be destroyed, neither in anger, nor in battle.

21. And in his estate shall stand up a vile person, to whom they shall not give the honour of the kingdom: but he shall come in peaceably, and obtain the kingdom by flatteries.

22. And with the arms of a flood shall they be overflown from before him, and shall be broken; yea, also the prince of the covenant.

23. And after the league made with him he shall work deceit-

fully: for he shall come up, and shall become strong with a
small people.
24. He shall enter peaceably even upon the fattest places
of the province; and he shall do that which his fathers have
not done, nor his fathers' fathers; he shall scatter among them
the prey, and spoil, and riches: yea, and he shall forecast his
devices against the strong holds, even for a time.
25. And he shall stir up his power and his courage against
the king of the south with a great army; and the king of the
south shall be stirred up to battle with a very great and mighty
army; but he shall not stand: for they shall forecast devices
against him.
26. Yea, they that feed of the portion of his meat shall destroy him, and his army shall overflow: and many shall fall
down slain.
27. And both these kings' hearts shall be to do mischief,
and they shall speak lies at one table; but it shall not prosper:
for yet the end shall be at the time appointed.
28. Then shall he return into his land with great riches;
and his heart shall be against the holy covenant; and he shall
do exploits, and return to his own land.
29. At the time appointed he shall return, and come toward
the south; but it shall not be as the former, or as the latter.
30. For the ships of Chittim shall come against him: therefore he shall be grieved, and return, and have indignation against
the holy covenant: so shall he do; he shall even return, and
have intelligence with them that forsake the holy covenant.
31. And arms shall stand on his part, and they shall pollute
the sanctuary of strength, and shall take away the daily sacrifice, and they shall place the abomination that maketh desolate.
32. And such as do wickedly against the covenant shall he
corrupt by flatteries: but the people that do know their God
shall be strong, and do exploits.
33. And they that understand among the people shall instruct
many: yet they shall fall by the sword, and by flame, by captivity, and by spoil, many days.
34. Now when they shall fall, they shall be holpen with a
little help: but many shall cleave to them with flatteries.
35. And some of them of understanding shall fall, to try
them, and to purge, and to make them white, even to the time
of the end: because it is yet for a time appointed.
36. And the king shall do according to his will; and he shall

exalt himself, and magnify himself above every god, and shall speak marvellous things against the God of gods, and shall prosper till the indignation be accomplished: for that that is determined shall be done.

37. Neither shall he regard the God of his fathers, nor the desire of women, nor regard any god: for he shall magnify himself above all.

38. But in his estate shall he honour the God of forces: and a god whom his fathers knew not shall he honour with gold, and silver, and with precious stones, and pleasant things.

39. Thus shall he do in the most strong holds with a strange god, whom he shall acknowledge and increase with glory: and he shall cause them to rule over many, and shall divide the land for gain.

40. And at the time of the end shall the king of the south push at him: and the king of the north shall come against him like a whirlwind, with chariots, and with horsemen, and with many ships; and he shall enter into the countries, and shall overflow and pass over.

41. He shall enter also into the glorious land, and many countries shall be overthrown: but these shall escape out of his hand, even Edom, and Moab, and the chief of the children of Ammon.

42. He shall stretch forth his hand also upon the countries: and the land of Egypt shall not escape.

43. But he shall have power over the treasures of gold and of silver, and over all the precious things of Egypt: and the Libyans and the Ethiopians shall be at his steps.

44. But tidings out of the east and out of the north shall trouble him: therefore he shall go forth with great fury to destroy, and utterly to make away many.

45. And he shall plant the tabernacles of his palace between the seas in the glorious holy mountain; yet he shall come to his end, and none shall help him.

History in Advance

Verses 1 and 2: "Also I in the first year of Darius the Mede, even I, stood to confirm and to strengthen him. And now will I shew thee the truth. Behold, there shall stand up yet three kings in Persia; and the fourth shall be far richer than they all: and by his strength through his riches he shall stir up all against the realm of Grecia."

Man writes history *after* it happens; God writes history *before* it happens. In this chapter we have the pre-written history of the kings of the north and the kings of the south. Also in this chapter we find a detailed report of the wars of the Ptolemies of Egypt: *"the kings of the south"*; and the wars of the Seleucidae of Syria: *"the kings of the north."*

Critics claim that the book of Daniel could not have been written as early as 533 B. C., but that it was written *after* the wars of the Ptolemies and the Seleucidae were ended, which was about 160 B. C. The critics declare that it would have been physically and humanly impossible for Daniel or any other person to so accurately describe these wars before they were fought. This is the place where critics and the Scriptures part.

When we admit the sovereignty of God and the verbal inspiration of the Scriptures, we have no trouble believing and receiving the fact that God can and does write history in advance–even to the description of battles in every detail. In II Timothy 3:16 and 17 we read, "ALL SCRIPTURE is given by inspiration of God, and is profitable for doctrine, for reproof, for correction, for instruction in righteousness: That the man of God may be perfect, throughly furnished unto all good works."

II Peter 1:19–21 tells us, "We have also a more sure word of prophecy; whereunto ye do well that ye take heed, as unto a light that shineth in a dark place, until the day dawn, and the day star arise in your hearts: Knowing this first, that no prophecy of the Scripture is of any private interpretation. For the prophecy came not in old time by the will of man: but holy men of God spake as they were moved by the Holy Ghost."

Since God is omniscient and knows the end in the beginning, it is not a hard matter for Him to write history in advance, unveiling and making things known in minute detail, centuries before they happen literally.

We might say the relation of history written by man, to prophecy given by Almighty God through holy men, is not that of interpretation, but of *verification.* History verifies what God declared centuries before it occurred. Prophecy is "a light that shineth in a dark place" (II Pet. 1:19). Prophecy illuminates centuries ahead of the occurrence that is prophesied.

Notice the opening words of verse 2: "*And now will I shew thee the truth.*" The prophecy set forth here is not clothed in symbols or figures, as were previous visions given to Daniel. We have here the literal language concerning the historical events of the Jews and the Holy Land, and we have literal language describing historical events having to do with the Jews and the Holy Land from Daniel's day down to the second coming of the Lord Jesus Christ. The prophecy begins with verse 2.

This prophecy was given to Daniel in the third year of Cyrus (Dan. 10:1 – in 533 B. C.) Therefore the three kings who were to "stand up yet" (after Cyrus) were Ahasuerus, Artaxerxes, and Darius (Ezra 4:1–24).

Here the spirit of prophecy returns to the events which concerned Daniel and his royal masters in their day, having to do with the coming days of the empire in which Daniel was such a great and outstanding person. Four kings were to follow in Media-Persia, after which Alexander the mighty king of Grecia would arise (verse 3). The division of Alexander's empire would be in four parts (verse 4), already prophesied in Daniel 8:22.

The account of these kings is found in Ezra 4:1–24. Please study this passage carefully, as space will not permit the quoting of the verses here. The first king

Ahasuerus, is known in history as Cambyses, who reigned from 529 to 522 B. C. The second king, Pseudo-Smerdis, reigned from 522 to 521 B. C.; and the third king, known in secular history as Darius Hystaspes, reigned from 521 to 485 B. C.

The fourth king was Xerxes, the son of Darius Hystaspes, and he reigned from 485 to 465 B. C. He was very rich, and his unusual wealth enabled him to build up vast armies and put them into the field, well equipped for his day. He stirred up the Persians against Greece, and in 480 B. C. he invaded that country but did not conquer her.

Prophecy always touches the important events in God's dealings with His people and the earth; therefore the remaining kings of Persia are omitted, and prophecy leaps over almost 150 years, to the time of the great and mighty king, Alexander the Great, who reigned from 336 B. C. to 323 B. C., a short reign of only 13 years.

Verses 3 and 4: "And a mighty king shall stand up, that shall rule with great dominion, and do according to his will. And when he shall stand up, his kingdom shall be broken, and shall be divided toward the four winds of heaven; and not to his posterity, nor according to his dominion which he ruled: for his kingdom shall be plucked up, even for others beside those."

These verses take us back to Daniel's vision of the ram and the he-goat recorded in Daniel 8:3–8 and 8:20–22. In this person known as the "mighty king" we recognize the "notable horn" of the he-goat, the horn which was broken off and in its place came up four horns. This mighty kingdom was divided toward the four winds. The *mighty king* was Alexander the Great, and the division of his kingdom toward the four winds of heaven was the time when at his death his kingdom was divided among four of his outstanding generals:

Cassander took Macedonia and the western part of the kingdom; *Lysimachus* took Thrace and the northern part of the kingdom; *Seleucus* took Syria and the eastern portion, while *Ptolemy* took Egypt and the southern part of the kingdom. Not one of Alexander's kinsmen succeeded him to the throne, and within a period of fifteen years his family was extinct.

Verse 5: "And the king of the south shall be strong, and one of his princes; and he shall be strong above him, and have dominion; his dominion shall be a great dominion."

Bear in mind that this prophecy had to do with Daniel's own people and the "glorious land" of Palestine. (Note verses 16, 41, and 45.) History substantiates the teaching of these verses; and though these dates and historical facts of kings and their wars may be a little wearisome, we must turn to the pages of history to follow through in our interpretation. The prophecy now narrows down to two of the four kingdoms into which the empire of Alexander the Great was divided. Palestine lies between Syria on the north and Egypt on the south, so the prophecy narrows to the wars between the kings of the north and the kings of the south. It was revealed to Daniel that from 320 B. C. to an unknown date A. D., the Jews would be persecuted and killed. They would suffer severely in the horrible wars between the kings of the north and the kings of the south. Desolation would come to Palestine and to the people of Israel, and Daniel was to know that it would be "many days" before his people would again become a nation and be out from under the bondage, destruction, and sufferings imposed upon them by the Gentiles.

God gave this vision to Daniel and made known its interpretation so that Daniel would understand that eventually his people would be a great and mighty nation;

but they must first pass through the fires of many years of persecution, finally to be cast into the winepress of the Antichrist, when blood would run like water in the streets. (This will be the time of which Jesus speaks in Matthew 24, when for the sake of the "elect" God will shorten the horrible days of persecution.)

Of the four kingdoms prophesied, Egypt was first to appear and come into prominence. It was founded and grew under the leadership of Ptolemy, one of the generals under Alexander the Great. Another of his generals, Seleucus Nicator, was appointed vicegerent of Babylonia. However, he was driven out by Antigonus, and fled to Egypt. He was received by Ptolemy and was made one of his princes, and with the assistance of Ptolemy he recovered his province, enlarged it, and took in Indus and Syria as well as Assyria. Eventually he became stronger than Ptolemy and his domain became greater and more powerful than Ptolemy's domain.

Verse 6: "And in the end of years they shall join themselves together; for the king's daughter of the south shall come to the king of the north to make an agreement: but she shall not retain the power of the arm; neither shall he stand, nor his arm: but she shall be given up, and they that brought her, and he that begat her, and he that strengthened her in these times."

There was a season of peace between the Egyptians and the Syrians during the reigns of these two generals. However, Ptolemy abdicated the throne in favor of his son, Ptolemy Philadelphus, whose half-brother had married a daughter of Antiochus Soter, who had succeeded Seleucus Nicator as king of Syria. The marriage of these two brought about war between Egypt and Syria; and the war was continued after Antiochus Soter's death by Antiochus Theos, the king who succeeded him. Finally, "at the end of years," Ptolemy offered Theos a handsome bribe if he would make peace.

The bribe was his daughter, Berenice, with a very large dowry–but there was a condition attached, that condition being that the king of Syria should declare his former marriage to Laodice void and declare her two sons by him illegitimate. This was finally agreed upon, the bribe was carried out, and the plan got under way to bring about peace.

But Ptolemy Philadelphus died, and then his daughter, Berenice, could no longer "retain the power of her arm," for Antiochus Theos put her away and went back to his former wife, Laodice. In Daniel's day, as in our day, they that sowed to the flesh reaped corruption, and Antiochus Theos did not stand. Laodice did not trust him, she wanted the crown for her own son–so she poisoned Theos and he passed out of the picture.

The throne was then taken over by Seleucus Callinicus. After he took the throne, Laodice persuaded him to have Berenice and her child assassinated–and along with her and her child, all who had helped her were killed in the same manner!

Verses 7 and 8: "But out of a branch of her roots shall one stand up in his estate, which shall come with an army, and shall enter into the fortress of the king of the north, and shall deal against them, and shall prevail: And shall also carry captives into Egypt their gods, with their princes, and with their precious vessels of silver and of gold; and he shall continue more years than the king of the north."

Notice: "*Out of a branch of her roots shall one stand up . . . .*" This means an offspring of the parents of Berenice, and refers to her brother, Ptolemy Euergetes, who succeeded his father, Ptolemy Philadelphus. He was naturally very angry about the treatment his sister had received, and he marched into Syria with a massive army. He arrived there too late to save Berenice and her son from assassination, but he took revenge by putting Laodice to death and capturing Seleucia, the fortress of the king of the north. He would have taken the entire kingdom had he not been recalled by an insurrection in Egypt which demanded his immediate attention. Having to leave the battle, he failed to conquer the entire kingdom at that time; but he did not return home empty-handed. He carried back many princes, 40,000 talents of silver, and 2500 precious vessels and images of gold. Because of his rich bounties taken in battle, the Egyptian priest bestowed an honorary degree upon Ptolemy and they surnamed him Euergetes, meaning "BENEFACTOR."

Verses 9 and 10: **"So the king of the south shall come into his kingdom, and shall return into his own land. But his sons shall be stirred up, and shall assemble a multitude of great forces: and one shall certainly come, and overflow, and pass through: then shall he return, and be stirred up, even to his fortress."**

The meaning here is simply this: The king of the south shall come into the territory of the king of the north, and shall "*return into his own land*"–which would be Egypt. We have seen in previous studies that he did just this. "But his sons (the sons of the king of the north) shall be stirred up" by the invasion of the king of the south, "and shall assemble a multitude of great forces."

We know that, according to history, this occurred exactly as stated here. The sons of Seleucus Callinicus and Antiochus (later surnamed *Magas*, meaning "the Great") assembled great armies. Seleucus Ceraunus sat on the throne after his father, and he, too, assembled a large army with the thought in mind to recover what his father had lost. But he was not a mighty warrior; he was weak, and unable to discipline his army and train men capable of fighting victorious battles. He was poisoned by two of his generals after he had reigned between two and three years.

His brother Antiochus then ascended the throne and assembled a large army which he led in person. This is the king referred to in verse 10 of our text. He is the one who should "overflow, and pass through." With his powerful army, he threw everything he had against the king of the south–who at that time was Ptolemy Philopater (successor to Ptolemy Euergetes).

Antiochus was a mighty warrior. He led his troops successfully, seized Tyre and Ptolemais, and kept advancing until he finally passed through Palestine. He marched on against Gaza, conquering as he went, right into the fortress of the king of the south, which is the limit pointed out in the prophecy. This happened in 218 B. C.

Verses 11 and 12: "And the king of the south shall be moved with choler, and shall come forth and fight with him, even with the king of the north: and he shall set forth a great multitude; but the multitude shall be given into his hand. And when he hath taken away the multitude, his heart shall be lifted up; and he shall cast down many ten thousands: but he shall not be strengthened by it."

The king of the south was furious. He was aroused to hatred and anger that was immeasurable because the king of the north had invaded his land. He immediately assembled a mighty army, and in 217 B. C. he defeated the army of Antiochus in a battle which occurred at Raphia, not too far from Gaza. Because of this tremendous victory, Ptolemy's heart "was lifted up," and had he been a man of character he might have followed up this victory by fighting Antiochus and seizing his kingdom; but he was too anxious to return to his drinking and sensual pleasures, and thereby lost the opportunity to drive on to complete victory and become a world ruler. Therefore, he was "*not strengthened*" by his great victory over Antiochus. He defeated the king–but he did not take the kingdom.

Verse 13: "For the king of the north shall return, and shall set forth a multitude greater than the former, and shall certainly come after certain years with a great army and with much riches."

There was a period of thirteen years of peace between Ptolemy Philopater and Antiochus. During these years, Antiochus strengthened himself in his kingdom. When he had armies powerful enough and sufficiently equipped, he began conquest and many victories were his. He took much spoil, and his treasury was filled with gold and silver.

In the meantime, he learned of the death of Ptolemy Philopater and of the succession to the throne of Ptolemy's infant son, Ptolemy Epiphanes. This led him to believe that the time was ripe for him to become a world conqueror. He therefore marched against Egypt with "a great army and with much riches," expecting a very easy victory. We will see what happened, a little later in the chapter.

As we study these two kingdoms, keep in mind the fact that while the *kingdoms* remain the same, the *kings* do not. As personages, the king of the north and the king of the south change many times, even though their official title does not change.

Verse 14: "And in those times there shall many stand up against the king of the south: also the robbers of thy people shall exalt themselves to establish the vision; but they shall fall."

Among the "many that stood up" against the infant king of the south was Philip, king of Macedon, who entered into an agreement with Antiochus to divide the kingdom of Ptolemy Epiphanes between them. At the same time, *Egypt* was a hotbed of sedition, and there were many wicked Jews in Palestine who hoped to gain the favor of Antiochus. These wicked Jews were called "robbers," and their conduct made the situation very difficult for their brethren, and thus they "established the vision" (the prophecy) of the extreme suffering and hardships of the Jews, Daniel's people. The king turned against these robber-Jews and caused them to fall. Verse 14 was literally fulfilled in the wars of Antiochus that followed.

Verses 15–19: "So the king of the north shall come, and cast up a mount, and take the most fenced cities: and the arms of the south shall not withstand, neither his chosen people, neither shall there be any strength to withstand. But he that cometh against him shall do according to his own will, and none shall stand before him: and he shall stand in the glorious land, which by his hand shall be consumed. He shall also set his face to enter with the strength of his whole kingdom, and upright ones with him; thus shall he do: and he shall give him the daughter of women, corrupting her: but she shall not stand on his side, neither be for him. After this shall he turn his face unto the isles, and shall take many: but a prince for his own behalf shall cause the reproach offered by him to cease; without his own reproach he shall cause it to turn upon him. Then he shall turn his face toward the fort of his own land: but he shall stumble and fall, and not be found."

We shall study these verses together, because they cover the remainder of the bloody wars of King Antiochus the Great, who was "the king of the north." As we study these last wars of Antiochus, we must keep in mind that the Holy Land is referred to as "*the glorious land.*" The glorious land was under the dominion of the king of the south—who at this particular time was Ptolemy Epiphanes.

In order to reach Egypt, it was imperative that Antiochus pass through the Holy Land. He must therefore conquer the Holy Land before he could conquer Egypt. This he determined to do; but as he crossed the border of that country he encountered Scopas (a great general in the army of Ptolemy). Scopas was forced to retreat and he sought refuge in the strongly fortified city of Sidon.

The Egyptians made a desperate attempt to relieve the city, but all such efforts failed and Sidon was forced to surrender to Antiochus. Then the king was able to do "*according to his own will and none were able to stand before him.*" He moved forward rapidly, conquering as he went, and finally took possession of the entire land of Palestine.

After conquering "the glorious land" he then set his face toward Egypt, determined to conquer and become ruler of that country. He massed his armies and accumulated all the power he could, preparatory to his drive against Egypt. But the Egyptians were not asleep – they had contacted Rome and begged for assistance against the powerful king of the north. The Romans were rapidly rising in power, and they promised support to the king of Egypt.

When the king of the north heard of this alliance between Rome and Egypt, he changed his plans; and instead of marching quickly against the king of the south, he sought to conquer them by diplomacy. He had a daughter named Cleopatra whom he suggested become espoused to the infant king Ptolemy Epiphanes–a lad only seven years old at the time. Cleopatra herself was very young; and because she was so young, still under the care of her mother and a nurse, she was called "*daughter of women*" (verse 17). The marriage took place about 193 B. C.

The statement, "*corrupting her,*" has to do with the scheme of Antiochus to cause her to play into his hands and give *him* her loyalty, rather than to be loyal to her own husband—but his plan failed. Cleopatra not only was faithful to her husband, she *joined him* in sending congratulations to the Romans on their victories over her father!

Such conduct on the part of his daughter infuriated Antiochus. So great was his hatred for the Romans that he determined to defeat both them AND Egypt. He fitted out a fleet of three hundred vessels and assailed the coast of the Isles of Asia Minor, only to meet with another sad disappointment. At Magnesia in 190 B. C. he was defeated by Scipio Asiaticus, "*the prince*" mentioned in verse 18.

Brokenhearted over his defeat, the king returned home and sent messengers to seek terms of peace. The terms offered him were hard: He lost Europe, he lost Asia on the European side of the Taurus, and he was commanded to give up all his ships of war but ten and to make an initial payment of 15,000 talents—500 to Eumenes.

A few months later he made his final mistake: In order to replenish his exhausted treasury, he attempted to plunder the temple of Bel in the city of Elymais, which so angered the people that they rose up in unison, rushed upon him with one accord, and slew him. Thus, "*he stumbled and fell and was found no more*" (verse 19).

Verse 20: "Then shall stand up in his estate a raiser of taxes in the glory of the kingdom: but within few days he shall be destroyed, neither in anger, nor in battle."

Antiochus the Great was succeeded by his son, Seleucus Philopater. When the new king ascended the throne the country was in such dire need and finances were at such low ebb, he was forced to become "a raiser of taxes," which was necessary in order to pay the fine that had been imposed upon his father for plundering.

Toward the end of his reign, he became so hard

pressed for money that he made the sad mistake of sending his treasurer to Jerusalem (referred to in our present verse as "the glory of the kingdom") with instructions to rob the temple and confiscate the silver and the gold there. But "within few days" the king was mysteriously poisoned, and thus he died, as prophesied in our verse, "neither in anger, nor in battle!" He reigned about twelve years.

In each instance concerning the battles, the victories, and the defeats of these kings of the north and of the south, we see over and over again that *the wages of sin is death, and God is not mocked*! Sowing to the flesh brings a harvest of corruption. When sin is finished, it brings forth death. Sin and death are synonymous; flesh and corruption are synonymous. Whether we be king or peasant, if God be for us, who can be against us? But by the same token, whether we be king or peasant, if God is against us we are defeated.

The Forerunner of Antichrist

Verses 21–31: "And in his estate shall stand up a vile person, to whom they shall not give the honour of the kingdom: but he shall come in peaceably, and obtain the kingdom by flatteries. And with the arms of a flood shall they be overflown from before him, and shall be broken; yea, also the prince of the covenant.

"And after the league made with him he shall work deceitfully: for he shall come up, and shall become strong with a small people. He shall enter peaceably even upon the fattest places of the province; and he shall do that which his fathers have not done, nor his fathers' fathers; he shall scatter among them the prey, and spoil, and riches: yea, and he shall forecast his devices against the strong holds, even for a time. And he shall stir up his power and his courage against the king of the south with a great army; and the king of the south shall be stirred up to battle with a very great and mighty army; but he shall not stand: for they shall forecast devices against him. Yea, they that feed of the portion of his meat shall destroy him, and his army shall overflow: and many shall fall down slain.

"And both these kings' hearts shall be to do mischief, and they shall speak lies at one table; but it shall not prosper: for yet the end shall be at the time appointed. Then shall he return into his land with great riches; and his heart shall be against the holy covenant; and he shall do exploits, and return to his own land. At the time appointed he shall return, and come toward the south; but it shall not be as the former, or as the latter. For the ships of Chittim shall come against him: therefore he shall be grieved, and return, and have indignation against the holy covenant: so shall he do; he shall even return, and have intelligence with them that forsake the holy covenant. And arms shall stand on his part, and they shall pollute the sanctuary of strength, and shall take away the daily sacrifice, and they shall place the abomination that maketh desolate."

The next king of the north is very significant: *He is a type or shadow of Antichrist . . . the little horn of Daniel 8.* His name was Antiochus Epiphanes, and he was the younger son of Antiochus the Great. He was a vile person, and in many ways he did the same things Antichrist will do.

He was by nature a despot, eccentric and unreliable—extreme in all of his passions, unscrupulous and cruel. He was an educated sadist—not a jungle man, but a king with a savage heart. He was, however, a man of great courage and outstanding ability. He was extraordinary in every way—even in his wickedness. He was debased, deplorable; nothing was too low and despicable for him to do.

"The honour of the kingdom" was not given to him because his nephew, Demetrius, should have been king. But Antiochus Epiphanes was assisted by the Pergamene monarchs, Eumenes and his brother Attalus; and with their help, his enemies (referred to in our Scripture as "the arms of a flood") were annihilated, and "the prince of the covenant" (the Jewish high priest) was deposed and put down.

Antiochus Epiphanes was a cruel man and a deceitful one. He broke the agreement ("the league") that he made with the monarchs of Pergamum. He had persuaded the Romans to recognize him, and while he was doing this he was at the same time working "deceitfully," making it appear that he had only a small army and a small following. However, in a very short time he became "strong with a small people," and with this small (but strong) army he entered "peaceably even upon the fattest places of the province."

Epiphanes was shrewd and cunning–*so* cunning, in fact, that he practiced the same tactics the devil used when he came into the Garden of Eden to tempt Eve. (He also used the same technique the Antichrist will use when he rides out on a white horse as described in Revelation 6:1,2.) He was unlike the kings who preceded him. He was extravagant with his gifts, and "scattered the spoil" of the riches taken in victories over his enemies. All the while he was doing this, he was, in the words of the Scripture, "forecasting his devices against the strong holds," referring to the land of Egypt.

A little later he overran and conquered Memphis, Naucratis, and Pelusium, but he failed to take Alexandria. Victory followed victory for a time, but he was finally stopped by the Romans.

Antiochus Epiphanes was determined to conquer every square inch of Egypt. He gathered together a great army and when he was ready, he marched against that country. He was *met* with a great *Egyptian* army, and both sides suffered tremendous losses. However, Ptolemy Philometer, king of Egypt, was betrayed by those who "fed of the portion of his meat," sold out by men who were supposed to be his friends and members of his cabinet and palace–and thus Epiphanes won the battle and the king of Egypt fell into his hands.

Ptolemy Philometer was dethroned, and his brother, Physcon, was then declared king. But Antiochus Epiphanes was a liar and a schemer. After defeating the king of Egypt and allowing his brother to sit on the throne, he made a covenant with the former king whom he had defeated and on the pretense of taking his part against his brother who was then king, Antiochus Epiphanes attacked Alexandria, but without success. He was defeated.

Because of that, Philometer became suspicious and made peace with his brother who was then on the throne. These two agreed to a joint sovereignty, then declared war against Antiochus Epiphanes, thereby literally fulfilling the prophecy set forth here: "THESE KINGS' (Antiochus Epiphanes and Philometer) hearts shall be to do mischief (scheming one against the other), and they shall speak lies at one table (as they sit at the same table they will lie to each other)." This literally took place, as history proves, just as Daniel prophesied it long before it came to pass.

After these battles in Egypt, Antiochus Epiphanes returned to Syria, bringing with him riches of gold and silver–spoils taken in Egypt. As he was returning to Syria he learned that someone had reported his death in the land of Palestine. Jason (who had been deprived of his priestly office), in the absence of Antiochus Epiphanes attacked Jerusalem, and endeavored to recover his office by force.

Antiochus Epiphanes regarded this as a revolt of the Jews, and when he learned that they rejoiced greatly because of his supposed death, he determined to make them pay for it. He therefore attacked Jerusalem, murdered

40,000 Jews, and sold thousands more into slavery. He plundered the city and the temple, took everything of value, and left Jerusalem–carrying with him much gold and treasure, and continued his march on into the city of Antioch.

In 168 B. C. Antiochus Epiphanes decided to make another attempt to conquer Egypt. But the two brothers were still on the throne and they appealed to Rome. Rome gave them armies and treasure, and Antiochus Epiphanes was driven back. He left Egypt defeated, and because of his defeat there, he was furious against the Jews and Palestine. He plundered the land and massacred thousands of Jews, causing thousands of others to become slaves. He then repaired the walls and towers of the citadel of David, put Syrian soldiers on guard and commanded all of the Jews and the people in the Holy Land to be one people, one religion, with the same laws, and he refused to allow the Jews to worship in their temple and pray to their God. Instead, he set up an idol altar and offered swine's flesh on that altar, which of course was an abomination beyond description to the Jews.

Epiphanes is a perfect picture of the Antichrist. When he offered swine meat on the altar in the temple, it was "the abomination that maketh desolate" spoken of in our present verses; however, this was NOT "the abomination of desolation" mentioned by the Lord Jesus in Matthew 24:15. The prophecy given by Jesus is still future. It is true that Antiochus Epiphanes was definitely a picture, and a good one, of the Antichrist who will BE "the abomination of desolation," and will stand in the holy place announcing that he is God and commanding all to worship him.

The terrible treatment of the Jews, and the terrible way Antiochus Epiphanes desecrated the Holy City and the temple, caused the Maccabean revolt. In the meantime he had left the city with an army, traveling into Persia. He gained many victories as he went, but later was driven back to Babylon. The news of the Maccabean revolt in Palestine crushed him. He died a natural death at Tabae, in 164 B. C.

Verses 21–31 have to do with Antiochus Epiphanes and his wars – they do not refer to the Antichrist who will come after the Rapture of the Church. The battles named here were literally fought and carried out as prophesied. These wars–the wars of the Persian and Grecian empires, and more in detail the war of the Syrian and Egyptian division of the Grecian empire–extended from 536 to 164 B. C., a period of 372 years. The marvelous prophetic foreview here is one of the most outstanding in the entire Bible, and goes into details such as only an omniscient God could possibly write down before they occur. Yet Bible antiquity and the history of Josephus and of the Maccabees definitely bears out the fact that these battles were literally fought exactly as prophesied in Daniel, many years before they took place.

The Period Between Antiochus Epiphanes and the Coming of Jesus, the Messiah

Verses 32 and 33: "And such as do wickedly against the covenant shall he corrupt by flatteries: but the people that do know their God shall be strong, and do exploits. And they that understand among the people shall instruct many: yet they shall fall by the sword, and by flame, by captivity, and by spoil, many days."

These verses describe the behaviour of some of the Jews under the severe persecution and oppression of Antiochus Epiphanes. Some of the Jews lived wickedly, and under the terrible persecution–and influenced by flatteries from the king–they were led to forsake their God and the religion of their fathers, and worship idols. However, there was a remnant of Jews who knew God, who believed, as did Daniel and his friends, that God was able to deliver them. These were made strong, and they did "exploits."

In Bible history and the history of the Maccabees, we learn of a good priest named Mattathias, who, with his sons, known as the Maccabees, fought from 166 to 47 B. C. to restore national life in Israel, and to restore the temple worship of the Jews. This faithful priest was persecuted by Antiochus Epiphanes, and was driven into the mountains, whence a number of faithful Jews followed him.

Two years later, Mattathias died and his power passed to his third son, Judas, known as "the Hammer," a very shrewd and capable leader. He avoided the guerrillas sent against him, defeated or dodged every Syrian *army* sent against him, and in 165 B. C., with a group of his followers he captured Jerusalem, purified the temple, and restored the daily sacrifice.

Judas "the Hammer" was killed in battle in 160 B. C. and was succeeded by his younger brother, Jonathan. At this time the Syrians were engaged in civil war; they were busy fighting among themselves, and Judaea enjoyed a season of peace. Meanwhile, Jonathan became stronger by making a treaty with the Romans and the Spartans. He was betrayed and slain by a Syrian general in 143 B. C., and his brother Simon succeeded him in the priesthood—the last of the sons of the faithful old priest, Mattathias.

Simon had two sons, one of which, along with Simon himself, was betrayed and slain by a son-in-law in 135 B. C. One of Simon's sons, John Hyrcanus, escaped death and became the high priest of Israel, with a very long and prosperous reign. Others followed him, until the Maccabeans came into disfavor with the people and were succeeded by the Idumaean, Antipater, in 47 B. C. After the murder of Antipater in 43 B. C., history tells us that

Marc Antony visited Syria and appointed two of Antipater's sons, Phasaelus and Herod, the latter to be known as Herod the Great, whose reign lasted from 37 B. C. until 4 B. C. Herod the Great was king when Christ was born in Bethlehem of Judaea. You can read the record in Matthew 2:1–15. The Maccabees bridged the greater part of the span of years between Antiochus Epiphanes and the birth of Christ.

At the very close of the period known to most of us as "the silent years" between Malachi and Matthew, God raised up a nucleus of spiritual leaders to whom He gave understanding and wisdom. They understood the prophecies of the Scriptures, they knew how to instruct others, and they taught the people as they were permitted to do so. Among these were Simeon and Anna (Luke 2:25–38), who waited for "the consolation of Israel."

The Period Between Messiah and the Time of the End

Verses 34 and 35: "Now when they shall fall, they shall be holpen with a little help: but many shall cleave to them with flatteries. And some of them of understanding shall fall, to try them, and to purge, and to make them white, even to the time of the end: because it is yet for a time appointed."

In Genesis 3:15 God promised the seed of the woman who would bruise the head of the serpent; and Paul tells us in Galatians 4:4 that in the fulness of time Jesus came, born of a woman, born under the law, to redeem them that were under the law. Jesus came to the Jew first. He offered Himself to them as their Messiah; but they said, "Give us Barabbas; we will not have this man to reign over us. Let Him be crucified! Let His blood be upon us and upon our children." They rejected their Christ and He was cut off.

However, 40 years later, in 70 A. D., the Holy City

was laid waste and destroyed by the Romans led by Titus, thus beginning the fulfillment of the last part of verse 33: "They shall fall by the sword, and by flame, by captivity, and by spoil, many days." These "many days" are the days of this dispensation which has been going on now for more than 1900 years. Jesus referred to them when He said, in Luke 21:24, "They (the Jews) shall fall by the edge of the sword, and shall be led away captive into all nations: and Jerusalem shall be trodden down of the Gentiles, until the times of the Gentiles be fulfilled."

Jesus spoke those words 1900 years ago, and we have seen them literally fulfilled in our lifetime! The Jews have been scattered through every nation under the sun and to every island of the sea. They have repeatedly been robbed, butchered and murdered. Their material possessions have been taken away from them "many days." Millions have fallen by the sword. They have been roasted in Hitler's ovens, they have been persecuted around the world; but they have not been exterminated–nor will they ever be!

They have been flattered, and promised many things; but these promises have very seldom, if ever, been fulfilled as promised. Even today, as I prepare these messages, the Jews have their faith in what the United Nations can do for them. They have been given back a small portion of the ground God gave to Abraham, and they are rebuilding that land; but this is not the real return of the Jew to Palestine . . . it is only the beginning–the forerunner of the real thing. But "a nation will be born in a day" when Jesus returns in the Revelation and every eye shall see Him. They will see the scars in His hands and they will fall at His feet and worship Him. They will then truly cry out, "Hosanna to our King!"

These verses cover the period between Messiah the

Prince and the time of the end. They correspond to the period between the 69th and 70th weeks of Daniel's seventy sevens of prophecy. They show the consistency of the vision God gave Daniel, and prove beyond the shadow of a doubt that these visions relate to the Jews, *NOT to the Church.* The Church is not once mentioned in any way.

The End Time – The Antichrist

Verses 36–45: "And the king shall do according to his will; and he shall exalt himself, and magnify himself above every god, and shall speak marvellous things against the God of gods, and shall prosper till the indignation be accomplished: for that that is determined shall be done. Neither shall he regard the God of his fathers, nor the desire of women, nor regard any god: for he shall magnify himself above all. But in his estate shall he honour the God of forces: and a god whom his fathers knew not shall he honour with gold, and silver, and with precious stones, and pleasant things. Thus shall he do in the most strong holds with a strange god, whom he shall acknowledge and increase with glory: and he shall cause them to rule over many, and shall divide the land for gain. And at the time of the end shall the king of the south push at him: and the king of the north shall come against him like a whirlwind, with chariots, and with horsemen, and with many ships; and he shall enter into the countries, and shall overflow and pass over. He shall enter also into the glorious land, and many countries shall be overthrown: but these shall escape out of his hand, even Edom, and Moab, and the chief of the children of Ammon. He shall stretch forth his hand also upon the countries: and the land of Egypt shall not escape. But he shall have power over the treasures of gold and of silver, and over all the precious things of Egypt: and the Libyans and the Ethiopians shall be at his steps. But tidings out of the east and out of the north shall trouble him: therefore he shall go forth with great fury to destroy, and utterly to make away many. And he shall plant the tabernacles of his palace between the seas in the glorious holy mountain; yet he shall come to his end, and none shall help him."

Verse 36 is stupendous as having to do with prophecy. Suddenly and abruptly we have the appearance of "THE KING," which implies that this king has been heard of before. He is not a new character on the scene; he does not need to be introduced; he has already been introduced. He is not brought on the scene as "A king," but as "THE king." He has been pointed out several times previously, as we will learn as we study these verses which have to do with the time of the end–the time when the willful king will reign supremely upon this earth.

The little horn of the fourth wild beast in Daniel chapter 7, and in chapter 8 the little horn which comes up on one of the four horns of the he-goat (Dan. 8:9–12), and the willful king of this present chapter are one and the same person. They point to the Antichrist. These three personalities–the two "little horns" and the "willful king"–reign at the same time . . . the time of the end. They display the same willful disposition, and all three are destroyed in exactly the same manner. They could not be anything but the same person.

This king comes on the scene at the close of the gap between Messiah the Prince and "the time of the end" (verses 33–35). We have seen that this corresponds with the gap between the 69th and 70th weeks of Daniel's seventy sevens of prophecy. This willful king is therefore identified with "the prince that shall come" (Dan. 9:26,27), and he will definitely be the last Roman dictator or emperor. He is "the little horn" of the fourth wild beast of Daniel's vision (chapter 7).

The willful king will be self-willed–he will do according to his OWN will. First, he will "exalt himself and magnify himself above every god." He will openly speak marvellous things against the God of gods, Jehovah. He will prosper until "the indignation (the Great Tribulation) be accomplished: FOR THAT THAT IS DETERMINED SHALL BE DONE" (verse 36).

Since God is sovereign, since He knows the end in the beginning–and all that will transpire between the beginning and the end–no power in heaven or on earth can stop that which He has determined to take place in "the time of the end." The willful king will not regard the "God of his fathers"–the God of Abraham, Isaac, and Jacob. It stands to reason that the Antichrist will be a Jew since Jesus was a Jew–and the Antichrist will be the counterfeit Christ. Also, in order to present himself to the Jews in an acceptable manner, it is only reasonable that he should be a Jew.

This king will have no regard for *"the desire of women."* Bible scholars do not fully agree on the meaning of this statement. If this has to do with the desire of the Jewish women, it probably means the hope of the Jewish women to become the mother of Messiah. To the Jews, Messiah has not yet come. Today they are looking for Him, and they will be looking for Him when Antichrist comes on the scene of action. This could very well be the meaning of the prophecy here.

If *"the desire"* relates to the king, it means that he does not possess the natural desire for the companionship of women. Others believe that he will have no mercy on women, as well as on men, during the horrible days of slaughter and persecution of the Jews. Matthew 24:19–21 tells us, "Woe unto them that are with child, and to them that give suck in those days! But pray ye that your flight be not in the winter, neither on the sabbath day: for then shall be great tribulation, such as was not since the beginning of the world to this time, no, nor ever shall be." This could also be the meaning of the statement. It could be that mothers with small children and mothers-to-be will beg for mercy but will not be regarded by the Antichrist. They will be butchered and slaughtered, and as Herod slew the babies when he learned that a king had been born, the Antichrist may practice the same unmerciful killing–not only of babies, but of mothers as well.

If the meaning is that he shall not regard the desire of Jewish women to be the mother of Messiah, then of course he will have no regard for the Messiah, and this is one of the characteristics of Antichrist. John tells us, "He is antichrist who denieth the Father and the Son" (I John 2:22). This willful king will honor the God of forces: his only god will be force and power. He will go to every extreme to conquer and rule the world: ". . . He went forth conquering and to conquer" (Rev. 6:2).

We know Satan is "the god of this world," and on the Mount of Temptation he offered the kingdoms of this world to Jesus–but Jesus refused the offer (Matt. 4:8–10). Jesus knew that He would receive the kingdoms of this world at the appointed time, from the hand of God the Father (Dan. 7:13,14).

In Revelation 11:15 we read, "And the seventh angel sounded; and there were great voices in heaven, saying, The kingdoms of this world are become the kingdoms of our Lord, and of His Christ; and He shall reign for ever and ever."

Concerning Antichrist we read, ". . . The dragon gave him his power, and his seat, and great authority" (Rev. 13:2b). The willful king will come into possession of the strongholds of the fortified cities and fortresses of the ten federated kingdoms which will quickly rise after the Rapture, making up the old Roman empire; and the willful king will garrison these ten kingdoms with tens of thousands of troops, on the pretense of maintaining peace and unity. He will flatter the people, and through his flatteries will win their respect and confidence. Thus "he shall increase with glory." He will also bestow glory, honor, and power upon whom he will, himself being the god of the hour, having no respect for Jehovah God nor any other emblem of worship employed by the people.

However, all will not continue to go well with this willful king because at this time the king of the south will again appear on the scene of action, and the king of the north "shall come against him like a whirlwind."

It is not easy to determine the activities of all the nations involved in chapter 11. There are many Bible scholars who feel that this invasion records that of only the king of the north and the king of the south; but in verse 36 we read of the "willful king" whom we previously identified as the beast, and the activities of this "willful king" seem to me to be outlined in the things that follow. I believe that if you will prayerfully study verses 40 through 45 you will see that these verses can hardly describe only the activities of the armies of the kings of the north and the south. The singular pronoun "*he*" is used; therefore the passage must describe not only the activities of the kings of the north and the south, but the further activities of the "willful king."

We have here a sudden transition from one person to another. If there were no more prophecy, if we were left only to *this* prophecy, it would be impossible to decide from this clause just what king is to enter into "the glorious land" and the countries. We could not clearly and dogmatically declare whether the king of the north, the king of the south, or the Roman empire would enter into the glorious land and conquer many countries. But we have other prophecies that deal with this particular point. Therefore, when we compare Scripture with Scripture, prophecy with prophecy, we can see and understand which king it is.

We know the king who is victorious at the time of the end is described in Daniel chapters 2 and 7, and also in Revelation 17. The king who will be victorious in all his battles is definitely and specifically identified with the fourth beast (the Roman empire which will be revived immediately after the Rapture). By taking all prophecies and using them as interpreters of *this* prophecy, we see clearly that the statement "he shall enter" (in verse 40) refers to the Roman power under its last mighty world dictator, the beast. It is he who will invade these countries, thus leading us to see that the king of the south and the king of the north have been unsuccessful in their battles against him.

This gigantic battle begins when the king of the south declares war and moves against the beast-false-prophet coalition (Dan. 11:40), and will take place "at the time of the end." This powerful king of the south is joined by the king of the north and his armies, and together they attack "the willful king" with great force—both on the land and on the sea (Dan. 11:40).

According to Zechariah 12:2, the Holy City Jerusalem will be destroyed in this battle: "Behold, I will make Jerusalem a cup of trembling unto all the people round about, when they shall be in the siege both against Judah and against Jerusalem."

From Zechariah 12:4 and Ezekiel 39 we learn that the armies of the northern confederacy will also be destroyed. Study carefully the entire 39th chapter of Ezekiel, and Zechariah 12:4: "In that day, saith the Lord, I will smite every horse with astonishment, and his rider with madness: and I will open mine eyes upon the house of Judah, and will smite every horse of the people with blindness."

Then the entire army of the beast will move into the Holy Land: "He shall enter also into the glorious land, and many countries shall be overthrown: but these shall escape out of his hand, even Edom, and Moab, and the chief of the children of Ammon" (Dan. 11:41).

No doubt it is at this time that the coalition described in Revelation 17:13 is formed: "These have one mind, and shall give their power and strength unto the beast." As the beast pushes on and carries his battle into Egypt, he receives a report that causes him alarm and much anxiety (Dan. 11:44). No doubt the report received informs the beast of the approaching of the gigantic masses of the kings of the east: "And the sixth angel poured out his vial upon the great river Euphrates; and the water thereof was dried up, that the way of the kings of the east might be prepared" (Rev. 16:12). These armies of the east have assembled because of the destruction of the great northern confederacy and are moving in to challenge the power and authority of the beast. At this time, the beast will move his headquarters into the Holy Land and will call all of his armies together in Palestine (Dan. 11:45). It is in "the glorious land" that he will meet his doom and destruction: "And he shall plant the tabernacles of his palace between the seas in the glorious holy mountain; yet he shall come to his end, *and none shall help him*" (Dan. 11:45).

The Armies of the East Invade Palestine

"And the sixth angel poured out his vial upon the great river Euphrates; and the water thereof was dried up, that the way of the kings of the east might be prepared" (Rev. 16:12).

Here we learn that through a miracle of supernatural power, the barriers are removed which kept the armies of Asia from coming into Palestine to challenge the beast. There are those who spiritualize and symbolize the drying up of the Euphrates; but personally, I believe the waters of the Euphrates will be *literally* dried up, and that this will take place through a miracle by an act of Almighty God.

The drying up of this great river will open the way for the kings of the east to move into the glorious land in battle against the beast. I believe that these multimillions who will move in from the east will be the Red Chinese. We have light on this Scripture today that God's ministers and teachers did not have fifty years ago. China is becoming one of the most dangerous communist nations on earth, and with all of her multiplied millions she could produce an army that could not be matched by any other nation in existence.

In this passage we see four great armies:

1. The armies made up of the federation of the Roman empire.
2. The armies of the north, made up of Russia and her satellite nations.
3. The armies of the south, made up of the Arab nations. (The Arabs are becoming more than ever a world problem. Under the leadership of their present dictators, and with Russian aid, they are becoming a danger to freedom and to the way of life we have always enjoyed in America.)
4. The armies of the east, made up of the yellow nations—China and her satellites.

The Invasion by the Armies of the Lord

Before this last all-out bloody battle begins, there

will appear a sign in heaven–the sign of the Son of man:

"And then shall appear the sign of the Son of man in heaven: and then shall all the tribes of the earth mourn, and they shall see the Son of man coming in the clouds of heaven with power and great glory" (Matt. 24:30).

This sign in heaven causes the armies to cease hostilities against each other and unite to fight against the Lord Jesus Christ and His army. John describes this event in Revelation 19:19: "And I saw the beast, and the kings of the earth, and their armies, gathered together to make war against Him that sat on the horse, and against His army."

We also have a prophetic picture of this great battle in Zechariah 14:3: "Then shall the Lord go forth, and fight against those nations, as when He fought in the day of battle."

"For they are the spirits of devils, working miracles, which go forth unto the kings of the earth and of the whole world, to gather them to the battle of that great day of God Almighty" (Rev. 16:14).

"These shall make war with the Lamb, and the Lamb shall overcome them: for He is Lord of lords, and King of kings: and they that are with Him are called, and chosen, and faithful" (Rev. 17:14).

"And I saw heaven opened, and behold a white horse; and He that sat upon him was called Faithful and True, and in righteousness He doth judge and make war. His eyes were as a flame of fire, and on His head were many crowns; and He had a name written, that no man knew, but He Himself. And He was clothed with a vesture dipped in blood: and His name is called The Word of God. And the armies which were in heaven followed Him upon white horses, clothed in fine linen, white and clean. And out of His mouth goeth a sharp sword, that with it He should smite the nations: and He shall rule them with a rod of iron: and He treadeth the winepress of the fierceness and wrath of Almighty God. And He hath on His vesture and on His thigh a name written, KING OF KINGS, AND LORD OF LORDS.

"And I saw an angel standing in the sun; and he cried with a loud voice, saying to all the fowls that fly in the midst of heaven, Come and gather yourselves together unto the supper of the great God; that ye may eat the flesh of kings, and the flesh of captains, and the flesh of mighty men, and the flesh of horses, and of them that sit on them, and the flesh of all men, both free and bond, both small and great. And I saw the beast, and the kings of the earth, and their armies, gathered together to make war against Him that sat on the horse, and against His army. And the beast was taken, and with him the false prophet that wrought miracles before him, with which he deceived them that had received the mark of the beast, and them that worshipped his image. These both were cast alive into a lake of fire burning with brimstone" (Rev. 19:11–20).

At this time, the armies of the beast and the gigantic armies of the east will be destroyed by the Lord Jesus and His army: "And the remnant were slain with the sword of Him that sat upon the horse, which sword proceeded out of His mouth: and all the fowls were filled with their flesh" (Rev. 19:21).

This will be the day spoken of by Jesus when He said, "When ye therefore shall see the abomination of desolation spoken of by Daniel the prophet stand in the holy place, (whoso readeth, let him understand:) then let them which be in Judaea flee into the mountains. (We believe this to be the mountains of Petra, where there is a natural rock fortress. This is only a very short distance from Israel as we know Israel today.) Let him which is on the house top not come down to take any thing out of his house: Neither let him which is in the field return back to take his clothes. And woe unto them that are with child and to them that give suck in those days! But pray ye that your flight be not in the winter, neither on the sabbath day. FOR THEN SHALL BE GREAT TRIBULATION, SUCH AS WAS NOT SINCE THE BEGINNING OF THE WORLD TO THIS TIME, NO, NOR EVER SHALL BE. And except those days should be shortened, there should no flesh be saved: but for the elect's sake those days shall be shortened" (Matt. 24: 15–22).

During these days, the horror, fury, death and destruction, the misery, anguish, and pain will be such as has never been nor will ever be again upon this earth. If God did not stop the slaughter there would be no flesh saved–but Jehovah God will destroy Antichrist and his armies, thus, for the sake of the "elect," putting a stop to the bloody destruction. This will be the final battle of the "willful king," also to be known as "the king of fierce countenance . . . the Man of Sin . . . the son of perdition . . . the Antichrist–the devil in flesh!"

The Personal Antichrist

Before going into the last chapter of Daniel I think it would be well worth our time to look closely at the Antichrist and see from God's Word exactly WHAT he is, WHO he is, WHY he is, and why God allows this personal counterfeit messiah. There are scores of preachers, teachers, and evangelists who do not believe that there will be the Rapture of the Church, the reign of a personal Antichrist, and, after his reign, a glorious Millennium–one thousand years of uninterrupted peace. But it is utterly impossible to understand God's plan of the ages unless we understand the book of Daniel—and especially the "willful king" referred to several times in this prophecy.

"He shall enter peaceably even upon the fattest places of the province; and he shall do that which his fathers have not done, nor his fathers' fathers; he shall scatter among them the prey, and spoil, and riches: yea, and he shall forecast his devices against the strong holds, even for a time" (Dan. 11:24).

This important verse of Scripture is very near the middle of the eleventh chapter of Daniel's prophecy, and in part describes the Man of Sin, the superhuman Antichrist who will appear after the Rapture of the Church. The first thirty-five verses of chapter 11 have to do with the history of the nations *after* Daniel's time.

In chapter 10 we learned much about angelic beings and their relationship to God and His people on earth today. There is a great host of angels around God's throne, ever ready to do His bidding in regard to His people on earth and His dealings with the earth. The angels are ministering spirits to the heirs of salvation; but just as truly as there is a mighty host of GOOD angels, there is also a mighty host of *fallen* angels. Satan is the leader of the fallen angels, but he has millions of lesser subjects known in the Bible as demons. Since the time when Satan fell, to become the loathsome creature that he is, his one purpose has been to disrupt the program of God, and if possible, prevent the program of Jesus concerning salvation and the eventual redemption of all creation.

As previously pointed out, from the Garden of Eden to the Mount of Calvary, Satan did all in his diabolical power to stop the seed of the woman; and after the birth of Jesus he did all in his power to destroy Him. During the Lord's public ministry, Satan tried to keep Him from reaching the cross by causing His enemies to attempt to stone Him or push Him over a precipice; but Jesus came into this world with His eye singled on Calvary, and He died according to the Scriptures (I Cor. 15:1–4).

Satan knows that Jesus will have a kingdom. When he offered Him all the kingdoms of the world, he was suggesting that there was no need for Calvary with all the suffering the Saviour would go through to purchase redemption for mankind and all creation. He declared that if Jesus would only fall down and worship him, he would give Him these kingdoms; but the Son of God conquered every temptation the devil hurled at Him. He finally said, "Get thee hence, Satan," and angels came and ministered unto Him (Matt. 4:1 ff). Jesus WILL sit on the throne of David in Jerusalem when He comes the second time with His bride, the Church.

Satan is not omniscient . . . he is not equal with God in knowledge; but he definitely knows that his head is to be crushed by Jesus, and that there will be a literal kingdom here on earth over which Jesus will reign as King. Satan has counterfeited everything good that God has ever done; he will produce a counterfeit messiah–and just as Jesus was *GOD in flesh*, the counterfeit messiah will be *the DEVIL in flesh*. Just as Jesus in the flesh fulfilled every jot and every tittle of the law (Matt. 5:17; Rom. 8:1–3), Satan in the counterfeit Christ will attempt to undo all that Jesus did. He will attempt to set up his kingdom right here on this earth, and he will stop at nothing to destroy every righteous person on earth and take this earth for himself and his followers.

We learned in Daniel 10:12 and 13 that the prince of Persia, one of the more powerful of the devil's henchmen, hindered Daniel's prayer for 21 days. This record is given in God's Word that we might be forewarned and not underestimate the power of Satan and his kingdom of evil spirits. In Jude 9 even Michael the archangel would not rebuke the devil, but said, "The LORD rebuke thee!"

The Antichrist will come into prominence suddenly—which is the way Jesus came; and the Man of Sin, though opposite, yet will copy the actions of Jesus as nearly as possible. Jesus was born in Bethlehem of Judaea, the wise men came and offered gifts—and then we hear nothing more of Him until the age of twelve, when He came to the temple. He then dropped from sight until He came to John the Baptist to be baptized. So the first thirty years of His life were years of obscurity; we know very little about them.

When Jesus came to be baptized of John in the river Jordan, and after His experience on the Mount of Temptation, He revealed Himself by performing miracles. The disciples believed on Him and followed Him.

Likewise, Antichrist will come upon the scene suddenly. He will pull fire down out of heaven; he will make an image and will cause that image to speak (Rev. 13). And because of his wondrous miracles the whole world will go after him—with the exception of those who are sealed in their foreheads. But through the preaching of this 144,000 (Rev. 7), many will hear the Gospel of the Kingdom and will refuse to worship the Antichrist.

When the Church is taken out, "then shall that Wicked (one) be revealed." Study II Thessalonians chapter 2. We do not know when this will take place. For all we know, the Antichrist may be in the world today. I personally believe that he will be born of a harlot . . . he will be conceived of the spirit of Satan just as the Holy Ghost overshadowed Mary and she conceived and brought forth God's Son. The devil will overshadow some woman upon the face of this earth and she will bring forth *his* son. This is my firm belief concerning the appearance of Antichrist. I believe the same spirit dwelt in Nimrod, Pharaoh, Judas, and others. The Antichrist will be the last great impostor to make an all-out attempt to frustrate the program of God.

When Jesus came on the scene of His public ministry He announced, "I am the Light of the world." Concerning the coming of the Antichrist upon the scene of action, we read, "Even him, whose coming is after the working of Satan with all power and signs and lying wonders, and with all deceivableness of unrighteousness in them that perish; because they received not the love of the truth, that they might be saved. And for this cause God shall send them strong delusion, that they should believe a lie" (II Thess. 2:9–11).

The Antichrist will not make his appearance wielding a shining sword nor displaying a weapon. He will make his appearance upon a white horse, and in his hand he will carry a bow (no arrow) which will also be a symbol of peace (Rev. 6:1,2).

Remember, Jesus came as the Prince of Peace. He WAS the Prince of Peace. The Antichrist will come offering peace, and will bring peace for a season. But then he will break every promise to the Jews and all hell will break out upon this earth. "And in his estate shall stand up a vile person, to whom they shall not give the honour of the kingdom: but he shall come in peaceably, and obtain the kingdom by flatteries. And with the arms of a flood shall they be overflown from before him, and shall be broken; yea, also the prince of the covenant. And after the league made with him he shall work deceitfully: for he shall come up, and shall become strong with a small people" (Dan. 11:21–23).

The stage is set, the world is ready, and the peoples of earth are anxiously awaiting this superman who will appear in miraculous form and offer peace to the earth. His first move will be to win the people—especially the nation of Israel. He will show every favor possible to the Jews back in the new state of Israel at the time of his appearance, and he will scatter among them the prey and the spoil and the riches of his victorious campaigns.

And do not forget that when the Rapture takes place, multibillions in wealth will be left by the Christians who are caught out. These treasures will be confiscated and distributed by the government. Today the stage is set for such action, and the people think nothing of calling upon the government to feed them and provide clothing for them, especially in the time of disaster. When the Rapture takes place and the millions are missing, certainly many areas will be declared disaster areas and there will be much food stuffs and many riches left by Christians, to be distributed among the unbelievers; and the Antichrist will direct much of this to the nation Israel to win their favor.

The master stroke of Antichrist will be to bring peace and *guarantee* peace to Israel. He will promise them all the land that was promised by God to Abraham. The greater part of this land today is occupied by Gentiles, not by the sons of Abraham. There will be peace and favors to Israel for a short time of three and one-half years, and then Antichrist will break his pledge: "Then shall he return into his land with great riches; and his heart shall be against the holy covenant; and he shall do exploits, and return to his own land" (Dan. 11:28).

Then we learn that "arms shall stand on his part, and they shall pollute the sanctuary of strength, and shall take away the daily sacrifice, and they shall place the abomination that maketh desolate" (Dan. 11:31). This is the time when Antichrist will announce to the world that he is God Almighty and will command all to worship him. This is the time of the red horse, as described in Revelation 6:4: "And there went out another horse that was red: and power was given to him that sat thereon to take peace from the earth, and that they should kill one another: and there was given unto him a great sword."

The religion of the Man of Sin will be a combination of atheism, ungodliness, lawlessness, and idolatry. He will deny all gods, all authority, all power except his own. He is "the lawless one." And at the very zenith of his power he will once again attempt to dethrone God Almighty and take God's throne. He attempted this in Isaiah 14 and in Ezekiel 28:14–and he will try the second time, only to be defeated.

His religion is described in II Thessalonians 2:3,4: "Let no man deceive you by any means: for that day shall not come, except there come a falling away first, and that man of sin be revealed, the son of perdition; who opposeth and exalteth himself above all that is called God, or that is worshipped; so that he as God sitteth in the temple of God, shewing himself that he IS God."

His political status is described in Daniel 11:36: "And the king shall do according to his will; and he shall exalt himself, and magnify himself above every god, and shall speak marvellous things against the God of gods, and shall prosper till the indignation be accomplished: for that that is determined shall be done."

But Antichrist will meet THE Christ, and that meeting is described in Revelation 19:11–19: "And I saw heaven opened, and behold a white horse; and He that sat upon him was called Faithful and True, and in righteousness He doth judge and make war. His eyes were as a flame of fire, and on His head were many crowns; and He had a name written, that no man knew, but He Himself. And He was clothed with a vesture dipped in blood: and His name is called The Word of God. And the armies which were in heaven followed Him upon white horses, clothed in fine linen, white and clean. And out of His mouth goeth a sharp sword, that with it He should smite the nations: and He shall rule them with a rod of iron: and He treadeth the winepress of the fierceness and wrath of Almighty God. And He hath on His vesture and on His thigh a name written, KING OF KINGS, AND LORD OF LORDS.

"And I saw an angel standing in the sun; and he cried with a loud voice, saying to all the fowls that fly in the midst of heaven, Come and gather yourselves together unto the supper of the great God; that ye may eat the flesh of kings, and the flesh of captains, and the flesh of mighty men, and the flesh of horses, and of them that sit on them, and the flesh of all men, both free and bond, both small and great. And I saw the beast, and the kings of the earth, and their armies, gathered together to make war against Him that sat on the horse, and against His army."

What a sight! The sky will roll back, outer space will be opened up–and a giant white horse will appear. The One sitting upon him is named Faithful and True. He is coming to judge, and to make war. His eyes are as a flame of fire, His head wears many crowns, He has a new name written that no man knows, and His raiment is dipped in blood. The rider of this white horse is called The Word of God–but look! There is another sight:

Many more horses follow Him–great armies of horses with riders. These are the armies of heaven, clothed in fine linen, white and clean. Can your imagination picture such a host?

The rider of the white horse leading the armies of heaven is unique: Out of His mouth goes a sharp sword, and with that sword He will smite the nations, ruling them with a rod of iron. He treadeth the winepress of the fierceness of Almighty God. And on His vesture there is a name: KING OF KINGS AND LORD OF LORDS.

And then John said he saw an angel standing in the sun. Imagine that! The brightness of the sun grows dim, the brilliance begins to fade. Why? An angel takes a position in the sun, and the sun with all its power and light becomes dim as the angel is seen standing in the sun. Oh yes – this is literal. There is nothing symbolic here. An angel stands in the sun, and calls all the vultures, buzzards, and fowls of the air to come to the battlefield for a feast. They will be fed the flesh of kings and captains, the flesh of mighty men, the flesh of free men, bondsmen, small and great.

And then John declares, "And I saw the beast and the kings of the earth . . . ." These are the ten kings of the revived Roman empire, with their armies. They are gathered together and united TO MAKE WAR AGAINST HIM THAT SAT ON THE HORSE, AND AGAINST HIS ARMY. Imagine that!

Imagine the devil declaring war on the rider of the beautiful white horse with the millions who ride with Him. Then John tells us in advance what will happen: The beast will be taken, along with the false prophet who wrought miracles, deceiving them who received the mark of the beast–and both the beast AND the false prophet will be cast alive into the lake of fire, burning with brimstone! (Rev. 19:20).

You believe what you want to; but I personally believe that Jesus Christ the Son of God will literally lay His hands on the beast, who is Antichrist, and on the false prophet (the third person of the Satanic trinity) and will personally put these two into the lake of fire, while the millions who are dressed in beautiful, white linen look on. Not only will *they* look upon the event, but *those who rode with Antichrist* will see their leader put into the pit. And after Jesus Christ has personally cast Antichrist into the lake of fire, the soldiers who followed him will be slain with the sword of Him who sat upon the horse, which sword proceeded out of His mouth, and the fowls will devour their flesh!

Yes, Jesus will be the Victor. Satan will be defeated in his last gigantic attempt to keep King Jesus from sitting on the throne of His father David in Jerusalem, to reign right here upon this earth for one thousand glorious years! (Rev. 20:5,6).

There Will Be a Literal Kingdom on Earth, With a Literal King Sitting on a Literal Throne

"Behold, the day of the Lord cometh, and thy spoil shall be divided in the midst of thee. For I will gather all nations against Jerusalem to battle; and the city shall be taken, and the houses rifled, and the women ravished; and half of the city shall go forth into captivity, and the residue of the people shall not be cut off from the city. Then shall the Lord go forth, and fight against those nations, as when He fought in the day of battle. And His feet shall stand in that day upon the Mount of Olives, which is before Jerusalem on the east, and the Mount of Olives shall cleave in the midst thereof toward the east and toward the west, and there shall be a very great valley; and half of the mountain shall remove toward the north, and half of it toward the south. And ye shall flee to the valley of the mountains; for the valley of the mountains shall reach unto Azal: yea, ye shall flee, like as ye fled from before the earthquake in the days of Uzziah king of Judah: and the Lord my God shall come, and all the saints with thee. And it shall come to pass in that day, that the light shall not be clear, nor dark: But it shall be one day which shall be known to the Lord, not day, nor night: but it shall come to pass, that at evening time it shall be light. And it shall be in that day, that living waters shall go out from Jerusalem; half of them toward the former sea, and half of them toward the hinder sea: in summer and in winter shall it be.

"And the Lord shall be king over all the earth: in that day shall there be one Lord, and His name one. All the land shall be turned as a plain from Geba to Rimmon south of Jerusalem: and it shall be lifted up, and inhabited in her place, from Benjamin's gate unto the place of the first gate, unto the corner gate, and from the tower of Hananeel unto the king's winepresses. And men shall dwell in it, and there shall be no more utter destruction; but Jerusalem shall be safely inhabited. And this shall be the plague wherewith the Lord will smite all the people that have fought against Jerusalem; Their flesh shall consume away while they stand upon their feet, and their eyes shall consume away in their holes, and their tongue shall consume away in their mouth. And it shall come to pass in that day, that a great tumult from the Lord shall be among them; and they shall lay hold every one on the hand of his neighbour, and his hand shall rise up against the hand of his neighbour. And Judah also shall fight at Jerusalem; and the wealth of all the heathen round about shall be gathered together, gold, and silver, and apparel, in great abundance. And so shall be the plague of the horse, of the mule, of the camel, and of the ass, and of all the beasts that shall be in these tents, as this plague.

"And it shall come to pass, that every one that is

left of all the nations which came against Jerusalem shall even go up from year to year to worship the King, the Lord of hosts, and to keep the feast of tabernacles. And it shall be, that whoso will not come up of all the families of the earth unto Jerusalem to worship the King, the Lord of hosts, even upon them shall be no rain. And if the family of Egypt go not up, and come not, that have no rain; there shall be the plague, wherewith the Lord will smite the heathen that come not up to keep the feast of tabernacles. This shall be the punishment of Egypt, and the punishment of all nations that come not up to keep the feast of tabernacles. In that day shall there be upon the bells of the horses, HOLINESS UNTO THE LORD; and the pots in the Lord's house shall be like the bowls before the altar. Yea, every pot in Jerusalem and in Judah shall be holiness unto the Lord of hosts: and all they that sacrifice shall come and take of them, and seethe therein: and in that day there shall be no more the Canaanite in the house of the Lord of hosts" (Zechariah chapter 14).

The Quality of the Kingdom

"The wolf also shall dwell with the lamb, and the leopard shall lie down with the kid; and the calf and the young lion and the fatling together; and a little child shall lead them. And the cow and the bear shall feed; their young ones shall lie down together: and the lion shall eat straw like the ox. And the sucking child shall play on the hole of the asp, and the weaned child shall put his hand on the cockatrice' den" (Isaiah 11:6–8).

"And I saw thrones, and they sat upon them, and judgment was given unto them: and I saw the souls of them that were beheaded for the witness of Jesus, and for the Word of God, and which had not worshipped the beast, neither his image, neither had received his mark upon their foreheads, or in their hands; and they lived and reigned with Christ a thousand years. . . Blessed and holy is he that hath part in the first resurrection: on such the second death hath no power, but they shall be priests of God and of Christ, and shall reign with Him a thousand years" (Rev. 20:4,6).

(The group described in verse four were martyred by Antichrist during the tribulation period. The martyrs for Jesus *before* the Rapture will be taken at that time. *These* are those who were slain for their testimony during the tribulation because they refused to receive the mark of the beast, as described in Revelation 13.)

CHAPTER TWELVE

THE APPROACHING END

1. And at that time shall Michael stand up, the great prince which standeth for the children of thy people: and there shall be a time of trouble, such as never was since there was a nation even to that same time: and at that time thy people shall be delivered, every one that shall be found written in the book.

2. And many of them that sleep in the dust of the earth shall awake, some to everlasting life, and some to shame and everlasting contempt.

3. And they that be wise shall shine as the brightness of the firmament; and they that turn many to righteousness as the stars for ever and ever.

4. But thou, O Daniel, shut up the words, and seal the book, even to the time of the end: many shall run to and fro, and knowledge shall be increased.

5. Then I Daniel looked, and, behold, there stood other two, the one on this side of the bank of the river, and the other on that side of the bank of the river.

6. And one said to the man clothed in linen, which was upon the waters of the river, How long shall it be to the end of these wonders?

7. And I heard the man clothed in linen, which was upon the waters of the river, when he held up his right hand and his left hand unto heaven, and sware by him that liveth for ever that it shall be for a time, times, and an half; and when he shall have accomplished to scatter the power of the holy people, all these things shall be finished.

8. And I heard, but I understood not: then said I, O my Lord, what shall be the end of these things?

9. And he said, Go thy way, Daniel: for the words are closed up and sealed till the time of the end.

10. Many shall be purified, and made white, and tried; but the wicked shall do wickedly: and none of the wicked shall

understand; but the wise shall understand.

11. And from the time that the daily sacrifice shall be taken away, and the abomination that maketh desolate set up, there shall be a thousand two hundred and ninety days.

12. Blessed is he that waiteth, and cometh to the thousand three hundred and five and thirty days.

13. But go thou thy way till the end be: for thou shalt rest, and stand in thy lot at the end of the days.

The Great Tribulation

Verse 1: "And at that time shall Michael stand up, the great prince which standeth for the children of thy people: and there shall be a time of trouble, such as never was since there was a nation even to that same time: and at that time thy people shall be delivered, every one that shall be found written in the book."

Notice the beginning of this last chapter: "*And at that time . . . .*" The conjunction "and" links this chapter with that which has gone before. "At that time" refers to the events recorded in chapter 11 concerning the willful king, his battles, his final defeat and destruction. The close of the previous chapter brought us to the end of the Great Tribulation as it applies to the Antichrist and the powers of the world. In the chapter before us, we return to go over the tribulation period as it will affect the Jewish people.

"And at that time *shall Michael stand up . . . .*" This is the time of the willful king, the time of the end. Michael will stand up on behalf of the people of Daniel.

Just who IS Michael? He has been twice mentioned previously—in chapter 10, verses 13 and 21—and in our present verse he is called "the great prince." He is said to stand for Daniel's people, the Jews. In the book of Jude Michael is called "the archangel," and in Revelation 12:7 we read where Michael and his angels fight against Satan and his angels. It seems that the work of Michael is to deliver God's people–particularly the children of Israel–from the power of the archenemy, the devil. In the battle which he finally leads against the devil and his angels in the heavenlies, Michael will be victorious and will cast the devil down to earth:

"And there was war in heaven: Michael and his angels fought against the dragon; and the dragon fought and his angels, and prevailed not; neither was their place found any more in heaven. And the great dragon was cast out, that old serpent, called the Devil, and Satan, which deceiveth the whole world: he was cast out into the earth, and his angels were cast out with him" (Rev. 12:7–9).

Michael is also associated with the resurrection, as we will see in the next verse of our present chapter. It seems that probably he has something to do with the resurrection of all peoples at all times. We know that he contended with the devil about the body of Moses (Jude 9), and we are told that the first resurrection will take place when the voice of the *archangel* sounds: "For the Lord Himself shall descend from heaven with a shout, *with the voice of the archangel*, and with the trump of God: and the dead in Christ shall rise first" (I Thess. 4:16).

Since Michael is the only archangel (so named) in the Scriptures, it seems that HIS voice will sound out at the resurrection of the righteous when the Rapture occurs.

At the time Michael stands up, there will be "a time of trouble," *terrible trouble* such as never was since the beginning of the world; and at that time the people shall be delivered–"*every one that shall be found written in the book.*" (This is the same period of time referred to in Matthew 24:15–22, when the "abomination of desolation" will announce in the temple in Jerusalem that he is God, and such terrible tribulation will be upon the earth that except for God shortening those days for the elect's sake, there would be no flesh saved.)

Some teachers would have us believe that the destruction of Jerusalem in 70 A. D. by Titus the Roman is the time described in Matthew 24 and also in our present Scripture, but this is impossible. The destruction of Jerusalem under Titus had to do with but one city and one people, whereas the Great Tribulation will be upon the whole world, and is to be followed by drastic physical changes upon the earth:

"Immediately after the tribulation of those days shall the sun be darkened, and the moon shall not give her light, and the stars shall fall from heaven, and the powers of the heavens shall be shaken: And then shall appear the sign of the Son of man in heaven: and then shall all the tribes of the earth mourn, and they shall see the Son of man coming in the clouds of heaven with power and great glory" (Matt. 24:29,30).

Notice that verse 29 of Matthew 24 begins, "*Immediately after the tribulation.*" The Holy Spirit then points out that the sun will be darkened, the moon will not give her light, the stars will fall from heaven, and Jesus will be seen coming in clouds. We know that this certainly did not happen in 70 A. D. when Titus destroyed Jerusalem.

Again, some teachers spiritualize these things and declare that it does not mean the literal sun, moon, stars, etc., but that this points to the downfall of rulers and governments. But this is not spiritual; it is physical, and there will be physical changes in the sun, moon, stars, and here upon the earth.

Exodus 10:21–23 tells of God's command to Moses, "Stretch out thine hand toward heaven, that there may be darkness over the land of Egypt, even darkness which may be felt. And Moses stretched forth his hand toward heaven; and there was a thick darkness in all the land of Egypt three days: They saw not one another, neither rose any from his place for three days . . . ."

There will be darkness again when the vials of the wrath of God are poured out upon this earth. Revelation 16:1–21 describes a horrible time of judgment when the vials of God's wrath will be poured out and suffering and torment such as this earth has never known will be right here on earth, *physically*.

Both the Old and the New Testaments describe this horrible time of suffering and death here on earth during the reign of the Antichrist, which will end when Jesus comes in final destruction. Jeremiah calls this "the time of Jacob's trouble," and compares the sufferings to the "*birth pangs*" of a woman in travail. (Study Jeremiah 30:4–7.)

Ezekiel also enlightens us concerning this time of suffering. He declares that Israel shall "pass under the rod" (Ezek. 20:34–38). God shall gather Israel into the midst of the Holy City, and the nation shall be cast into God's melting pot to be refined as silver:

"And the word of the Lord came unto me, saying, Son of man, the house of Israel is to me become dross: all they are brass, and tin, and iron, and lead, in the midst of the furnace; they are even the dross of silver. Therefore thus saith the Lord God; Because ye are all become dross, behold, therefore I will gather you into the midst of Jerusalem. As they gather silver, and brass, and iron, and lead, and tin, into the midst of the furnace, to blow the fire upon it, to melt it; so will I gather you in mine anger and in my fury, and I will leave you there, and melt you. Yea, I will gather you, and blow upon you in the fire of my wrath, and ye shall be melted in the midst thereof. As silver is melted in the midst of the furnace, so shall ye be melted in the midst thereof; and ye shall know that I the Lord have poured out my fury upon you'' (Ezek. 22:17–22).

Zechariah 13:9 tells us, "And I will bring the third part through the fire, and will refine them as silver is refined, and will try them as gold is tried: they shall call on my name, and I will hear them: I will say, It is my people: and they shall say, The Lord is my God.''

In Malachi 3:1–3 we read, "Behold, I will send my messenger, and he shall prepare the way before me: and the Lord, whom ye seek, shall suddenly come to His temple, even the messenger of the covenant, whom ye delight in: behold, He shall come, saith the Lord of hosts. But who may abide the day of His coming? and who shall stand when He appeareth? for He is like a refiner's fire, and like fullers' soap: And He shall sit as a refiner and purifier of silver: and He shall purify the sons of Levi, and purge them as gold and silver, that they may offer unto the Lord an offering in righteousness.''

In the Old Testament the prophets did not go into detail concerning this terrible time, because it was not necessary in their particular day; but in the New Testament, God gave John on the Isle of Patmos minute details about this time of great tribulation. Revelation 6:1 through 19:21 gives a picture of the terrible judgment and horrible refining process in the melting pot, through which the nation Israel (primarily) and the peoples of the earth (generally) will pass.

The Great Tribulation has nothing to do with the Church; the Church will not enter nor go through any part of that terrible time. Any preacher or teacher who suggests that the bride of Christ will be subjected to any part of the reign of the Antichrist is definitely wrongly dividing the Word of Truth. God pity the preacher who will accuse Jesus of allowing Antichrist to reign over His bride—and the Church IS the bride of Christ!

We have the blessed promise, "Because thou hast kept the word of my patience, I also will keep thee from the hour of temptation, which shall come upon all the world, to try them that dwell upon the earth" (Rev. 3:10).

In the writings of Paul we are promised, "*For God hath not appointed us to WRATH*, but to obtain salvation by our Lord Jesus Christ" (I Thess. 5:9). The Great Tribulation period has to do with the nation of Israel, not with the Church.

If the Church were to enter or go through any part of the tribulation, believers would be commanded to watch for *Antichrist,* not for THE CHRIST. We would be commanded to watch for great tribulation, not to wait for God's Son from heaven (I Thess. 1:10).

The godly remnant of Daniel's people will be delivered in the end time. *Their names are written in "the book."* God has always kept books, and He always will. He never does anything without a plan or a blueprint.

This Is a Jewish Resurrection

Verse 2: "And many of them that sleep in the dust of the earth shall awake, some to everlasting life, and some to shame and everlasting contempt."

In the Word of God we read of three resurrections:

1. *The spiritual resurrection:* "And you hath He quickened who were dead in trespasses and sins" (Eph. 2:1). Also study Ephesians 2:1–18; 5:14, and Romans 6:11.

Every believer has been spiritually raised from the dead; every *unbeliever* is dead in trespasses and sins. "She that liveth in pleasure is dead while she liveth"

(I Tim. 5:6). When a person believes on the Lord Jesus, that person is born into God's family and raised from the deadness of sin to the newness of life:

"Verily, verily, I say unto you, He that heareth my word, and believeth on Him that sent me, hath everlasting life, and shall not come into condemnation; but is passed from death unto life" (John 5:24).

2. We read much in the New Testament concerning the *physical (bodily) resurrection.* The *spirit* of man never dies; there is no such thing as "soul sleep." All that goes into the grave is the *body.* Man's spirit is eternal, it will never cease to be, it will never cease to *know*; but the body goes back to dust. There will be a resurrection of the righteous and of the unrighteous. The bodies of the righteous will be raised at the Rapture—this is the first resurrection—but the rest of the dead will live not again for a thousand years. The second resurrection will be for the wicked (Rev. 20:1–6).

Study the fifteenth chapter of I Corinthians and you will see the New Testament teaching concerning the bodily resurrection of the righteous. There is no such thing in the Word of God as a "general resurrection"—a time when all of the dead will come out of the graves at the same time. The doctrine of a general resurrection is foreign to the Word of God.

3. There will be a *national resurrection* of the nation of Israel. They are now nationally dead, buried in the graveyard of the nations of earth and the islands of the sea. But they will be revived, raised, and restored to their own land as a nation: "Therefore, behold, the days come, saith the Lord, that it shall no more be said, The Lord liveth, that brought up the children of Israel out of Egypt; But, The Lord liveth, that brought up the children of Israel from the land of the north, and from all the lands

whither He had driven them: and I will bring them again into their land that I gave unto their fathers" (Jer. 16: 14,15). Also study Romans 11 in connection with this.

When God resurrects the children of Israel and they are restored to their own land, the whole twelve tribes will return. Paul distinctly tells us that ". . . all Israel shall be saved: as it is written, There shall come out of Sion the Deliverer, and shall turn away ungodliness from Jacob" (Rom. 11:26).

In Ezekiel's vision of the valley of dry bones we are clearly told that these dry bones represent the whole house of Israel–not just a few of the tribes, but all twelve tribes: ". . . Behold, O my people, I will open your graves, and cause you to come up out of your graves, and bring you into the land of Israel. . . Behold, I will take the children of Israel from among the heathen, whither they be gone, and will gather them on every side, and bring them into their own land: And I will make them one nation in the land upon the mountains of Israel; and one king shall be king to them all: and they shall be no more two nations, neither shall they be divided into two kingdoms any more at all" (Ezek. 37:12, 21, 22).

This does not mean that God will bring every Israelite out of graves dug in the ground–not at all; the dry bones Ezekiel saw were scattered all over the valley . . . they were not in literal graves. God is speaking here of the graves of nations where the Jews have been scattered. Nothing is said in these verses about graves in Israel where the patriarchs, judges, kings, and prophets are all buried. This Scripture refers to the nations where the twelve tribes have been scattered and buried AS A NATION, not as individuals. Ezekiel explains this in Ezekiel 37:13, 14:

"And ye shall know that I am the Lord, when I have

opened your graves, O my people, and brought you up out of your graves, and shall put my Spirit in you, and ye shall live, and I shall place you in your own land: then shall ye know that I the Lord have spoken it, and performed it, saith the Lord."

This prophecy is in accord with many other Scriptures in the Old Testament that clearly teach that Israel as a nation will be brought back to her own land of Palestine. Study Jeremiah 16:14,15; Isaiah 43:5–7; and Amos 9:14,15. The Scriptures further state that Israel as a nation will go through fiery judgment, they will go through the "time of Jacob's trouble"–the Great Tribulation period (Ezek. 20: 34–38; 22:19–22; Zech. 13:9; Mal. 3:1–3). Because of these sufferings and tribulation, Israel will call on the Lord for deliverance. God will hear their prayer, He will pour out His Spirit of grace and mercy upon them, and will save them:

"And I will pour upon the house of David, and upon the inhabitants of Jerusalem, the spirit of grace and of supplications: and they shall look upon me whom they have pierced, and they shall mourn for Him, as one mourneth for his only son, and shall be in bitterness for Him, as one that is in bitterness for his firstborn. In that day shall there be a great mourning in Jerusalem, as the mourning of Hadadrimmon in the valley of Megiddon. And the land shall mourn, every family apart; the family of the house of David apart, and their wives apart; the family of the house of Nathan apart, and their wives apart; the family of the house of Levi apart, and their wives apart; the family of Shimei apart, and their wives apart; all the families that remain, every family apart, and their wives apart" (Zech. 12:10–14).

God has promised, and He cannot and will not break His promise. Therefore, ". . . I will take you from among the heathen, and gather you out of all countries, and will bring you into your own land. Then will I sprinkle clean water upon you, and ye shall be clean: from all your filthiness, and from all your idols, will I cleanse you. A new heart also will I give you, and a new spirit will I put within you: and I will take away the stony heart out of your flesh, and I will give you an heart of flesh. And I will put my Spirit within you, and cause you to walk in my statutes, and ye shall keep my judgments, and do them'' (Ezek. 36:24–27).

When this prophecy is fulfilled literally, then will be brought to pass the fulfillment of Isaiah's words, "Who hath heard such a thing? Who hath seen such things? SHALL THE EARTH BE MADE TO BRING FORTH IN ONE DAY? OR SHALL A NATION BE BORN AT ONCE? For as soon as Zion travailed, she brought forth her children'' (Isaiah 66:8). *Zion (Israel) will travail* as a woman about to be delivered. She will certainly experience birth pangs during the Great Tribulation which we have just discussed, when the king of fierce countenance does all in his diabolical power to annihilate Israel. Yes, a nation will be born in a day . . . the nation of Israel. Thus the vision of the valley of dry bones will be fulfilled.

The vision of the valley of dry bones is confirmed in Ezekiel 37:15–28, where God gives a beautiful object lesson concerning two sticks. Ezekiel was instructed to take a stick and write on the stick, "For Judah and for the children of Israel, his companions"–which were the two tribes, Judah and Benjamin, known as *Judah*. Ezekiel was further instructed to take *another* stick, and on the second stick he was to write, "For Joseph, the stick of Ephraim." (Ephraim was the son of Joseph for whom the ten tribes were sometimes called, after Jeroboam's insurrection.) When Ezekiel had taken the two sticks and had marked them as instructed, he was told to join the two together—but note: *He was to join them END TO END* (not lay them side by side) *thus making ONE stick.*

"And when the children of thy people shall speak unto thee, saying, Wilt thou not shew us what thou meanest by these? Say unto them, Thus saith the Lord God; Behold, I will take the stick of Joseph, which is in the hand of Ephraim, and the tribes of Israel his fellows, and will put them with him, even with the stick of Judah, and make them one stick, and they shall be one in mine hand. And the sticks whereon thou writest shall be in thine hand before their eyes. And say unto them, Thus saith the Lord God; Behold, I will take the children of Israel from among the heathen, whither they be gone, and will gather them on every side, and bring them into their own land: And I will make them *one nation* in the land upon the mountains of Israel; and one king shall be king to them all: and they shall be no more two nations, neither shall they be divided into two kingdoms any more at all" (Ezek. 37:18–22).

From these clear Scriptures we see that the whole house of Israel, the entire twelve tribes, will be gathered back into their own land of Palestine and will dwell there. Study Ezekiel chapter 48.

Listen to this clear, enlightening statement of Jeremiah: "In those days the house of Judah shall walk with the house of Israel, and they shall come together out of the land of the north to the land that I have given for an inheritance unto your fathers" (Jer. 3:18). "The land of the north" could refer to no other place but Russia, and the land of the "inheritance" could refer to no land but Palestine.

The second verse of our present chapter refers to the national resurrection of the nation of Israel. The phrase "*sleep in the dust*" seems to imply physical death, and under ordinary circumstances would do so; but we must not forget that the verse refers to the condition of Daniel's people in the *latter days*–not a condition of death, but of national existence. Notice that it does not say that many who sleep in GRAVES in Palestine shall awake, but "many of them that sleep in the *dust of the earth* shall awake" . . . yea, unto the ends of the earth and every island of the sea where the Jews have been scattered as was prophesied by God when they rebelled against Him and turned to strange flesh and dumb idols. We need to see clearly that this resurrection is NOT physical (from the grave) nor spiritual (from the deadness of sin), but a NATIONAL resurrection before the beginning of the Millennium:

"Immediately after the tribulation of those days shall the sun be darkened, and the moon shall not give her light, and the stars shall fall from heaven, and the powers of the heavens shall be shaken: And then shall appear the sign of the Son of man in heaven: and then shall all the tribes of the earth mourn, and they shall see the Son of man coming in the clouds of heaven with power and great glory. And He shall send His angels with a great sound of a trumpet, and they shall gather together His elect from the four winds, from one end of heaven to the other" (Matt. 24:29–31).

We know that the "*elect*" mentioned here are not those of the Church, because this occurs *after* the Tribulation–and the Church will be caught out *before* the Tribulation. This is not a "catching up to be with the Lord in the air," but a *gathering together*. The scene is here on earth. We must remember that Israel is an earthly people with earthly promises, while the Church is a heavenly people with heavenly promises. As a nation, the Jews have been asleep in the dust of the earth for more than 2,500 years; but even though they dwell in the dust, they shall yet awake and sing:

"Thy dead men shall live, together with my dead body shall they arise. Awake and sing, ye that dwell in dust: for thy dew is as the dew of herbs, and the earth shall cast out the dead" (Isa. 26:19).

Paul said, "For if the casting away of them be the reconciling of the world, what shall the receiving of them be, but life from the dead?" (Rom. 11:15).

In the threefold parable in the fifteenth chapter of Luke, we have the story of a lost sheep, a lost coin, and a lost son. The prodigal son, while in the far country, was referred to as *dead*; but when he returned to the home of his father, he was said to be "*alive again*" (Luke 15:24). As a nation–insofar as their relationship to God is concerned–Israel is dead, although *physically* they live. If we do not interpret the second verse as a *national* resurrection, then we have a mixed resurrection of the righteous and the wicked, which is foreign to the Word of God. Many of the Israelites will be gathered back to Palestine, but many will die in shame and contempt outside the Holy Land. "*Some to everlasting life . . . .*" Many will turn to Messiah, but many will follow Antichrist "to shame and everlasting contempt." Daniel 12:2 has nothing to do with the resurrection of the righteous as pertaining to the first resurrection when the Rapture occurs.

The Reward of the Wise

Verse 3: "And they that be wise shall shine as the brightness of the firmament; and they that turn many to righteousness as the stars for ever and ever."

Who ARE the wise? Paul tells us that the wisdom of this world is foolishness with God, and the foolishness of God is wiser than the wisdom of this world. He also tells us, ". . . If a man think himself to be something, when he is nothing, he deceiveth himself" (Gal. 6:3). Solomon declares, "The fear of the Lord is the beginning of knowledge . . . ." (Prov. 1:7). In James 5:20 we read, "Let him know, that he which converteth the sinner from the error of his way shall save a soul from death, and shall hide a multitude of sins." In James 1:5 we are told, "If any of you lack wisdom, let him ask of God . . . and it shall be given him." All true wisdom comes from God.

We learn from Scripture that true wisdom, the gift of God, comes by studying God's Word. We learn from Scripture that the fear of the Lord is the beginning of knowledge, he who winneth souls is wise, and the wise (soulwinners) shall shine as the brightness of the firmament. Daniel is speaking primarily of the teachers of Israel. In the 24th chapter of Matthew Jesus pointed out that one of the signs of the end will be false prophets and false teachers, preaching error and wrongly dividing the Word.

Matthew 24:14 is a verse that has confused many in this day of Grace; but if we rightly divide the Word, comparing spiritual things with spiritual, there is no need for confusion. Jesus said, "*This Gospel of the kingdom shall be preached in all the world for a witness unto all nations; and then shall the end come.*" The Rapture is not the end. The end is when Antichrist is destroyed and Jesus comes in the Revelation with the Church to set up the kingdom. The Gospel of the kingdom is not the Gospel we preach today: WE preach the Gospel of the grace of God.

Four Gospels are named in the New Testament:

1. The Gospel of the Kingdom. This is the good news

that God is going to set up a kingdom on this earth over which David's Son Jesus will reign (Luke 1:32,33).

2. *The glorious Gospel* – which is the message of the glorious appearing of Jesus in the Rapture (Tit. 2:13).

3. *The everlasting Gospel.* This will be preached by an angel just before the vial judgments are poured out upon the earth, and will be "good news" to those who are passing through the Great Tribulation because it declares that their suffering will soon be over. It will be *bad* news to the Antichrist and his followers because it will declare that the hour of God's judgment for them has come. The everlasting Gospel is mentioned in Revelation 14:6,7, as an angel flies through the midst of heaven, having the everlasting Gospel to preach unto them that dwell on the earth–every nation, kindred, tongue, and people.

This everlasting Gospel is to be preached to the peoples on earth at the end of the Great Tribulation period, immediately preceding the judgment of the nations when the sheep will be divided from the goats (Matt. 25:31–46). This is not the Gospel of the Kingdom; it is not the Gospel of the grace of God. The message is judgment–not salvation. The saved ones will rejoice to hear the message of the everlasting Gospel!

4. *The Gospel of the Grace of God.* Paul preached this Gospel and declared that if anyone preach another gospel, "let him be accursed" (Gal. 1:8,9). The Gospel of Grace is the good news that the Redeemer has come, settled the sin-question, paid the sin-debt in full, and fully satisfied the righteousness of God. Now God can be just and yet justify the ungodly through the shed blood of the Son of His love, the Lord Jesus Christ:

"But now the righteousness of God without the law

is manifested, being witnessed by the law and the prophets; even the righteousness of God which is by faith of Jesus Christ unto all and upon all them that believe: for there is no difference: For all have sinned, and come short of the glory of God; being justified freely by His grace through the redemption that is in Christ Jesus: whom God hath set forth to be a propitiation through faith in His blood, to declare His righteousness for the remission of sins that are past, through the forbearance of God; To declare, I say, at this time His righteousness: that He might be just, and the justifier of him which believeth in Jesus. Where is boasting then? It is excluded. By what law? of works? Nay: but by the law of faith. Therefore we conclude that a man is justified by faith without the deeds of the law. Is He the God of the Jews only? Is He not also of the Gentiles? Yes, of the Gentiles also: Seeing it is one God, which shall justify the circumcision by faith, and uncircumcision through faith. Do we then make void the law through faith? God forbid: yea, we establish the law" (Rom. 3:21–31).

The Gospel is always good news. If you would like to study these four Gospels further, you will find the Gospel of the Kingdom in Matthew 3:2. The Gospel of the Grace of God you will find in Romans 1:1; II Corinthians 4:4 and 10:14; Acts 20:24; I Timothy 1:11; Ephesians 1:13 and 6:15; Hebrews 2:9 and Galatians 2:7.

You will find the Everlasting Gospel in Revelation 14:6. Also read Matthew 25:31; Luke 21:28; Psalm 96; Isaiah 35:4–10, and Revelation 7:9–14.

In Romans 2:16 Paul speaks of "my Gospel." That which Paul calls "my Gospel" is the Gospel of the Grace of God in its fullest development, because it revealed the Church, the *calling out* of the Church, the relationship of the Church to Jesus, the head, and the privileges and the responsibilities of the Church of God. Paul's Gospel was truly the "glorious Gospel"–his messages to the churches to whom he wrote directly; but since all Scripture is profitable, regardless of the day or age, the message is to us, also.

To make the statement that the Gospel of the Kingdom must be preached to every nation, every tribe, every person, *before Jesus comes,* is to wrongly divide the Word. Certainly there is no ground for such a statement. *Gospel* means "good news." The Gospel of the Kingdom which will be preached ("and then the end come") will be the good news announced by the 144,000 during the Great Tribulation–the good news that Jesus the King is coming to reign.

In Luke 1:31–33 the virgin Mary was informed that she would be the mother of the Son whose name was to be called Jesus, and that He would sit on the throne of His father, David, and reign forever. John the Baptist announced, "The kingdom of heaven is at hand." Jesus announced the kingdom–but the Jews rejected their King and crucified Him. Thus the setting up of the kingdom was postponed or set aside until the fulness of the Gentiles be accomplished.

The Church will be caught out, the Dispensation of Grace will be ended, the Holy Spirit will go out with the Church–and then God will seal 12,000 out of each of the twelve tribes of Israel. They will have the seal of God in their foreheads, and they will announce to the world the coming kingdom. They will call the people to repentance in preparation for the setting up of the "stone kingdom" which Daniel revealed to Nebuchadnezzar from his dream in Daniel 2:34,35,44 and 45. All who hear the Gospel of the Kingdom–and refuse to receive the mark of the beast–will either be killed or forced to hide until the Tribulation is over; and then they will enter the Kingdom which will be set up here on earth after the Great Tribulation.

The Gospel of the Kingdom was preached by John the Baptist, it was preached by Jesus–and by the disciples until the King was crucified. Then God called and anointed Paul a minister to the Gentiles to preach the Grace of God, announcing that the middle wall of partition has been broken down, and now "whosoever will"–Jew or Gentile, rich or poor, bond or free–can be saved through the Gospel of the Grace of God.

These wise teachers in the end time will have understanding of the Scriptures–primarily the Old Testament and prophecies relating to the children of Israel, the setting up of the kingdom, and the "peace on earth, good will toward men" that was promised but has never been fulfilled. There will be a day when the knowledge of the Lord will cover this earth as the waters cover the sea, and there *will be* peace on earth, good will toward men. Warriors will beat their swords into plowshares and their spears into pruning hooks, and this earth will be one magnificent Garden of Eden (Isaiah 2:4; 11:1–9). King Jesus will sit on the throne in Jerusalem and we, the bride, will reign with Him over this earth during one thousand glorious years!

I am sure every Christian is familiar with the old song, "*Will There Be Any Stars in My Crown?*" There is no Scripture to indicate that the saints will wear "starry crowns," but there is Scripture which is much greater: We are promised that "the *wise* (he that winneth souls is wise) *shall shine as the brightness of the firmament, and they that turn many to righteousness as the stars for ever and ever!*" And this promise is to the soulwinners of ANY age–whether it be an Old Testament Isaiah, Ezekiel, Moses, or Daniel, a New Testament Matthew, Mark, Luke, John, or Paul, or a Spurgeon, Moody, Finney, Livingstone–or yourself! "He that winneth souls is wise," and the wise shall shine–not as just a little star in a crown, but as the brightness of ALL the stars that shine above us! And they will shine–not just for a little season and then flicker out: *They will shine forever and ever*!

"It pays to serve Jesus, it pays every day; it pays every step of the way"–and then it keeps ON paying–every moment of time throughout the endless ages of eternity! The greatest investment mortal man can make is the investment of time, talent, and money in turning men to God, winning souls, giving out the good news that salvation has been brought down to man, and is for "whosoever will."

God's Last Message to Daniel

Verse 4: "But thou, O Daniel, shut up the words, and seal the book, even to the time of the end: many shall run to and fro, and knowledge shall be increased."

God instructed Daniel to shut up the words and seal the book until the time of the end, when "*many shall run to and fro, and knowledge shall be increased.*" Daniel was to seal up the message God had given him, until the appointed time for the message to be made known, at which time God would open up the book; but in Revelation 22:10 John the Beloved on the Isle of Patmos was instructed, "*Seal NOT the sayings of the prophecy of this book: for the time is at hand.*"

During the public ministry of Jesus here on earth, He frequently spoke in parables. Of course, the multitude to whom He spoke was primarily Jews, and one day the disciples asked Him, "Why speakest thou unto them in parables? He answered and said unto them, Because it is given unto you to know the mysteries of the kingdom of heaven, but to them it is not given. For whosoever hath, to him shall be given, and he shall have more abundance: but whosoever hath not, from him shall be taken away even that he hath. Therefore speak I to them in parables: because they seeing see not; and hearing they hear not, neither do they understand. And in them is fulfilled the prophecy of Esaias, which saith, By hearing ye shall hear, and shall not understand; and seeing ye shall see, and shall not perceive: For this people's heart is waxed gross, and their ears are dull of hearing, and their eyes they have closed; lest at any time they should see with their eyes and hear with their ears, and should understand with their heart, and should be converted, and I should heal them" (Matt. 13:10–15).

According to this Scripture, the Jews in the days of Jesus were "willingly ignorant," for He said, "In them is fulfilled the prophecy of Esaias," referring to Isaiah 6:9–12:

"And He said, Go, and tell this people, Hear ye indeed, but understand not; and see ye indeed, but perceive not. Make the heart of this people fat, and make their ears heavy, and shut their eyes; lest they see with their eyes, and hear with their ears, and understand with their heart, and convert, and be healed. Then said I, Lord, how long? And He answered, Until the cities be wasted without inhabitant, and the houses without man, and the land be utterly desolate, and the Lord have removed men far away, and there be a great forsaking in the midst of the land."

We are told in Peter's second epistle that the time will come when men will again be "willingly ignorant," and we are living in that day. The Jews had the books of the Old Testament that clearly outlined the coming of their Messiah. They had ears to hear—but *they did not hear.* They had hearts to understand—but they did not WANT to understand. Therefore, in order not to add to their sin and heap added damnation upon them, Jesus spoke in parables of the mysteries of the kingdom. The disciples understood Him, but the masses of the people did not understand. They were blinded simply because they had *refused to see* when God would have shown them:

"But their minds were blinded: for until this day remaineth the same vail untaken away in the reading of the old testament; which vail is done away in Christ. But even unto this day, when Moses is read, the vail is upon their heart. Nevertheless when it shall turn to the Lord, the vail shall be taken away" (II Cor. 3: 14–16).

To the Jews, primarily, to all and sundry generally, the book of Daniel has been a sealed book, but it is sealed only until the time of the end; and when that time comes, the Jews will hear the words of the prophecy, they will understand, and when they see their Messiah they will receive Him, asking where He received the scars in His hands.

"The time of the end" in the book of Daniel is a statement definitely referring to God's dealings with the Jews after the Rapture, during the time of "Jacob's trouble." We read concerning the time of the end, in Daniel 8:17–19; 9:26; 11:35,40,45; and then in our present chapter, verses 4, 6, and 9.

The time of the end begins with the revelation of "the prince that shall come," the son of perdition, the Man of Sin, the beast. He will make a covenant with the Jews, restoring their temple worship and sacrifice (Dan. 9:27). He will present himself to the Jews as God, announcing that he is their messiah (Dan. 11:36,38;

Matt. 24:15; II Thess. 2:4; Rev. 13:4–6).

The time of the end will close with the destruction of Antichrist when Jesus comes in the Revelation, when every eye shall see Him and all the kindreds of the earth shall wail because of Him (II Thess. 2:8; Rev. 19:19,20).

The Length of the Time of the End

Verses 5–12: "Then I Daniel looked, and, behold, there stood other two, the one on this side of the bank of the river, and the other on that side of the bank of the river. And one said to the man clothed in linen, which was upon the waters of the river, How long shall it be to the end of these wonders? And I heard the man clothed in linen, which was upon the waters of the river, when he held up his right hand and his left hand unto heaven, and sware by Him that liveth for ever that it shall be for a time, times, and an half; and when He shall have accomplished to scatter the power of the holy people, all these things shall be finished. And I heard, but I understood not: Then said I, O my Lord, what shall be the end of these things? And He said, Go thy way, Daniel: for the words are closed up and sealed till the time of the end. Many shall be purified, and made white, and tried; but the wicked shall do wickedly: and none of the wicked shall understand; but the wise shall understand. And from the time that the daily sacrifice shall be taken away, and the abomination that maketh desolate set up, there shall be a thousand two hundred and ninety days. Blessed is he that waiteth, and cometh to the thousand three hundred and five and thirty days."

From chapter 10 through chapter 12, Daniel was standing by the river Hiddekel (the Tigris). The record given to us in these chapters constitutes one vision. The man clothed in linen here is the same one mentioned in chapter 10, verses 5 and 6, where he is minutely described. However, at this point in his vision, Daniel sees two other angelic beings–one on either side of the river; and one of these two creatures begins a conversation with "the man clothed in linen." He asked, "HOW LONG SHALL IT BE TO THE END OF THESE WONDERS?" With both hands lifted high toward heaven, the man clothed in linen answered and sware by the Almighty that it should be for "TIME, TIMES, AND AN HALF"–meaning three and one-half years.

The book of Revelation is the best commentary available on Daniel. I repeat what I declared earlier in this study: *the only way to understand the Word of God is to compare Scripture with Scripture and spiritual things with spiritual.* Men do not agree in their interpretations, but holy men of old agree. There is no discrepancy and no contradiction in the Word of God.

We notice two significant things in the statement in verse 7: First, *the oath.* The man clothed in linen lifted both hands and sware "by Him that liveth forever." (He could swear by none higher!) Second, *the length of the time.* In Revelation 10:1–6 we read:

"And I saw another mighty angel come down from heaven, clothed with a cloud: and a rainbow was upon his head, and his face was as it were the sun, and his feet as pillars of fire: And he had in his hand a little book open: and he set his right foot upon the sea, and his left foot on the earth, and cried with a loud voice, as when a lion roareth: and when he had cried, seven thunders uttered their voices. And when the seven thunders had uttered their voices, I was about to write: and I heard a voice from heaven saying unto me, Seal up those things which the seven thunders uttered, and write them not. And the angel which I saw stand upon the sea and upon the earth lifted up his hand to heaven, and sware by Him that liveth for ever and ever, who created heaven, and the things that therein are, and the earth, and the things that therein are, and the sea, and the things which are therein, that there should be time no longer."

These verses shed much light on the closing words of Daniel. The description John gives of the mighty angel standing on the land and on the sea, with His hand raised toward heaven–His actions, His appearance, His message–is in perfect harmony with that of Daniel's "man clothed in linen." There is no doubt that these two personages are one and the same. I personally believe that this is none other than the Lord Jesus Christ. Certainly the description given by Daniel in chapter 10 corresponds to Him who is seen standing in the midst of the lampstands in Revelation 1:12–16. In the Old Testament He was called "the angel of the Lord" (Ex. 3:2–18). When Moses asked Jehovah whom he should say sent him, God answered, "Tell Pharaoh that 'I AM' sent thee."

The "I AM" of the Old Testament is the "I AM" of the New Testament. Jesus is the great "I AM." He appeared as the angel of the Lord in the Old Testament, why not in the New? In these closing chapters of Daniel, Jesus comes to the people of Israel as the angel of the Lord. Since that is true, what could be more fitting in the end time described in Revelation chapters 6 through 19 than that Jesus appear to Israel during this terrible time of "Jacob's trouble" as "*a mighty angel*"?

The mighty angel in Revelation 10:3 cried with a loud voice, "as when a lion roareth." This certainly identifies the mighty angel as *the Lion of the tribe of Judah:* "And one of the elders saith unto me, Weep not: behold, the Lion of the tribe of Juda, the Root of David, hath prevailed to open the book, and to loose the seven seals thereof" (Rev. 5:5).

The mighty angel in Revelation 10 and the man clothed in linen in Daniel 12 swear by Jehovah God *that there should be time no longer.* The literal Greek in Revelation reads, "delay no longer"–that is, "the time of the end has arrived." The mighty angel made His announcement in the middle of Daniel's seventieth week of prophecy; therefore, there were only three and one-half years (forty-two months) remaining (Rev. 13:5). This corresponds to the announcement made by "the man clothed in linen." Forty-two months equals "time, times, and an half" (Dan. 12:7). Revelation and the prophecy of Daniel are in perfect harmony concerning *the length* of the time of the end. The length was given to both men by the same Person–the Lord Jesus Christ, Israel's king.

Daniel heard perfectly well what was said, but he did not understand. He asked, "O my Lord, what shall be the end of these things?" The man in linen did not repeat the revelation – he simply said, "*Go thy way, Daniel:* For the words are closed up and sealed till the time of the end." In other words, "Daniel, you have seen, you have heard, and you have obeyed. You have penned down the words. Now close the book, seal it up–and do not worry or fret about it. This vision is for the time of the end. *You go your way and rest.*"

"*Many shall be purified, and made white, and tried*" (verse 10). As the end of this dispensation of Grace comes nearer, true believers will become more dedicated and separated. They will live pure, separated lives, knowing that at any moment the Rapture may occur. There will not be an international revival, but because of the dedicated lives of the believers, many will be saved ("made white") by the blood.

Those who are dedicated unto the Lord shall suffer persecution – they will "*be tried.*" ("Yea, and all that will live godly in Christ Jesus shall suffer persecution"–II Tim. 3:12.) At this same time, wicked men will become more wicked: ". . . Evil men and seducers shall wax worse and worse, deceiving, and being deceived" (II Tim. 3:13).

The wicked will not understand; they will be blinded (II Cor. 4:3,4). Every major judgment has been preceded by extreme ignorance concerning God and righteousness. At the time of the flood, the people were eating, drinking, marrying, buying, selling – "AND KNEW NOT until the flood came, and took them all away" (Matt. 24:39).

In Sodom and Gomorrah poor Lot was counted crazy by his sons-in-law, and he lost all he had except his two daughters. Yet Sodom "knew not" (Gen. 19). When Jesus was born, King Herod and those in high places "knew not." But the humble shepherds heard the announcement of His birth, and *believed it.*

So it is today: The masses know not what is taking place all around us–throughout the entire world . . . "*but the wise shall understand.*" The wise know and understand that Jesus is coming the second time, just as He promised. Those whose "eyes of understanding" have been opened by the Holy Spirit, see the end of this age approaching; but the wicked who are blinded by "the god of this age" see nothing about which to be alarmed. They live as though they plan to stay here forever. They have no time for God, and no desire to prepare to meet Him. Things will continually grow worse as the end approaches.

We will study several of these verses a little more and go into them a little deeper a bit later. But I want to keep the line of thought until we finish this particular part of the prophecy before going into the signs of our time that point to the soon return of Jesus.

In verses 11 and 12 two other measures of time are made known to Daniel: 1290 days and 1335 days. These days were to begin when the daily sacrifice is taken away and the "abomination of desolation" set up. We know that *the abomination of desolation* will stand in the holy temple of God and announce that he IS God in the middle of Daniel's seventieth week (Dan. 9:27). That is the time when the daily sacrifice will be taken away, and he will break every promise he made to Israel when he rode to prominence on the white horse (Rev. 6:2), bringing peace. Therefore we have three measures of time in Daniel, and each of the three *begins in the middle of the seventieth week* (Dan. 9:27).

First, we have 2300 days (Dan. 8:13,14). Then we have here 1290 days and 1335 days. Each of these go beyond the end of Daniel's seventieth week. The 2300 days in Daniel 8 go beyond 3½ years, 1040 days. 1290 days go beyond 30 days, and 1335 days go beyond 75 days. We read clearly that the 2300 days have to do with the cleansing of the sanctuary. The Holy Spirit did not see fit to reveal to us what events these last two measures of days lead up to. No doubt after Jesus returns in the Revelation at the end of the week, there will be other events concerning the Jews (nationally) that will take place before the Millennial Kingdom begins. (Study Revelation 19:17–19.)

We need not fret over these days mentioned here. Daniel did not understand what he had written, but God told him not to worry about it, to go his way and rest. If God had wanted us to know the full meaning of the 1290 days and the 1335 days, He would have made it known—either here, or in some other place in the Bible. These days have nothing to do with the Rapture of the Church, nor with the saints who make up the Church; and at the appointed time, God will reveal to wise men exactly the meaning of these days. There is an answer, and there is no contradiction—but there is no need for us to speculate on what God has not seen fit to reveal to us in understandable language.

Verse 11 clearly states that *from the time the daily sacrifice shall be taken away*, which will occur after three and one-half years of peace brought about when the Antichrist appears, there will be a thousand two hundred and ninety days. This was in answer to Daniel's question, "What shall be *the end of these things*?" For three and one-half years there will be worldwide Utopia – peace. And then when the Antichrist seemingly has all peoples of earth under his thumb, he breaks every promise and the abomination of desolation will be set up. Jesus refers to this in Matthew 24. Verse 12 goes 45 days beyond the "*end of these things*" and says, "Blessed is he that waiteth, and cometh to the thousand three hundred and five and thirty days."

Let me attempt once more to sum up these three periods of days: The three periods of days date from the day when the "abomination of desolation" is set up. The "abomination of desolation" is the blasphemous assumption of deity by the beast referred to in verse 11, also in Matthew 24:15 and II Thessalonians 2:4. Note carefully that there are 1260 days up to the destruction of the beast who announces that he is God (Dan. 7:25; 12:7; Rev. 13:5; 19:19,20). This period of time is also the duration of the *Great Tribulation* (Dan. 9:27), which has to do with the last three and one-half years of the *overall* tribulation. As I have pointed out several times, the first half will be peaceful, the last half will be a deluge of blood. In verse 6 of chapter 12 one of the men asked the question, "How long shall it be to *the end of these wonders*?" The wording of his question differs from that of Daniel in verse 8. The answer to the question in verse 6 is "that it shall be for a time, times, and an half"–or three and one-half years, which corresponds to Daniel 9:27.

Three and one-half prophetic years, each month 30

days, adds up to exactly 1260 days. Notice in verse 11, 30 days are added, making a total of 1290 days. And again, 45 days are added with them to the promise recorded in verse 12. We have 1335 days. The Holy Spirit did not give us an account of just what happens during these additional 75 days between the end of the Great Tribulation and the blessing promised in verse 12. Bible scholars suggest that the explanation may be found in the prophetic description of the events that will follow the battle of Armageddon in the Valley of Megiddo when the armies of Antichrist and the armies of the Christ come together for a final battle, and a victory over Antichrist and his armies.

"For they are the spirits of devils, working miracles, which go forth unto the kings of the earth and of the whole world, to gather them to the battle of that great day of God Almighty" (Rev. 16:14).

"And the remnant were slain with the sword of Him that sat upon the horse, which sword proceeded out of His mouth: and all the fowls were filled with their flesh" (Rev. 19:21).

The beast who set himself up as God is at that time totally destroyed. The Gentile world dominion is ended. The end comes when the stone cut out of the mountain without hands as seen by Nebuchadnezzar, strikes at the end of 1260 days. Of course, at the close of this great battle, the earth will be filled with chaos and debris, and the "WIND" must carry away this debris before the blessing of the Millennium comes and King Jesus sits on the throne of David in Jerusalem:

"Then was the iron, the clay, the brass, the silver, and the gold, broken to pieces together, and became like the chaff of the summer threshingfloors; *and the wind carried them away*, that no place was found for them: and the stone that smote the image became a great mountain, and filled the whole earth" (Dan. 2:35).

I do not suggest that I fully know the meaning of these periods of time. I have searched in Bible dictionaries and encyclopedias, and I find that even the greatest of scholars do not agree on the subject. But I DO know that these days have nothing to do with our salvation! Jesus Christ died on the cross, "according to the Scriptures." He was buried and rose again, "according to the Scriptures." *Believing in the death, burial, and resurrection of Jesus, according to the Scriptures, brings salvation to all.* It is interesting to study these prophetic truths and see them fall into place to the glory of God. If I have not made these days and dates plain, read your Bible and study more. I trust that these lessons will whet your appetite and give you a hunger such as you have never had to study prophecy.

The Lord God Makes Known to Daniel His Glorious Lot

Verse 13: "But go thou thy way till the end be: for thou shalt rest, and stand in thy lot at the end of the days."

Through the Holy Spirit, God dictated to Daniel 12 chapters of the Word of God; and in these chapters He made known to Daniel through revelation, symbols, and visions, the times of the Gentiles and God's dealings with Daniel's people, Israel. Up to the beginning of the glorious reign of Jesus (seen in the book of Daniel as the stone cut out of the mountain without hands), Daniel understood some of the things revealed to him. Others he did not understand, and this troubled him. But in the closing chapter, God told him, "Go thy way, for the words are closed up and sealed until the time of the end."

In the closing chapter of this series of studies, I want to point out just how up-to-date the last chapter of Daniel is, even though it was written almost 2,600 years ago, five and one-half centuries before the birth of Christ. God revealed to Daniel exactly what would be going on in our day, just before the Rapture of the Church.

Verse 1 of this chapter is extremely rich and illuminating. It begins with "And at that time," the "and" linking it with that which has been given previously, especially the events recorded in chapter 11.

In chapter 11, Daniel saw a vision and received revelation concerning the activities of the archenemy of the Lord Jesus Christ (the Antichrist) and the people Israel during the tribulation period. I have previously pointed out the political and religious policies of this counterfeit messiah, and stated that the world is looking and yearning for just such a person—a superhuman to bring about "peace on earth, good will toward men." He will appear immediately after the Rapture of the Church, he will be hailed and acclaimed as the saviour of the world, and world leaders will fall at his feet, declaring that he is the person for whom they have longed and waited.

To God's chosen people Israel, Antichrist will proclaim himself messiah. He will be clever and cunning; he will be *the devil in flesh*! Israel will be restored to their own land and allowed to worship in their own temple. They will put their trust in the counterfeit messiah, but after approximately three and one-half years of peace and prosperity he will break every promise he has made to Israel:

"And he shall confirm the covenant with many for one week: and in the midst of the week he shall cause the sacrifice and the oblation to cease, and for the overspreading of abominations he shall make it desolate, even until the consummation, and that determined shall be poured upon the desolate" (Dan. 9:27).

Antichrist will come, he will promise peace–and he will *bring* peace for a season. Then his true nature will be revealed. He will desecrate the temple of God, he will turn against God's ancient people, and he will become the most bitter enemy Israel has ever had. However, they will accept his promises, they will believe in him, until he proves to them that he is their archenemy.

May 1948 marked the birth of the new state of Israel. For the first time in more than 2,500 years, Israel has her own government, her own capital, her own coins, in her own land. The stage is set for the appearing of the false messiah. When Jesus was here on earth He declared to His people, "I am come in my Father's name, and ye receive me not: if another shall come in his own name, him ye will receive" (John 5:43). And it will happen exactly that way.

The Jews today are ready to receive someone to lead them out of the sufferings they have gone through–and are presently going through–in the nations around the world. A small remnant has already returned to the homeland, and others are going back as rapidly as they are allowed to return. I have seen the quarantine camps in Trans-Jordan and in Israel where the Jews are being brought in from other nations. Around the world they are anxious to return home, and will do so just as soon as they are allowed.

Not only will the *Jews* accept the false messiah–this superhuman who will come–but *the world at large* will also receive him. We are living in a world that is anxious. These are the most trying days man has ever known. Today's world is a powder-keg. Man has finally discovered and manufactured tools with which he can annihilate himself from the face of the earth. All major nations live in fear of each other. The world is longing and praying for someone to save civilization. The Antichrist will make such promises, and through his miracles he will draw the peoples of earth to him—with the exception of those who are sealed in their foreheads as mentioned in Revelation chapter 7, and the few who will believe the message of the coming kingdom, preached by the 144,000 sealed ones.

When Antichrist comes, he will make world government a reality. The *United States of the World* will come to pass. Today men are planning and looking forward to one world government. Not only will Antichrist unite the *political factions* of the world, but he will also bring together the *religious* bodies and unite the faiths. We have today the World Council of Churches, which is definitely the forerunner of the church of Antichrist.

The program of Antichrist will be to do away with all differences that separate people—both politically and religiously. He will advocate the brotherhood of man, and in the middle of the tribulation period he will announce himself as God. He will actually bring about a man-made millennium—but after three and one-half years of peace, all hell will break out and blood will run in the streets like water.

Since the day God created Adam He has longed for and sought a people to honor Him supremely, every way and in all things. The devil has always been jealous and envious of God . . . that is the reason he is a devil today. In his original state he was the anointed cherub, Lucifer, the shining one; but jealousy cost him his glorious estate and he became the loathsome liar and murderer that he is today. He came into the Garden of Eden and suggested to Eve that if she would eat the fruit God had forbidden her to eat, she would become as a god. She was deceived by the devil's lie, she and Adam ate, and through their disobedience they lost their perfect estate.

They saw themselves naked and shameful, and immediately attempted to correct their mistake by the labor of their own hands, just as man has been busy *for more than 6,000 years* trying to correct his mistakes! The Antichrist will, in a counterfeit way, bring the Utopia and the good will which man has attempted to bring to pass on earth these many centuries; but there will never be *lasting* peace until King Jesus sits on the throne of David in Jerusalem.

A river of blood flows from Genesis to Calvary. The greatest battle of the ages has been fought between Satan and Jehovah God. Satan attempted to stop the seed of the woman before the birth of Jesus, and then in his mad attempt to thwart God's plan immediately *after* the birth of the Saviour he caused Herod to command the butchering of all the children three years old and under.

Just before Calvary, Satan attempted to shed the blood of Jesus–not on the cross, but in the Garden of Gethsemane. He also attempted to prevent the resurrection–but when Jesus walked out of the tomb, Satan knew that he was defeated – and since that day he has made an all-out attempt to damn every soul he possibly can!

This battle between God and Satan has been going on for centuries and centuries. The battle between God and Satan concerning the soul of man has been going on for six thousand years and will continue for the duration of man's day, until the seed of the woman finally crushes the head of the serpent.

Satan himself will be cast into the lake of fire at the end of the Millennium, but his personal representative, the Antichrist, will be cast into the lake of fire at the *beginning* of the Millennium.

The Antichrist will be the incarnation of Satan, just as the Lord Jesus Christ was the incarnation of God.

Jesus was *God* in flesh; Antichrist will be *Satan* in flesh.

"And the beast was taken, and with him the false prophet that wrought miracles before him, with which he deceived them that had received the mark of the beast, and them that worshipped his image. These both were cast alive into a lake of fire burning with brimstone" (Rev. 19:20).

"And the devil that deceived them was cast into the lake of fire and brimstone, where the beast and the false prophet are, and shall be tormented day and night for ever and ever" (Rev. 20:10).

"And then shall that Wicked be revealed, whom the Lord shall consume with the spirit of His mouth, and shall destroy with the brightness of His coming: Even him, whose coming is after the working of Satan with all power and signs and lying wonders" (II Thess. 2:8,9).

"And he shall plant the tabernacles of his palace between the seas in the glorious holy mountain; yet he shall come to his end, and none shall help him" (Dan. 11:45).

It is true that Satan will be placed in the bottomless pit for one thousand years–the duration of the Millennium: otherwise there could BE no Millennium. In Revelation 20:1–3 we read of an angel descending from heaven with a great chain in His hands, "and He laid hold on the dragon, that old serpent, which is the Devil, and Satan, and bound him a thousand years, and cast him into the bottomless pit, and shut him up, and set a seal upon him, that he should deceive the nations no more, till the thousand years should be fulfilled: and after that he must be loosed a little season."

After this "little season" Satan will be placed into the lake of fire–the eternal abode of the damned.

I find that believers are tragically mixed up as to

the chronology of events preceding the coming of the Lord in the Rapture, the Tribulation period, the Revelation of the Lord, the Millennium, and the ages of ages. To clearly understand these things we need to read, re-read, and carefully study the truths laid down in the prophetic books of the Bible.

I believe that we are now living in the very closing hours (prophetically) of this dispensation. I believe the next great event in store for this old world is the coming of the Lord Jesus Christ in the Rapture of the Church. If there is one thing clearly taught in the Bible it is that at the close of this Dispensation of Grace, the Church will be caught out of this earth to meet Jesus in the clouds in the air – and the Holy Spirit will be caught out with the Church. Then will the Man of Sin, the son of perdition, be revealed. Antichrist *cannot* be unveiled until the Holy Spirit is taken out of the earth (II Thess. 2:7,8); but when "He who now letteth" be taken out with the Church, Satan will then unveil his masterpiece–his incarnation, the Antichrist!

Then will follow the period of the Great Tribulation (which corresponds to the *last week of years* pointed out in the seventy weeks in Daniel 9). This week will be shortened for the sake of the elect; if not, there would be no flesh saved. The first half of the reign of the Antichrist will be peace; the last half will be blood. The last half of blood will be shortened a few days, perhaps a few weeks, and then the battle of Armageddon will be fought. The nations of earth will gather for the last great battle to be fought between *men* upon this earth.

The battle of Gog and Magog will be between God Almighty and the armies of Gog and Magog. Fire will come down from heaven and completely annihilate the enemies of God. Their bodies will be cremated with fire and their spirits will be cast into the lake of fire. *But the battle of Armageddon will be a battle of blood.*

All the armies of earth will be gathered north of Palestine to destroy Israel in her own land. They will be anxiously anticipating total victory, but the battle will end when Jesus comes and destroys them with the sword of His mouth. Blood will run to the horses' bits in the battle of Armageddon!

At the close of that battle, Jesus will personally put Antichrist into the lake of fire. Satan will be placed into the bottomless pit and sealed for one thousand years. The horrible reign of terror of the Great Tribulation will end in the battle of Armageddon when the king of the south, the king of the north, and the king of the east will meet on the great historical battleground of Armageddon, where many bloody battles have been fought in the centuries behind us.

It will take seven months to clean up the land and bury the dead after the battle of Armageddon. (Study Ezekiel chapters 37, 38, and 39.) And then we will have one thousand years of glorious peace on earth, good will toward men. The curse will be lifted from all creation, and the knowledge of the Lord will cover the earth.

We see the things Daniel prophesied more than 2,500 years ago, being literally fulfilled before our very eyes this moment. In Europe, we see the formation of two gigantic power blocks, one consisting of the territory which corresponds almost exactly to the old Roman empire, the other consisting of the Communist nations, with Russia as the head, with her many satellites. There is tremendous unrest among the Arab nations, and where could you find more unrest and demon hatred than in China, with her godless leaders today?

We are living in the hour of the fulfillment of those

things which Daniel did not understand, even though God gave them to him and he penned them down. Surely we are living in the last days of the Dispensation of Grace. The Lord Jesus Christ is coming soon!

Daniel 12:4 gives a prophecy that has been literally fulfilled in the last few years, and most of you who read these lines will remember the beginning of the fulfillment of this prophecy.

"Many shall run to and fro." A fleet-footed horse was probably the fastest mode of travel in Daniel's day. The kings had horses and chariots which were very fast in that day, but compared with the speed of today they were slower than a tortoise. This is a statement revealed to Daniel by the Holy Ghost concerning "the time of the end."

Notice that "MANY"–not just a few, but *multitudes*–shall run to and fro. My father lived to be seventy years of age. He left his home state only once during those years, and the only reason he traveled so far from home that one time was because my brother, out of the state in an army camp, was preparing to go overseas. Had it not been for the fact that my brother was going to war, I doubt that my dad would have left his native state during his lifetime.

Fifty years ago, very few people traveled very far; but today almost everyone travels. Millions travel even across the seas, and a trip around the world is nothing unusual today. Regardless of where you go on this earth, many are running to and fro. I visited the jungles of Africa, and in Leopoldville we purchased a ticket for the native train that ran a hundred miles back into the jungle. I supposed there would be an abundance of room, but the next morning when we went down to the station to board the train we found people standing, hanging out the windows, and riding everywhere they could find a place to stand or sit. Wherever you may go today, people are on the move, traveling, going and coming.

In the early days of our country, people traveled from east to west, but as a rule they traveled only one way – most of them never returned. But Daniel was instructed to write that many would run *"to and fro"*: They will go, and they will return.

Notice that *"many will RUN to and fro."* When I was a boy, I walked five miles to school. Today, the average child who goes as far as two city blocks to school either rides in the family automobile, or has his own bike or motor scooter. There is a minimum of walking.

Wherever you go, people are running, they are in a hurry–and *for what*? Most of them could not tell you. They are hurrying to get – *where*? Most of them do not know–but they are always in a hurry. The only way to stay alive today is to run–even in the supermarket. If you are not careful, someone will run a grocery-cart right over you if you stop moving!

This is the age of speed. As I dictate these lines, the President of the United States has just announced that we have a jet fighter plane that flies more than 2,000 miles per hour . . . think of it! It makes one *dizzy* to think of such speed. It has just been announced that France is building a transport that will carry 200 people across the Atlantic ocean in one hour and twenty-five minutes.

If Daniel could have read a statement such as I have just made, he could not have understood the words he read. Thus the Lord God instructed him to seal up the book and close up the words until the time of the end. WE can understand because we have *seen* these things come to pass. We live in the days of the fulfillment of this prophecy.

The days just before the end of this age will be days of greatly increased speed. My grandfather used oxen, and I well remember riding in my father's buggy. I was a lad in the horse-and-buggy days, but *in my day* I have seen man move from the buggy to the airplane, to the jet plane – yea, even into outer space! Books written on this chapter of Daniel fifty years ago are out of date now. They spoke of automobiles traveling at the rate of 40 miles per hour, and airplanes at the rate of 200 miles per hour; but today most automobile speedometers have 120 miles on them and many planes fly at the rate of 1000, 1500–and the latest one more than 2000–miles per hour! Certainly Daniel 12:4 fits our day.

Not only will many be running to and fro, but *"knowledge shall be increased."* It will suffice to say that there has been a tremendous increase of knowledge in literature, inventions, medicine, science, chemistry, surgery, farming, mining, shipping–any field you wish to name. Knowledge has been increased more in the past fifty years than in any dozen of the preceding centuries. Radio became an accepted reality just about twenty-five years ago, and today we have radio, television, jet propulsion, travel in outer space. Doctors are transplanting bones, kidneys, hearts, eyes, and other vital organs from one body to another. A staggering advance has been made in every field in the last fifty years, especially in the last decade.

The heavenly messenger who was speaking to Daniel continued the revelation: *"Go thy way, Daniel: for the words are closed up and sealed till the time of the end. Many shall be purified, and made white, and tried; but the wicked shall do wickedly: and none of the wicked shall understand; but the wise shall understand."*

Summary

These verses give additional information concerning the end time, and when we consider these things we know all the more surely that these are the closing days of this Age of Grace, and that they point to the nearness of the Lord's return. In addition to the multitudes running to and fro, we must face the fact that there has been a tremendous increase of knowledge and education. Men are not only educated for *good* – they are also educated for *wickedness.*

"Many shall be *purified*, many shall be *made white*, many shall be *tried.*" In the end time, many will separate and dedicate themselves unto the Lord as never before, and I think you will agree that in this hour we are seeing a separation. The modernists and liberals are separating themselves from the fundamentalists – they want no part of fundamental Christianity; and of course the same is true on the part of the fundamentalists. We are refusing to walk with those who deny the fundamentals of the faith. The end time will be (and IS) an age of separation among God's people and worldly church members; and because the *spiritually* minded refuse to go along with the program of the *world*, the spiritually minded will suffer. They will be persecuted, they will be ignored, they will be tried.

Surely we are living in the age when true Christians are being laughed at and persecuted on every hand, and when the lines between Atheism and true Christianity are being drawn very, very tightly. The line is becoming more and more evident between those who believe the Word of God–the old-fashioned Gospel of the blood atonement, the virgin birth, the Rapture of the Church, the bodily resurrection–and those who deny the truth. If a person believes in old-fashioned Christianity today he is branded as a fanatic, a foolish crackpot. Ministers who get ahead today are those who are "good mixers," not good separators. These are the signs of the end.

". . . But the wicked shall do wickedly, and none of the wicked shall understand; but the wise shall understand."

In the light of this revelation we see that there is no such thing taught in the Bible as a world-wide revival, or the conversion of the world, before the Rapture. Wickedness, violence, immorality, ungodliness, war, hatred, divisions, strife, and murder will increase more and more the nearer we come to the end, until the day Jesus comes. "The wicked shall do wickedly." In other words, the wicked shall become MORE wicked and more ungodly. Why? Because they do not understand. They do not know what God is doing, they do not know His plan. They have no thought concerning the end; they are beyond feeling, spiritually. They are working toward that great Utopia. The motto is "Eat, drink, and be merry." They are deluded by Satan, their eyes are blinded, their mind is closed and they are madly rushing on to horrible destruction and everlasting torment in the lake of fire. But "THE WISE SHALL UNDERSTAND."

I realize there are multitudes who do NOT believe in the Millennial coming of Jesus; they deny the second coming of Christ; but percentage-wise, more believers believe in and study the second coming of Jesus Christ than ever before in the history of the world. Hardly a Christian magazine is published today without at least one message on some phase of the second coming of Jesus Christ. Most fundamental preachers mention the Lord's return in almost every sermon they preach. There have been scores of wonderful books written by some of God's greatest preachers today on the return of Jesus as taught in the Scriptures. Yes, during the end of this age, multitudes will come and go. They will run to and fro. Knowledge shall be increased. Many will be purified. Many will be tried – but the wicked will not understand, and will continue to be even more wicked. But the wise will understand and will be looking up always, *"occupying" until He comes*!

Knowledge and Ignorance

Every major judgment God has poured out upon this earth has been preceded by extreme wisdom in one direction and extreme ignorance in another. In the Garden of Eden, it was Eve's desire to be wise, to be as a god, that caused her to succumb to the temptation of the devil and eat the forbidden fruit. She wanted "to KNOW"—and she found out, to her sorrow!

Cain fell because he thought he knew more than God. He had a mind of his own and he walked according to his own will. He brought his own choice of offering and refused to obey God's command. His punishment was greater than he could bear (Gen. 4:13).

In the days of Noah there were giants in the land, men of renown, mighty men. That does not necessarily mean that they were physical giants, although they could have been that. But certainly they were mental giants, men of knowledge. We have many mental giants today—giants in the field of education, in the field of science. Knowledge has been increased.

The disciples asked Jesus what should be the sign of His coming and of the end of the world. He gave them a list of events in Matthew 24:4–14, and warned them concerning the "abomination of desolation" spoken of by Daniel. And then He gave them the parable of the fig tree—which we know is a figure of Israel:

"Now learn a parable of the fig tree; When his branch is yet tender, and putteth forth leaves, ye know that summer is nigh: So likewise ye, when ye shall see all these things, know that it is near, even at the doors. Verily

I say unto you, This generation shall not pass, till all these things be fulfilled. Heaven and earth shall pass away, but my words shall not pass away. But of that day and hour knoweth no man, no, not the angels of heaven, but my Father only. But as the days of Noe were, so shall also the coming of the Son of man be. For as in the days that were before the flood they were eating and drinking, marrying and giving in marriage, until the day that Noe entered into the ark, and knew not until the flood came, and took them all away; so shall also the coming of the Son of man be" (Matt. 24:32–39).

Jesus said, "When HIS (Israel's) branch is yet tender and putteth forth leaves, ye know that summer is near. Likewise (in the same way, after the same fashion), when you see all these things, know that (the second coming) is near, even at the doors."

And then He said, "*As the days of Noe were*, so shall also the coming of the Son of man be." Before the flood, people were eating, drinking, marrying and giving in marriage until the very day Noah entered the ark. And then we read these significant words from the lips of Jesus: "AND KNEW NOT UNTIL THE FLOOD CAME and took them all away! So shall also the coming of the Son of man be." The people of Noah's day were extremely intelligent, yet they "knew not" until the flood waters came and took them all away.

Jesus said, "*As the days of Noe were*, so shall also the coming of the Son of man be." The best way I know to find out what people were doing and how they were living in those days is to read the account of "Noah-days":

First, the age just before the flood was an age of city building. Cain built the first city ever built upon this earth (Gen. 4:17).

Second, it was an age of polygamy. Lamech was the first man to have two wives (Gen. 4:19).

Third, it was an age of agriculture and cattle raising–big business. Up to that time the people had been raisers of sheep (Gen. 4:20).

Fourth, it was an age of music. Jubal was the first man to play the harp and the organ (Gen. 4:21).

Fifth, it was an age of metal–a steel and copper age, instructers in iron and brass (Gen. 4:22).

Sixth, it was an age of crime. Lamech followed in Cain's footsteps: he killed two men instead of one (Gen. 4:23,24).

Seventh, it was an age not only of violence, murder, and killing, but an age when men bragged about killing more than one man (Gen. 4:24).

I think you will agree that our day is a repetition of the very thing I have just pointed out. Today we are building cities, cities, cities! And certainly all we need do is visit the divorce courts to learn that this is an age when men and women marry many times. Today agriculture is prevalent and "big business" is on the rise everywhere.

Do we have music? Everywhere one may go, it is music, music, music–that is, if the term "music" can be applied to some of the jungle boogie-woogie we hear today.

Needless to say, this is the age of metal. It seems that everything is at least partially metal. Skyscrapers are being built today without one splinter of wood in them–they are aluminum, copper, brass, steel, glass. And this is the age of wholesale killing. Murder is on every hand; life is cheap. War and bloodshed prevail in almost every corner of the world. Surely, this is a repetition of Noah-days.

Most significant is the fact that in Noah's day, the people "KNEW NOT." They knew how to build cities, marry wives, develop agriculture and raise cattle. They knew how to make music, work with brass and iron and all kinds of metals. They knew how to kill and then brag about it–but they did not know God. They laughed, scoffed, and jeered at Noah – nevertheless, it rained!

As it was, so shall it be! Surely this is the age of extreme wisdom in material things and extreme ignorance toward God.

Everything that needs to be fulfilled before the Rapture of the Church *has been literally fulfilled*, and is going on now before our very eyes. Every newspaper, every newscast and periodical carry new fulfillments of Scripture. The space age is a definite fulfillment of Scripture. Every field and every avenue of life show signs of His coming. Surely the day is upon us.

Writing to Timothy, Paul said: "THIS KNOW ALSO, that in the last days perilous times shall come. For men shall be lovers of their own selves, covetous, boasters, proud, blasphemers, disobedient to parents, unthankful, unholy, without natural affection, trucebreakers, false accusers, incontinent, fierce, despisers of those that are good, traitors, heady, highminded, lovers of pleasures more than lovers of God; having a form of godliness, but denying the power thereof: from such turn away. For of this sort are they which creep into houses, and lead captive silly women laden with sins, led away with divers lusts, ever learning, and never able to come to the knowledge of the truth. . . Yea, and all that will live godly in Christ Jesus shall suffer persecution. But evil men and seducers shall wax worse and worse, deceiving and being deceived" (II Tim. 3:1–7, 12, 13).

This passage speaks for itself. *Are these perilous*

times? Look at the front page of your morning paper—especially on Monday morning: wrecks, murder, rape, suicide, tragedy!

Look all around you – in the religious world, the world of business, politics, finances. Are men in love with themselves? How many people do you know personally who attempt to practice the Golden Rule? How many people do you know who keep the second great commandment – "Love thy neighbour as thyself"? This is the most selfish, self-centered age that history has ever known.

Are people covetous? Not only individuals, but governments are covetous. *Communism covets the world!* – and not only Communism, but some other "isms" as well. Are men boasters? Read your paper, listen to the radio – and yes, listen to some preachers. Boasters indeed! This is an AGE of boasting.

Is mankind proud? Is this an age of blasphemers? All we need do is watch and listen—or perhaps you had better NOT listen unless you want to be embarrassed if you are a lady and disgusted if you are a gentleman. This is the "cussin'est" age God ever permitted upon this earth, when man breathes God's air and spits it back in His face in blasphemy!

"*Incontinent*"—"not restraining the passions or appetites, particularly the sexual appetites." Are people incontinent today?

Fierce? Men are fierce. They are demonstrating the barbaric jungle nature as they have never demonstrated the fierceness of the flesh.

Despisers of those that are good? If you want to be hated today, you live a consecrated, dedicated, spirit-filled life and you will not have too many friends. If you are a good mixer, if you are a regular fellow, you are "somebody." But if you believe in a dedicated life, most people—even many church people—will treat you like you have a bad case of smallpox.

Traitors? Indeed, I should say! Heady? Yes. High minded? To be sure.

Lovers of pleasure more than lovers of God? On Sunday nights, while the lights are out in thousands of churches, theatres are packed. Televisions are busy, drive-ins are flooded, while churches are dark. Lovers of pleasure? Indeed!

"*Having a form of godliness, but denying the power thereof.*" All one need do is visit most of the big, fashionable churches—and they have form—indeed they do. They have beauty—indeed they do! But where is the Spirit? God pity us! We are commanded to turn away from such! Have you? If you have not, you should. You would not want the Lord Jesus to come and find you in any such church as that, I am sure.

"Ever learning, and never able to come to the knowledge of the truth." We have more educated preachers today than ever in the history of the world, and yet, percentage-wise, we have fewer preachers who know how to tell people how to be saved.

We have too many ministers who are manufactured in the seminaries of the denomination. God save us from assembly-line preachers! All they know is what they learn at the seminary. God pity us today when such a man pastors the church in our community. Yes, they go to school – and then they go to school some more, and then they go away and get another degree. I am not against education, but education that takes the fire out of a minister and the Spirit out of a sermon is definitely the wrong kind of education. Men are studying, preparing, going to school, getting degrees; but many of them *never "come to the knowledge of the truth."*

What IS the truth? Jesus said, "I am the truth." What IS the truth? "Sanctify them through thy Word: thy Word is truth." The Word of God is truth. "Ye shall know the truth and the truth shall make you free." The devil does not care how long, loud, or fervently a man preaches, just so long as he does not preach the truth.

Yes, we have educated preachers by the tens of thousands, but many of them have never come to the knowledge of the truth. Godly people are suffering persecution today as they have never suffered before, and evil men and seducers are waxing worse and worse, deceiving and being deceived. Even while I prepare this message, men are working *around the clock* to invent and manufacture some device to damn the unborn if Jesus tarries. Millions are spent by industry every year to damn souls. How much are we spending to get people saved?

As for me and my house, I can say what John the Beloved said to the last testimony in the Bible–which is this: "He which testifieth these things saith, Surely I come quickly. Amen." John replied, "*Even so, come, Lord Jesus*!" This may be the day the trumpet will sound!

Can YOU say, "Even so, come, Lord Jesus"? Does it frighten you to think of His coming? If it does, I fear you have never been saved. Will you not bow your head this moment and invite Jesus to come into your heart? He will – and you will know it!

Fear hath torment – but perfect love removes fear. Salvation does not torment us – it gives us peace that surpasses all understanding, joy unspeakable and full of glory. If you fear and tremble at the thought that Jesus may come within the next sixty seconds, the next hour, or the next twenty-four hours, I would advise you to seek the Lord while He may be found, and let Jesus come into your heart.

May God richly bless these messages to your life, is my prayer. Amen.